ANCIENT CUZCO

Joe R. and Teresa Lozano Long Series in Latin American and Latino Art and Culture

ANCIENT CUZCO

Heartland of the Inca

BRIAN S. BAUER

UNIVERSITY OF TEXAS PRESS

Austin

First edition, 2004

Requests for permission to reproduce material from this work
should be sent to Permissions, University of Texas Press, Box
7819, Austin, TX 78713-7819.

∞ The paper used in this book meets the minimum require-
ments of ANSI NISO Z39.48-1992 (R1997) (Permanence of Paper).

Library of Congress Cataloging-in-Publication Data

Bauer, Brian S.
    Ancient Cuzco : heartland of the Inca / Brian S. Bauer. —
1st ed.
        p.   cm. — (Joe R. and Teresa Lozano Long series in
Latin American and Latino art and culture)
Includes bibliographical references and index.
    ISBN 0-292-70243-4 (hardcover : alk. paper)
    ISBN 0-292-70279-5 (pbk. : alk. paper)
1. Indians of South America—Peru—Cuzco (Province)—
History. 2. Indians of South America—Peru—Cuzco (Province)—Antiquities. 3. Incas—Peru—Cuzco (Province)—
History. 4. Incas—Peru—Cuzco (Province)—Politics and
government. 5. Inca architecture—Peru—Cuzco (Province)
6. Cuzco (Peru : Province)—History. 7. Cuzco (Peru : Province)—Antiquities. I. Title. II. Series.

F3429.B38 2004
985'.3700498—dc22   2003018415

. . . Yo me acuerdo a ver visto por mis ojos a indios viejos, estando a vista del Cuzco, mirar contra la ciudad y alzar un alarido grande, el cuál se les convertía en lágrimas salidas de tristeza contemplando el tiempo presente y acordándose del pasado, . . .

. . . I remember seeing with my own eyes old Indians who, upon seeing Cuzco, stared at the city and gave a great cry, which then turned to tears of sadness, as they contemplated the present and recalled the past, . . .

PEDRO DE CIEZA DE LEÓN 1553

This work is dedicated to

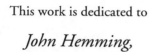

John Hemming,

whose books have inspired a generation of researchers.

CONTENTS

ACKNOWLEDGMENTS

IN THIS BOOK I present an overview of the cultural developments that took place in the Cuzco Valley from the time when the first hunter-gatherers entered the region to the fall of the Inca Empire.

I owe a great many thanks to numerous people who have supported and aided me in different stages of this research. Both Alan Covey and Bradford Jones played critical roles in helping me direct various seasons of field research in the Cuzco Valley. Mary Glowacki and Sara Lunt have frequently provided me with advice on ceramic styles of the region. Cindy Klink conducted the Archaic projectile-point analysis. Terence D'Altroy, Jean-Jacques Decoster, Joyce Marcus, Michael Moseley, Katharina Schreiber, and Charles Stanish have also been strong supporters of the general research program.

Throughout the years I have also benefited greatly from discussions with colleagues in Cuzco, including Percy Ardiles, Fernando Astete, Luis Barreda, Raymundo Béjar, Claudio Cumpa, Octavio Fernández Carrasco, Arminda Gibaja, José Gonzales, Italo Oberti, Wilbert San Román, Alfredo Valencia, Wilfredo Yépez, Julinho Zapata, and other members of the National Institute of Culture and the Universidad Nacional San Antonio Abad del Cuzco. Additional thanks go to Wilton Barrionuevo, Cosme Caceres, Christina Elson, Javier Flores, Silvia Flores, Ricardo Huayllani, Rene Pillco, Eva Santa Cruz, Patricia Milena Vega Centeno, and many others with whom I have had the pleasure of working. Drafts of this book have been read by Alan Covey, Clark Erickson, Sabine Hyland, Bradford Jones, Jeffrey Parsons, Helaine Silverman, and Nancy Warrington. Major funding has been provided by various organizations, including the National Science Foundation, the National Geographic Society, the National Endowment for the Humanities, the John Heinz III Charitable Trust, and the University of Illinois at Chicago (Institute for the Humanities, Office of Social Science Research, and the Department of Anthropology).

Because this book is a summation of many years of research in the Cuzco region, certain sections have appeared elsewhere. Chapter 2 (The Inca Heartland) was first printed in *The Development of the Inca State* (University of Texas Press, 1992), and various sections that pertain to the pottery styles of the Cuzco region have appeared in *The Early Ceramics of the Inca Heartland* (*Fieldiana Anthropology:* The Field Museum of Natural History, 1999), and *The Early Intermediate and Middle Horizon Ceramic Styles of the Cuzco Valley* (*Fieldiana Anthropology:* The Field Museum of Natural History, 2003). Chapter 8 (The Development of the Inca State) appeared in *American Anthropologist* (10: 3 [2002]: 846–864). They are reproduced here with permission.

ANCIENT CUZCO

CHAPTER 1

Introduction to the Inca

THE INCA EMPIRE was the largest state to develop in the Americas. Last in a series of complex Andean societies, it emerged in the south-central mountains of Peru, expanded across the western highlands and coast of South America, and ultimately encompassed a territory that stretched from modern-day Colombia to Chile. By the time of European contact in 1532, the Inca ruled a population of at least eight million from their capital city in the Cuzco Valley.

The Cuzco Valley was the sacred center of the empire and the royal seat of the dynastic order that ruled the realm. Despite the importance of the Cuzco Valley in the prehistory of the Americas, it has been one of the last great centers of civilization in the Americas to be systematically studied. As the heartland of the Inca, the Cuzco Valley has frequently been discussed in the literature, and anthropologists, historians, and archaeologists have long speculated on the locations and importance of its numerous archaeological sites. Yet there has been a surprising lack of archaeological field research in the Cuzco Valley itself.[1]

Until recently, there had been no attempt to systematically survey the Cuzco Valley or to document all of its archaeological sites. As a result, critical issues concerning the cultural history of the valley and the development of the Inca Empire have remained unexplored. Furthermore, we know little about the social complexity of groups that occupied the region before the Inca Empire developed and how the achievements of these earlier people helped to form the foundations upon which the Inca built their great state.

Witnessing the recent rapid urban growth of the city and realizing the need for a systematic regional survey of the Inca heartland, I began the Cuzco Valley Archaeological Project in 1994. The project was designed as a multi-stage regional study of the Inca heartland, dedicated to documenting and interpreting the distribution of its archaeological sites. The systematic documentation of site types, locations, sizes, and ages in the region has yielded new information on the ancient cultures of this important area. The overall objective of the project was to reconstruct the settlement history of the Cuzco Valley by combining the results of a systematic survey of the valley with data gathered from excavations at a number of sites and information recovered from various historic documents.

In this book I present the major results of that project and offer an overview of the cultural developments that occurred in the Cuzco Valley from the time of its first occupants, soon after the retreat of the Pleistocene glaciers, to the arrival of the Spaniards and the subsequent collapse of the Inca Empire. The goal of the book is to extend our knowledge of the area well beyond the generalized descriptions currently available for the prehistory of the region and to address a series of research questions concerning both the general processes of cultural development and the specific historic patterns of the region. In the first half of the book, I attempt to answer several basic questions: How has the climate of the region changed over time (Chapter 3)? When was the valley first occupied (Chapter 4)? How did settlement strategies change with the establishment of the first villages (Chap-

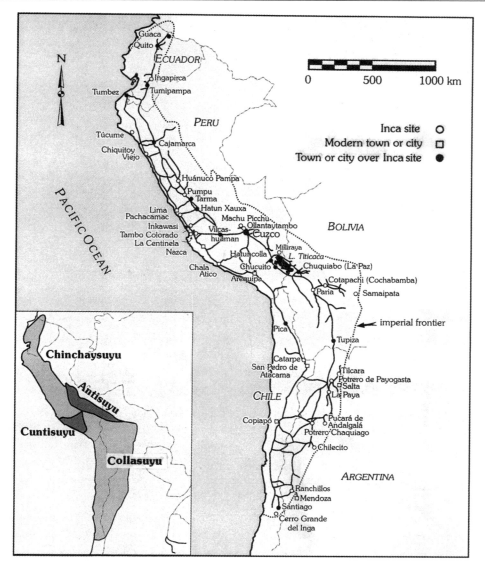

MAP 1.1. The Inca Empire on the eve of European contact [1531]
(Courtesy of Terence N. D'Altroy)

ter 5)? What effects did the conquest of the region by the Wari Empire (ca. AD 600) have on the indigenous populations (Chapters 6 and 7)? and When did the Inca state first develop in the Cuzco Valley (Chapter 8)?

Detailed descriptions of the Cuzco region at the height of Inca rule are also presented. Issues addressed include: How is the heartland of the Inca defined (Chapter 2)? What was the valley and the imperial city of Cuzco like during Inca times (Chapters 9 and 10)? and finally, What do we know about the most famous sanctuary of the Inca (the Coricancha) and about the Inca practice of mummifying and worshiping their dead kings (Chapters 11 and 12)?

In sum, this book provides a regional context within which we can study the development of social complexity in the Cuzco Valley for the first time. By combining systematic survey data with information collected from excavations as well as historic documents, we are able to reconstruct the settlement history of the valley from preceramic times to the fall of the Inca Empire (Map 1.1).

The analysis of the data takes place within the confines of a cultural evolutionary model that anticipates that with strong population growth, there will be a greater dependence on domesticated foods, larger settlements, and increased specialization over time. In this way, the populations of a region are seen as transitioning from being hunter-gatherers living in seasonal camps to agriculturists and herders living in hamlets and small villages. In time, these villages grow larger, and hierarchical differences may develop between individuals. The appearance of two-tiered societies (also called ranked societies), composed of a small number of elite families and a large number of commoners, in the archaeological record is generally interpreted as marking the formation of chiefdoms in a region. Especially successful chiefdoms may in time incorporate other nearby societies into their sphere of influence and emerge as states. Through the use of this cultural evolutionary model, the results of this investigation can be compared with those of other regional studies that have recently been completed in Peru, such as those conducted by Timothy K. Earle et al. (1980) and Jeffrey R. Parsons et al. (2000a, 2000b) in the Upper Mantaro region, by Charles Stanish (2003) in the Lake Titicaca region, by Helaine Silverman (2002) in the Nazca region, as well as by Brian Billman (1996) and David J. Wilson (1988) on the north coast. The results of the work also provide comparative information for the study of chiefdoms and states elsewhere in the ancient Americas (e.g., Marcus and Flannery 1996; Marcus 1998; Blanton et al. 1999).

The Cuzco Valley at the Time of the Inca Empire: A Brief Overview

The large and agriculturally rich Cuzco Valley emerged preeminent in the fifteenth century AD as the heartland of the Inca. Near the north end of the valley lies the sacred city of Cuzco. The region immediately surrounding the Cuzco Valley was occupied by a number of different ethnic groups that were absorbed into the Inca state during an early period of state formation. By about AD 1400, the Inca had united the region under their rule, and the city of Cuzco had emerged as their capital (Bauer 1992a; Bauer and Covey 2002). The Inca then expanded from this well-integrated heartland and quickly formed one of the greatest polities to develop in the Americas. Within three generations, the Inca Empire grew to control a vast area of South America. Yet, as a result of regional and ethnic conflict, conquest by the Spaniards, and the spread of deadly European diseases, the last and largest of the

indigenous states of the Americas collapsed even more quickly than it began. By 1572, thousands of Spaniards occupied the important cities of the former empire, and the last direct heir to the Inca crown, Tupac Amaru, had been executed. In 1650 an earthquake flattened the city of Cuzco, and in its aftermath the city was rebuilt following norms of European architecture. By that time, the Inca Empire had long since fallen, and Lima had come to dominate the social, political, and economic spheres of the land. The Cuzco region, home to thriving local societies for thousands of years and the former capital of the Inca Empire, began to fade from the world's view.

INCA CUZCO

At its height, the city of Cuzco was home to more than 20,000 people (Valverde, cited in Porras Barrenechea 1959: 312–313 [1539]), with many thousands more located in numerous large villages scattered across the valley. Besides being the royal seat for the ruling dynasty and the political heart of the Inca polity, Cuzco represented the geographical and spiritual center of the empire. At the center of the city stood the Coricancha[2] (Golden Enclosure) or what the Spaniards later referred to as the Templo del Sol (Temple of the Sun). This elaborate complex, built with the finest Inca stone masonry and metalwork, was the focal point for the major imperial religious rites that were staged in the city. After the conquest, the church and monastery of Santo Domingo was built on this site. Nevertheless, many of the former structures and the superb Inca stonework of the temple complex can still be seen.

The central plaza of Cuzco was also an important ceremonial area in the city. During major rituals, the mummies of the dead Inca rulers were placed in the plaza, and thousands of people gathered to see them. The city center also held temples for various gods, several palaces, numerous royal storehouses, and a wide range of other state institutions and facilities. For example, the large complex of the Acllahuaci (House of Chosen [Women]), which housed hundreds of women who dedicated their lives to serving the state, stood near the center of Cuzco.

Just outside the city was the monumental structure of Sacsayhuaman. World famous for the massive stones that form parts of its walls, Sacsayhuaman is frequently referred to as a "fortress." Some early accounts of Cuzco (Cieza de León 1976: 154 [1554: Pt. 2, Ch. 51]) indicate that Sacsayhuaman contained a sun temple, suggesting that it was the focus of ritual activities. Further outside the city, but still within the valley, were other state facilities, royal estates, and a large number of villages and towns.

DYNASTIC ORDER OF THE INCA

At the time of the European invasion, the royal Inca traced their ancestry back eleven generations from the last undisputed ruler of the empire, Huayna Capac, to the mythical founder of Cuzco, Manco Capac (Table 1.1). Traditionally, the Inca are thought to have expanded their state beyond the limits of the Cuzco region under Pachacuti Inca Yupanqui, the ninth ruling Inca. A warrior king of legendary proportions, Pachacuti Inca Yupanqui is frequently credited with having reorganized the economic, social, and calendric systems of the empire. According to oral tradition recorded by the Spaniards, Pachacuti Inca Yupanqui's eldest son, Amaru Topa, was passed over as heir to the throne, and the rule was given to his younger son, Topa Inca Yupanqui. Decades later, Huayna Capac, a son of Topa Inca Yupanqui, inherited the rule from his father and continued expanding the empire until his sudden death in an epidemic that swept the empire in the 1520s, shortly before European contact. Following the death of Huayna Capac, the rule of Tahuantinsuyu was disputed between two half brothers, Atahualpa and Huascar. The Spanish forces of Francisco Pizarro arrived in Peru in 1532, just as Atahualpa defeated Huascar. Pizarro captured Atahualpa in the highland city of Cajamarca and, after holding the ruling Inca hostage for most of a year, executed him.

For some forty years after the execution of Atahualpa, the Spaniards established and supported a series of puppet Inca kings in Cuzco. During this period the Spaniards fought a protracted war against Manco Inca (a half brother of Atahualpa) and his descendants, who attempted to maintain an independent Inca state with a capital in the remote area of Vilcabamba. The end of indigenous rule came in 1572 with the capture and execution of Tupac Amaru, the last surviving son of Manco Inca, by the Spaniards.

TABLE 1.1. Traditional list of Inca kings

	RULER
(1)	Manco Capac
(2)	Sinchi Roca
(3)	Lloque Yupanqui
(4)	Mayta Capac
(5)	Capac Yupanqui
(6)	Inca Roca
(7)	Yahuar Huacac
(8)	Viracocha Inca
(9)	Pachacuti Inca Yupanqui
(10)	Topa Inca Yupanqui
(11)	Huayna Capac
(12)	Huascar
(13)	Atahualpa
(European Invasion of 1532)	
(14)	Manco Inca
(15)	Paullu Inca

The Cuzco Valley and Its Natural Resources

The Cuzco Valley is defined in this work as the area drained by the Huatanay River (Map 1.2), which flows southeast from above the modern city of Cuzco, through the area of the Angostura (the Narrows) at approximately mid-valley, and into the Lucre Basin, where it turns northeast and enters the Vilcanota River. So defined, the Cuzco Valley is about 40 kilometers long and 15 kilometers wide at its maximum (Photo 1.1). For analytical purposes, the Cuzco Valley is frequently divided into three parts or basins: the Cuzco Basin, the Oropesa Basin, and the Lucre Basin.

The Cuzco Basin represents the northwest end of the valley and is defined as the region between the headwaters of the Huatanay on the mountain of Huaynacorcor, northwest of Cuzco, and the distinct narrowing of the valley below the modern-day town of San Jerónimo called the Angostura, southeast of Cuzco. The Oropesa Basin represents a long and narrow stretch of the river valley between the Angostura and a second constriction of the valley just southeast of the town of Oropesa. The Lucre Basin entails the drainage area for Lake Lucre near the

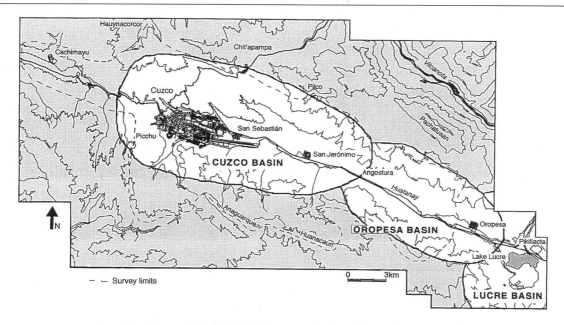

MAP 1.2. The Cuzco Valley is divided into three basins: Cuzco, Oropesa, and Lucre.

PHOTO 1.1. The Cuzco Basin looking southeast (Courtesy of Servicio Aerofotográfico Nacional, Peru)

5

conjunction of the Huatanay and the Vilcanota Rivers. The southeast end of the Cuzco Valley, in the Lucre Basin, lies at 3,100 m, while Cuzco rests at 3,400 m. The highest mountain surrounding the valley is Pachatusan, which rises to 4,842 m. A series of diverse climatic zones are located along the slopes of the Cuzco Valley.[3] During Inca times, the lowest-lying areas were inundated from January through March by annual flooding. Thus, although the valley bottom supported a wide range of faunal and floral life, it was unsuitable for permanent human occupation.

The most agriculturally productive and intensively occupied environmental zones in the Cuzco Valley are the large alluvial terraces that rest some 20–50 meters above the valley floor. Being flat and relatively easily irrigated, these regions are excellent for maize cultivation. It should be noted, however, that the alluvial terraces are not distributed evenly across the valley. For example, the north side of the Cuzco Basin is characterized by steep mountain slopes, entrenched streams, and small areas of alluvial terraces. In contrast, the southern side of the Cuzco Basin contains broad expanses of alluvial terraces, wide tributary valleys, and gentler slopes. For these rea-

sons, the first agriculturists focused their settlements on the south, rather than the north, side of the basin. It was not until the Killke Period (AD 1000–1400), and the advent of large-scale irrigation systems built as public works projects, that the agricultural potential of the north side could be fully and effectively exploited. The settlement preference for the south side of the valley was immediately clear to us while conducting the survey, and it is even notable in the first archaeological map of the basin, made when the locations of only a handful of sites were known (Map 1.3).

A variety of Old and New World crops, including wheat, broad beans, and potatoes, are currently grown on the valley slopes (3,500–3,900 m). Daniel Gade (1975: 105–106), working in the nearby Vilcanota Valley, notes that in Inca times this zone was characterized by the cultivation of tubers (such as *oca, añu,* and *ullucu*) and native seed crops (such as *quinoa* and *tarwi*). Harvests on the valley slopes vary greatly from year to year because of frost and hail damage.

The highest environmental zone in the Cuzco Valley is characterized by rounded ridges and scattered rock outcroppings. The lower reaches of this zone are occa-

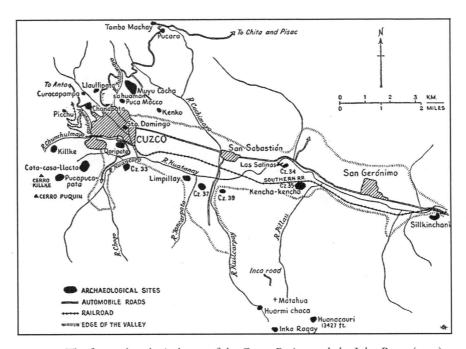

MAP 1.3. The first archaeological map of the Cuzco Basin, made by John Rowe (1944), highlights the fact that many of the largest prehistoric sites are located along its south side.

sionally used for tuber cultivation (3,900–4,000 m.) while the upper parts are covered with the hearty Andean *ichu* grass used extensively for pasture. Gade (1975: 104) writes of this zone: "Undoubtedly the most important single grass species is *Stipa ichu,* the basic food of llamas and alpacas, as well as a plant used directly by man in a number of ways. The low temperatures and short growing season rule out full-scale agriculture, and in this zone one finds the uppermost limits of crop cultivation." A variety of frost-resistant tubers, including various "sweet" and "bitter" potatoes, are cultivated in the Cuzco region. From June to August, when the nights are cold and frosts frequent, *chuño* and *moraya,* two different forms of freeze-dried potatoes, are produced in this zone.

Rising above the upper limits of crop cultivation are several important mountain peaks, most notably Pachatusan, where snow survives year-round in the deeply shaded spots near its summit. Other important mountains adjacent to the valley include Huanacauri (4,089 m), Anaguarque (4,000 m), Picchu (4,050m), and Huaynacorcor (formally known as Sinca [4,400 m]), which were all considered sacred by the Inca (Sarmiento de Gamboa 1906: 69 [1572: Ch. 31]). Evidence of Inca offerings has been found at the summits of most of these mountains.

It is also important to note that although the Cuzco Valley is now greatly deforested, during late prehistoric times this was not the case. Garcilaso de la Vega witnessed the rapid deforestation of the valley that occurred soon after the arrival of the Spaniards:

> I remember that the valley of Cuzco used to be adorned with innumerable trees of this valuable variety, but within the space of a very few years it was almost stripped of them, the reason being that they provide excellent charcoal for braziers. (Garcilaso de la Vega 1966: 504 [1609: Pt. 1, Bk. 8, Ch. 12])[4]

Perhaps the largest concentration of forest lay to the northwest of Cuzco, in a vast and rolling area between the city and the slope of Huaynacorcor. Based on the large number of projectile points found during our survey work in these hills, it seems that the northwestern end of the valley continued to be a favored hunting region throughout prehistory. This remained true even in Inca times, as we

know that the Inca maintained a royal hunting lodge there (Cobo 1990: 63 [1653: Bk. 13, Ch. 14]).

Salt springs are common features of the Andes, and when the concentration of salt in the water is high enough, the streams are exploited for their minerals. During the dry season, wide, shallow basins are dug into the earth and repeatedly filled with the saline water. Through numerous evaporation and refilling events, deposits of salt develop on the basin floors which are then harvested at the end of the dry season. Such salt production continues today in the area of Maras, some 30 kilometers northwest of Cuzco, and there were once similar, although much smaller, salt pans just outside the village of San Sebastián in the Cuzco Basin. Various early colonial writers note the production of salt at this location, and it was at this spot that Hernando Pizarro defeated Diego Almagro in 1538 in what is called "the Battle of the Salt Flats." Bingham recorded the salt pans in a 1912 photograph, and a few survived until the early 1970s, when they were finally destroyed by urban growth (Photo 1.2).

Overview of Cuzco Archaeological Research

Following Peru's independence from Spain in 1824, Cuzco became a mecca for those interested in the Inca.[5] American and European explorers began arriving and subsequently publishing accounts of their travels. At the same time, Peruvian educational and research institutions began to develop, and their members also journeyed to the former imperial capital to report on its antiquities.

NINETEENTH-CENTURY WORKS

With the publication of William Prescott's *History of the Conquest of Peru* (1847), interest in the Inca was renewed worldwide. Building on the success of Alexander Humboldt's explorations into Ecuador at the turn of the century, the French were especially active in explorations. In 1847 Léonce Angrand (1972) traveled from Lima to Cuzco, recording his journey in a series of fine-line drawings.[6] Peruvian-born Mariano Eduardo de Rivero and his colleague Johann Jakob von Tschudi described the general antiquities of Peru, first in Spanish in 1851 and then in English in 1854, and included a discussion of Cuzco. Their work contains a rough but early illustration of the

PHOTO 1.2. The salt pans of San Sebastián in 1912
(Neg. no. 2586, Hiram Bingham, courtesy Yale Peabody Museum and the National Geographic Society)

Dominican church that was built upon the Coricancha as well as a crude drawing of a stone wall in the city. British explorer Clements Markham arrived in Cuzco in 1853 and spent several weeks visiting the city and the nearby countryside (Markham 1856). He, too, provides a number of rough drawings of the city and its ancient monuments (Blanchard 1991). Charles Wiener was commissioned by the French government to travel through and report on Peru and Bolivia in 1877. His book contains many engravings of Cuzco and various artifacts that he saw while in the city (Wiener 1880). Peruvian researchers were also active during this time. Among the most important was Antonio Raimondi, who recorded his impressions of the Cuzco countryside in his multivolume work *El Perú* (1874–1879).[7]

Ephraim George Squier, perhaps the most celebrated nineteenth-century explorer of the Andes, visited Cuzco in 1865 and lived for two weeks with the Dominican monks within the confines of the former Coricancha. He traveled to Peru as part of a special negotiating commission appointed by President Lincoln to settle a variety of issues with the Peruvian government. After com-

pleting his official work in Lima, Squier spent over a year (1864–1865) exploring the Andes. On returning from South America, Squier wrote his classic study *Peru: Incidents of Travel and Exploration in the Land of the Incas.* His book is filled with detailed discussions of the places he saw, maps of many of the sites he visited, and numerous engravings of the lands, ruins, and peoples he encountered. In all, Squier provides three maps (including the earliest map of the Coricancha) and more than twenty engravings related to the city of Cuzco and its surrounding ruins.

An equally significant contribution by Squier, although largely unpublished, is a collection of photographs that he took during his travels.[8] His pictures of the coast are of extremely high quality and represent the earliest photographs of many important archaeological sites. Unfortunately, Squier's photographer died as soon as they arrived in the Bolivian highlands, so he was forced to take his own pictures during the later months of his trip. But Squier had little photographic experience, and his pictures of the Lake Titicaca Basin and Cuzco region are of poor quality. Nevertheless, they preserve important architectural information, and several are published for the first time in the second half of this book.

EARLY-TWENTIETH-CENTURY WORKS

One of the "fathers" of Andean archaeology, Max Uhle, conducted active fieldwork in Peru for several decades after his first visit to Peru in 1892.[9] He spent time in 1905, 1907, and 1911 in the Cuzco region, where he conducted excavations (Uhle 1912; Valencia Zegarra 1979), as well as in the city itself, where he produced an early map of the Coricancha (Uhle 1930). The great turning point in Cuzco archaeology occurred, however, with the work of Yale University's Hiram Bingham. Although Bingham was a Latin American historian rather than a trained archaeologist, he led a series of three archaeological expeditions over the course of five years (1911–1916) that brought Machu Picchu to the world's attention. This spectacular find placed Cuzco in the limelight for world travelers, where it has remained ever since. Bingham's numerous publications and those produced by other members of the expeditions also marked the beginning of scientific literature for the Inca heartland.[10]

By 1920 the Cuzco region—with the imperial city of the Inca, the so-called Sacred Valley of the Vilcanota, and the newly cleared site of Machu Picchu—was established as a world-famous tourist destination. Guide books (Zárate 1921; García 1922), postcards, and images for lenticular stereoscopes showing the ancient monuments of the region were being produced on a large scale. In 1934, to increase tourism and to mark the fourth centenary of Spanish Cuzco, the Peruvian government began a series of large-scale restoration projects at the largest and most famous sites of the region, such as Sacsayhuaman, Kenko, Tambomachay, Pikillacta, and Pisaq. Unfortunately, with the exception of a few brief accounts by Luis E. Valcárcel (1934, 1935), the results of these massive projects have not been published. However, other studies conducted in Cuzco over the course of the 1930s, particularly those supervised by Luis Pardo, director of the Archaeological Museum in Cuzco (1938, 1939, 1941, 1946, 1957), were completed and published.

The 1940s brought many advances to Cuzco archaeology, which was at that time still largely focused on studying Inca remains. Starting in 1941, John H. Rowe began

an investigation of the region to identify its pre-Inca materials (Rowe 1944). Working closely with local archaeologists, Rowe (1956) produced the first ceramic sequence for the region, which spans the time between the appearance of large agricultural villages (ca. 500 BC) to the fall of the Inca Empire. In the post–World War II period, there has been a steady increase in research interest in the Inca and pre-Inca remains of the region. Much of this more recent research is discussed in detail in later chapters of this book that present the various historic periods of the Cuzco region in chronological order.[11]

The Cuzco Valley Archaeological Project

With the rapid population growth of Cuzco, dozens of its archaeological sites are being destroyed each year, and there is little time left to collect information on the heartland of the Inca. In the early 1980s, the National Institute of Culture (INC, Instituto Nacional de Cultura) in Cuzco funded a project to document the largest sites of the area. In the course of this project, the INC produced a series of outstanding maps that have successfully been used to defend many areas of cultural importance against the advancement of urban growth. Nevertheless, with the construction of new homes, roads, sewer lines, and other support facilities for Cuzco, many sites are destroyed each year. In 1994 I began the Cuzco Valley Archaeological Project, which included both a regional survey and an excavation program, to understand the settlement history of the valley before much of the evidence was destroyed by urban growth.

THE REGIONAL SURVEY PROGRAM

A research methodology based primarily on systematic survey data was selected for this project in the belief that the developmental processes of culture change are best investigated through regional archaeological investigations (Hutterer and MacDonald 1982). Regional archaeological surveys suppose that the spatial distribution of the sites of a prehistoric society will reflect fundamental organizational features of that society, and that a systematic examination of settlement patterns is a logical beginning point in the investigation of prehistoric social and economic systems. Assuming that the settlement patterns in a region reflect indigenous patterns of resource use, subsistence procurement, and social organization, archaeological surveys are now widely conducted in the Andes (Browman 1970; Earle et al. 1980; Schreiber 1987a; Wilson 1988; Bauer 1992a; Billman 1996; Stanish et al. 1997; Parsons et al. 2000a, 2000b; Stanish 2001, 2003; Silverman 2002). By comparing the regional settlement patterns obtained for each period of the valley's history, we can view regional changes over space and time and model the kind of changes brought about by a number of important processes, such as the formation and expansion of a centralized state.

The archaeological survey of the Cuzco Valley was designed as a 100 percent coverage survey, which was necessitated by the fact that the survey data were to be analyzed in conjunction with historic information concerning the distribution of kin groups and their landholdings in the valley at the time of the Spanish Conquest. The combination of archaeological survey data and extensive historic information provides the database to document the social organization of the valley on the eve of European conquest and to analyze the changes that occurred in its social organization through time.

The study area encompassed approximately 350 km².

It ran from the area of Cachimayu in the west to the town of Oropesa in the east. In the north it extended to the Cuzco-Chit'apampa ridge and in the south to the ridges of Anaguarque and Huanacauri (Map 1.4). In 1994, while holding a Fulbright-Hays Teaching/Research Fellowship, I covered approximately 10 percent of the valley. This pilot project allowed me to test the survey methodology and to develop time estimates for the coverage of the entire valley. In 1997, with the aid of a Campus Research Board grant from the University of Illinois at Chicago and with funds from the Heinz Foundation, Alan Covey and I then extended the survey to cover an additional 30 percent of the valley. With support from the National Geographic Society, the National Science Foundation, and the National Endowment for the Humanities, we completed the entire survey during 1998 and 1999.

The goal of the fieldwork was to identify the locations of all prehistoric occupation sites and support facilities in the research zone (including terraces, canals, roads, bridges, and storehouses). To conduct the survey, teams of three to four persons, spaced at 50-meter intervals, walked assigned areas identifying the locations of prehistoric sites (Photo 1.3). When a site was found, its location was marked on aerial photographs (approximate

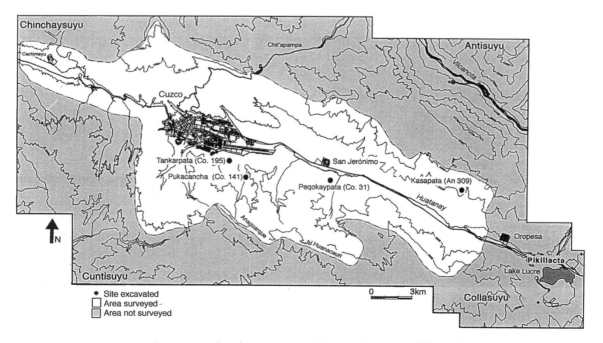

MAP 1.4. Area surveyed and sites excavated during the Cuzco Valley Archaeological Project

PHOTO 1.3. Surveying the area near Larapa in the Cuzco Valley

scale 1: 10,000) and on topographical maps (scale 1: 10,000) that the surveyors carried in the field. Its location was also plotted with a Global Positioning System. Standardized survey forms were completed and photographs taken of each site. The Inca divided the Cuzco region into four geopolitical parts (or *suyus*): Chinchaysuyu (Ch.), Antisuyu (An.), Collasuyu (Co.), and Cuntisuyu (Cu.). During the Cuzco Valley Archaeological Project, sites were assigned numbers according to the Inca *suyu* divisions of the valley. For example, the site of Kasapata, which lies within the area of Antisuyu, was given the number of An. 309, and the site of Pukacancha, located in Collasuyu, was labeled as Co. 141.

One of the most challenging aspects of regional survey work is estimating the dimensions of specific components within multicomponent sites. That is to say, if a site was occupied during two or more time periods, it may be difficult to estimate site sizes for each of the occupations. To address this problem, we implemented an additional step, which we simply called second collections. Second collections involved revisiting sites larger than 100 x 50 m and all sites that had evidence of two chronological components. The goal of the second collections was to gather additional information on the distribution of artifacts at the sites.

We timed the second collections so that at least one year had passed between visits to the site. This was so that agricultural work and natural forces would bring new artifacts to the surface. During the second collections, the surveyors walked the sites marking the locations of certain styles of ceramics with small flags. The flag distributions were then used to help estimate the size and density of the various components of the site. The second collection also provided an opportunity to recheck other important information recorded on the survey forms. Although this additional procedure—which involved revisiting hundreds of sites—required additional time and resources, it enabled the survey teams to check, improve, and further strengthen previous observations, and it has greatly increased our ability to model prehistoric change in the Cuzco Valley through time.

After the surface materials were collected from the sites, they were brought to Cuzco to be washed and processed. In the laboratory, the diagnostic sherds from each site were separated into homogeneous groups based on wares, design elements, pigment colors, and surface treatments.

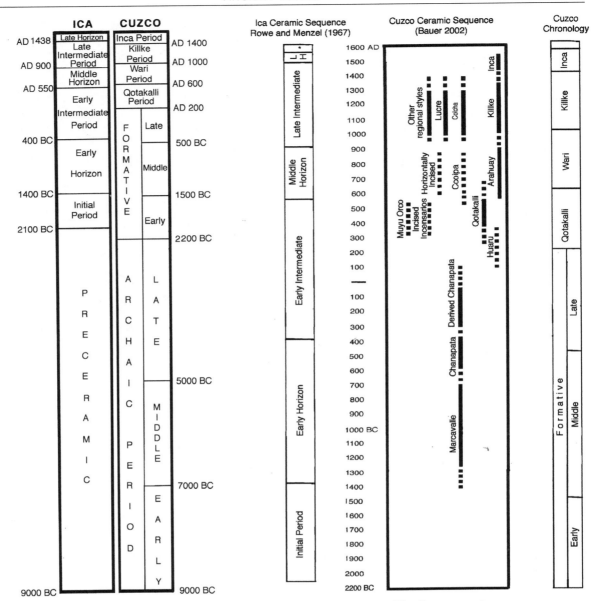

FIGURE I.I. The Cuzco Chronology

FIGURE I.2. The Cuzco ceramic sequence

These groups were then further subdivided according to vessel forms. Pottery samples were then analyzed to determine the periods of site occupation. At the close of the project in 2001, the artifacts were deposited in the Institute of Culture in Cuzco in specially constructed wooden containers for permanent storage.

THE EXCAVATION PROGRAM

As recently pointed out by Stanish (2001), it is a common misunderstanding that regional studies confine themselves to survey data and do not include excavation components. On the contrary, many of the most successful regional studies actively incorporate excavations as a critical research tool within their multiphase research programs. The primary purpose of survey work is to locate, describe, and date all archaeological sites. Such survey data are inherently important as a means to characterize the settlement history of a research area. They also serve as a database for additional stages of research. That is, once a settlement history is defined, strategically important sites can be chosen for excavations based on the anthropological and historical problems researchers consider most important (Stanish 2001). In other words, once the full range and number of sites in a region are known, investigators are able to select particular sites to answer very specific research questions, rather than simply conducting their work at the largest or at the best-known sites of the area.

Building on the results of our systematic survey (1994, 1997–1999) of the Cuzco Valley, which documented the locations of more than 1,200 archaeological sites, we chose three small- to medium-sized sites for test excavations in 1999: Peqokaypata (Co. 31), Pukacancha (Co. 141), and Tankarpata (Co. 195). These three sites were selected for excavation because they contained different combinations of ceramic styles dating from AD 200 to AD 1000 (Map 1.4). By conducting test excavations at multiple small sites, we hoped to isolate and date the various ceramic styles used in the Cuzco Valley during this era (Bauer and Jones 2003).

During the course of our systematic survey of the Cuzco Valley, we also recorded the surface remains of numerous lithic sites. Accordingly, the results of the survey challenged the long-held view that there were no preceramic cultures in the valley and that the area was occupied relatively late in prehistory. A tentative comparison of the surface remains from these newly discovered sites with projectile points found elsewhere in the Andean highlands, especially in the Lake Titicaca Basin, pushes back the date of the first occupants of the valley from around 1000 BC to 7000 BC, a time when much of the southern Andean highlands was being colonized. Thus, systematic identification of and collection from lithic sites in the Cuzco Valley provided the opportunity to define a new lithic tradition for the region and to study the lifeways of its earliest inhabitants. Building on this new data, we conducted excavations at the preceramic site of Kasapata (An. 309) in 2000. This site was selected for excavation because it was the largest and the best-preserved lithic site in the Cuzco Valley.

The Cuzco Chronology

In the 1950s and early 1960s, through a series of excavations in the Ica Valley on the south coast of Peru, John

Rowe and his colleagues developed a "master ceramic sequence" that divides Peruvian prehistory into a series of temporal periods based on absolute dates (Rowe 1962; Rowe and Menzel 1967). The beginning date for each period is defined by the appearance of specific ceramic types in the Ica Valley. Divisions within each period are defined by more subtle changes in local pottery styles. For example, Rowe (1962: 50) writes, " . . . the Early Intermediate Period represents the time covered by Phases 1 to 8 of the Nasca style at Ica. We can therefore divide the Early Intermediate Period into eight subdivisions ('epochs'), each corresponding to one of the Nasca Phases." Some scholars have attempted to use the Ica sequence to organize archaeological settlement data recovered in the Cuzco region (Kendall 1997); however, the sequence proves to be problematic in discussing cultures and events that occurred before the arrival of the Wari (ca. AD 600). This is not a problem unique to the Cuzco region. Stanish et al. (1997: 9) describe similar circumstances in the Lake Titicaca region: "The basic problem with using this framework (i.e., the Ica sequence) is that the cultural history of the south coast is simply too different prior to the Middle Horizon to be directly applicable to the Titicaca Basin in any but the most general manner. Our research indicates that a modification of the existing chronologies for the Titicaca Basin is warranted."

Because this book is about the development of cultures in the Cuzco region, I use a Cuzco-based chronology to organize the archaeological materials rather than the Ica-derived sequence (Figures 1.1 and 1.2). The temporal periods used in this book are largely defined by the appearance of specific artifact styles in the Cuzco region. The projectile-point styles used in this book are derived from examples recovered in our survey and excavations in the Cuzco Valley as well as from known styles of the Lake Titicaca region. The ceramic classifications are based on an updated ceramic sequence for the Cuzco region (Bauer 1999, 2002; Bauer and Jones 2003).[12] The calendar years assigned to each period are based on the most recent radiocarbon dates and are open to reassessment as more information becomes available (Appendix). As noted above, the latter periods of the Cuzco Chronology are very similar, though not identical, to those defined in the Ica sequence, but the early periods are distinctly different.

CHAPTER 2

The Inca Heartland

THIS CHAPTER DEFINES the Inca heartland as it was described to the Spaniards by native informants. It also provides an introduction to the ethnic groups of the Cuzco region and an overview of the social hierarchy of the region as seen at the time of the European invasion. I am specifically concerned with the hierarchical and spatial relationship that existed between the Inca of Royal Blood, the Inca of Cuzco, and what are called the Inca of Privilege (Inca de Privilegio), the ethnic groups living within the Cuzco region but outside the capital city.

The identification of the various groups that once inhabited the Cuzco region is an important first step in understanding the development of the Inca state because the processes of state formation do not simply affect a single "capital" city or just the populations that are immediately adjacent to it. Social transformations occur on a *regional* level, affecting dozens of ethnic groups and hundreds of villages. The development of the Inca state is largely about the creation of a heartland: how the many ethnic groups of the Cuzco region were forged into a single entity and how that entity was then able to expand across much of South America. In the chapters that follow, I examine the long process of indigenous cultural development in the Cuzco region that led to the formation of these various groups and their eventual unification into the Inca state.

The Social Hierarchy of the Cuzco Region

Detailed information concerning the ethnic groups of the region and the social relationships that bound them

to the Inca of Cuzco is provided by three independent indigenous chroniclers—Guaman Poma de Ayala, Garcilaso de la Vega, and Juan de Santa Cruz Pachacuti Yamqui Salcamayhua—as well as one Spanish writer, Baltasar Ocampo Conejeros. The indigenous chroniclers were personally familiar with the Cuzco social hierarchy as it existed in the immediate postconquest period. Consequently, they offer unusually accurate information on the spatial distribution of ethnic groups in the Cuzco region (Table 2.1, Map 2.1). In addition, the range and depth of information that is provided by the indigenous chroniclers is enhanced by their differing ethnic backgrounds, which lead each of them to view the same social reality through differing perspectives. The Spanish writer provides a slightly different yet complementary view of the boundaries of the Inca heartland as seen through European eyes.

GUAMAN POMA DE AYALA AND THE SOCIAL HIERARCHY OF THE CUZCO REGION

Felipe Guaman Poma de Ayala was an indigenous writer who wrote a thousand-page letter to the king of Spain in the early seventeenth century. This work, called *El primer nueva corónica y buen gobierno,* has become famous not only for the information found within its text but also for its several hundred fine line drawings. In several passages of his letter, Guaman Poma de Ayala describes the social hierarchy of the Cuzco region and the administrative organization of the empire in terms of ranked kin

TABLE 2.1. Inca of Privilege as described by Garcilaso de la Vega,
Guaman Poma de Ayala, and Santa Cruz Pachacuti Yamqui Salcamayhua

GARCILASO	GUAMAN POMA	SANTA CRUZ	LOCATION
Antisuyu			
Poques			Paucartambo
Cuntisuyu			
Masca	Masca	Mascas	Paruro
Chillque	Chillqui	Chillques	Paruro
Pap'ri	Papri	Papres	Acomayo
	Tanbo	Tambos	Paruro
	Acos		Acomayo
	Yana Uara		Tambobamba
Chinchaysuyu			
Mayu	Mayu	Mayos	Anta
Cancu	Cancu	Tancos	Anta
Chinchapucyu			Anta
Rimactampu	Rimactampu		Anta
Y'úcay			Anta
Tampu		Tanbo	Urubamba
	Anta		Anta
	Equeco/Sacsa Uana		Anta
	Quilis Cachi	Quilliscches	Anta
	Quichiua	Quicchguas	Curawasi
	Lare		Urubamba
	Uaro Conde		Anta
Collasuyu			
Ayamarca			Quispican. Cz.
Quespicancha			Quispican. Cz.
Muina			Quispican. Cz.
Urcos			Quispican. Cz.
Quéhuar	Queuar	Quiguares	Quispican. Cz.
Huáruc	Uaroc		Quispican. Cz.
Cauiña	Cauina		Quispican. Cz.
Location unknown			
	Chilpaca		?

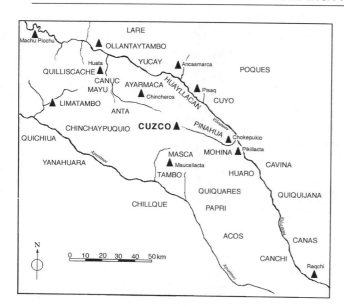

MAP 2.1. The Inca heartland and its ethnic groups

groups. For the purpose of this investigation, I will concentrate on four separate but nearly identical lists in which he describes his vision of the social divisions that existed in the Cuzco region during Inca rule. The first of these lists is presented in Guaman Poma de Ayala's conception of the Pacariqtambo origin myth (Guaman Poma de Ayala 1980: 62–66 [1615: 79–85]; Bauer 1991). In this account he describes how the first mythical Inca, Manco Capac, and his three brothers and four sisters emerged from a cave called "Tanbo Toco" (Tampu-toco), or "Pacaritanbo" (Pacariqtambo), and made their journey to the Cuzco Valley via the mountain of "uana cauri" (Huanacauri).[1] Guaman Poma de Ayala also describes how a large number of people traveled with the royal siblings on their mythical journey to Cuzco. This entourage included representatives of the groups that Guaman Poma de Ayala (1980: 66 [1615: 84–85]) calls the *uaccha* (poor) Inca of the Cuzco region, or what other chronicles have described as the Inca of Privilege:

All those who have pierced ears are called Incas, but not all are perfect, rather some are poor Indians and low people who are not gentlemen, but tribute payers. Of those mentioned who have pierced ears, only one was the first Inca king, Manco Capac. Because of this they called him *capac*;[2] that is, Inca is com-

mon, it is not king, but *capac apu*[3] means king, and so the first Inca was Manco Capac, the second Anta Inca, Caca Guaroc Inca, Quiuar Inca, Masca Inca, Tambo Inca, Lari Inca, Equeco, Xaxa Uana Inca, Uaro Conde Inca, Acos Inca, Chillque Inca, Mayo Inca, Yanahuara Inca, Cauina Inca, Quichiua Inca.[4] (Translation by author)

In this description Guaman Poma de Ayala takes care to explain that although Manco Capac and his royal siblings traveled with other groups, there was, nevertheless, a clear hierarchical order among them.

The "poor Inca" (or the Inca of Privilege), described by Guaman Poma de Ayala as living in the Cuzco heartland, formed the lower class of producers who supported the ruling elite of the capital through their tribute. Guaman Poma de Ayala (1980: 96 [1615: 117–118]) specifically describes the subservient position and image of the Inca of Privilege in comparison to the ruling Cuzco elite:

In the law of the Inca they ordained "Capac Apo Inca" to be king. Inca does not mean king. Instead as Inca there are low-status people like Chillque Inca potter; Acos Inca cheater; Uaroc Inca Llulla Uaroc liar; Mayo Inca false witness; Quillis Cachi and Equeco Inca, bearers of rumors and lies; Poquis Colla *millma rinre*.[5] These are Inca. Therefore they are neither lord nor king nor duke nor count nor marquis nor gentlemen Inca, but rather they are common Inca people and tribute payers.[6] (Translation by author)

According to Guaman Poma de Ayala, these low-status, tribute-paying Inca of the territories surrounding the Cuzco Valley were "Inca" by virtue of two salient features. First, ancestral representatives of these ethnic groups had accompanied Manco Capac on his mythical journey from the royal origin place of Tamputoco to Cuzco. Second, various ethnic groups of the Cuzco region, like the Inca of Cuzco and the imperial ruler himself, wore earspools. The Inca custom of wearing earspools and the journey of Manco Capac from Tamputoco to Cuzco are intimately related. The *huaca* (shrine) of Huanacauri is said to be one of the brothers of Manco Capac that was turned to stone during their journey to Cuzco, and it was this shrine that, according to Inca mythology, introduced the custom of ear piercing to the Inca.

In a later section of his *Primer nueva corónica . . .,* Guaman Poma de Ayala, a native of the Huánuco region, presents another list of Cuzco ethnic groups very similar to the two outlined above. In this passage, Guaman Poma de Ayala (1980: 310 [1615: 337]) suggests that the Cuzco ethnic groups were classified as Inca by the people living outside the Cuzco region, and he stresses the symbolic linkage between Inca ear perforations and their hierarchical status:

> As they had their courts [vices], ear perforations, and ancient customs of the Incas Capac Apu Inca[7] and other Auquiconas[8] Incas and Inca commoners: Hanan Cuzco, Hurin Cuzco, Anta Inca, Tambo Inca, Queuar Inca, Uaroc Inca, Quillis Cachi Inca, Uaro Condo Inca, Lari Inca, Masca Inca, Acos Inca, Chillque Inca, Cauina Inca, Quichiua Inca, Yanahuara Inca, Chilpaca Yunga, Uro Collo, Puquis Colla, *milma rinri.*[9] Each one of them, according to his rank, pierced his ears according to the law and ceremonies that they used in the time of the Inca.[10] (Translation by the author)

The social hierarchy of the various ethnic groups in the Cuzco region is emphasized in the above quote. Of paramount importance in the social hierarchy of the imperial capital, according to Guaman Poma de Ayala, were the royal and noble Inca by birth, the Capac Apu Inca (Royal Lord Inca) and Auquiconas (Nobles), respectively. Below them were the people of Hanan (Upper) and Hurin (Lower) Cuzco, who held a variety of different privileges and obligations to the Inca Empire. Below the Inca of Hanan and Hurin Cuzco, on the lowest level of the regional social hierarchy, were the ethnic groups living outside the Cuzco Valley.

Later in his chronicle, Guaman Poma de Ayala presents a fourth description of the social hierarchy in the Cuzco area within a model of Inca kinship.[11] In this description, he expands on the social divisions that he presented earlier, stating that the Auqui Capac Churi (Powerful Royal Children), were the "princes" of the kingdom. These included the sons, grandsons, and great-grandsons

of the ruling Inca. Below this social strata were the Incacona (Inca people), who included the high-status individuals of Hanan and Hurin Cuzco who were symbolically called the great-great-grandchildren and cousins of the Inca. The lowest stratum was composed of a large number of Inca who Guaman Poma de Ayala calls *haua* (outside) or *uaccha* (poor) Inca. These ethnic groups represented the tribute-paying citizens of the state who lived in regions surrounding the city of Cuzco. They are listed by Guaman Poma de Ayala (1980: 690 [1615: 740]) in relation to the four great *suyu* divisions that surrounded the imperial capital:

> Auqui capac churi, princes of this kingdom, sons and grandsons and great-grandsons of the Inca Kings of these kingdoms, Don Melchor Carlos Paullo Topa Ynca, Don Cristóbal Suna, Don Juan Ninancuro, Don Felepe Cari Topa . . . They are caste and generation and royal blood of this kingdom.
>
> Incaconas gentlemen lords Hanan Cuzco, Hurin Cuzco Incas, great-great-grandsons and cousins, *ñustas,* princesses of royal caste of this kingdom.
>
> Haua Inca, Uaccha Inca, Chinchay Suyo Inca, Anta Inca, Sacsa Uana Inca, Quilis Cachi Inca, Mayu Inca, Quichiua Inca, and their wives, *palla* (noblewomen), *aui* (common women): are tribute-paying Indians.
>
> Anti Suyo Inca, Tambo Inca, Lare Inca and their wives, *palla, aui:* are tribute-paying Indians.
>
> Colla Suyo Inca, Queuar Inca, Uaroc Inca, Cauina Inca, Masca Inca, Tambo Inca, Acos Inca, Chillque Inca, Papri Inca, and their wives, *palla, aui:* are tribute-paying Indians.[12]
>
> Conde Suyo Inca, Yanahuara Inca, and their wives they call *ynaca aui* and are tribute-paying Indians.[13] (Translation by author)

These four discussions by Guaman Poma de Ayala stress different essential aspects of Inca social hierarchy. The first discussion, set in the context of the Pacariqtambo origin myth, suggests that the social hierarchy of the Cuzco region was determined in a distant time, when the mythical Manco Capac emerged from the cave of Tamputoco and journeyed to Cuzco. The ethnic groups of the Cuzco region followed Manco Capac. As such, the hierarchical social order for the Cuzco region is presented as both divinely sanctified and unchangeable, since the events that determined the various social ranks took place in a primordial setting and involved the operation of powers outside the normal realm of human experience. The second passage describes the subservient, tribute-paying status that the Inca of Privilege held in relation to the royal inhabitants in Cuzco. The third discussion, which focuses on the earspools of the Inca, emphasizes the importance of symbolic emblems in the representation of Inca cultural identity as well as the physically distinguished internal ranks in that same identity. The origin of the earspools, like the social hierarchy of the region, is linked to the Pacariqtambo origin myth and the migration of the first, mythical Inca to the Cuzco Valley. The fourth discussion depicts the social hierarchy for the Cuzco region in terms of a descent system. This system begins with the ruling monarch, symbolically located in the center of Cuzco, and radiates from the imperial capital into the four *suyus* of the Cuzco region. The ethnic groups located farther from the sacred capital, were given the ambiguous title by Guaman Poma de Ayala of "poor" or "outside" Inca.

GARCILASO DE LA VEGA AND
THE SOCIAL HIERARCHY OF THE CUZCO REGION

Inca Garcilaso de la Vega was the son of a Spanish captain and a noble Inca woman. He was born in Cuzco in 1539 and lived there until he departed for Spain in 1560. In his old age, he finished an immense work titled *Comentarios reales de los incas,* which has become the best-known description of the Inca and of the Spanish invasion of the Andes. Within this work, Garcilaso de la Vega presents a detailed description of the social hierarchy of the Cuzco region and lists the major ethnic groups of the area. Like Guaman Poma de Ayala, Garcilaso de la Vega associates the social structure of the Cuzco region with the mythical acts of Manco Capac. However, this Cuzco-born chronicler presents a different version of the Pacariqtambo origin myth and the founding of the imperial city of Cuzco from that of the chronicler from Huánuco. In Garcilaso's version, Manco Capac and his sister/wife leave Lake Titicaca and travel to Pacariqtambo. From Pacariqtambo they walk to the mountain of Huanacauri and then descend into the Cuzco Valley. After founding the city and organizing its inhabitants, Manco Capac walks through the four *suyus* (divisions) of the Cuzco region organizing the ethnic groups who are later called Inca of Privilege:

> Thus to the east of the city, with the people he [Manco Capac] brought from that direction, in the region that stretches to the side of the river called Paucartampu, he ordered thirteen towns to be settled on either side of the royal road of Antisuyu. We omit their names to avoid prolixity; they are all or almost all of the tribe called Poques. To the west of the city, in an area eight leagues long by nine or ten broad, he ordered thirty towns to be established scattered on either side of the royal road of Cuntisuyu. These were peoples of three tribes with different names: Masca, Chillqui, and Pap'ri. To the north of the city he settled twenty towns with four names: Mayu, Cancu, Chinchapucyu, Rimactampu . . . The remotest of these towns is seven leagues from the city, and the rest are scattered on both sides of the royal road of Chinchasuyu. South of the city thirty-eight to forty towns were set up, eighteen of the Ayarmaca tribe, which are scattered on both sides of the royal road of Collasuyu for a distance of three leagues beginning from the place called Las Salinas, a short league from the city . . . The remaining towns are of people with five or six names; Quespicancha, Muina, Urcos, Quéhuar, Huáruc, Caviña . . .
>
> Now in our own times, during the last twenty years or so, the villages founded by the Inca Manco Capac and almost all the others in Peru are not in their ancient sites, but in completely different ones, because one of the viceroys, as we shall relate in its place, had them reduced to large towns, bringing together five or six at one place and seven or eight in another, the number varying according to the size of the villages that were concentrated . . . (Garcilaso de la Vega 1966: 52–53 [1609: Pt. 1, Bk. 1, Ch. 20])[14]

Garcilaso de la Vega's version of the Pacariqtambo origin myth and the founding of Cuzco implies that the Inca of Privilege were non-noble indigenous occupants of the region. Garcilaso de la Vega does not suggest, as does Guaman Poma de Ayala, that the Inca of Privilege originated with Manco Capac at Pacariqtambo and traveled with him to Cuzco. Instead, Garcilaso de la Vega's depiction asserts that the Inca of Privilege were genealogically and geographically outsiders to Cuzco and at the same time subservient to it.

Garcilaso de la Vega describes a hierarchy of genealogy and of space that mythically determines the social divisions in the Cuzco region. According to Garcilaso de la Vega, Manco Capac traveled from Lake Titicaca to Cuzco via Pacariqtambo. The descendants of this mythical founder became the Inca of Royal Blood, and the descendants of the inhabitants of Cuzco became the Incacuna (Inca people) of Hanan and Hurin Cuzco. Manco Capac then recognizes the ethnic groups of the Cuzco region. According to Garcilaso de la Vega's mythology, these groups were not present at the founding of the imperial capital and could therefore not be called Inca.

Later in his chronicle, Garcilaso de la Vega describes how Manco Capac gradually began to give privileges to the inhabitants of Cuzco and the surrounding region. The first privilege awarded to these loyal subjects was the right to wear certain clothes. The second was the right to have their hair cut short, like the Inca of Royal Blood. The third, and apparently the most important, was the privilege to pierce their ears and to wear earspools:

> There was however, a limitation as to the size of the hole, which was to be less than half that of the Inca's, and they were to wear different objects as earplugs according to their various names and provinces. Some were given as a token a splinter of wood as thick as the little finger, as were the tribe called Mayu and Çancu. Others were to have a little tuft of white wool which stuck out of the ear on both sides the length of the top of the thumb: these were of the tribe called Poques. The Muina, Huáruc, and Chillqui tribes were to have earplugs of the common reed the Indians called *tutura*. The Rimactampu tribe and their neighbors had them made of a plant called maguey in the Windward Islands and *chuchau* in the general tongue of Peru. When the bark is removed, the pitch is quite light, soft and

spongy. The three tribes bearing the name Urcos, Y'úcay, and Tampu, all dwelling down the river Y'úcay, were given special privilege and favor of wearing larger holes in their ears than the rest, though they were still to be less than half as large as those of the Inca. (Garcilaso de la Vega 1966: 56–57 (1609: Pt. 1, Bk. 1, Ch. 23])[15]

In this description Garcilaso de la Vega supports Guaman Poma de Ayala's observations that the hierarchical ranking of various ethnic groups of the Cuzco region was determined by their genealogical and spatial relationship to the Cuzco elite. Nevertheless, the ascribed social status of the various ethnic groups in the Cuzco region appears to have differed with the perspective of the observer. Guaman Poma de Ayala (1980: 66, 117–118, 310, 690), born in the Huánuco region and thus an outsider to the Cuzco area, is very specific in his description of the ethnic groups that surrounded the Cuzco Valley as Inca. On the other hand, Garcilaso de la Vega, the great-grandson of the last undisputed Inca ruler, Huayna Capac, saw the Inca of Privilege as outsiders to Cuzco. Garcilaso de la Vega (1966: 58 [1609: Pt. 1, Bk. 1, Cp. 23]), as an "Inca of Royal Blood," perceived the Inca of Privilege as non-Inca who were given special privileges and a minor ceremonial status only because of their proximity to the imperial capital.

SANTA CRUZ PACHACUTI YAMQUI SALCAMAYHUA AND THE SOCIAL HIERARCHY OF THE CUZCO REGION

A third possible description of the social order for the Cuzco region is briefly presented by the indigenous chronicler Juan de Santa Cruz Pachacuti Yamqui Salcamayhua as he describes the departure of Atahualpa from Cuzco (also see Zuidema 1977: 278). In this chronicle, the inhabitants of the Cuzco region loyal to the Cuzco-born Atahualpa in the civil war against his half brother Huascar are portrayed as leaving Cuzco in specific ranks, which may have served as symbolic expressions of their social order. Santa Cruz Pachacuti Yamqui Salcamayhua (1950: 273 [ca. 1613]) writes:

> And in this way Atahualpa left Cuzco, taking with him in his company all the *apocuracas*[16] and

Lord Chiefs

Manco Copac's sons of Cuzco

auquiconas for his soldier(s), and to support him, all the (pierced-) ear (people) of *mancopchurincuzco*,[17] who are gentlemen, and *acacacuzcos*[18] and *ayllon-cuzcos*,[19] who are special gentlemen; and as front runners he brings the Quiguares and Collasuyos, and Tambos, Mascas, Chillques, Papres, and Quicchguas, Mayos Tancos, Quilliscches, and as personal guards he brings the Chachapoyas and Cañares in the position of vanguard or rearguard, all in good order.[20] (Translation by author)

Although the terminology is slightly different, the relative order and composition of the social categories presented by Santa Cruz Pachacuti Yamqui Salcamayhua are consistent with those presented in the other indigenous chronicles. Like Guaman Poma de Ayala and Garcilaso de la Vega, Pachacuti Yamqui places the Inca of Royal Blood first, the Nobles of Cuzco second, the Citizens of Cuzco third, and the Inca of Privilege fourth.

BALTASAR DE OCAMPO CONEJEROS AND THE BAPTISM OF MELCHOR INCA

The fourth description that helps us to define the Inca heartland comes from an unlikely source. Some time after 1607, Baltasar de Ocampo Conejeros, an aging Spaniard who had fallen on hard times, petitioned the Viceroy of Peru, Juan de Medoza y Luna, for financial support. In his request letter, Ocampo Conejeros describes an elaborate baptism that he witnessed in Cuzco. In 1571, shortly after Viceroy Toledo arrived in Cuzco, Mari de Esquivel, the wife of the Spanish-supported Inca "ruler" Carlos Inca, gave birth to a son. As this was their first child and his birth provided a legitimate heir to the royal line of Inca kings, there was a great celebration in the city. Carlos Inca, who was the grandson of Huayna Capac, requested that the newly arrived viceroy baptize the child.[21] Titu Cusi Yupanqui and his young brother Tupac Amaru, both contenders to kingship, attended, as did many members of nearby parishes. From the list that Ocampo Conejeros presents, it is clear that all the major groups within the Cuzco region sent representatives:

Invitations were sent out over all the land for more than forty leagues round Cuzco, and there as-

sembled for the occasion all the Incas of the following parishes: Accha, Anta, Antahuayllas, Araypalpa, Ataras, Chinchero, Colcha, Concacalla, Cucharay-pampa, Equequo, Cuzco, Huanuquiti, Huayhua-cunca, Marco, Paccaritambu, Pacopata, Palpa, Pam-pacuchu, Parcos, Paruro, Pilpinto Pisaq, Pocoray, Puquiura, Quiquisana, Rimactampu, San Salvador, San Gerónimo de Corama, Surite, Urcos, Uru-pampa, Xaquizahuana, Yaurisca, Yucay.

All these are places where Incas reside. Canas, Canchis, and Collas were also invited, and men of all other nations that could be got together. Among the rest there came to the christening Titu Cusi Yupanqui Inca and his young brother Tupac Amaru Inca, who came from the province of Vilcapampa. (Baltasar de Ocampo Conejeros 1907: 208–209 [1610])

As a Spaniard involved in a baptism, Ocampo Conejeros presents the participants in terms of recently established parishes. Nevertheless, the area covered by these churches is very similar to the area covered by the indigenous lists of Inca of Privilege. They were, after all, in the words of Ocampo Conejeros, the "places where Incas reside."

Summary and Discussion

Although the details of the classificatory systems presented by Guaman Poma de Ayala, Garcilaso de la Vega, and Juan de Santa Cruz Pachacuti Yamqui Salcamayhua may vary in detail, it is important to note that the categories of hierarchically ranked genealogical sets that result from these chroniclers are nearly identical. Of utmost importance in these classificatory systems is the Royal Inca and his divine ancestors in Cuzco. The lowest tier of the Cuzco social hierarchy is held by the Inca of Privilege, who are genealogically and geographically distant from the emperor and the capital. Thus, although the system is grounded on genealogy, the actual territorial relationships that existed among the various hierarchically ranked groups reaffirm the prevailing Cuzco-centric social hierarchy. The social hierarchy of the Cuzco region is also legitimated through references to the mythical actions of Manco Capac, who is said to have established the regional ranking during the primordial creation of human existence.

After the formation of the Inca state, the Inca of Privilege continued to play important roles in the organization of the empire. For example, it appears that the Inca of Privilege held a wide range of administrative positions throughout the newly conquered territories of the empire. Guaman Poma de Ayala (1980: 318–335 [1615 f. 346–363]) presents a detailed discussion of administrative functions held by Inca of Privilege. Although his list should not be interpreted literally as a description of state organization based on a series of highly specialized ethnic groups, it does emphasize the wide range of administrative positions the various members of the Inca of Privilege groups could hold, including regional and provincial governors, judges, messengers, surveyors, administrators of the royal roads and bridges, and inspectors.

Inca of Privilege also played a critical role within Inca policies of colonization. After the conquest of a new region, the Inca frequently transferred part of the indigenous population of the region to a different area and brought colonists of differing ethnic backgrounds into the newly conquered province. Although the Inca institution of *mitmaes* (colonist) is still little understood and demands an extensive study, it has become evident that the Inca of Privilege were frequently resettled in recently incorporated areas. Closely affiliated with the ruling social hierarchy in Cuzco and loyal to the Inca state, the Inca of Privilege were ideal colonists.

The area that was once covered by the Inca of Privilege will be used in this study to define the Inca heartland. It is a region that covers approximately 60 kilometers in radius from Cuzco. Within the heartland are several discrete geographical areas, such as the Cuzco Basin, the Lucre Basin, the Huaro Basin, and the Plain of Anta, that supported very large populations in late prehistoric times. Groups from these areas, such as the Inca (Cuzco), Xaquixaguana (Anta), Ayarmaca (Anta and Chinchero), Mohina (Lucre), Pinahua (Lucre), and Huaro (Huaro), played different but critical roles in the final formation of the Inca state. Other groups such as those of Chit'apampa and the Cuyo located north of Cuzco in the Vilcanota River Valley, and even smaller groups such as the Tambo, Chillque, and Masca of the regions to the south of Cuzco, also played notable roles. Nevertheless, these various groups only become archaeologically recognizable relatively late in prehistory during the Killke Period (AD 1000–1400). The full story of Cuzco and the development of complex societies in the south-central Andes begins much earlier, with the arrival of the first bands of hunter-gatherers in the region soon after the end of the last Ice Age. Before we examine their lives, however, it is necessary to understand the general climatic conditions for the region in which the cultures developed.

Is Mimilaque
a mitima
colony?

If so, what ethnohistoric
sources are there?

· Garci Diez

· Katherine Julien (?)

· anything from Arequipa?

CHAPTER 3

Human Impact and Environmental History of the Cuzco Region

Alex Chepstow-Lusty, Brian S. Bauer, and Michael Frogley

THE CLIMATE of the central Andes has varied throughout prehistory. Recent research indicates that substantial fluctuations in rainfall and temperature have occurred over the past several millennia that greatly affected the plant and animal resources available to the people occupying various regions and altitudes. Although studies of past climate change in the central Andes are just beginning, some data are already available that can be used to assess the broad climatic conditions that have existed in the Cuzco region since the end of the last glaciation.

To understand the subtleties of past climatic change and its effects on societies, we must compare our archaeological data with climatic models developed using a variety of different Holocene records. In this chapter, we provide a summary of our current understanding of climate change in the Cuzco region since the end of the Pleistocene. Although changes in climatic conditions should not necessarily be seen as the direct cause of cultural change in the region, they did present limitations and, in a few cases of severe drought, considerable challenges to the existing societies.

Ice Cores

Our information on the paleoclimatology and paleoecology of the central Andes comes from various ice and lake-sediment cores of several different research projects. Currently the best-known record of past climatic conditions comes from ice cores extracted from permanent ice caps on the high peaks of the Andes Mountains. The Quelccaya ice cap (Photo 3.1), located at 5,670 m roughly midway between the Cuzco Valley and the Lake Titicaca Basin, is a major repository of environmental data on precipitation, temperature, and dust events at annual resolution for the last 1,500 years (Thompson et al. 1985, 1988; Thompson and Mosley-Thompson 1987; Shimada et al. 1991). In addition, ice cores taken from the Huascaran glacier in the north-central highlands of Peru have yielded important information on past climatic conditions dating as far back as fifteen thousand years (Thompson et al. 1995). By tracing the rate of ice accumulation, changes in oxygen isotope ratios, and the amount of dust particles deposited in the ice over time, these continuous records provide critical data to model the past climate of the Andes. Records such as these, especially those from the Quelccaya ice cores, will be referred to in this study for assessing climate change within the Cuzco region through time. Because these ice cores have been extracted from deposits at extremely high altitudes in remote areas of the Andes, we assume that many of the changes they record reflect broad regional environmental variability, rather than human-induced changes brought about by the activities of local societies.[1]

Lake-Sediment Cores

Other substantial suites of data concerning the paleoecology of the central Andes have been derived from sediment cores extracted from various lakes. The pollen, macrofossils, phytoliths, charcoal, and sedimentological records in

PHOTO 3.1. The Quelccaya ice cap provides
a remarkable record of climatic change in the Andes over
the past 1,500 years. (Courtesy of Lonnie G. Thompson)

these cores can act as a proxy for human impact as well as vegetation and climatic changes. Undoubtedly, the most important lake cores currently available for reconstructing the paleoecology and paleoclimatology of the Cuzco region have been extracted from Lake Marcacocha in the area of Ollantaytambo. Because this small lake forms the basis for much of our climate reconstruction and our understanding of the impact of human activities on the environment in the Cuzco region, it is important to describe it and the sediment cores in some detail.[2]

MARCACOCHA

Marcacocha is a small, recently infilled lake at an altitude of 3,355 m and currently about 40 meters in diameter (Photo 3.2). It is situated 12 kilometers from the town of Ollantaytambo, where the Patacancha River joins the Urubamba Valley.[3] Having most likely formed in the Late

Pleistocene, the lake basin is surrounded by Inca and pre-Inca terraces and lies near the agricultural boundary for maize and potato cultivation. The nearby valley slopes contain a number of archaeological sites, the earliest of which dates to ca. 800 BC (Kendall 1992; Early 1995).

In 1993 two overlapping series of cores, reaching a maximum depth of 8.25 m, were taken from near the center of the lake. The lowest 2 m of these sequences contained well-rounded gravels of fluviatile origin, which were almost barren of organic remains; in contrast, the upper 6 m were rich in organic sediments. These were sampled for pollen analysis to reconstruct the vegetation history of the area. Microcharcoal content (Clark 1982) as well as the ratio of organic to inorganic material were evaluated to understand the burning and erosional history of the catchment.[4] Five bulk radiocarbon dates were taken at regular intervals down the six organic meters of the cores, which gave an internally consistent chronology. The oldest of these samples yielded a calibrated date of around 2200 BC (Chepstow-Lusty et al. 1997: 129). In addition, an inorganic horizon was identified at 50 cm, separating the upper peats from the lower lake muds. This was deposited at the time of infilling ca. AD 1960, according to local sources. Hence, this extra time horizon markedly improves the chronology above the topmost radiocarbon date of ca. AD 1400.

The Marcacocha lake cores, which cover the last 4,000 years, provide the first proxy record of vegetation change from the Cuzco region. Most of the pollen is considered to be from plants that were within the immediate vicinity of the lake. Using the Marcacocha data to compare with events recorded in other lake-sediment and ice cores from the Andes, we can begin to reconstruct the late prehistoric environmental history of the Inca heartland. It should be noted, however, that we do not expect a one-to-one correlation between the events recorded in the lake-sediment cores and those documented in the ice cores. Paleoecological records from small lakes at lower altitudes, such as Lake Marcacocha, are generally assumed to register mostly local events.[5]

The Cuzco Environment and
Human Impact: 10,000–2000 BC

Environmental evidence for the Early and Middle Holocene Epochs has not yet been recovered from the Cuzco

PHOTO 3.2. Overview of the Patacancha Valley showing Lake Marcacocha surrounded by Inca and pre-Inca terraces
(Photograph by Alex Chepstow-Lusty)

region. This is unfortunate, since it was during the Middle Holocene, perhaps sometime between 7000 and 5000 BC that hunter-gatherers first arrived in the Cuzco Valley (Chapter 4).[6] Nevertheless, it seems that throughout the central Andes this may have been a time of drier conditions. Lake basins in Bolivia and northern Chile support the evidence for drier conditions during the Middle Holocene, though the timing of this subregional hydrological response varies (Abbott et al. 1997; Schwalb et al. 1999; Abbott et al. 2000; Cross et al. 2000; Baker et al. 2001).

By around 3000 to 2000 BC, the climate in the Andean highlands was becoming not unlike that of the modern day. In Peru, the coasts became much drier and the highlands started getting more regular annual rainfall. It may also be during this interval that El Niño events began (Sandweiss et al. 1996). This had major implications for people and may even be the time when agriculture began to be firmly established in the Andes. This would be consistent with the pollen data examined from both Lake Marcacocha (Chepstow-Lusty et al. 1998) and Lake Paca, as well as macrofossil evidence also from the Junín area, which indicates cultivation beginning around this time (Pearsall 1980, 1983; Hansen et al. 1994).

The Cuzco Environment and Human Impact: 2000 BC–AD 100

Since the Lake Marcacocha cores provide the best record of past climate change in the Cuzco region during the Late Holocene (Figure 3.1), their temporal divisions are used here (Chepstow-Lusty et al. 1998). These divisions include the following: 2000 BC–AD 100; AD 100–1100; and AD 1100–1993.

The Marcacocha cores suggest that even before 2000 BC the forests that covered the upper slopes of the Patacancha Valley had already been cleared[7] or had never

[handwritten margin note: 3000–2000 BC: 1) drier coast 2) more-regular sierra rain 3) possibly initial agriculture]

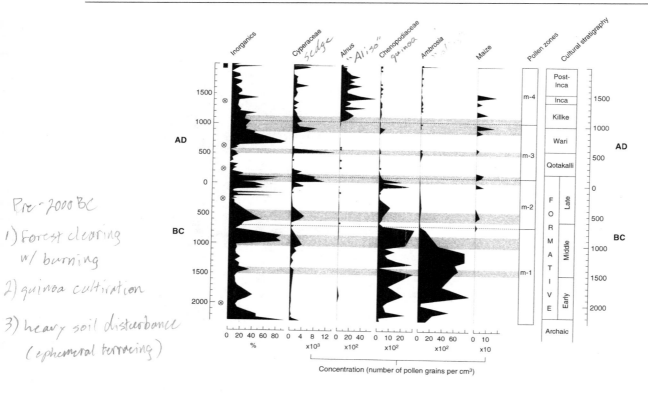

FIGURE 3.1. Selected results from the Marcacocha cores. The shaded areas show periods of possible aridity.

[Handwritten margin note:]
Pre- 2000 BC
1) forest clearing w/ burning
2) quinoa cultivation
3) heavy soil disturbance (ephemeral terracing)

fully recovered from the Early to Middle Holocene period of sustained aridity experienced before human impact began. The charcoal record indicates that the landscape was subjected to regular burning during most of this time interval. This burning, which is still practiced today, was probably done to maintain the soil fertility for agriculture, as well as the quality of pasture for herds of llamas and alpacas.

Pollen types indicate that local crops included *Chenopodium quinoa*, in the family Chenopodiaceae, confirming that cultivation was taking place in the Cuzco region at least as early as 2200 BC.[8] The significant occurrence of pollen from *Ambrosia arborescens* is an indicator of soil disturbance[9] and suggests that agricultural terraces were poorly developed during this period. The first ephemeral terrace works, which may have been used during this period, would have been erased when stone terraces were constructed in later prehistory.

Around 900 BC there is a marked increase in sedges (Cyperaceae), whose increased presence may reflect shrinking (i.e., drier) lake conditions. This is followed by a significant inorganic peak (Chepstow-Lusty et al.

2002), accompanied by a major permanent decline in *Ambrosia* toward 700 BC. These events may be linked to an abrupt climatic change around 850–760 BC that has been noted in other archaeological and paleoecological studies conducted elsewhere in the world (e.g., Van Geel et al. 1996). A second phase of sedges (Cyperaceae) centered on 500 BC corresponds with a peak of inorganic material, as does a third phase developing between 10 BC and AD 100. These phases may reflect general drought conditions for the region during these periods (Chepstow-Lusty et al. 2002).

The production of Chenopodiaceae crops may have reached its peak around 800 BC at the same time that *Ambrosia* was experiencing a rapid decline. Droughts may well have been superimposed on what was generally a long-term decline in temperature. Shortly after 800 BC, the Chenopodiaceae also experienced a massive decline. Subsequently, there appear to have been minor surges of Chenopodiaceae-oriented agriculture centered on 350 BC and between about 10 BC and AD 100.

Maize, the most important crop of the Cuzco region today, is observed for the first time in the Marcacocha

[margin note: Maize 2]

sedimentary deposits at around 600 BC. Its presence is noted throughout the rest of the sequence, albeit in a seemingly erratic fashion. The presence of maize at Lake Marcacocha is especially noteworthy because this is approximately the altitudinal limit of maize cultivation in the Patacancha Valley today. This may make the lake an especially sensitive repository for climatic information affecting the altitudinal distribution for maize in the region. Nevertheless, because maize's relatively large-sized pollen is poorly dispersed and, therefore, under-represented in cores, additional work is needed to establish its antiquity and continuity through the Marcacocha record.

The timing of potato cultivation in the Cuzco region and elsewhere in the Andes remains open to debate. Since most tuberous families in the Andes are insect pollinated, tangible remains of these plants are rarely observed in the pollen record. Potato remains are also more difficult to detect archaeologically than quinoa or maize, since their soft celluloid structure tends to preserve poorly, even after being burned. Excavations in Chile at the Late Pleistocene site of Monte Verde (Dillehay 1989) and at the Early Holocene site of Guitarrero Cave (Lynch 1980) indicate that hunter-gatherers collected wild tubers from an early date. Nevertheless, their importance in prehistoric diets and the timing of their domestication are still being researched.

The Cuzco Environment and Human Impact: AD 100–1100

[margin notes: EIP, MH]

During this period, evidence for Chenopodiaceae-oriented agriculture in the Marcacocha region sharply declines. Quinoa returns in low abundance at the end of this interval, possibly amongst a number of crops, including maize, but it never again reaches the high levels of cultivation experienced in the pre–AD 100 interval. The low proportion of Chenopodiaceae and *Ambrosia* suggests that temperatures were suppressed during much of this period, and it is possible that agriculture shifted to the production of hardier tuberous crops as well as pastoralism.

It is important to note that within the Marcacocha record a distinct Cyperaceae (sedge) event, currently thought to reflect a dry period, is centered on AD 550 (Figure 3.1). This is the largest and most defined peak within the Cyperaceae record, although it does not cor-

respond with any major inorganic peak (Chepstow-Lusty et al. 2002). Meanwhile, in the Quelccaya ice core there is a decrease in the ice accumulation record (a proxy for reduced precipitation) and an increasing abundance of dust particles between AD 540 and 600 (Thompson et al. 1985, 1988, 1992).

[margin note: AD 550: peak of an extreme aridity event ↓ 1) drought + El Niño exacerbate Moche collapse]

The distinct AD 550 Cyperaceae (sedge) peak in the Marcacocha sediment cores and the concurrent indications of a regional decline in precipitation and increase in dust in the Quelccaya ice cores appear to reflect a period of major climatic disruption during the latter half of the sixth century AD. These climatic episodes may have had significant effects on the coastal cultures of Peru. It has been suggested that a series of droughts, as well as several El Niños, were major factors in the dramatic collapse of the Moche polity between AD 560 and 600 on the northern Peruvian coast (Shimada et al. 1991; Thompson et al. 1992). Although the effects of these climatic events on the highland cultures are still not well understood (Paulson 1976; Isbell 1978), it is worth noting that it was during this period that the Wari state expanded from the Ayacucho region of Peru and began a centuries-long occupation of the Lucre Basin near Cuzco (see Chapter 7).

[margin note: 2) Wari expansion during this period]

The Quelccaya ice cores record that a second period of major droughts occurred between AD 1000 and 1100. Supporting evidence for this prolonged period of aridity comes from hiatuses and other sedimentological changes, indicative of low lake levels, in the Lake Titicaca cores. Kolata (1996) and his associates (Binford et al. 1997; Kolata et al. 2000) have proposed that these climatic changes resulted in the large-scale abandonment of the raised-field systems that surrounded Lake Titicaca, which supported the Tiwanaku state (Binford et al. 1996, 1997; Abbott et al. 1997). It is suggested that the Tiwanaku became overly dependent on their raised-field systems and that the state collapsed as a result of these droughts (Ortloff and Kolata 1993; Kolata and Ortloff 1996).

[margin note: Another severe dry spell AD 1000–1100]

Unlike the AD 550–600 drought, the prolonged drought of AD 1000–1100 is less clearly recorded in the Marcacocha cores. Even with minor problems in the Marcacocha chronology caused by assuming a constant sedimentation rate between the two top radiocarbon dates (through an interval including rapid inorganic deposition), the Marcacocha cores reflect an increased sedge abundance from about AD 900 onward. This is well before the Quelccaya record registers a marked reduction in precipitation. The two records may be recording different environmental information at this time, as the major declines in precipitation in the Quelccaya ice core occur during the post–AD 1000 era.

The Cuzco Environment and Human Impact: AD 1100–1490

Numerous studies have suggested that globally there was an increase in temperature during the first few centuries of the second millennium AD. This increase, called the Medieval Warm Period (ca. AD 1100–1490), is clearly marked by a period of reduced precipitation in the Quelccaya record. The establishment and dramatic success of the tree *Alnus acuminata* (*aliso* in Spanish) throughout the Medieval Warm Period may mark the warming of the climate in the Cuzco region (Chepstow-Lusty and Winfield 2000). From the decrease in grasses, it may also be suggested that the slopes of the Patacancha Valley became too valuable to be used for camelid pasture during this period. It is plausible that many of the slopes in the valley were first formally terraced at this time and that the construction of irrigation canals was begun then as well. These fluctuations in climate and environmental resources are currently under study. They are of special interest to archaeologists working in the Cuzco region, since it was during this period that the Inca state (ca. AD 1200–1400) developed (see Chapter 8).

Toward the end of the Medieval Warm Period there is a significant dust peak centered on AD 1450 in the Quelccaya record. Around this same time, there is also a distinct inorganic layer at Marcacocha. In both cores, these are the largest events of their kind of the last six hundred years; however, their cause(s) is still undetermined. These phenomena are also important to understand, since it was in the early to mid-1400s that the Inca expanded beyond the Cuzco region.

The Cuzco Environment and Human Impact during the Little Ice Age: AD 1490–1880

The existence of an appreciably colder period dating from the late fifteenth to the late nineteenth century, known as the Little Ice Age, is now widely recognized by scholars. The Little Ice Age has been identified in the Quelccaya ice cores by a decrease in the oxygen isotope values (from AD 1520 to 1900), an increase in the dust content (from AD 1490 to 1880), and an initial increase in precipitation (from AD 1500 to 1700)[10] followed by a dry period (AD 1720–1860; Thompson et al. 1986). The ice cores also appear to record a series of strong El Niño events across the Little Ice Age.

Both the beginning and the end of the Little Ice Age were very abrupt, as indicated by distinct and dramatic increases in the climate indices for the ice cores. The end of the Little Ice Age is placed at AD 1880, with the modern climate characterized by increased annual mean temperatures (Thompson and Mosley-Thompson 1987: 107). It is also suggested that although the onset of this period began around AD 1490, the most extreme effects did not begin for several centuries (Thompson and Mosley-Thompson 1987: 105). Thus, it was during the initial, comparatively milder decades of the Little Ice Age that the Inca Empire grew to its maximum size and came to control most of western South America.

Summary and Discussion

Although the study of past climate in the Cuzco region and concomitant anthropogenic modifications of the landscape is still just beginning, several important observations can be made. The first hunter-gatherers arrived in the Cuzco Valley during the Middle Holocene. At this time it is likely that conditions drier than exist today prevailed. By 2000 BC, precipitation had increased and the climate conditions resembled those of the modern day. During this period we may see the widespread cultivation of Chenopodiaceae-oriented agriculture, and settlements began to become larger and more permanent.

The Marcacocha sediment cores suggest that although Chenopodiaceae production may have dominated local agriculture for more than a millennium, it suddenly declined around 700 BC. About this same time, the first maize pollen appears in the lake cores. It is possible, although additional research needs to be conducted, that these events document the arrival of maize in the Cuzco region and a dramatic shift in agricultural practices that would have accompanied it.

Periods of droughts may have occurred around 1500 BC, 900 BC, and 500 BC. These remain to be investigated through additional cores in the Cuzco region. Around AD 100 two important changes occur in the archaeological record of the Cuzco region. First, there is a shift from the occupation of knolls and ridges to settlements located near the valley bottom. Second, there is the development and use of a new ceramic style called Qotakalli. The Marcacocha core indicates that large-scale Chenopodiaceae production essentially stops at this time and maize appears to take on an increasingly important role in the local economy. Although additional research needs to be done, it is possible that all of these events may be related to an arid event that also occurred at this time.

It is also important to note that within the Marcacocha sediment cores there is a distinct Cyperaceae (sedge) event, thought to reflect a dry period, centered on AD 550. This prolonged drought may also be recorded in the Quelccaya ice cores as a decrease in the ice accumulation record and an increasing abundance of dust. The timing of this drought is of particular interest to Andean archaeologists, since it appears to be correlated with the spread of the Wari from Ayacucho into the south-central Andes.

It has been reported that another prolonged drought occurred in the Lake Titicaca region between AD 1000 and 1100. This event is not well recorded in the Marcacocha sediment cores. Instead, the lake appears to have experienced a period of diminishing water intake in the pre-1000 era, starting around AD 900. The reasons for these inconsistencies are currently not understood.

It was during the Medieval Warm Period (AD 1100–1490) that the Inca state developed in the Cuzco Valley and started its expansion across the Andes. Perhaps beginning as early as AD 1200, a large polity had formed and was in control of the greater Cuzco region by around AD 1400 (Bauer 1992a; Covey 2003). The previously independent groups that inhabited the Cuzco region were brought into the emergent Inca state through a variety of mechanisms, including alliance formations, wife exchange amongst chiefs, and outright conquest (Bauer and Covey 2002). The Inca then began to expand from the Cuzco region, and by the end of the Medieval Warm Period, they had established control over much of western South America and had become the largest empire to develop in the Americas.

AD 100 - 550:
1) settlement shift to valley bottoms
2) maize agr. common
3) Qotakalli ceramics
4) ends w/ dry period, Wari occupation

climatic periods & Inca State:
1) MCO (AD 1100-1490) → state formation, political consolidation of Cuzco Valley
2) LIA (AD 1490-1880) → imperial expansion in early period, when conditions were more mild. Spanish Conquest = 1532.

CHAPTER 4

The Archaic Period
and the First People of the Cuzco Valley (9500–2200 BC)

Brian S. Bauer, Bradford Jones, and Cindy Klink

WITH THE FINAL RETREAT of the Pleistocene glaciers between 10,000 and 8,000 BC, much of the Andean region became open to human occupation for the first time. Although initially the climate was cooler and moister than it is today, small groups of hunter-gatherers soon began to colonize the mountains. Presumably migrating from the western slopes and Pacific coastal areas where occupations are known to date as far back as 10,500 BC (Dillehay 1984, 1997), these earliest peoples ventured into the vast uninhabited highlands of Peru, Bolivia, and Chile.[1]

Excavations by John Rick (1980) in caves and rock-shelters in the high-altitude area of Junín have yielded evidence of camelid hunting perhaps as early as 9000 BC. Caves in the more montane areas of Ayacucho (MacNeish et al. 1980) and Callejón de Huaylas (Lynch 1980) provide evidence of upland occupations dating to at least 8000 BC that were supported by a broader spectrum of plant and animal resources. Extensive research on high-mountain environments and early human habitation has also been carried out in the upper Moquegua region. Aldenderfer (1998) has conducted excavations at various rock-shelters as well as at the open-air site of Asana, which was first occupied by hunter-gatherers just after 8000 BC.

In the south-central and southern highlands, the long period of preceramic occupations is frequently referred to as the Archaic Period (9500–2200 BC). Aldenderfer (1996, 1997, n.d.) and Klink (1998, 1999, n.d.) have directed surveys and excavations at various Archaic Period sites in the Lake Titicaca region. The Archaic-era economy was based on hunting large and small game as well as collecting wild plants. Terrestrial resources dominated the economy, and sites concentrated in the interior river valleys and surrounding plains and mountains. A true "lacustrine" adaptation, with land use and resources focused on Lake Titicaca itself, apparently did not develop until the end of the Archaic Period or the early part of the Formative Period. Currently, the oldest excavated occupations at the site of Quelcatani date to 6200–6400 BC (Aldenderfer n.d.); however, initial settlement of the region clearly occurred much earlier (Klink 1998, n.d.).

Despite the fact that few studies have been conducted at early sites in the central highlands, it is clear that hunting and foraging bands were moving through and beginning to inhabit the Andean mountains and high grassland areas (*puna*) relatively soon after the end of the glacial period (Núñez et al. 2002). Following the general outline provided by Aldenderfer (1998: 51; n.d.), I provisionally divide the Cuzco Archaic into Early (10,000–8000 BP [calibrated 9500–7000 BC]), Middle (8000–6000 BP [calibrated 7000–5000 BC]), and Late (6000–4000 BP [calibrated 5000–2200 BC]) Phases. The Cuzco Archaic remains a vast and unexplored time period. It is widely recognized that the high grassland regions south and southeast of Cuzco, including the Provinces of Chumbivilcas and Espinar, hold numerous caves and rock-shelters with extensive lithic materials (Astete 1983; S. Chávez 1988; Lantarón 1988). The dates of these sites are, however, not known.

Until recently, the Cuzco Valley was believed to be

[handwritten margin notes:]
Archaic:
1) 9500-2200 BC
2) broad-spectrum H/G economy
3) initial sierra occupants came up from Pacific coast
4) little/no evidence for Titicaca Area occupant until Terminal Archaic

devoid of Archaic Period materials and occupations. A lack of prominent caves, rock-shelters, and rock art, combined with an image of Archaic peoples being confined to the high grassland areas where wild camelids would have flourished, supported the notion that the Cuzco Valley was occupied relatively late in prehistory. In addition, since nearly one hundred years had passed since the first archaeological studies concerning the Cuzco region were published and no Archaic finds had been reported, it became the standard view that there were simply none to be found (K. Chávez 1980).

However, soon after initiating our systematic survey of the Cuzco Valley we began finding evidence of Archaic Period remains. The first artifacts included isolated projectile points. Later, occupation sites marked by scatters of andesite debitage were also identified. Working in collaboration with Cindy Klink, who had just finished a projectile-point sequence for the Lake Titicaca region (Klink and Aldenderfer n.d.), we were able to assign many of our points tentative temporal affiliations. The Lake Titicaca Basin Archaic Period projectile sequence was selected as a working model for developing and testing a Cuzco-based sequence because the Lake Titicaca region

is relatively near to Cuzco and it currently has some of the best-researched Archaic Period remains in the central Andes.

Our database for the Archaic Period in the Cuzco Valley is rudimentary at best. Although we found more than thirty sites that contain strong lithic components, the majority of these cannot be definitively dated to the Archaic Period because of a lack of diagnostic artifacts (i.e., projectile points). Our survey and test excavations suggest that andesite was widely used in the Cuzco region to make stone tools from the Middle Archaic Period through the Formative Period and perhaps even later. Because of this, Archaic Period sites cannot be identified simply by the presence of stone tools and debris. In theory, sites with lithic materials could date to any prehistoric period. Thus, we classify a site as dating to the Archaic Period only when diagnostic projectile points have been recovered from it (Map 4.1).

Furthermore, our survey methodology was not ideal for the identification and reconstruction of Archaic Period cultures. Surveys dedicated to mapping the distribution of preceramic-period remains frequently involve crew members walking in lines no more than 5 meters

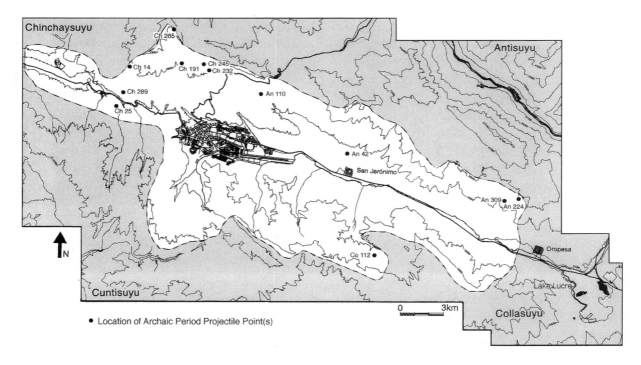

MAP 4.1. Known Archaic Period sites in the Cuzco Valley

apart, rather than the wider-spaced transects used in our research. This is because preceramic sites frequently represent the remains of hunting stations and base camps, which are often quite small.

It should also be mentioned that the landscape of the Cuzco Valley is dynamic. Millennia of erosion have destroyed or buried many Archaic Period sites. We also note that people have been farming and reshaping the Cuzco landscape through their settlements as well as through terraces and irrigation works for well over three thousand years. These activities can easily destroy or distort beyond recognition the relatively delicate remains of Archaic Period sites.

Despite these limitations, our survey did provide important information on the previously unknown preceramic cultures of the Inca heartland. The identification of Archaic Period remains in the Cuzco area more than doubles the length of known occupations in the valley and provides a foundation for larger and more systematic studies to be conducted on the first peoples of the region.

The Cuzco Archaic Period

Ten thousand years ago the Cuzco Valley would have been a tempting environment for hunter-gatherers. Its numerous springs and natural salt pans would certainly have been alluring. Equally important, its broad river valley bottom, gently sloping valley sides, and accessible, although not especially high, grassland areas, would have supported a wide variety of flora and fauna. Although no Late Pleistocene or Early Holocene studies have been conducted in the region, we can safely state that a variety of large mammals, including wild ruminants (camelids and deer) and their carnivorous predators, such as pumas, lived in the valley and high grassland. Smaller mammals, for example, fox, viscacha, and guinea pig, as well as various rodents were also common. Birds, attracted to the floodplains and river edge, would also have thrived in these swampy regions.

The Cuzco Valley, which ranges in elevation from 3,100 m to 4,800 m, contained hundreds of plants species. The high grassland was dominated by bunchgrasses that provided the food for camelids. The higher valley slopes may have held stands of wild chenopods. The mid- to lower

valley slopes were covered with Andean trees, including *queñua* and *quishuar,* which provided a prime habitat for deer. The valley bottom, floodplain, and river edge contained a dense patchwork of perennial shrubs. As we will see, this valley, with its diverse wealth of wild plant and animal resources, supported hunter-gatherers for more than two hundred generations before the advent of agriculture.

THE EARLY ARCHAIC PHASE (9500–7000 BC)

The remains of Early Archaic Phase hunter-gatherers in the Andes are exceptionally rare. The small size of their bands, their light impact on the environment, and their high mobility make Early Archaic Phase peoples exceedingly difficult to detect in the archaeological record. With results similar to many other highland surveys, we recovered projectile points dating to this period but were not able to identify the camps of these earliest peoples (Aldenderfer 1989b).

During the survey phase of the project, two projectile points were found that, based on stylistic comparisons with other points found in the south-central Andes, appear to date to the Early Archaic Period (Klink and Aldenderfer n.d.). Both are spine-shouldered diamond points with rounded bases (Figure 4.1). One of the projectile points (Ch. 191 L-4) is made on a high-quality chert. The other (Ch. 245 L-1), which is an especially elegant projectile point, is made on high-quality chalcedony. Both were recovered in the northwest corner of

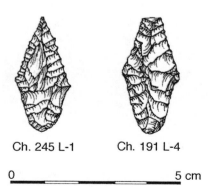

Ch. 245 L-1   Ch. 191 L-4

0   5 cm

FIGURE 4.1. Early Archaic Phase projectile points from the Cuzco Valley. Both of these are made with imported material.

the valley, at an elevation around 3,950 m (Map 4.1). With its gently rolling hills, numerous springs, and deep ravines, this region of the valley may have been particularly well suited for deer during the Early Archaic Phase.

Although little can be concluded on the basis of a few isolated tools, it is worth noting that both Early Archaic Phase projectile points are made with materials that are not found in the Cuzco Valley. In addition, it may be significant that no Early Archaic Phase occupation sites have been found in the study area. From these observations, it can be proposed that the Early Archaic Phase peoples may not have intensively occupied the Cuzco Valley, but instead included it within a larger hunting and foraging migratory cycle.

MIDDLE ARCHAIC PHASE (7000–5000 BC)

The Middle Archaic is described as a time when hunter-gatherers were "settling down" across the Andes (Richardson 1994: 39). With population levels increasing over several millennia, archaeological sites dating to the Middle Archaic Phase are far more common than those dating to the Early Archaic Phase. In some regions, such as in Callejón de Huaylas and in Junín, a shift from deer to camelid remains occurs during this period, reflecting an intensification of camelid exploitation. Likewise, evidence from the Callejón de Huaylas and Ayacucho areas indicates that certain plant species were beginning to be se-

lected intensively for use. In other words, across the Andean highlands the Middle Archaic Phase is a time of slow transition from an era of nomadic hunters and foragers to a time of more sedentary existence based on the intensive use of local plants and animals (Figure 4.2).

Paleoclimatic research conducted in the Lake Titicaca Basin suggests that the period of the Middle Archaic Phase as well as the early Late Archaic Phase was a time of exceptional aridity in the highlands. The notably drier-than-present conditions would have impacted the range of resources available to the hunter-gatherers in the Cuzco region. Based on both stylistic comparisons of projectile points and radiocarbon dates, our survey of the valley yielded two locations (An. 42 and An. 309) with late Middle Archaic (or early Late Archaic) remains (Map 4.1). These sites contained broad scatters of lithic debitage suggestive of camps, although both of unknown duration. The sites, located at 3,650 m and 3,450 m, are significantly lower than the Early Archaic Phase remains. At these mid-valley elevations, the occupants of the sites had easy access to all of the ecological zones of the region.

During the course of the Cuzco Valley Archaeological Project, excavations were conducted at the site of Kasapata (An. 309) to gain additional information on the lifeways of the early inhabitants of the Cuzco Valley. Although the analysis is still under way, some general conclusions can be presented concerning its early occupants. Two dates were obtained from a single piece of carbon found

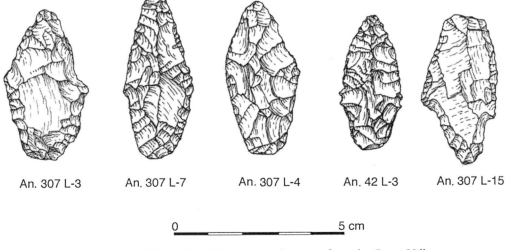

An. 307 L-3   An. 307 L-7   An. 307 L-4   An. 42 L-3   An. 307 L-15

0 _____ 5 cm

FIGURE 4.2. Middle Archaic Phase projectile points from the Cuzco Valley

at the lowest occupation: 5645 ± 76 BP (calibrated 95.4% probability: 4690–4340 BC),[2] and 5567 ± 38 BP (calibrated 95.4% probability: 4460–4330 BC).[3] This stratum provides evidence of a series of temporary, perhaps seasonal, camps. Stratified sheet middens containing andesite debitage and several obsidian flakes were found. Projectile points, bone tools, unworked bone, and burned stones were also recovered in the middens. The faunal remains included numerous large (camelid and deer) and small mammal remains. The postholes of a small circular structure with a possible hearth were identified as well as various pits and two adult burials (Jones et al. 2001; Klink et al. 2001). Although this specific deposit dated to the early Late Archaic Phase, we believe that it is typical of the earlier Middle Archaic occupations at the site as well.

LATE ARCHAIC PHASE (5000–2200 BC)

The Late Archaic Phase began as a time of aridity but ended with a climate not unlike that of the modern day. Equally gradual yet dramatic shifts in cultural organization took place during this period (Rick 1988; Aldenderfer 1989a). Like their predecessors, the Late Archaic peoples of the central highlands are archaeologically identifiable as small groups that hunted and harvested wild plants. However, by the end of the Late Archaic Phase, many of these groups had grown large and had become semi-sedentary, engaging in some forms of early horticulture and incipient animal domestication. In an overview of Andean preceramic cultures, Lynch notes that the Late Archaic marked a time of profound changes:

> Broadly based subsistence systems were accompanied by experimental horticulture, varying degrees of sedentism (with seasonal transhumance in some cases), and technological proliferation, including many styles of projectile points, other artifacts for processing plant foods and industrial materials, and luxury artifacts intended to change one's personal state (objects of adornment, status, and hallucinogenic paraphernalia) . . . We know now that the process of agriculturalization was gradual, [and] that it took up much of the Archaic period . . . (Lynch 1999: 257)

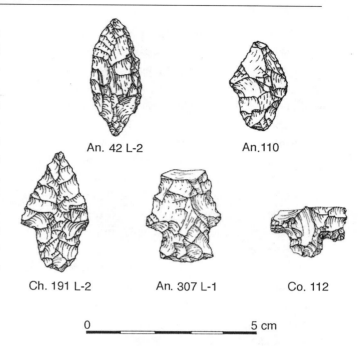

An. 42 L-2   An. 110

Ch. 191 L-2   An. 307 L-1   Co. 112

0   5 cm

FIGURE 4.3. Late Archaic Phase projectile points from the Cuzco Valley

We have recovered survey and excavation information to begin to outline the many social changes that occurred in the Cuzco Valley during this seminal period (Figure 4.3). Seven sites (Ch. 25, Ch. 191, Ch. 232, An. 42, An. 110, An. 309, and Co. 112) were found with Late Archaic Phase remains (Map 4.1). To these we might conservatively add three additional sites that contained points that were classified as "general" Archaic (Ch. 14, Ch. 265, and Ch. 289). This set of ten sites ranged in size and elevation from an isolated point found above 4,200 m to a moderately dense scatter of lithics at 3,450 m.

The largest Late Archaic Phase site so far identified is that of Kasapata (An. 309), which measures some 100 by 40 meters. As noted above, this site was selected for test excavations by our project because it contained both late Middle and Late Archaic Phase remains (Jones et al. 2001). A dense midden deposit, which in places was more than 50 cm thick, defined much of the Late Archaic Phase component of the site. A carbon sample from the midden yielded a radiocarbon date of 4428 ± 37 BP (calibrated 95.4% probability: 3330–2910 BC).[4]

Although the analysis of the materials from these excavations is still being conducted, some general conclusions can be presented. For example, the Late Archaic

Phase midden contains large quantities of andesite debitage, as well as appreciable quantities of obsidian and a few fragments of chert.[5] Numerous projectile points and other bifaces, bone tools, and bone ornaments as well as examples of ground-stone bowls, mortars, and a stone hoe were also found (Klink et al. 2001). Burned small- to medium-sized stones are also common in the Late Archaic Phase stratum. Faunal remains included abundant burned and unburned bones of various large mammals, small mammals, and birds. There appears to be, however, an increase in the relative quantity of camelid bones in comparison to other large mammals (i.e., deer) through time.

Although no structures were found, several large postholes and various large pits were identified. Various burials were recovered from the Late Archaic Phase contexts, including numerous infants as well as several youths, young adults, and adults. Although most of the burials did not contain grave goods, one youth was buried with twelve bone beads and one infant had been covered with red ocher.

The Cuzco Late Archaic Phase remains support general trends that have been identified elsewhere in the Andean highlands (e.g., Callejón de Huaylas, Ayacucho, and Lake Titicaca) as occurring during this time period. These include a population increase, as reflected in the greater number of sites; sites that are both larger in size and appear to have been inhabited for longer durations; and a greater variety of stone and bone implements as well as personal ornaments. Furthermore, there is evidence of intensification of plant resources and a possible change to pastoralism.

It should also be noted that the one set of petroglyphs found during our survey work in the Cuzco Valley is located relatively near the site of Kasapata (An. 309). Although these petroglyphs have been known locally for some time, they remain to be described or studied in detail and cannot be dated to the Archaic Period with certainty.[6] The petroglyphs are situated on top of a steep hill called Cruz Moco (An. 224), directly north of the Inca ruins of Tipón and west of Kasapata. At the summit of the hill is a group of large boulders on which sets of spirals, dots, and irregularly running lines have been carved (Map 4.1 and Photo 4.1).

PHOTO 4.1. At the summit of a steep hill is a group of large boulders on which sets of spirals, dots, and irregularly running lines have been carved.

Summary and Discussion

Currently, we can only map the general contours of culture change that occurred in the Cuzco Valley during the long Archaic Period. Nevertheless, based on newly available survey and excavation data, we can state that the differences between the Early, Middle, and Late Archaic Phase remains in the valley reflect the gradual and, no doubt, uneven development of sedentary life during this period. The Early Archaic Phase begins with small groups of highly mobile hunters and foragers. The population levels and the impact of these migratory groups on the environment are so low that their campsites are almost undetectable. Nevertheless, we know that their hunting tools were made of high-quality, exotic materials, and we can propose that these groups included the Cuzco Valley within larger seasonal movements.

The Middle Archaic and Late Archaic Phases bring with them larger bands with greater archaeological visibility. These early cultures appear to have had favored sites in the valley. Although the bands were still mobile, they returned repeatedly to preferred locations in the Cuzco Valley and most likely stayed for longer periods. Excavations at the site of Kasapata provided evidence of an early occupation (ca. 4400 BC) with small structures, pits, burials, and stratified sheet middens. The vast majority of the tools and lithic debris were produced from local andesite resources. Nevertheless, travel to, or trade with, other regions also occurred, since some exotic materials, such as fine chert and obsidian, are present in the collections. Faunal remains indicate that a broad range of animals were being hunted, with an emphasis on the deer of the forested valley slopes and the camelids of the higher grasslands.

The later preceramic occupations of the valley, represented by the Late Archaic Phase sites, reflect a more sedentary lifestyle. Thick middens and larger sites are suggestive of large band sizes. Excavations at the site of Kasapata, which encountered various burials that reflected the full mortality range (infants, youths, young adults, and adults), also bespeak of a more sedentary lifestyle. The increase in camelid remains over those of other large mammals may reflect the beginnings of animal domestication. The remains of stone grinding tools for seed plant processing, as well as a stone hoe, are suggestive of more intensive utilization of wild plants. Thus, although hunting and gathering had provided well for the inhabitants of the Cuzco Valley for thousands of years, it currently appears that as early as 3000 BC groups had become larger in size and had begun to change their resource strategies to include long-term occupations, early animal domestication, and perhaps incipient agriculture.

3000 BC:

1) climate less arid, more amenable to human occupation in highlands

2) groups in Cuzco start becoming more sedentary, subsistence shift toward farming & herding

CHAPTER 5

The Formative Period
and the Emergence of Ranked Societies

(2200 BC–AD 200)

LIKE OTHER RECENT AUTHORS working in the Cuzco region (e.g., Zapata 1998), I have elected to call the period of time between the advent of ceramic production and the appearance of Qotakalli pottery in the Cuzco region the Formative Period.[1] During this era, profound changes occurred in the region, including the gradual shift from a mobile life to a sedentary one and the concomitant transition from wild to domesticated food resources. The appearance of permanent residential structures, which were aggregated into hamlets and villages, occurs during this period. The existence of permanent villages implies a reliance on stable food sources as well as population levels above those of most hunting-and-gathering societies. As the population levels grow, the organizational needs and material demands of these larger groups also increase. From these humble origins, craft specialization, public architecture, and social ranking emerge over time. *How?*

The development of fully sedentary villages, subsisting predominantly on agricultural and animal husbandry, was a long and uneven process in the Andes. Although our knowledge is elementary at best, I will summarize what we currently know concerning this process in the Cuzco region. The period during which this process took place will be divided into three phases: the Early, Middle, and Late Formative.[2] The phases represent the gradual cultural transformations that begin with the establishment of the first fully sedentary, autonomous villages and that end with the development of several chiefdoms in the greater Cuzco area.

The Early Formative Phase (2200–1500 BC) and the Beginnings of Ceramic Production

The Early Formative Phase in the Cuzco region starts around 2200 BC, with the beginnings of ceramic production, and ends around 1500 BC, with the establishment of large permanent villages. The Early Formative Phase cultures developed successful agricultural systems and presumably maintained herds of domesticated camelids. Cores taken from Lake Marcacocha in the Patacancha Valley suggest that forest clearance by burning had taken place and that agriculture was established by the Early Formative Phase. There is evidence of successful Chenopodiaceae cultivation (most certainly including quinoa) as early as 2200 BC. After 800 BC, Chenopodiaceae cultivation rapidly declined (Chepstow-Lusty et al. 1997), although there appear to have been minor resurgences around 350 BC and between about 10 BC and AD 100 (Figure 3.1).

Within our survey of the Cuzco Valley, we recorded a dozen or so sites that contained large lithic components as well as the remains of heavily eroded pottery. Five of these sites contained a sand-tempered pottery that has not previously been described in the Cuzco region. The pottery is relatively thin, and the most common vessel form is a curved-sided pot with flaring rims. Although this theory is untested, I suggest that this sand-tempered ware, or perhaps another unidentified ware, represents the earliest ceramics for the Cuzco region. The central point is that the currently oldest-dated ceramic style for the Cuzco Valley, Marcavalle, certainly does not repre-

EF:
1) ceramics ca 2200 BC
2) large, perm. villages ca 1500 BC
3) Agr. fields cleared by burning
4) herds of domesticated camelids

sand-tempered pottery

sent the *first* pottery style to have been produced in the region. As carefully documented by Karen Chávez (1980), Marcavalle ceramics are relatively sophisticated in their forms, surface finishes, paste-temper groups, and decorative techniques. They appear nothing like the poorly fired and unslipped first ceramics of other Andean regions, such as the Pasiri ceramics of the Lake Titicaca Basin (Stanish et al. 1997: 40–42). As additional research unfolds concerning the Late Archaic Phase and Early Formative Phase occupations of the Cuzco region, it is most certain that new ceramic types will be identified that will substantially predate the Marcavalle series.

The Middle Formative Phase and the Establishment of Autochthonous Village Leadership (ca. 1500–500 BC)

The beginning of the Middle Formative Phase is marked by the development of Marcavalle ceramics and the establishment of the first villages. With the gradual establishment of the first villages in the Cuzco Valley, the lifeways of its early occupants were transformed. The Middle Formative Phase in the valley is represented by a series of undifferentiated settlements, which began as hamlets and grew increasingly large through time. We can speculate that these villages would have had leaders (so-called Big Men), whose positions of authority were highly unstable. Particularly successful leaders may have gained considerable authority over their lifetime. Repetitively successful individuals, family groups, or lineages would have given rise to the beginnings of ranked village societies throughout this long period.

This era of developmental growth in the Cuzco area is best represented in the detailed analysis of the site of Marcavalle by Karen Chávez and her colleagues. The site is located between Cuzco and San Sebastián, on the west bank of the Cachimayu River well above the floodplain of the Huatanay River. It is on good agricultural land, close to both the salt springs of Cachimayu (Photo 1.2) and the rich clay deposits of Sañu (K. Chávez 1980: 226–227; Bauer 1998: 86, 103).

THE SITE OF MARCAVALLE

Manuel Chávez Ballón and Jorge Yábar Moreno first noted the prehistoric occupations at the site of Marcavalle

in 1949. Chávez Ballón and Rowe conducted surface collections there in 1954 (K. Chávez 1980: 211), and Rowe concluded correctly in his 1956 article that the site contained the earliest ceramics found in the valley.

Luis Barreda Murillo and Patricia Lyon directed the first excavations at Marcavalle in 1963 and 1964. The preliminary results of that work are presented in Barreda Murillo (1973), along with the first detailed description of the ceramics from the site. K. Chávez (1980: 213) reports that various other surface collections and excavations were conducted at the site during the 1960s and 1970s by members of the Cuzco academic community and by other professionals. Despite its important position in the prehistory of the Cuzco region, the site is now nearly destroyed. Alfredo Valencia Zegarra and Arminda Gibaja Oviedo (1991) have chronicled the slow destruction of the site of Marcavalle and have pleaded for its preservation.

Karen Chávez directed the largest study at Marcavalle from 1966 through 1968. Her research is described in a number of publications (K. Chávez 1977, 1980, 1981a, 1981b, 1982). On the basis of extensive attribute study, K. Chávez defined ten major vessel forms and divided the Marcavalle collections into four phases. She also provided descriptions of a number of surface finishes, paste-temper groups, and decorative techniques.

Considerable effort has been made to date Marcavalle pottery. A carbon sample from Barreda Murillo and Lyon's 1963 excavations yielded a date of 2645 ± 115 BP (calibrated 95.4% probability 1050–400 BC; Patterson 1967: 143; Lawn 1971: 373).[3] K. Chávez furnished five dates for Marcavalle ceramics that ranged from 2916 ± 55 BP to 2571 ± 45 BP.[4] To these, we may be able to add a date, 3330 ± 240 BP (calibrated 95.4% probability 2300–900 BC), provided by Frederick Engel (Krueger and Weeks 1966: 155) from materials found at the site of Chanapata.[5] These dates suggest that the production of Marcavalle ceramics may have occurred as early as 1200 BC and continued perhaps until about 700 or 500 BC.

MARCAVALLE AND THE FORMATION OF VILLAGE LIFE

Excavations by K. Chávez at the site of Marcavalle provided important information on the lifeways of the early villagers who lived there. A large number of faunal re-

---

[Handwritten margin notes:]

MF:
1) Marcavalle ceramics
2) 1ˢᵗ villages, grown from hamlets
3) domesticated camelids
4) beans & maize Agr.
5) extensive regional trade, particularly w/ Titicaca
6) adobe walls around Marcavalle, but no public/ceremonial architecture

[next to text:] How?!

mains from the site were analyzed by Elizabeth S. Wing (1978) and George R. Miller (1979). The majority (<84%) of the faunal remains were camelids (K. Chávez 1980: 244–246). The sizes of the camelids indicate that they were domesticated, and the broad animal age span in the collection suggests that they were being used and killed for a variety of purposes, including wool, beasts of burden, food, and sacrifices (K. Chávez 1980: 246–248). Other domesticated animals in the collection included guinea pigs and dogs. Wild species were represented by deer, pumas, small rodents, birds, and toads in decreasing percentages (K. Chávez 1980: 244, 247).

Lithics from the site document trade with other localities of the southern highlands. Two fragments of obsidian have been traced to the Chivay source, near the Colca Valley, and four additional obsidian pieces have been identified as coming from the Alca sources, near Qotahuaci (K. Chávez 1980: 249–253; Burger et al. 2000: 289).[6] K. Chávez (1980: 243–244) also recovered direct evidence of agriculture, with bean remains being dated at 800 BC and maize at 200 BC. Other imported materials included a peccary tooth from the lowlands and green stone bowls of an uncertain source (K. Chávez 1980: 247, 254–255). Finally, although some adobe walls were identified, no large architectural features that could be classified as public works were found. K. Chávez (1980: 259) summarizes what the valley-wide settlement pattern would have been like during Middle Formative times: "While each village, including Marcavalle, was likely relatively self-sufficient, each developed its own local specialties, as the restrictions accompanying sedentism limited direct or easy access to resources. . . . No direct evidence was found to indicate social stratification, or craft specialization based on principles other than age or sex." She also emphasizes that the people of Cuzco and the Lake Titicaca Basin lay within the same broad interaction sphere and that trade and exchange occurred between the two regions from an early period in prehistory. It was an interaction that would continue to grow for many centuries, until the arrival of the Wari in the Cuzco Valley.

Marcavalle was not, of course, the only village in the Cuzco Valley. There were many other villages like it. For example, test excavations by Edward B. Dwyer (1971b) at the site of Minaspata in the Lucre Basin revealed evidence of a similar, although slightly smaller, village. This occu-

pation, writes K. Chávez (1980: 215), "was associated with beans, corn, camelids, and guinea pigs . . ." Through a comparison of materials recovered at Marcavalle and Minaspata, she concludes: "The relationship with the Lucre Basin inhabitants appears to have been one of *stable, mutual reciprocity in a context of mundane interaction as between kinsmen or neighbors* involving perhaps many persons from various segments of the populations. . . ." (K. Chávez 1981b: 343; emphasis in original). An additional small village site dating to the Middle Formative Phase has been identified at Batan Orco in the Huaro area (Patterson 1967; K. Chávez 1980; Zapata 1998). As research continues, and as we are better able to distinguish different ceramic styles within the Formative Period, there is little doubt that many others sites will be found.

The Late Formative Phase and the Development of a Valley-wide Chiefdom (500 BC–AD 200)

During his seminal 1940s research, Rowe identified a pre-Inca ceramic style that he named Chanapata. In 1942 Rowe excavated at the type-site of Chanapata, just north of the city of Cuzco, and found a series of retaining walls, various burials, and vast amounts of ceramics and animal bones (Rowe 1943, 1944: 10–23). He was also able to document similar pottery on the surfaces of two other sites in the Cuzco Valley (Picchu and Limpillay [Wimpillay]), and at a third site near the community of Maras (Pacallamocco), approximately 30 aerial kilometers northwest of Cuzco. Summarizing his excavation and exploration findings, Rowe writes: "The locations of the known sites near good agricultural land where game is not particularly plentiful suggest that the people of Chanapata practiced agriculture, and great quantities of llama bones show that they kept large numbers of domestic animals. Pottery is well made and abundant, and a high percentage of decorated ware is found in the refuse, . . . " (Rowe 1946: 198). It is through the pottery style defined at the site of Chanapata that we can identify the Late Formative Phase sites of the Cuzco Valley and other nearby regions.

CHANAPATA AND DERIVED CHANAPATA CERAMICS

During his work at Chanapata, Rowe was able to define the first pre-Inca ceramic style of the Cuzco region (1944:

stable reciprocity btw peer villages

LF;

1) chanapata
ceramics

2) many,
many
LF sites

3) site-size
hierarchy

4) intensified
Agr. w/
maize,
beans,
quinoa +
potatoes

5) camelid
herding,
but still
hunting
deer

15–16).[7] Combining decorative elements (plain, incised, punctated, burnished, etc.) and ware color (red and black), he divided the Chanapata collection into several subtypes. Continued research by Rowe in the Cuzco region in the mid-1950s identified several additional Chanapata sites, some of which contained a greater frequency of fine red ware than black ware. These findings caused Rowe to review his data from Chanapata, and he found that there was a decrease in the frequency of polished black ware from the bottom to the top of the excavations. Rowe writes, "This situation suggests that the sites with red fired ware only are later than the main occupation at Chanapata. We gave the name 'Derived Chanapata' to the newly identified red phase . . ." (1956: 143).[8] Radiocarbon dates from various Chanapata-containing sites support the proposition that there is a shift through time from black to red wares in the sequence.

Because Rowe's initial report on the archaeology of Cuzco contained an extensive description and numerous drawings of Chanapata ceramics, this style is relatively well known and has been found at various sites in the Cuzco region. For example, Chanapata ceramics have been found at the site of Huillca Raccay in the Cusichaca Valley (Kendall 1976; Hey 1984; Lunt 1984), at Chokepukio in the Lucre Basin (McEwan 1987), at Muyu Orco in the Cuzco Valley (Zapata 1998), at Batan Orco in the Huaro Basin (Zapata 1998), and across the area of Paruro (Bauer 1999, 2002).

We also have numerous radiocarbon dates from excavation levels with Chanapata ceramics (see Appendix). Work done in 1960 by Chávez Ballón at Chanapata furnished two dates (Yamasaki, Hamada, and Fujiyama 1966: 337). The first sample dated to 2520 ± 150 BP (calibrated 95.4% probability 1000–200 BC),[9] but the second yielded the less useful date of 2360 ± 760 BP (calibrated 95.4% probability 2300 BC–AD 1200)[10] due to a small sample size. A sample from the site of Chanapata is mentioned by Patterson (1967: 143) as dating to 2600 ± 150 BP (calibrated 95.4% probability 1150–350 BC). Another sample from the type-site submitted by Engel (Krueger and Weeks 1966: 155) provided a date of 3330 ± 240 BP (calibrated 95.4% probability 2300–900 BC).[11] This date seems too early for Chanapata ceramics but may well date a lower stratum of Marcavalle materials at the site. Work

in the Cusichaca region has supplied another sample with a date of 2380 ± 70 BP (calibrated 95.4% probability 800–200 BC)[12] from the site of Huillca Raccay (Burleigh, Ambers, and Matthews 1983). Two samples from the site of Chokepukio (McEwan et al. 1995: 15) date Chanapata and Derived Chanapata remains at 2130 ± 70 BP (calibrated 95.4% probability 380 BC–AD 10)[13] and 2190 ± 60 BP (calibrated 95.4% probability 390–90 BC).[14]

Several dates are also available for Derived Chanapata ceramics. Two are from excavations at the site of Marcavalle (Lawn 1971: 373; K. Chávez 1980: 241): 2131 ± 55 BP (calibrated 95.4% probability 390–90 BC)[15] and 2096 ± 51 BP (calibrated 95.4% probability 360 BC–AD 30).[16] The third date, 2073 ± 29 BP (calibrated 95.4 percent probability 180 BC–AD 10), is from Zapata's excavations at Batan Orco.[17] To these we can add two additional dates from our recent excavations (Bauer and Jones 2003) at the site of Peqokaypata toward the eastern end of the Cuzco Basin: 1881 ± 42 BP (calibrated 95.4% probability AD 20–240)[18] and 1985 ± 43 BP (calibrated 95.4% probability 100 BC–AD 130).[19] On the basis of these findings, it can be suggested that the production of Chanapata and related ceramics started around 500–300 BC and continued until after the turn of the first millennium AD.

The Late Formative Phase in the Cuzco Valley

The Late Formative Phase, Chanapata, and Derived Chanapata ceramics are among the best-described and the best-understood early ceramics of the Cuzco area (Rowe 1944, 1956; Bauer 1999, 2002). As a result, numerous Late Formative sites have been identified in the region. In a recent overview of the Cuzco Formative Period, Zapata (1998) plots the location of some forty Late Formative Phase sites spread along the Vilcanota River drainage between the site of Machu Picchu and the city of Sicunai. To this sum, we can add thirty additional Late Formative Phase sites in the Province of Paruro and those that have recently been found in the Cuzco Valley.

The number of Formative Period sites in the Cuzco Valley is well over eighty (Map 5.1). Most of these sites date to the Late Formative Phase. Because so many Late Formative Phase sites have now been identified, and several have been sampled through test excavations, they provide us with a database to develop theories concerning the indigenous social and political organization of the valley during these times. The Cuzco Valley Formative Period sites fall within several site-size categories: hunting stations defined by Formative Period projectile points, single homesteads, hamlets, villages, and a single center. The hamlet- and village-level sites contain dense trash middens and most likely held populations from a few dozen to several hundred persons each. Many of these sites are located on hilltops, knolls, promontories, and the ends of ridges. This pattern is found elsewhere in the surrounding area, including the Province of Paruro (Bauer 1999, 2002), the Cusichaca area (Hey 1984), and the Huaro Basin (Zapata 1998).

Among the most intriguing of the Late Formative Phase occupations of the Cuzco Valley are the two adjacent sites of Wimpillay and Muyu Orco (Photo 5.1).[20] Wimpillay is located on a broad river terrace, south of the Huatanay River, a relatively short distance from Cuzco. Adjacent to Wimpillay is the steeply rounded hill of Muyu Orco.[21] The hill is a prominent feature of the landscape and was considered a sacred place by the Inca

(Bauer 1998: 114). Both Wimpillay and Muyu Orco have been greatly damaged in recent years by the rapid urban growth of Cuzco.

Wimpillay and Muyu Orco have long attracted the attention of archaeologists. They were first noted as archaeological sites by Rowe (1944: 22–23), who documented Chanapata and later ceramics on them. Since that time, numerous test excavations have been conducted at these two sites by the students and faculty of the Universidad San Antonio Abad del Cuzco. Most recently, Zapata (1998: 320–328) directed excavations on the summit as well as on the northwestern slope of Muyu Orco. On the summit of the hill, he found evidence of what appears to be a Late Formative sunken court, similar to courts constructed in the Lake Titicaca region during this same period.

During our survey, Wimpillay not only proved to be the largest Late Formative Phase site in the Cuzco and Oropesa Basins, but it also provided the finest Late Formative Phase pottery. The association of finer craft production with the largest village of a basin to serve the demands of a developing elite class is frequently observed in the archaeological record. It lends support to the unique

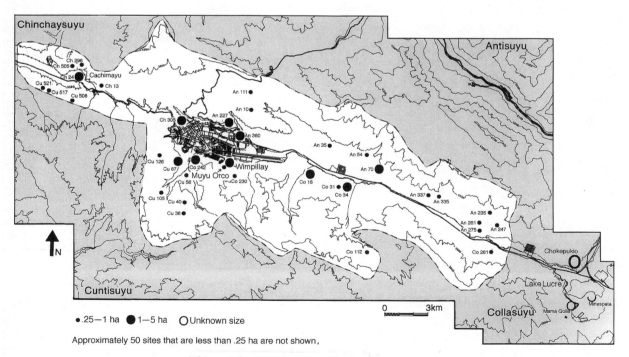

MAP 5.1. Thirty-eight important Formative sites in the Cuzco Valley

PHOTO 5.1. The site of Wimpillay (center left), which lies on the lower slope
of the hill of Muyu Orco (center right), is now largely destroyed by urban growth.

importance that Wimpillay may have held among the Late Formative Phase sites of the basin. Based on our surface collections and the test excavations by Zapata, I currently interpret the site of Wimpillay to be the center of a valley-wide chiefdom during the Late Formative Phase. Closely associated with this center was a ritual precinct, Muyu Orco, which continued to hold special significance in the valley until the arrival of the Spaniards.

THE SOCAL ECONOMY
OF THE LATE FORMATIVE PHASE

Agricultural intensification continued during the Late Formative Phase, and we know that quinoa, beans, and presumably potatoes held critical roles in the local economy. It is clear, however, that maize also played a part in the Late Formative diet. Maize pollen, dating to 500 BC, has been recovered in Lake Marcacocha (Chepstow-Lusty et al. 1997: 131). Furthermore, excavations at the site of Marcavalle recovered carbonized corn in deposits dating to 200 BC (K. Chávez 1980: 243–244). The maize fields near Marcavalle and elsewhere across the lower elevations of the Cuzco Valley would have been supported by seasonal rains and perhaps by small irriga-

tion ditches that were constructed to bring water from adjacent springs or streams.

Camelid herds would also have been kept in the upper elevations of the valley during this era. As in earlier times, these herds met a wide variety of needs for the people, including food, wool production, and beasts of burden. Nevertheless, deer hunting still continued throughout this period as well. This is documented by numerous Late Formative projectile points found on the upper valley slopes during the survey and by the deer remains recovered in the course of excavations (Figure 5.1).

Summary and Discussion

The Formative Period was a critical period in the prehistory of the Cuzco Valley. A sand-tempered ceramic style found in the valley may represent the initial stages of ceramic production and may mark the transition from the Late Archaic Phase to Early Formative times. The Middle Formative Phase is represented by small independent villages. K. Chávez's research at the site of Marcavalle exemplifies village life during this period. She writes, "The abundance and concentration of refuse at known Marcavalle sites, well documented at Marcavalle itself, appear to indicate Marcavalle settlements were *sedentary villages having fairly dense populations*" (1980: 257; emphasis in original).

The Late Formative Phase is a time of special interest in the prehistory of the Cuzco Valley, since it is during this period that a clear settlement hierarchy developed. Our regional survey data document a multitiered settlement pattern for the Late Formative Phase, with numerous small sites, a variety of bigger settlements, and a single center (Map 5.2). Within the anthropological literature, such a pattern is considered a classic hallmark of early chiefdom societies (e.g., Marcus and Flannery 1996). Timothy Earle notes that a similar, although slightly later, pattern emerges in the Mantaro region: "During the Huacrapukio Period (AD 200–500), simple chiefdoms appear to have developed in the valley. The best evidence for these chiefdoms is the distinctly rank-sized distribution of settlements. Around a few larger sites cluster smaller sites, forming delimited regional groups" (1997: 55).

An analogous, although slightly earlier, process occurred in the Lake Titicaca region (Stanish 2003). Two of the Lake Titicaca chiefdoms grew quickly, and perhaps as early as 200 BC both the site of Pucara, in the northern basin, and the site of Tiwanaku, in the south-

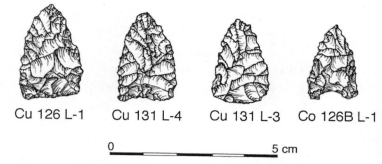

Cu 126 L-1   Cu 131 L-4   Cu 131 L-3   Co 126B L-1

0   5 cm

FIGURE 5.1. Formative Period obsidian projectile points

ern basin, emerged as regional powers. The paramount villages of these chiefdoms grew to unparalleled sizes for the south-central Andes and held many thousands of inhabitants, including elites, attached retainers, craft specialists, and resident farmers and herders. These large chiefdoms brought adjacent polities under their direct control and cast their political, economic, and artistic influence over many others at greater distances. A diffuse form of this influence would eventually extend into the Cuzco region during the Qotakalli Period (AD 200–600).

During the Late Formative Phase, a site hierarchy developed in the Cuzco Basin, most likely reflecting the growth of a small chiefdom society. From the village of Wimpillay, the chiefdom may have controlled the lower-level settlements throughout the valley. Broad areal excavations are needed at Wimpillay as well as at a number of other Late Formative Phase sites to gain a better understanding of the political organization that developed in the valley at this time. If this model of the Late Formative Phase is correct, excavations at Wimpillay should find evidence of sumptuary goods,[22] elite burials, and gradients in household status, craft production, and additional public works projects.

It may also be noted that there is a distinct clustering of sites in the Cachimayu area, in the northwest extreme of our survey area (Map 5.1). This cluster is made all the more notable by the fact that there are no Formative sites in the high watershed area between the Cachimayu area and the Cuzco Basin. These sites most likely represent a small village cluster that paid allegiance to the elites of Cuzco or a similar chiefly society developing in or near the Plain of Anta, farther to the west.

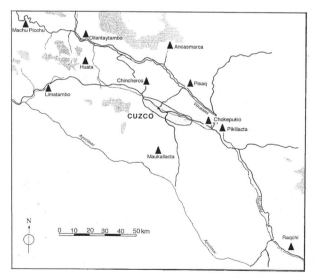

▲ Archaeological site

MAP 5.2. Hypothetical area under the influence of Cuzco-based chiefdom during the Late Formative Phase

Explorations and survey work across the Cuzco region provide evidence of other chiefdoms. Regional survey work south of Cuzco in the Province of Paruro suggests that there may have been important villages near the modern towns of Yaurisque and Paruro (Bauer 1999: 128; 2002).[23] There is also evidence to suggest that a polity may have existed in the Cusichaca area, focused around the site of Huillca Raccay (Hey 1985). As more surveys are completed in the Cuzco region, many more centers and their affiliated villages will be documented. For example, Covey's work to the north of Cuzco has identified a possible Late Formative Phase chiefdom in Chit'apampa and another in the Cuyo Basin (Covey 2003).

Nor is there any doubt that a chiefdom also existed in the Lucre Basin during the Late Formative Phase. Work by Gordon F. McEwan (1987) at the site of Chokepukio has recovered substantial Late Formative remains suggesting that it represented the center of Late Formative power in the Lucre Basin. Its influence must have extended some distance toward the Cuzco Valley. Since periods of chiefdom development are frequently marked by conflict as many roughly equal polities compete for dominance, it is possible that additional research in the Cuzco region will not only help us to better define the political divisions of the area, but will also bring forth evidence of conflict and alliance formations between the many different chiefly centers.

Chiefdoms rarely, if ever, develop in isolated settings. Rather, they are the outcome of broad processes of societal transformations—uneven processes to be sure, but ones that affect the social landscape of large regions. In our case, we can now see that much of the south-central Andes, from Cuzco to Lake Titicaca, was being transformed during the Middle to Late Formative times, and that by the end of the millennium most of the population was being incorporated into chiefly societies of varying levels of social complexity.

CHAPTER 6

The Qotakalli Period:

Time of Regional Development (AD 200–600)

THE QOTAKALLI PERIOD in the Cuzco region covers an era between the rise of the first chiefly societies and invasion of the area by the Wari Empire. Unfortunately, this is one of the least-understood time periods of the Cuzco region. No major projects have been dedicated to understanding this era, and the basic ceramic styles of the period are still being defined and debated. Nevertheless, from what little evidence we have, it is clear that it was an important time of regional development, population growth, and settlement shifts, as well as a time of contact and exchange with surrounding regions.

Previous Research on the Qotakalli Period

For about a half-century the name Huaro has appeared on ceramic sequences in association with the period before Wari influence in the Cuzco region. Chávez Ballón identified this ceramic style in 1952 during his excavations at the site of Batan Orco, located approximately 50 kilometers southeast of Cuzco in the Huaro Basin. Huaro ceramics are thought to resemble a style of ceramics called Carmenca identified by Rowe in the early 1940s at the site of Chanapata (Rowe 1944: 19–20; 1956: 142). However, the Huaro ceramic style remains virtually unknown, since no illustrations or descriptions of it have been published. In short, for decades the name Huaro has been used largely as a placeholder in the ceramic sequence, without reflecting a clear ceramic style or cultural affiliation.

Although the specific characteristics of Huaro ceramics continue to be debated, significant progress has been made in recent years in identifying and describing several other ceramic styles of the Qotakalli Period. It is currently recognized that when the Wari began the eastward expansion of their empire from the Ayacucho region, the dominant local ceramic style of the Cuzco Valley was a cream-slip ware that we call Qotakalli (Barreda Murillo 1982; Glowacki 1996; Bauer 2002; Bauer and Jones 2003). The origins of this local style are unclear, but excavations suggest that a rapid transformation occurred in local ceramic production from the burnished earthen Chanapata and Derived Chanapata styles of the Formative Period to the distinctly different Qotakalli style some time after the beginning of the modern era. Similar shifts appear to have occurred elsewhere in the central Andes, for example, in Junín (Morales Chocano 1998) and Ayacucho (Knobloch 1983).[1]

The type-site for Qotakalli ceramics, located south of the modern airport across the Huatanay River, was first excavated by Lyon and Rowe in the 1970s. Barreda Murillo published the first description of Qotakalli pottery in 1982. Since that time, Qotakalli ceramics have been found at numerous sites in the Cuzco region, although we still lack an intensive study of this important style.

The exteriors of most currently recognized Qotakalli vessels are covered with a cream or white slip and are well burnished. The slip provides a surface on which the decorations are painted and assures relatively strong color-tone contrasts. Several variations of Qotakalli ceramics have been identified (Glowacki 1996). By far the most

[Handwritten marginal notes:]

Qotakalli Ceramics:
1) abrupt transition from Chanapata to Qotakalli
2) dominant ceramic style until Wari;
3) cream/white slip over exterior, high contrast w/ decorations
4) bichrome is most common ↓ black-on-cream or (rarely) red-on-cream
5) also polychrome (black & red on cream), usually higher quality than bichromes
6) designs are basic geometric

PHOTO 6.1. Qotakalli black-on-cream ceramics

PHOTO 6.2. Qotakalli black-and-red-on-cream ceramics

common substyles are bichromes (black-on-cream or, more rarely, red-on-cream [Photo 6.1]) and polychromes (black-and-red-on-cream [Photo 6.2]). In general, the polychromes tend to be of a higher quality than the bichromes. The major designs of Qotakalli ceramics are usually defined in black, and the minor ones are executed in either red or black. Qotakalli ceramics have a limited variety of geometric decorations. The most common elements are straight horizontal and vertical lines, zigzagging lines, diamonds, triangles, and dots.

Although Qotakalli ceramics have been found at numerous sites in the Cuzco region, until recently little detailed information on their production dates has been available. It is clear that Qotakalli ceramics were being produced when the Wari arrived, and that certain substyles continued to be in production for a considerable time afterward. For example, black-on-cream Qotakalli ceramics have been found in structures and middens at the Wari center of Pikillacta (Barreda Murillo 1982; McEwan 1984; Glowacki 1996) as well as in Wari Period tombs at Batan Orco (Zapata 1997).[2] Evidence suggests, however, that the production of Qotakalli materials may have begun several centuries before the time of Wari expansionism. Excavations by Ann Kendall (1996: 153) at the site of Huillca Raccay in the Cusichaca Valley recovered Qotakalli-style pottery in a midden that yielded a radiocarbon date of 1580 ± 60 BP (calibrated 95.4% probability AD 340–620).[3] Two other projects in the Lucre Basin, including research at the site of Chokepukio (McEwan et al. 1995) and at the site of Minaspata (E. Dwyer, personal communication, 1997), as well as work conducted in the Province of Paruro (Bauer 1999; 2002)

have found Qotakalli materials directly above strata with Chanapata and Derived Chanapata ceramics.

As part of the Cuzco Valley Archaeological Project, we conducted test excavations at a series of small- to medium-sized sites in the Cuzco Valley in 1999 and 2000 to investigate the ceramic styles of the Qotakalli and Wari Periods (Map 1.4). These ceramic styles, especially those of the Qotakalli Period, were selected for additional research because they represented some of the least-known ceramic styles of the Cuzco Valley. We also wanted to address a series of interrelated questions concerning the Wari and pre-Wari cultures of the valley. Most importantly, we wanted to know when the Wari and Altiplano influences in the Cuzco Valley began and ended. The sites chosen for test excavations included the following:

Pukacancha (Co. 141): A medium-sized site on the western slope of Taucaray Hill with a small cluster of Inca buildings. Numerous Inca and Arahuay ceramic fragments as well as a few Qotakalli sherds were recovered from the surface of the site. The large number of Arahuay sherds at Pukacancha suggested that its major pre-Inca occupation dated to the Wari Period. By excavating at this site, we hoped to better understand the timing of Wari influence in the Cuzco region.

Tankarpata (Co. 195): A medium-sized site beside the village of Tankarpata with no visible architectural remains. Located one ridge to the west of the original type-site of Qotakalli, the site of Tankarpata contained numerous fragments of Qotakalli and Arahuay ceramics, as well as minor amounts of many other styles. From the surface collections retrieved there, we believed that the site was continually occupied throughout the Qotakalli and Wari Periods.

Peqokaypata (Co. 31): A small site with no visible architectural remains. The dominant ceramic styles represented in the surface collections were Qotakalli and Formative pottery. Some Muyu Orco and incised *incensario* sherds, along with various other later (Killke and Inca) styles, were also recovered. The complete absence of Wari and Arahuay ceramics at Peqokaypata suggested that this site would yield information on the immediately pre-Wari occupation of the Cuzco Valley.

In other words, rather than excavating at a single large multicomponent site, we used our survey results to select particular sites that contained the specific combinations of pottery styles that we wanted to study. To investigate the Wari and pre-Wari ceramic styles of the Cuzco Valley, we selected what we believed to be a site that contained a clear Wari Period occupation with little evidence of earlier remains (Pukacancha), a site that had been occupied during both the Qotakalli and the Wari Periods (Tankarpata), and an immediately pre-Wari site (Peqokaypata). The results of these excavations are presented in Bauer and Jones (2003) and are summarized here and in Chapter 7.

Excavations revealed that the site of Pukacancha was first occupied at the beginning of the Wari Period. The ceramic collection from this site was dominated by Arahuay pottery, a local but heavily Wari-influenced pottery style that was produced during the time of the Wari occupation of Lucre Basin. However, a few black-on-cream Qotakalli fragments were found at the bottom of a shallow trash pit that provided a date of 1435 ± 65 BP (calibrated 95.4% probability AD 430–720)[4] and in a higher level that dated to 1322 ± 40 BP (calibrated 95.4% probability AD 650–780).[5]

Our work at Tankarpata indicated that it was occupied during the Qotakalli and Wari Periods. The earliest of seven radiocarbon dates for Qotakalli remains at this site came from a deeply buried midden with an age of 1404 ± 47 BP (calibrated 95.4% probability AD 540–710).[6] The latest samples came from a floor level that yielded a date of 1100 ± 45 BP (calibrated 95.4% probability AD 780–1030).[7]

The site of Peqokaypata contained dense deposits of Qotakalli materials and no evidence of Wari influence. We believe that it was abandoned just before, or as a result of, the arrival of the Wari in the Cuzco Valley (Bauer and Jones 2003). The site of Peqokaypata, discussed again below in reference to possible pre-Wari Altiplano influence in the region, contained Qotakalli ceramics in cultural contexts that dated from 1527 ± 40 BP (calibrated 95.4% probability AD 430–620)[8] and 1439 ± 39 BP (calibrated 95.4% probability AD 540–670).[9] Thus, dates from Peqokaypata suggest that the production of Qotakalli ceramics began before the expansion of the Wari from Ayacucho, and dates from Tankarpata and Pukacancha indicate that it continued to be produced into the time of the Wari occupation of the Cuzco region.

It should also be noted that a small pit that contained an unknown coarse buff ware with monochrome paint was found cut into the Formative Period deposit of the Peqokaypata site. Carbon from this feature yielded a date of 1615 ± 50 BP (calibrated 95.4% probability AD 260–570).[10] Additional research in Qotakalli Period sites such as Peqokaypata will aid us in understanding the transition that occurred from the burnished earthen wares of the Formative Period and the cream-slipped ceramics of the Qotakalli Period (Bauer and Jones 2003).

Our research has also documented that there is a temporal element to the Qotakalli subtypes of black-on-cream and red-and-black-on-cream (Bauer and Jones 2003). This is best illustrated by comparing the Qotakalli sherds found in surface collections and excavations at Peqokaypata and Pukacancha. Peqokaypata was abandoned just before the Wari entered the Cuzco Valley. At this site, approximately 33 percent of all Qotakalli sherds found were classified as red-and-black-on-cream. Pukacancha, on the other hand, is a Wari Period site established about the time that the Wari entered the Cuzco region, and it was occupied for some three hundred years afterward. A small percentage of this site's total ceramic collection was classified as Qotakalli, all of which fell into the substyle of black-on-cream. That is to say, not a single example of Qotakalli red-and-black-on-cream ceramics was recovered during the two surface collections or during our excavations at the site. It appears that the production of the Qotakalli black-on-cream pottery began early and continued throughout much of the Qotakalli Period and the Wari

Period, although the quantity of its production diminished after the Wari arrival. Qotakalli red-and-black-on-cream ceramics were also produced during the Qotakalli Period, but it seems that the production of this finer substyle ended around the time of the Wari occupation in the valley. These findings are consistent with the fact that only Qotakalli black-on-cream vessels have been found in the site of Pikillacta. I return to this issue in the next chapter when discussing the development of local Wari Period ceramics in the Cuzco Valley.[11]

PHOTO 6.3. Muyu Orco ceramics

Altiplano Influence in the Cuzco Region during the Qotakalli Period

During the Qotakalli Period, the site of Pucara, approximately 200 kilometers southeast of Cuzco in the Peruvian Altiplano near Lake Titicaca, reached its largest area of influence. It is widely believed that Pucara was the center of one of the earliest and largest complex societies in the south-central Andes. Pucara ceramics, characterized by incised vessels with complex yellow and black figures painted on a dark red background (Kidder 1943; Rowe and Brandel 1971) have been found in the upper Vilcanota and Apurímac River drainages. Reconnaissance by Juan Núñez del Prado (1972), Sergio Chávez (1988), and Lizandro Lantarón Pfoccori (1988) recovered examples of Pucara ceramics throughout the Province of Chumbivilcas, some 75 kilometers south of Cuzco. Most recently, Zapata's (1998: 313) excavations at the site of Batan Orco have provided examples of Pucara ceramics. The completion of his work will greatly increase our understanding of the relations between the Cuzco and Altiplano region during this early period of cultural development.

Two other, but slightly later, ceramic styles have been found in the Cuzco region that I believe record influence from the Altiplano area during the Qotakalli Period. The first style, called Muyu Orco, was identified in the Province of Paruro in the late 1980s (Bauer 1989; 1999; 2002).[12] During our more recent survey work in the Cuzco Valley, we found Muyu Orco pottery at seventeen sites. It has also been recovered in significant quantities during excavations at Batan Orco (Zapata 1998: 313) and Rachi (Bill Sillar, personal communication, 1999).[13] The proposed Altiplano connection is based on two observa-

PHOTO 6.4. Incised *incensarios* from the Cuzco Valley

tions.[14] First, Muyu Orco ceramics are decorated with bright white, black, and orange colors painted over a polished dark red background (Photo 6.3). These colors are also used in the Altiplano ceramic traditions of Pucara and Tiwanaku but are uncommon in Wari collections. Second, various vessel forms (annulated bowls) and vessel attributes (rim scallops and pedestal bases) found in the Muyu Orco collections are frequently seen in Altiplano collections of this time period but rarely displayed in Wari assemblages (Bauer 1989; 1999: 78–81; 2002).

Altiplano influence in the Cuzco region during the Qotakalli Period may also be recorded by the presence of incised *incensarios* at numerous sites.[15] Incised *incensarios* are annulated bowls that stand on pedestal bases; it is widely

[handwritten margin notes:]
In Huaro Basin

Altiplano Influence:
1) Muyu Orco ceramics & incised incensarios
2) both are stylistically similar to altiplano (i.e. Pukara), not Wari
3) both end abruptly at time of Wari occupation

believed that they were used as ceremonial burners (Photo 6.4). They are heavily burnished and then deeply incised with dense geometric patterns. They have scalloped rims and pronounced puma-head adornments. K. Chávez (1985) has documented the widespread distribution of incised *incensarios* at sites between Cuzco and Lake Titicaca.[16] Five additional sites with incised *incensarios* have been identified in the Province of Paruro (Bauer 1998), and Zapata (1998: 313) has also found them at Batan Orco. Our survey of the Cuzco Valley recorded two more sites, Co. 31 (Peqokaypata) and An. 328 (Huasao), with incised *incensario* fragments (Map 6.1).

As noted above, in 1999 and 2000 we conducted test excavations at the site of Peqokaypata to better understand the Qotakalli and Wari Period ceramics of the Cuzco Valley. The site was especially intriguing because it contained numerous Formative, Muyu Orco, Qotakalli, and incised *incensario* sherds but no Wari or Wari-related materials. The excavations revealed several structures as well as deep middens. Carbon extracted from the top of a small platform in direct contact with a shattered incised *incensario* provided a date of 1422 ± 151 BP (calibrated 95.4% probability AD 530–700).[17] Soon after

this date the site was abandoned. Until additional data are recovered, this date may also be used for the end of early Altiplano influence in the Cuzco region. As will be discussed in the next chapter, this date also corresponds with the arrival of Wari influence in the Cuzco Valley.

In sum, from the results of our excavations at the site of Peqokaypata, it appears that Muyu Orco ceramics and incised *incensarios* were contemporaneous styles that were either produced in the Cuzco region or imported from a nearby area.[18] They reflect southerly Altiplano artistic traditions and date to the Qotakalli Period. With the recovery of Muyu Orco ceramics and incised *incensarios* in the greater Cuzco region, it can be proposed that the long-established contacts between Cuzco and the Lake Titicaca region continued throughout the Qotakalli times. This interaction abruptly changed, however, with the expansion of the Wari into the Cuzco region.

The Cuzco Valley during the Qotakalli Period

Our systematic survey recorded the locations of approximately 115 sites that contained Qotakalli ceramics (Map 6.2). The sizes and distribution of these sites provide a

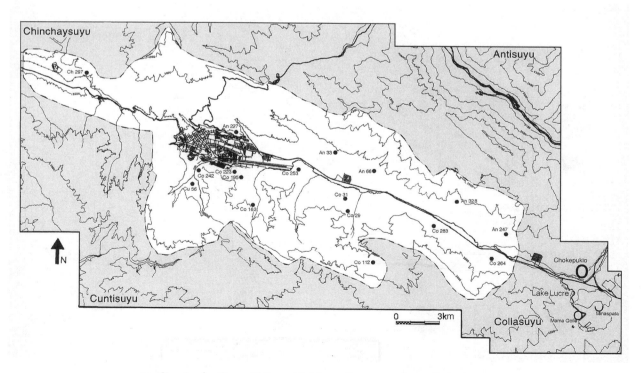

MAP 6.1. Sites in the Cuzco Valley with Muyu Orco ceramics or incised *incensarios*

number of insights into the social organization of the valley during the Qotakalli Period. For example, although the site of Wimpillay is still relatively large, it no longer dominates the settlement pattern of the Cuzco Basin as it did in Late Formative times.[19] Instead, what we see is a greater overall density of large sites at the western end of the Cuzco Basin. Some of these sites are still well preserved, but many others have been destroyed by urban expansion.[20] The location of these large Qotakalli Period sites surrounding Cuzco suggests that there may also have been a large village in the area now covered by the city. Based on these findings, it is proposed that local power was concentrated in the western end of the Cuzco Basin during the Qotakalli Period. In other words, although there was a continuation of a chiefly society in the basin from Late Formative times to the Qotakalli Period, the loci of elite occupation may have shifted slightly from the single site of Wimpillay to a dense array of sites in the area where Cuzco is now. The cluster of sites in this area during the Qotakalli Period suggests that the power and wealth of the valley may have become divided between groups of elite households located in a

series of separate but closely spaced kin-based (i.e., *ayllu*) settlements.

It is also important to note that there is a continuous spread of large Qotakalli sites along the southern slope of the Cuzco Basin from the city of Cuzco to the Angostura. As mentioned earlier, the two sides of the basin are geologically different. The southern side is better endowed for agricultural production, since it contains wide tributary valleys; large, flat river terraces; and numerous small streams. In contrast, the northern side contains fewer tributaries, steeper slopes, and deeply entrenched streams. Thus, the distribution pattern of Qotakalli Period villages closely reflects the areas of prime, easily irrigable agricultural land in the Cuzco Basin.

A similar correlation between the distribution of settlements and areas of good agricultural land can be seen in the Oropesa Basin. Between the Angostura and the modern town of Oropesa, the northern side of the valley becomes wider and less steep than the southern side. Consequently, in this stretch of the valley, the distribution of settlements is denser on the northern side than on the southern. Furthermore, the largest Qotakalli Period site

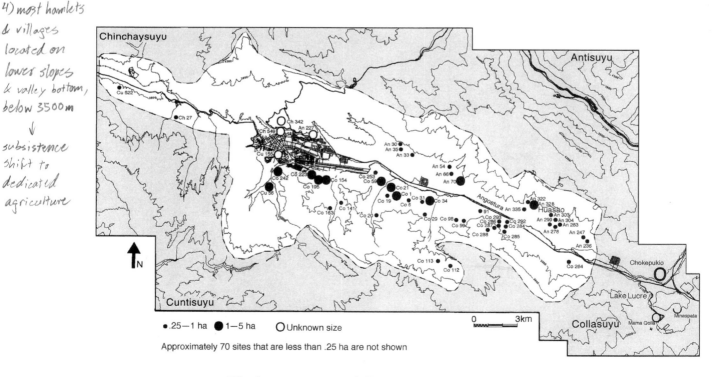

MAP 6.2. Fifty-five important Qotakalli Period sites in the Cuzco Valley (AD 200–600)

Handwritten margin notes:

Qotakalli Sites:
1) 115 recorded
2) large villages clustered around modern city ↓ possible locus of elite households separated into ayllus
3) many large sites spread along south slope, on prime farmland
4) most hamlets & villages located on lower slopes & valley bottom, below 3500 m ↓ subsistence shift to dedicated agriculture

in this section of the valley is in the area of Huasao (An. 328), which also contains the best agricultural land. The Huasao site may represent a secondary center that held a small group of elites who were subservient to Cuzco but who also held some authority over those living nearby. Or, alternatively, Huasao may have risen during this period of prehistory to hold a small chiefly society that was independent of those to the west in the Cuzco Basin and those to the east in the Lucre Basin.

Although the Lucre Basin has not been systematically surveyed, it is known to have contained several large Qotakalli Period sites. Most notable among these are the sites of Chokepukio and Mama Qolla. These sites may also have acted as chiefly centers during this period.

It should also be noted that there are important differences between the Late Formative Phase settlement pattern in the Cuzco Valley and that of the Qotakalli Period. Almost all of the highest Late Formative Phase village sites were abandoned and a host of new settlements were established along the lower valley slopes during the Qotakalli Period. Furthermore, the vast majority of the Qotakalli Period hamlets and villages were located below 3,500 m and formed a dense array of settlements along the lower valley slopes. This process of moving down to and filling up the lower valley area is suggestive of strong population growth as well as an important shift in the local economy. Although it remains to be tested through excavation, this shift from higher to lower site locations appears to represent a movement away from a mixed food economy during the Formative Period. Pollen from Lake Marcacocha suggests that Chenopodiaceae production would never again reach its Formative Period levels and that maize would hold a significantly larger role in the local economies.

The Distribution of Qotakalli Ceramics beyond the Cuzco Valley

Neutron activation analysis supports the proposition that Qotakalli ceramics were produced somewhere in the Cuzco Valley (Montoya et al. 2000), and our regional survey data suggest that a chiefly society, centered at the western end of the Cuzco Basin, flourished during the Qotakalli Period. This being so, then the distribution of Qotakalli materials outside the valley may well document

the areas that fell under its influence, if not direct control, during this period.

Alan Covey (2003) has surveyed the area north of Cuzco, from Chit'apampa to the far side of the Vilcanota River between Pisaq and Calca. He reports finding two large villages and associated smaller hamlets with strong Qotakalli assemblies south of the Vilcanota River. One of the large villages is located in Chit'apampa, which is adjacent to the Cuzco Valley. The other is near Patabamba, overlooking the Vilcanota River Valley. Covey (2003) suggests that these two sites represent the centers of two small chiefly polities that may have formed early alliances with Cuzco. Importantly, he also notes that the percentage of Qotakalli materials dramatically diminishes on the far, or northern, side of the Vilcanota River. This suggests to him that the influence of Cuzco waned at the river during the Qotakalli Period.

Similar distribution data have been recorded in the area due south of Cuzco. The number of sites that contain Qotakalli ceramics declines as one leaves the Cuzco Basin and enters the Province of Paruro. They all but disappear on the far, or southern, side of the Apurímac River (Bauer 1999: 74; 2002). This suggests that, as in the north, the influence of Cuzco during this period may have spread southward until it reached the largest river.

The distribution of Qotakalli ceramics to the west of Cuzco, in the Anta plain, is not well understood, although it is likely that Anta had its own chiefdom during this period. Considerable amounts of Qotakalli materials have also been recovered in the Lucre Basin, especially at the site of Chokepukio (Barreda Murillo 1973; McEwan 1987). As noted above, although the exact nature of this site is still under investigation, it seems likely that it was the center of another large chiefly society during the Qotakalli Period.

Summary and Discussion

In this chapter I have examined the distribution patterns of sites in the Cuzco Valley immediately before the arrival of the Wari (AD 200–600). As noted in the introduction, this is one of the least-studied periods of the valley's history, and there is still much research to be done. Nevertheless, by combining the results of our survey and test excavation programs in the valley with information pro-

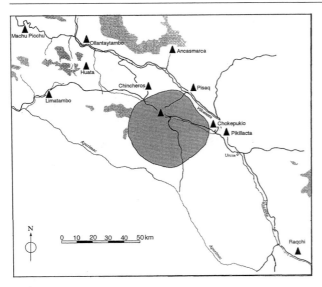

MAP 6.3. Hypothetical area under the influence of Cuzco-based chiefdom during the Qotakalli Period (AD 200–600)

The largest and most powerful of these were located in the areas of greatest agricultural production, including the Plain of Anta, the Cuzco Basin, the Lucre Basin, and the Huaro Basin. Elsewhere, smaller chiefdoms also developed. Depending on their locations, these were most likely in a constant state of conflict or alliance formation with the larger polities of the region.

The center of political power in the Cuzco Basin rested near its western end, localized in a dense cluster of large villages (Map 6.3). Though this Qotakalli Period polity cast its control over the inhabitants of the Cuzco Basin, its power was most likely limited to the east and west by similarly large chiefdoms in the Plain of Anta and the Lucre Basin. To the north and south, however, there were smaller, weaker entities that may have come under its influence, if not its direct control.

The settlement pattern data suggest that strong population growth occurred during this period as well as a shift from a mixed economy toward more intensive agricultural production. Small irrigation and terrace projects may have been started at this time to increase successful maize production. Finally, it is clear that the Cuzco region was not isolated from the rest of the Andes. During this period, contact and exchange between the inhabitants of the Cuzco region and those of Altiplano societies appear to have been particularly well developed.

duced by other researchers working in adjacent areas, I have attempted to establish a starting point for understanding this period of regional growth and development.

When the Wari entered the Cuzco region, they encountered thriving local societies. Based on a series of large villages established during the Formative Period, numerous chiefdoms had developed across the region.

Qotakalli Period Developments:

1) iconic ceramic style
2) small chiefdoms - peer polities competing for influence/control
3) urban centers occupied by wealthy elites
4) increased pop. density, settlements near valley bottom
5) subsistence shift from mixed farming/herding to more intensive agriculture
6) long-distance ties (& trade?) with altiplano societies (e.g. Pucara)

CHAPTER 7

The Wari Period

(AD 600–1000) in the Cuzco Region

THE WARI PERIOD (also generally known as the Middle Horizon) encompasses a broad span of time during which much of the Andean highlands came under the influence of two empires: Wari and Tiwanaku. Current research suggests that the Wari began to expand from their traditional homeland in the Ayacucho region of Peru sometime after AD 550 and that the expansion continued through at least AD 900, after which the empire appears to have suddenly collapsed. Though less is known concerning the development of Tiwanaku, it seems that by AD 300 the city of Tiwanaku, near the southwestern shore of Lake Titicaca in Bolivia, was of considerable importance. Expansion of Tiwanaku may have begun around AD 500 and waned, like Wari, near the end of the first millennium.

Researchers have long noted the presence of Wari materials in the Cuzco region, and it is recognized that Ayacucho influenced the thriving polities of the region for several centuries. Thus, the Wari Period is a fascinating phase for the Cuzco region. It is a time of both foreign occupation as well as indigenous development. Fortunately, it is also one of the better-studied periods of the region's history. In this chapter I outline the course of Wari Period research in the Cuzco region and examine the processes of culture change that occurred there as a result of its incorporation into the Wari Empire.

Indicators of Wari Influence

Wari influence in a region is commonly inferred from architectural remains as well as from the presence of Wari ceramics or other portable artifacts. The Wari built many of their buildings in a distinct architectural style that featured large high-walled rectangular enclosures. Made of fieldstones and mud mortar, these enclosures generally contained a central patio and a series of distinctly long and narrow galleries. Archaeologists frequently use the presence of these enclosures, along with their patios and galleries, to identify installations built by the expanding Wari Empire.

An even more common means of documenting Wari influence in a region is through ceramics. Among the various ceramic styles used in this book to identify Wari influence are a series of styles that were actually produced in the Ayacucho area and then imported into the Cuzco region. These include the Ayacucho styles of Chakipampa, Okros, Viñaque, Huamanga, and Robles Moco (Knobloch 1991; Glowacki 1996, 2002).[1] Various examples of possible imported Wari ceramics have been found in excavations at Pikillacta. Neutron activation analysis by Glowacki and her associates of selected pieces indicate that they were in fact produced in the Wari heartland and then imported into the Cuzco region (Montoya et al. 2000). During our 1999 excavations in the Cuzco Valley, we recovered various pieces of Wari ceramics (Bauer and Jones 2003). Carbon from a trash pit at the site of Tankarpata, which contained a fragment of Viñaque pottery, provided a date of 1290 ± 50 BP (calibrated 95.4% probability AD 650–880).[2] In addition, a midden at the site of Pukacancha containing a piece of Huamanga pottery dated to 1210 ± 45 BP (calibrated 95.4% probability AD 680–960).[3] These dates fall well within the time traditionally believed to frame the Wari expansion.

There are also a number of other ceramic styles in the Cuzco region that appear to be locally produced but that closely imitate ceramics of the Wari heartland. For example, the finer wares recovered at the site of Pikillacta have been shown to imitate the Okros ceramics of the Wari homeland, but they were produced in the Cuzco region (Knobloch 1991: 253–254; Glowacki 1996; Montoya et al. 2000). Another example is the recently defined style of Arahuay (Torres Poblete 1989; Glowacki 1996; Bauer 1999, 2002). Arahuay ceramics are characterized by the use of broad red bands outlined with narrow black lines over a buff slip (Photo 7.1). Glowacki (1996) has demonstrated that Arahuay pottery closely imitates the Huamanga ceramics of the Ayacucho region. Through neutron activation, she and her colleagues have also shown that Arahuay ceramics are made from local clays (Montoya et al. 2000). Surveys have found that Arahuay ceramics are widely spread in the Cuzco region, and we currently use them as a marker for Wari influence in the area. Because the physical composition of Arahuay pottery is similar to that of Qotakalli (Montoya et al. 2000), it appears that many of the ceramic workshops that produced Qotakalli vessels before the arrival of the Wari gradually accepted and began production of the Wari-style pottery, such as Arahuay, after the region fell under the influence of the Ayacucho state. Although Arahuay ceramics represented one of the dominant ceramic styles of the Cuzco region during the Wari Period, its period of production was little understood before our 1999 excavation season (Bauer and Jones 2003).

PHOTO 7.1. Arahuay pottery from the Cuzco Basin

Theodore McCown and John Rowe first proposed Wari influence in the Cuzco region in the early 1940s (Rowe 1944: 53). Manuel Chávez Ballón and Rowe later confirmed it in the early 1950s as they studied excavation and surface collections from a number of archaeological sites southeast of the city of Cuzco (Rowe 1956: 142). The most important information came from the site of Batan Orco, a small knoll that juts out into the Vilcanota River Valley near the town of Huaro (Reichlen 1954; Rowe 1956: 142). The discovery by looters of an elite tomb at Batan Orco in 1952 brought the site to the attention of Cuzco officials as well as the general public (*El Comercio* 1952a–k; Reichlen 1954). Chávez Ballón (personal communication, 1990) dug at the site that same year, but his collections were destroyed before he could finish his analysis. Barreda Murillo (1973) conducted additional excavations at Batan Orco in 1952, and Tom Patterson and Rowe made surface collections there in the 1960s (Patterson 1967). Initially, the finds at Batan Orco were classified as Tiwanaku-related (Reichlen 1954). However, further examination of the materials by Chávez Ballón and Rowe suggested a closer relationship to the Ayacucho state than to Tiwanaku. This conclusion is supported by recent work at Batan Orco by Zapata (1998) and at the nearby town of Huaro (Glowacki and Zapata 1998; Glowacki 2002).

The Development and Expansion of the Wari Empire

Developing out of a culture in the Ayacucho region currently known as Huarpa, the city of Wari grew to enormous proportions. At the height of its influence, around AD 700–800, the city covered many square kilometers with densely packed buildings and rectangular compounds. As Katharina Schreiber (1992: 80) describes it, "The site, as known today, is immense. The architectural core of the site, comprising diagnostic rectangular compound-style architecture, measures some 200 hectares. Around this core is an area of dense surface scatter; including this scatter, the site covers perhaps as much as 300 hectares." There is evidence of craft specialization within the city as well as indications of royal tombs and elite compounds (Benavides C. 1991; Isbell et al. 1991). Elaborate ceramic production was also occurring in villages near it (Pozzi-Escot B. 1991). With the current end to more than a decade of political upheaval in the re-

PHOTO 7.2. Aerial photograph of Pikillacta (Neg. no. 334819, photo by Shippee Johnson, courtesy the Library, American Museum of Natural History)

gion, we will soon learn a great deal more about the core region of Wari development.

Current scholarship suggests that the Wari rapidly expanded beyond their core area of development sometime in the late sixth or early seventh century AD. As the Wari conquered and incorporated various regions into their empire, they built a series of administrative centers across the central Andes. Two of these are qualitatively larger than the other centers, and, fascinatingly, they are positioned near what appear to be the northern and southern extremes of Wari influence in the highlands.

In the north, in the area of Huamanchuco, lies the extensive Wari ruin called Viracochapampa. The site covers more than 30 hectares and displays many classic features of Wari architecture, such as a great enclosing wall and large-scale rectangular courts with central patios and multiple long, narrow galleries. It also contains some local features such as niched halls. Research at the site indicates that Viracochapampa was never completed, although when construction began and when it stopped is not well understood (Topic and Topic 1985).

Near the southern extreme of the Wari Empire is the site of Pikillacta. As discussed below, this site shares many interesting features with Viracochapampa, not least of which is the fact that it was never completed. Other Wari

centers are known in the central highlands, but none come close to the dimensions of Viracochapampa, Pikillacta, and Wari (Schreiber 1992: 96–114). The relative sizes of the three largest Wari sites, and their geographical locations spread across the central Andes, have encouraged scholars to suggest that the capital of the Wari Empire was the city of Wari in the Ayacucho region and that the Wari attempted to build two large installations (Viracochapampa and Pikillacta) to serve as provincial capitals near the northern and southern borders of their empire.[4]

The Site of Pikillacta

The largest single Wari occupation in the Cuzco region is the site of Pikillacta, which is located in the Lucre Basin approximately 30 kilometers southeast of the city of Cuzco. Cieza de León (1976: 261 [1551: Pt. 1, Ch. 97]) visited this well-preserved site soon after the European invasion, and centuries later Squier (1877: 419–422) commented on its large size and apparent antiquity.[5] More than a thousand years after its abandonment, the site of Pikillacta is breathtaking in both its horizontal and vertical scales (Photos 7.2 and 7.3).

Because of its large size and remarkable state of preservation, Pikillacta remains an important feature of the

PHOTO 7.3. Aerial photograph of Pikillacta (Courtesy of Servicio Aerofotográfico Nacional, Peru)

landscape today (Photos 7.4 and 7.5). It has, neverthe-less, suffered at the hands of looters. Cieza de León notes that looting began at the site soon after the Spaniards arrived in Cuzco:

Pikillacta?

> There were great buildings in Mohina, but they are now destroyed and fallen down. When the Gover-nor Don Francisco Pizarro entered Cuzco with the Spaniards, they say they found near these buildings and in them a large amount of silver and gold, and even more of the fine, valuable clothing I have men-tioned on other occasions. And I have heard some of the Spaniards say that there was at this place a stone statue of a man with a kind of long robe and beads in his hand, and other figures and statues. (1976: 261 [1551: Pt. 1, Ch. 97])[6]

In the early 1920s, looting at Pikillacta produced two caches of turquoise figurines (Cook 1992). The figurines were part of two dedicatory offerings placed within a build-

ing in the central sector of the site. Various other offer-ings, although less elaborate, have been found in later ex-cavations (McEwan 1996). Over the past fifty years many individuals have conducted research at Pikillacta, includ-ing Emilio Harth-Terré (1959), Barreda Murillo (1964), William T. Sanders (1973), and Alfredo Valencia Zegarra. Beginning as early as the 1930s, the Peruvian government, most recently under the auspices of the National Insti-tute of Culture (Cuzco), has also directed a series of reno-vation projects at the site. Finally, McEwan supervised a long-term project at Pikillacta beginning in 1979.

PIKILLACTA AS A WARI ADMINISTRATIVE CENTER

Pikillacta is a well-planned and excessively large installa-tion that was built and occupied in a deliberate sequence. The site was constructed on a large mountain shelf—one that had not been occupied by previous cultures—overlooking Lake Lucre. Excavations in Pikillacta and in trash middens outside the massive walls of the site indi-

PHOTO 7.4. A thousand years after its abandonment, Pikillacta remains a very impressive site.

PHOTO 7.5. Some of the walls at Pikillacta still stand several stories high.

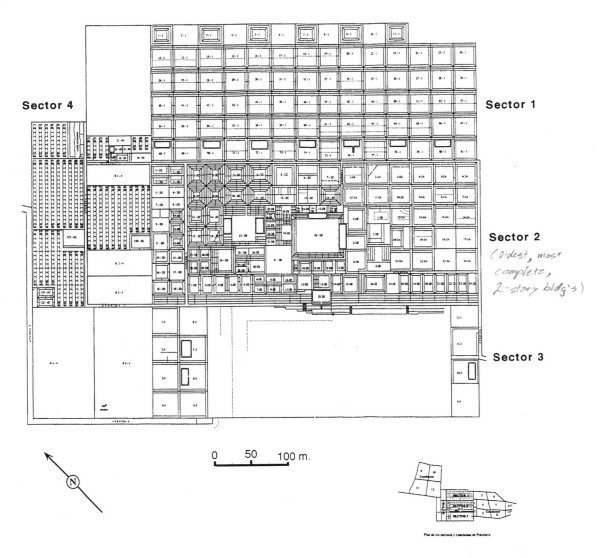

Handwritten margin note (left, near Sector 4 label): *oldest, most complete, 2-story bldg's* (near Sector 2)

MAP 7.1. Map of Pikillacta (Courtesy of Gordon McEwan)

cate that its occupants used several different ceramic styles, including a few exotic vessels imported from Nazca and Cajamarca (Knobloch 1991: 253; Glowacki 1996). Investigations have also revealed much about the construction sequence of the site. McEwan (1996) divides the central zone of Pikillacta into four sectors, each of which has a different construction and occupational history (Map 7.1). Sector 1, the northernmost sector, is composed of eighty-one large square compounds with some internal galleries and structures. The layout is remarkably rigid, with little variation in compound types. Research in this sector suggests that it was nearly complete at the time of site abandonment, although it was never occupied.

The central area of Pikillacta, Sector 2, is by far the most elaborate. It is composed of many large square and rectangular compounds and a mazelike collection of internal galleries. There is also an expansive central plaza and a smaller, secondary plaza to one side. Excavations indicate that Sector 2 was completed and occupied for a considerable period. Most of the walls and floors of the structures were covered with a thick, white gypsum plaster. McEwan (1996: 182–183) writes, "Excavation illustrates that Sector 2 was the first to be built, and featured fully plastered walls and floors in multi-story buildings with thatched roofs. This sector was occupied long enough for some buildings to have undergone at least

Handwritten margin notes (left):

Pikillacta as Admin Center:

1) built on previously-uninhabited landform

2) several ceramic styles, incl. exotic imports

3) 4 separate sectors, each w/ diff. construction + occupational history

4) large, formal layout & high walls reflect massive construction project

5) construction technique is very basic, probably built in separate chunks assigned to diff. ayllus

6) boom-and-bust pattern of imperial installation, similar to Inca provincial centers

two remodeling episodes." A large burning event in the sector resulted in the superimposition of the floors in the multistoried galleries as their crossbeams failed and the floors collapsed, one on top of the other.

The construction sequence and layout of Sector 3, the southernmost area of the site, is the least understood, partly because a large-scale remodeling of the area by the Peruvian government may have occurred in the early 1930s. The section seems vacuous in comparison to other parts of the site, and the fact that some of the walls appear unfinished suggests that the construction of this sector was still in progress when Pikillacta was abandoned.

The western area of the site, Sector 4, is composed of five compounds of densely packed single-room structures. Four of the compounds also contain large rectangular areas. Since the first mapping of the site, it has been suggested that this sector represents a storage area. This idea has been readily accepted, based on features of the sector such as its limited access, the five hundred identical cell-like rooms, and large rectangular areas perhaps used for the drying of products. However, excavations in the rooms have revealed domestic remains, including informal hearths and light trash middens (McEwan 1991).

THE CONSTRUCTION OF PIKILLACTA

The construction techniques used in building Pikillacta are not complex. Its walls are made of local fieldstones held together with mud mortar. The gypsum plaster that once covered many of its structures is also found locally. Nevertheless, its great size, formal layout, and impressively high walls mark Pikillacta as an unprecedented construction project in the south-central Andes.

The building of Pikillacta was an immense investment by the Wari Empire in the Cuzco region, and some unusual architectural features of the complex hint at how the local labor was organized during its construction phases. Traditionally, large public works projects in the Andes are organized around village-level *ayllus* (kin groups). Rather than organizing themselves into a single massive labor force when undertaking large public labor projects, Andean populations generally work in a multitude of small groups, the coordination of which is left in the hands of overseers. Each *ayllu* is assigned a distinct aspect of the larger project, and that section or task is to

be completed independently of the other groups' contributions. Evidence of such labor organization has been noted in the production of adobes at the Moche Pyramid of the Sun on the north coast of Peru (Hastings and Moseley 1975), and other facts suggest that similar labor and construction techniques were used to build Pikillacta.[7] For example, the great enclosure wall of the site is divided into a large number of uneven sections (Photo 7.6). These seams introduce a structural weakness to the wall, but they make sense if the seams represent the labor assignments of separate kin groups.

We can also assume, using well-documented Inca analogies, that the construction of Pikillacta occurred through *mit'a* (turn) labor. Under the Inca system of governance, each village was required to provide a certain number of workers for state projects for a set time period. When they had completed their turn, the workers were replaced by laborers from other settlements, and the first group of workers returned to their homes. Although we may never know which local groups were most heavily involved, there is no doubt that the construction of Pikillacta and the maintenance of the people who occupied it placed a tremendous strain on the local population.

THE ABANDONMENT OF PIKILLACTA

Unlike normal villages and towns, whose population may wax and wane over the years, imperial installations frequently experience a boom-and-bust cycle. For example, many of the largest Inca provincial centers, such as Huánuco Pampa (Morris and Thompson 1985), Pumpu (Matos M. 1994), and Machu Picchu, were abandoned soon after the Spanish invasion. The high-level Inca administrators fled, and the local, lower-level providers of the centers returned to their villages as the power of the Inca Empire collapsed. Many of the Inca provincial capitals were artificial cities, in the sense that there were no permanent residents with strong traditions that tied them to the centers. The provincial capitals were quickly built under the strong hand of the empire and even more quickly abandoned as soon as the hegemonic power of Cuzco waned.

A similar pattern of construction, habitation, and abandonment can be seen in Pikillacta. As a planned Wari center, Pikillacta appears on a mammoth scale in an area

PHOTO 7.6. Seams in the large exterior wall of Pikillacta may represent divisions between assigned labor units.

The Wari probably burned it themselves

of the Lucre Basin that had not attracted previous occupations. The resident population would have been made up of foreign elite, no doubt closely affiliated with those of the Wari heartland, as well as an untold number of locals serving their labor obligations. Further excavations may reveal the presence of lower-level administrators, craft specialists, and some military personnel as well.

The plans that the Wari held for the Cuzco region must have been immense to justify the building of such a massive complex. The large scale of Pikillacta can be interpreted as a reflection of what the Wari Empire eventually expected to gain from the region. The Wari would not have invested so much time and energy in its construction if they had not believed that the site and the region as a whole would provide significant rewards to the empire. Also, it appears that the Wari believed that the relatively low level of societal complexity in the Cuzco region would be inadequate to fulfill the demands that the empire would place on it, and thus they built their own center so that the region could be administered by Wari officials. Nevertheless, the great expectations, perhaps represented by the maize grown in this agriculturally important region or the establishment of a strong frontier with the Tiwanaku polity to the south, may never have been completely realized, as Pikillacta was abandoned in the midst of its great construction plan. Furthermore, excavations at the site indicate that parts of it

seems like they did this everywhere they went, though..

were burned soon after its abandonment, perhaps reflecting local resistance against the Wari in the Cuzco region.

There is evidence that other sites in the Cuzco region were also burned and abandoned at the same time as Pikillacta. For example, in 1999 we selected for excavation a small site called Pukacancha (Co. 141) near Cuzco to gain more information on the ceramic styles of the valley (Bauer and Jones 2003). The site, which had been occupied throughout the Wari Period, was abandoned after a burning episode that dated to around AD 780–1030 (95.4% probability).[8] This date is remarkably similar to the latest dates obtained from Pikillacta and may mark the termination point for Wari influence in the valley (see below).

The history of the Wari occupation of the Cuzco region also needs to be understood on a regional level. To accomplish this, we can now turn to the results of several other research projects in the Cuzco region and to the findings of our valley survey.

The Wari in the Cuzco Region

Pikillacta is not the only archaeological site in the Lucre Basin. During McEwan's work at Pikillacta, he explored the Lucre Basin and recorded the locations of thirty-two additional sites, approximately half of which appear to contain Wari Period components (McEwan 1984). He suggests that several of the Wari Period sites were so tightly integrated with Pikillacta that they should be considered annexes of it. McEwan proposes that together they formed a single urban-like zone in which different sites served separate functions.

WARI INFLUENCE IN THE HUARO BASIN

Because Pikillacta is the largest Wari site in the Cuzco region, it has long been assumed to be the earliest Wari occupation in the area. However, recent research in the Huaro Basin, to the southeast of the Lucre Basin, suggests that the history of the region may not be as certain as current reconstructions imply. Many years ago, looting at the site of Batan Orco, just outside the town of Huaro, uncovered the remains of an elite Wari burial, and more recent excavations at the site by Zapata (1997) revealed the remains of a Wari Period cemetery. Glowacki and Zapata (1998) continued researching the Wari Period occupation of the Huaro Basin, conducting excavations in the town of Huaro itself as well as at several sites that surround it. The excavations in Huaro indicate that the town sits above a large Wari site that contains ceramics of especially high quality. Additional excavations at nearby sites found dense domestic materials. The combination of several large habitation sites, a cemetery with high-status graves, and a central area with fancy pottery (perhaps an elite residence or a ceremonial district) indicates that the Huaro Basin was of considerable importance to the Wari. Furthermore, survey work by Glowacki (2002) has shown, based on ceramic styles, that a number of large sites in the Huaro Basin were occupied throughout the Wari Period. Glowacki and Zapata (1998) have hypothesized that the Huaro Basin was occupied early on during the Wari expansion process and that it was from this "beachhead" that the Wari began to consolidate their hold over the Cuzco region. These researchers suggest that it was after the Wari had occupied the Huaro Basin that they selected the large unoccupied plain above Lake Lucre as the site for their future provincial center and began the construction of Pikillacta. Glowacki (2002) also proposes that certain sites in the Huaro Basin continued to be occupied even after the abandonment of Pikillacta.

The presence of elite burials and compounds, in ad-dition to several large domestic occupations in the immediate area, certainly indicates that the Huaro Basin was important for the Wari. Only future research will be able to determine if Huaro was the primary Wari administrative center before the construction and occupation of Pikillacta. Alternatively, Huaro could represent a secondary node of Wari administration in the Cuzco region, developed to administer the area along the upper Vilcanota River Valley between Lucre to the west and Sicuani to the east.

WARI INFLUENCE EAST AND SOUTHEAST OF THE HUARO BASIN

A series of other studies is helping to map the distribution of Wari influence east of Cuzco, beyond Huaro, toward the Altiplano and the Lake Titicaca Basin. Rowe and his colleagues found Wari-style ceramics at several sites near Sicuani in the early 1950s (Rowe 1956: 142–144). Recent work by Bill Sillar and Emily Dean (personal communication, 1999) in the region of Rachi has identified numerous sites that contain Wari-style materials and others that contain Altiplano-related artifacts. In other words, Pikillacta no longer stands as the last Wari site before entering the Altiplano, and there may have been considerable interaction between these two empires.

Sergio Chávez (1985, 1987) reports on an elaborate collection of 141 Wari-style metal objects from the Pomacanchi area, to the southeast of Cuzco. Within this collection also were two ceramic vessels, one of which is classified by S. Chávez (1987: 8) as Chakipampa B and the other appears to be a local style. Excavations conducted by Wilbert San Román Luna (1979, 1983) at the site of K'ullupata in Pomacanchi have recovered various Wari-style artifacts. Other isolated Wari-style finds have been recovered still farther to the southeast of Cuzco in the Province of Chumbivilcas by S. Chávez (1987, 1988) and Lantarón Pfoccori (1988), and in the Province of Espinar by Meddens (1989).

It should be noted that S. Chávez's (1987: 17) study of Wari-style metal objects recovered in the Pomacanchi area suggests that these objects may also reflect some Tiwanaku influence. Furthermore, S. Chávez indicates that he has found a provincial Wari-style beaker from Chumbivilcas that also contains some Tiwanaku features. These findings emphasize that there most certainly were people living in transitional zones, such as the Altiplano regions east and southeast of Cuzco, which were not directly controlled by either Wari or Tiwanaku but were influenced by both of these expanding states.

WARI INFLUENCE NORTHWEST AND SOUTHWEST OF THE LUCRE BASIN

Research has revealed several Wari sites in the upper course of the Vilcanota Valley between the area of Pikillacta and Sicuani. Other projects conducted to the northwest and southwest of the Lucre Basin have, however, revealed dramatically different patterns. For example, Wari or Arahuay ceramics have been found at relatively few sites in the Province of Paruro (Bauer 1999; 2002). Furthermore, all of the sites with Wari or Arahuay materials in the Province of Paruro lie north of the Apurímac River and none of them is especially large. One unusual site, Muyu Roqo, located on a mountain slope immediately west of the town of Paruro, deserves some special discussion. Surface collections from this small site, which measures approximately 50 m by 50 m, provided a large number of Wari-style fragments (Bauer 1999; 2002). Test excavations at the site yielded hundreds more and nearly two thousand camelid bone fragments. A radiocarbon date run on one of the bones yielded an age of 1135 ± 50 BP (calibrated 95.4 % probability AD 770–1000).[9]

The Muyu Roqo ceramic collection suggests that the site served a ceremonial function during the Wari Period. A high percentage of fine ware vessels were found at the site, most of which were large bowls and drinking vessels, which implies that extensive eating and drinking activities took place there. The great number of camelid bones recovered at the site reinforces this interpretation. Although the exact nature of the site cannot be determined until additional excavations take place, the current evidence strongly suggests that this site was used for ritual activities during the Wari Period.

Muyu Roqo is also noteworthy because it is one of a small number of sites in the Paruro Valley that contain significant Wari-style remains. The Lucre Basin and the Wari center of Pikillacta are located only 20 kilometers north of the Paruro Valley. These two areas are connected by several large trails, and the journey between them on foot takes only six to eight hours. Despite the close proximity of the Lucre and Paruro regions, it is clear that they hold different kinds and densities of Wari remains.

Similar survey results have been found in the lower Vilcanota Valley downstream from the Lucre Basin. While surveying the region between Cuzco, Pisaq, and Calca, Covey (2003) has detected few sites with Wari ceramics. It is becoming increasingly clear that the Wari occupation of the Cuzco region was highly uneven. People living one or two river valleys away from the Lucre Basin would have certainly been aware of the great political and social changes that were occurring in it, but their lives may have been affected to a much lesser extent.

WARI INFLUENCE IN THE CUZCO AND OROPESA BASINS

Our systematic regional survey found a relatively strong record of Wari influence west of the Lucre Basin. In all, around eighty-five sites were identified in the Oropesa and Cuzco Basins that contained Arahuay ceramics (Map 7.2). Several interesting observations can be made about these sites. First, unlike in the Lucre Basin, no sites in the Oropesa and Cuzco Basins contain Wari-style architectural remains. Thus, all Wari-site classifications in these areas of the Cuzco Valley have been done on the basis of recovered ceramics. In this regard it is also worth noting that in all of our surface collections and test excavations, we recovered only a handful of ceramics that appear to have been imported from the Wari homeland and none of the sites found contained any unusual proportions of domestic versus fancy wares. In other words, from the current database, we imagine a series of Wari Period settlements stretching across the Cuzco Valley that were simply using the ceramics of their time. No sites display remains of Wari architecture, and there were no distinct concentrations of extra fine or important vessels that might be reflective of an important political or ritual center for the Wari in either the Oropesa or Cuzco Basins.

A second, related point is that none of the sites containing Wari Period pottery in the Oropesa and Cuzco Basins is especially large. Although several of the sites measure 3–4 hectares in size, and most certainly represented substantial villages in their time, none are large enough to be considered a secondary center of Wari administration. Perhaps the largest Wari Period occupation in the valley was the site of Coripata (Cu. 155 on Map 7.2).[10] Urban growth of Cuzco has destroyed the site (Cumpa Palacios 1988), but it is fair to say that it was not over 5 hectares. Given the sheer magnitude of Pikillacta, it is not surprising that there is no secondary Wari center in the valley. The western end of the Cuzco Basin is some 30 kilometers from Pikillacta. The Wari could easily have administered this entire region and its population from the Lucre Basin, through the use of local elite already established in the preexisting Cuzco chiefdom. The surplus agricultural production from the valley was most likely sent straight to Pikillacta, and groups of villagers, perhaps functioning under a system of obligatory, rotating labor service, would have worked on its construction.

It should also be noted that the clusters of sites containing Arahuay materials in the Oropesa and Cuzco Basins are similar to those seen for the Qotakalli Period. There is a significant site cluster around site An. 326, near the village of Huasao in the Oropesa Basin. Not surprisingly, the Huasao area contains some of the best

maize-producing fields in this narrow section of the Huatanay drainage. Further up the river in the Cuzco Basin, near the modern city of Cuzco, there is a much heavier concentration of Wari Period sites on the southern side of the basin than on its northern slopes. There are also no sites at the far northwest end of the basin, but they pick up again on the other side of the watershed in the Cachimayu region. These patterns resemble those found for the distribution of Qotakalli Period remains.

Perhaps the most striking difference between the two periods is that during Qotakalli times, there appear to be more small sites scattered across the countryside than in the Wari Period. Although resolution of our site-size data is not especially high, it appears that many of the small and more isolated Qotakalli Period homesteads and hamlets were abandoned, and their inhabitants moved into the many village-level settlements located across the region. This may reflect the greater agricultural intensification that occurred during this era.

Unlike the Cuzco and Oropesa Basins, some areas of the Andes reflect clear shifts in settlement patterns before and after they were incorporated under Wari rule.

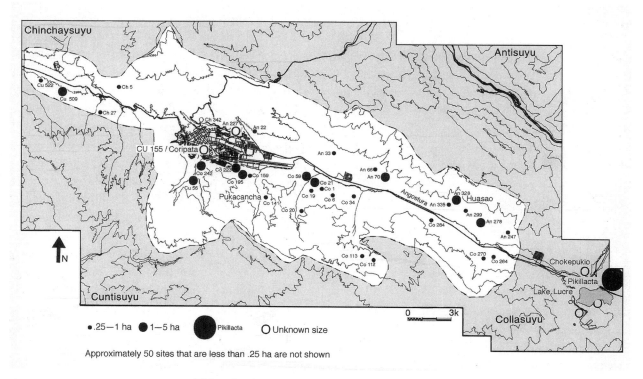

MAP 7.2. Thirty-five important Wari Period sites in the Cuzco Valley

5) some settlement aggregation from hamlets to small villages, but no wholesale restructuring of regional settlement like Wari occupations elsewhere

6) area was already intensively growing maize - a Wari priority

For example, in her regional study of the Carhuarazo Valley, Schreiber (1987b, 1991, 1992, 1999) has documented substantial changes in the local settlement pattern as the Wari consolidated the region into their expanding state. A large administrative center (Jincamocco) was constructed, along with at least three subsidiary centers. A series of new village settlements were established in the lower maize-growing region of the valley, and many of the villages located in the potato-growing elevations were abandoned. She writes:

> The picture that emerges in the Carhuarazo Valley is one of a small highland valley with a relatively low population engaged in tuber cultivation and camelid herding. Suddenly, in the Middle Horizon, a new culture appeared. A large center was built, after summarily destroying the local village that occupied the desired location. Terraces were built and maize cultivation increased. Some of the local villages were moved down to lower elevations, closer to the newly created maize zone. The increased labor inputs required to build the center and complete the terraces may have necessitated bringing in laborers from outside the valley. (Schreiber 1992: 161)

In the Cuzco and Oropesa Basins of the Cuzco Valley, we see a markedly different process of consolidation occurring. There is no evidence of a radical reorganization of the social landscape with the arrival of the Wari. Many of the smallest sites are abandoned, but few new sites of significant size (village or above) are established. For the most part, Wari Period materials simply appear in villages that had already been occupied during the previous era. This, in turn, is radically different from what has been found in the Lucre and Huaro Basins to the east, where large Wari installations appear to have been built and occupied.

The strong continuation of Qotakalli Period settlement patterns into and throughout the Wari Period in the Cuzco and Oropesa Basins provides important insights into their economic system. For example, it seems that the local economy already conformed to the priorities of the foreigners. Since Late Formative times, there had been a gradual concentration of the population into habitation sites in the lower elevation zones of the valley. The Wari were interested in maize, and the local economy of the region was already focused on its production. Rather than expending a large amount of time and energy in reorganizing the local economy, the Wari were satisfied with the status quo and quickly began a process of power consolidation through the occupation of the Huaro Basin and the construction of Pikillacta in the Lucre Basin.

It must be stressed, however, that maize production is not the whole story to explain the Wari presence in the Cuzco region. If it was, we would expect to find a series of large Wari sites stretching down the Vilcanota Valley, which holds some of the finest maize-growing areas of the Andean highlands. Recent work by Covey (2003) in the Vilcanota Valley between San Salvador and Calca has demonstrated that there are no imperial Wari centers in this highly fertile, frost-free zone of maize production. Rather than concentrating solely on the maize resources of the region, it seems that the Wari positioned Pikillacta to take advantage of a number of different local economic factors. From the Lucre Basin, the Wari could take advantage of tribute labor in the maize-growing areas of the Cuzco and Vilcanota Valleys to the northwest, without having to invest in building facilities in these areas. Furthermore, from the Lucre Basin, the Wari could gain access to, and perhaps even control over, the coca trade routes to the north, which brought this valuable leaf from the subtropical areas of Paucartambo into the highland valleys. Finally, the location of Pikillacta in the Lucre Basin also provided the Wari with an entry into the rich tuber-producing and herding economies of the upper Vilcanota Valley to the southeast as well as establishing a frontier with more remote regions that were under the influence of Tiwanaku.

The strong continuation of Qotakalli Period and Wari Period settlement patterns in the Cuzco and Oropesa Basins also yields information on the local-level political organization of the region at the time of Wari influence. Since the days of Menzel (1959), it is well recognized that the form and intensity of installations in an area of imperial expansion will vary in response to the preexisting social organization of the area. Using the Inca as an example, Menzel demonstrated that in areas that had well-established social hierarchies and centralized rule, the Inca co-opted members of the local elite to work for them

(damr

Wari wanted more than maize:
1) admin center at Pikillacta could oversee much
2) maize production in Cuzco & Vilcanota Valleys
3) coca trade routes north of Lucre
4) tubers & camelids in upper Vilcanota
5) establish frontier zone on Tiwanaku border
6) utilized intact social hierarchy in Cuzco for indirect admin

*Using Inca model to describe Wari imperial strategy — how does this **not** seem like Inca statecraft was based on Wari principles? (i.e. circular reasoning?)*

and left the existing institutions largely in place. In contrast, in the areas that lacked centralized authority, the Inca needed to construct their own administrative centers and support facilities. These observations can be used to provide some clarity on the Wari occupation of the Cuzco region.

It is clear that the Wari felt a great need to completely transform the Lucre Basin through the construction of Pikillacta and its numerous support facilities, which included large tracks of terraces, canals, and various satellite communities. In contrast, the Cuzco polity, concentrated at the northwest end of the valley some 30 kilometers away, was left relatively on its own. No secondary center was constructed in the Cuzco Basin, and the settlement pattern remained largely unchanged. It seems that the local population of the Cuzco Basin was brought under Wari influence through a variety of social mechanisms. Most importantly, the Wari needed the labor tribute of the Cuzco polity, as well as that of other surrounding ethnic groups, to build, maintain, and supply their emergent center of Pikillacta. As the Wari entered the Cuzco region, they would have attempted to form coalitions with certain members of the local elite families, and then, over time, tried to extend their direct administrative control over the region and its populace.

Dating the Period of Wari Influence in the Cuzco Region

We currently have two independent data sets to date the arrival and withdrawal of the Wari from the Cuzco region (Figure 7.1).[11] The first set consists of ten dates extracted from Pikillacta (McEwan 1984, 1996). The earliest dates are derived from excavated floor levels in the complex that suggest a foundation date of between AD 600 and AD 700.[12] The latest samples come from the wooden beams charred in a fire that destroyed the central sector of the site, and provide dates of between AD 800 and AD 1000.[13] It should be noted that since the wooden beam samples come from construction materials within Pikillacta, they do not date the destruction of the site, but instead date what appears to have been the last construction phase.

The second data set comes from our excavation program at Wari Period sites in the Cuzco Basin. In all, eight carbon samples have been dated from contexts with Wari (Viñaque and Huamanga) and Arahuay pottery. The earliest two samples date to between AD 650 and AD 850,[14] and the last two fall between AD 800 and AD 1000. These dates, taken from a series of small Wari Period sites in the Cuzco Basin, are similar to those from Pikillacta. The combined data sets suggest that the Wari arrived in the Cuzco region sometime around AD 600 and were active in the region until at least AD 900, and perhaps even till the turn of the millennium. The beginning date of Wari influence in the region also meshes well with the final appearance (1422 ± 51 BP [95.4% probability AD 530–700])[15] of Altiplano-influenced materials (Muyu Orco and incised *incensarios*) recovered at the site of Peqokaypata and thought to be in the valley before the arrival of the Wari.

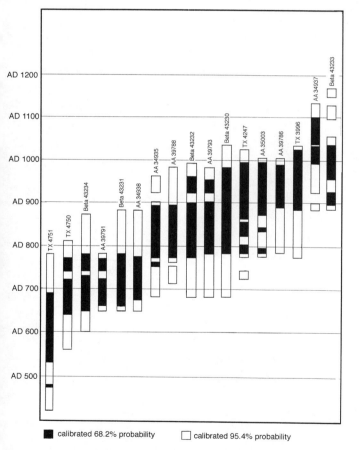

FIGURE 7.1. Calibrated radiocarbon dates from Wari and Wari-related contexts in the Cuzco region (from Bauer and Jones 2003)

Summary and Discussion

When the Wari entered the Cuzco region, they found it to be similar to many other areas of the south-central Andes. Small sets of ranked elites lived in a few chiefly villages spaced out along the river valleys. A significant percentage of the population also lived in numerous homesteads or hamlets densely scattered across the region. Local societies were thriving, but they had yet to reach a level of social or political complexity equal to that already achieved in the Ayacucho region.

The Wari were drawn to the Cuzco region because it was a rich area of agricultural potential relatively near to, but outside of, the direct control of Tiwanaku. In the Cuzco Basin they found a large concentration of people near its western end. In the Lucre Basin, Chokepukio appears to have been of importance as well. In between these basins, along the course of the Huatanay River, were numerous villages, hamlets, and homesteads. To the east of the Lucre Basin was the area of Huaro, which presumably also contained a significant population concentration. Many thousands of people lived in the region, but given its large size and rich climatic zones, large tracts of land were still available for agricultural expansion and, most importantly, intensification.

The Wari Empire was interested in maize and found that the local economy was already focused on its production. Because of this, they did not need to physically reorganize the indigenous settlement systems of the region, as they had done elsewhere. Instead, the Wari concerned themselves with consolidating their influence over the region and establishing a southern administrative center for their empire. During this period there appears to have been some minor concentration of peoples in the largest villages of the region, and many of the smallest Qotakalli Period sites were abandoned. Local potters shifted through time from producing the local style of Qotakalli to Wari-influenced styles, such as Arahuay. Burger et al. (2000) have also documented a clear shift in obsidian procurement patterns. For more than a thousand years, the peoples of the Cuzco region had obtained their obsidian from sources located in the Alca region. During the Wari Period, when Wari occupied parts of the Cuzco region, the obsidian flow from this source stopped. For this relatively brief period of time, obsidian was im-ported into the region from the Quispisisa area, which, like the Cuzco Valley, was under Wari control (Burger et al. 2000).

The Wari may have first established themselves in the Huaro Basin and then begun to expand their influence into the Cuzco Valley. Eventually, the area that felt the greatest Wari impact in the Cuzco region was the Lucre Basin. There the Wari built an architectural marvel, the site of Pikillacta. Enormous on any scale, the site of Pikillacta represented an unparalleled construction project in the region. The Wari selected a large mountain shelf above Lake Lucre, near the confluence of the Vilcanota and Huatanay Rivers, to build their administrative center. New terrace systems were built, canals constructed, and large tracts of previously marginal land were brought into full agricultural production.

Some 30 kilometers northwest of Pikillacta, the preexisting chiefdom in the Cuzco Basin was less affected. No secondary center was built in the Cuzco Basin, and the settlement pattern continued relatively unchanged. In this case, the Wari appear to have gained influence through more subtle means. Local elites would have played important roles in mediating Wari administration in the Cuzco Basin, at least in the beginning.

It is clear that the Wari ultimately hoped to control the entire Cuzco region and then rule the southern highlands directly from their administrative center at Pikillacta. Construction began at Pikillacta after AD 600, and the last known building phase occurred as late as AD 900. However, after centuries of occupation, the site was abandoned, with different sectors left in varying stages of construction. The fact that the center was never completed indicates that the Wari were never able to establish the kind of integration that they had envisioned when the expansion process began.

The concluding event at Pikillacta was a huge fire that destroyed much of the formally occupied area of the site. This is strong evidence that mediation with the local population had failed. In other words, the Wari had been unable to fully incorporate and indoctrinate the peoples of the region into their state. The political and economic authority that emanated from the large complex of Pikillacta was still seen as "foreign," despite the fact that the complex had existed for several centuries.

In recent years, it has been suggested that since Pikillacta was not completed, it never functioned on a scale that its large size suggests. Nevertheless, the fact that so much of the complex was built indicates that the Wari dominated the region and were able to extract a large amount of rotational labor for its projects. As has been noted for the construction of monumental architecture elsewhere in the Americas, the coordinators of these projects most certainly attempted to present them to the local populace as logical continuations of traditional labor practices, even though the scale of the operations had greatly changed (Pauketat 2000). The construction occurred at levels not seen before in the region, because the Wari could extract labor from different ethnic groups who had never before worked "collectively" on a project.

At the height of their power, the Wari controlled a vast, though discontinuous, area across the central Andes. With the construction of Pikillacta, parts of the Cuzco region fell under its influence. Contact with other parts of the Wari realm is reflected by the recovery of a few fragments of Nazca and Cajamarca ceramics at Pikillacta (Glowacki 1996). Slightly more numerous, however, are vessels that were imported into the Cuzco region from the Wari core area of Ayacucho.

Archaeological surveys in the Cuzco region indicate that the distribution of direct Wari control was highly uneven. Centered largely in the Lucre Basin, their direct control extended up the Vilcanota River Valley at least until the town of Huaro, where another, perhaps earlier, center was built. The Wari had markedly less influence in the areas to the south, and they worked closely with local leaders to the west to extend their influence over the preexisting Cuzco Basin chiefdom.

Although the Wari attempt to incorporate the Cuzco region into their expanding state eventually failed, the centuries-long Wari presence in the south-central Andes fostered many important local changes that influenced the course of future development in the area. For example, the Wari presence in the region must have altered local intellectual and administrative infrastructure as ethnic elites and their commoner populations both cooperated with and offered indigenous resistance against the newcomers. Furthermore, the construction of terraces and canals and the opening up of large tracts of agricultural land in the Lucre Basin must have impressed the local population. In fact, terrace construction and irrigation would become a major feature in the development of new agricultural lands and the formation of power in the next period. In addition, the Wari occupation also brought the production and standardization of local ceramics to a scale not seen before. Imported styles were reproduced, and after the fall of the empire, they served as the foundation for the development of new regional traditions. Successful cultural hegemony by the Wari over selected aspects of the Cuzco-based societies is reflected in the production of Wari-style (i.e., Arahuay) pottery in local workshops. Arahuay ceramics dominate the finer wares of the valley during the Wari Period and, perhaps most important, appear to form the ceramic tradition from which Killke (or Early Inca) ceramics develop after the Wari withdraw from the region.

The withdrawal of the Wari from the Cuzco region and the burning of Pikillacta set the scene for the rise of local ethnic groups. The next period, one of the most interesting times of local development in the Cuzco region, would witness the development of the Inca state and set the foundations for Cuzco's own course of expansionism across the Andean world.

Wari in Cuzco (AD 600-900)

probably entered from Huaro, older settlement, via Lucre Basin

high labor investment, settlement shift in Lucre, founding of Pikillacta

in NW of valley, local social system and intensified maize agr. resulted in little settlement shift, imposition of direct control (i.e. rule through local elites)

4) Wari presence opens up exchange routes w/ rest of Wari realm. Ceramics from Ayacucho, Nazca, Cajamarca. Obsidian from Quispisisa (instead of Alca).

5) Local ceramic production abandons altiplano influence (Muyu Orco) & picks up Wari influence (Arahuay). Wari ceramic style is very standardized. Arahuay is base for later Killke style.

6) Wari could mobilize labor from multiple ethnic groups to build Pikillacta, impressive terrace agr. systems. Large-scale public works become important political-economic strategy later on.

7) Wari suddenly abandon Cuzco ca. AD 1000. Clear way for new political succession of local elites.

★ Typical LIP demographic shift doesn't occur in Cuzco - is it because Wari left local sociopolitical system intact?

CHAPTER 8

The Development of the Inca State (AD 1000–1400)

Brian S. Bauer and R. Alan Covey

IN THIS CHAPTER we examine the dramatic social transformations that occurred in the Cuzco region between AD 1000 and 1400, during the Killke Period (also generally known as the Late Intermediate Period).[1] Conceptually, this encompasses regional developments following the decline of Wari influence in the south-central Andes and leading up to the first Inca territorial expansion outside the Cuzco region. As such, this era represents the critical time when the Inca transformed themselves from one of many competing complex polities on the post-Wari political landscape into a well-integrated state capable of dominating the central Andean highlands.

Because Inca imperialism occurred just before the Spanish Conquest of the Andean highlands (AD 1532), some information recorded in sixteenth- and seventeenth-century colonial documents can be compared critically with archaeological data recovered through excavations and settlement surveys in the Cuzco region. References to the interactions among Cuzco's ethnic groups during the Killke Period facilitate a more detailed discussion of Inca state development than would otherwise be possible.

In considering the ethnohistoric record, we acknowledge the problems inherent to the study of these documents (Rowe 1946: 192–197; Bauer 1992a; Julien 2000), at the same time asserting that their anthropological study can yield important perspectives on long-term regional processes. While specific Inca rulers are often credited with specific events or achievements, we combine information contained in the Spanish chronicles with excavation and survey data to construct multiple lines of evidence for state formation processes. In other words, we attempt to identify the particular conditions that favored social transformation in the Cuzco region during this period of state development, rather than develop biographies of the charismatic individuals who have come to be credited with such changes (Covey 2003:6).

In this context, the distribution of Inca of Privilege—groups in the Cuzco region to whom Inca ethnic status was extended—becomes the basis for our analysis of the development of the imperial heartland (Map 2.1). As discussed in Chapter 2, the Inca of Privilege were subservient to Cuzco and yet allied with it, and they represented a large, tribute-paying social stratum that supported the ruling elite in Cuzco and occupied low-level bureaucratic positions in Inca imperial institutions. This is to say, the state formation process promoted the development of an ethnically unified Inca heartland. The full ethnic integration of the Cuzco region corresponds to the first campaigns of Inca imperial expansion into neighboring non-Inca regions.

Previous Research on the Development of the Inca Heartland

Before the 1970s, many writers described Inca political origins in terms of the personal achievements of Inca rulers. Using certain Spanish chronicles, it has been proposed that the Inca emerged from obscurity in the early fifteenth century during the reign of Viracocha Inca and his son Pachacuti Inca Yupanqui. The catalyst for the sudden political growth in the Cuzco region is said to have been the ability of these two Inca kings to unite the various ethnic groups of the region and to score a decisive military victory over a traditional rival, the Chanka. Nigel Davies (1995: 59) summarizes the traditional interpretation of Inca political origins: "When he [Pachacuti] became ruler, the Incas formed only a modest village community; at his death they were the mightiest empire of South America."

Accepting the belief that the Inca state was largely the invention of Pachacuti Inca Yupanqui, many scholars have concentrated on reconstructing and analyzing the individual actions of this heroic leader rather than trying to understand the broader social contexts in which those actions took place. Here and elsewhere, we argue against the use of this traditional explanation of rapid state growth, and the methodological individualism that supports it, in favor of a more processual approach (Bauer 1992a; Bauer and Covey 1999; Covey 2003). Shifting the interpretive focus to processes of long-term change is the first step in moving beyond the "great man" paradigm of Inca origins to develop more anthropological perspectives on the Inca Empire (Covey 2003: 4).

In other words, although Inca imperial expansion appears to have occurred quite rapidly, researchers increasingly view this as the result of antecedent and long-term regional political processes rather than the serendipitous outcome of a single battle and the aspirations of specific individuals. A process-oriented interpretation requires that we work with a chronological scope exceeding that of the reliable ethnohistoric record. Still, some scholars have read the documents for more causal or processual perspectives on Inca state formation as the interests of scholars have shifted from singular events and individual agency to the long-term development of social, economic, military, and ideological power (Covey 2003). For example, Rostworowski (1978) suggests that the manipulation of institutionalized exchange relationships (and *not* military conquest) led to political integration and Inca territorial expansion. Conversely, Lumbreras (1978) emphasizes class conflict and traditional interregional hostilities between Cuzco and the Chanka. John Murra (1972), Richard Schaedel (1978), and William Isbell (1978) have each stressed the importance of economic management and redistribution systems in stimulating Inca po-

litical centralization, whereas others have suggested the Inca system of dual inheritance as the ideological impetus for territorial expansion (Conrad 1981; Demarest and Conrad 1983; Conrad and Demarest 1984; Patterson 1985). Through the investigation of broad categories of social and economic organization, these authors have shifted their interpretive focus from the actions of a single individual to more general processes of social change.

Certainly, earlier theoretical discussions of Inca origins have advanced our interpretive orientation, but they have been unable to test ethnohistorically generated hypotheses against independent archaeological data. As Geoffrey Conrad and Arthur Demarest (1984: 96) observed in the mid-1980s, "Archaeology could greatly further our understanding of the pre-imperial Inca by revealing the precise chronology of their cultural development and by serving as a means of evaluating conflicting hypotheses derived from the chronicles. The practical problem is that the archaeological data available at present are not very extensive." Fortunately, a large body of new survey and excavation data has been collected in the past two decades, and we can now evaluate Inca state formation with several independent lines of evidence.

Archaeological Surveys in the Inca Heartland

Understanding how various Cuzco ethnic groups were incorporated into the emerging Inca state is a necessary first step in the formation of a larger explanatory model for state development in the Inca heartland. Therefore, we first examine the settlement shifts that occurred in the Cuzco Valley during the Killke Period. Then, using results from additional survey projects that have been conducted to the south and north of the Cuzco Valley, and exploratory work that has been conducted to the east and west of Cuzco, we examine how various groups were incorporated into the emerging state.

Traditionally, there has been a general bias in the Cuzco region for conducting archaeological research at sites with monumental architecture. Great strides have been made in understanding large imperial Inca sites, such as Machu Picchu (Valencia Zegarra and Gibaja Oviedo 1992), Ollantaytambo (Protzen 1991), Chinchero (Alcina Franch et al. 1976), and Yucay (Niles 1999), but smaller, earlier

[Handwritten marginal notes:] Process-based interp. 1) longer time scope than ethno-historic accounts 2) political, economic, ideological explanations 3) testing hypotheses w/ archiv data

72

sites in the region—sites that played a role in early state development processes—have not been as extensively studied. Furthermore, until recently, the interpretation of excavation data has been hindered by a lack of regional settlement pattern data from intensive survey projects. Most archaeological projects in the Cuzco region have concentrated either on conducting excavations at a single site or on collecting surface pottery from a limited number of sites. With the possible exception of Kendall's (1976) work in the Cusichaca Valley, located some 60 kilometers northwest of the Cuzco Valley, no systematic survey work was conducted in the Cuzco region prior to the mid-1980s. Though excavation data are crucial for understanding site-level impacts of state formation, only regional settlement data can address the full scope of state formation processes and contextualize the occupations of individual sites.

The first large-scale systematic archaeological survey project in the Inca heartland was conducted by Brian Bauer between 1984 and 1987 in a 600 km² region directly south of the Cuzco Valley (Bauer 1992a, 1999, 2002).[2] The results of this work indicated a greater time depth to a regionally dominant Cuzco polity than suggested by some historical accounts (e.g., Rowe 1944; cf. Means 1931). Bauer expanded upon this work in 1994 in a second regional project, examining the long-term developmental processes within the Cuzco Valley proper. As noted in Chapter 1, the study of this 350 km² region was completed by Bauer and Alan Covey in 1997–2000.[3] A third survey, covering over 300 km² in the Vilcanota Valley to the north of Cuzco, was directed by Covey in 2000 (Covey 2003).[4] Combined, these three contiguous survey projects encompass a total area of over 1,200 km² and document the locations of more than 2,000 archaeological sites (Map 8.1).[5] Equally important, the three survey projects form an 80-kilometer north-south transect directly through the Inca heartland. As such, the surveys cover the center of the Inca polity in the Cuzco Valley, as well as the lands of several ethnic groups living to the north and south of its capital.

These three survey projects provide an unprecedented opportunity to examine the developmental processes of the Inca state. The survey data can be combined with the results of excavations and reconnaissance work conducted to the east and west of Cuzco to assess the chang-

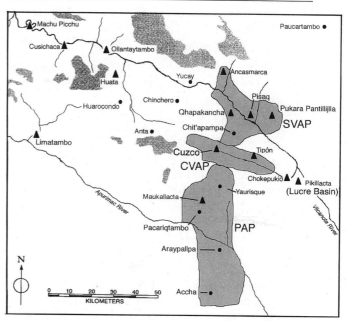

MAP 8.1. Regional settlement surveys in the Cuzco region. Three systematic regional surveys have been completed in the Inca heartland to understand the processes of state development. Research was conducted in the areas north and south of Cuzco, as well as within the Cuzco Valley itself.

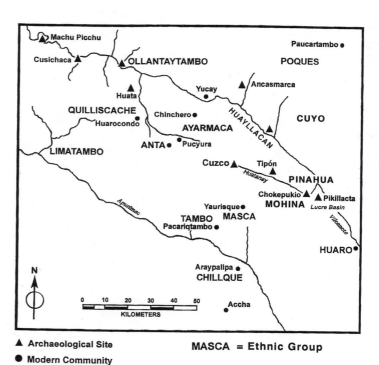

MAP 8.2. Overview of the Inca heartland

ing political interactions between the emerging Inca state and its neighbors of other ethnic identities. We find that during the period of state development, as well as for the better-understood period of imperial expansion, the Inca employed a wide range of strategies to extend their influence and consolidate their control.

Of special interest to this study are those groups identified as Inca of Privilege, to whom Inca ethnic status was extended at the onset of the imperial period (Map 8.2). Inca imperial expansion was predicated on the administrative and ethnic unification of what became the imperial heartland by means of a dramatic increase in "Inca" population in which different ethnicities participated unequally.

Through a series of case studies, we can now observe that these strategies targeted different local levels of social complexity and exploited patterns of elite interaction within the emergent heartland. Before we turn to the case studies, however, it is important to review the Killke ceramic styles of the Cuzco region, since it is through these ceramic remains that most of the Killke sites have been identified.

Ceramic Styles of the Killke Period

The most common local ceramic style produced and used by the inhabitants of the Cuzco Basin between AD 1000 and 1400 has been named Killke (Rowe 1944). Decorations on Killke vessels are generally geometric in form and composition (Photo 8.1). Among the wide variety of design motifs used in Killke pottery, the most frequent are broad red (or occasionally black) bands outlined by one to three narrow black lines. Other motifs include sets of nested triangles, often alternating in color from red to black; linked ovals with central dots, linked rectangles with solid interior ovals; large areas covered with black crosshatching; crosshatched diamonds; and pendant rows of solid or crosshatched triangles (Rowe 1944; Dwyer 1971a; Bauer and Stanish 1990; Bauer 1999, 2002).[6]

Killke pottery, as the immediate antecedent to Inca pottery, holds a unique position in the history of the Cuzco region. Changes in the production and distribution of this ceramic style through time provide archaeologists with a means to examine the development of the Inca state in the Cuzco region. Accordingly, it is worth

reviewing past research on this important ceramic style.

Among the earliest known excavations conducted in the Department of Cuzco were those of Max Uhle at the site of Q'atan, near modern Urubamba. Uhle's fieldwork at Q'atan and additional collections from other parts of the Cuzco region encountered a style of pottery quite different from those generally associated with the Inca. Since little was known of the pre-Inca cultures of the Department of Cuzco, Uhle (1912) could only suggest that this new pottery style dated to a pre-Inca but post-Tiwanaku period, and he proposed a broad AD 800 to 1400 time frame. Soon afterward, Jacinto Jijón y Caamaño and Carlos Larrea M. (1918) reproduced Uhle's findings in their work "Un cementerio incaico en Quito . . ." Later, in *Los orígenes del Cuzco,* Jijón y Caamaño (1934) again reproduced some of Uhle's material and presented additional examples of similar ceramics that he found in the Cuzco region and in museum collections. Like Uhle, Jijón y Caamaño suggested a broad pre-Inca, post-Tiwanaku time period for the production of this new ceramic style. These isolated finds by Uhle and Jijón y Caamaño would later be classified as Killke-related ceramics and dated to the immediate pre-Inca period of the Cuzco region (Rowe 1944: 61–62).

In 1941, John Rowe began to conduct archaeological reconnaissance in the Cuzco Basin, and he undertook a

PHOTO 8.1. Killke pottery

series of test excavations. One goal of this research was to identify and describe the pre-Inca ceramic sequence for the valley (Rowe 1944: 61). Test excavations conducted by Rowe in a courtyard of the Santo Domingo monastery, adjacent to the Inca "Temple of the Sun" (Coricancha), revealed an undisturbed deposit containing ceramic materials similar to those previously found by Uhle and Jijón y Caamaño (Rowe 1944: 61–62). Additional surface collections made by Rowe later that year at a number of archaeological sites found that this pottery style was not only present in the city of Cuzco but also widely distributed throughout the basin.

Rowe performed test excavations in and around the city of Cuzco during 1942 and 1943 to investigate further this ceramic style, which he had by then named Killke. The recovery of large quantities of Killke pottery at the site of Sacsayhuaman, just north of the city of Cuzco, was especially important in this research. Through the use of the Sacsayhuaman materials, Rowe developed a broad stylistic typology for what he called the Killke Series (Rowe 1944: 60–62). Although he did not find stratified Killke and Inca deposits, he inferred, on the basis of his surface collections, that Killke pottery was the antecedent to Inca pottery in the Cuzco Basin (Rowe 1944: 61).

The identification of the Killke ceramic style in the Cuzco Basin had a profound impact on the study of the Inca. Imperial Inca pottery of the Cuzco region had long been recognized (Bingham 1915; Eaton 1916; Valcárcel 1934, 1935; Pardo 1938, 1939). The discovery of a precursor to this pottery style provided a means to identify sites occupied during the period of state development. Future excavations of sites containing Killke pottery would yield information on the social and economic conditions in which state development took place.

Soon after Rowe's formal identification of the Killke style, Jorge Muelle led an expedition into the Province of Paruro. Near the hacienda of Ayusbamba, in the District of Pacariqtambo, Muelle identified three sites that contained pottery similar to the Killke materials identified by Rowe in the Cuzco Basin (Muelle 1945). Muelle's recovery of Killke materials outside the immediate confines of the Cuzco Basin suggested that the Killke-style pottery was distributed widely throughout the entire region. Despite this discovery, and the immediate academic acceptance of Killke pottery as the early Inca pottery style

in the region, an extensive study of Killke pottery was not conducted for another twenty years.

From 1966 to 1968, Edward Dwyer conducted test excavations at three sites in the Cuzco region: Minaspata in the Lucre Basin, Pukara Pantillijlla near Pisaq, and Sacsayhuaman. The purpose of Dwyer's research was to further investigate the Killke Series as earlier defined by Rowe. Of the three sites selected for excavation, Sacsayhuaman again provided the largest sample of Killke pottery, and carbon extracted from a hearth in a Killke context yielded a radiocarbon age of 770 ± 140 BP (calibrated 94.5% probability AD 990–1430).[7] Using this radiocarbon sample, Dwyer (1971a: 140) established the initial production of Killke pottery slightly earlier than Rowe, writing, "Killke culture was probably dominant in the Valley of Cuzco from around AD 1100 until the establishment of the Inca Empire." Bauer's (1992a) research in the Paruro region supports this view. A carbon sample from the site of Tejahuaci in Paruro provided a radiocarbon age of 940 ± 140 BP (calibrated 94.5% probability AD 750–1300),[8] a date similar to that obtained by Dwyer during his excavations of Killke materials at the site of Sacsayhuaman.[9]

Other Killke-Related Styles in the Cuzco Region

There were numerous centers of ceramic production in the Cuzco region between AD 1000 and 1400. Each of these centers produced its own ceramic style, but because the various ethnic groups of the Cuzco region shared close contacts, there is a great overlap between the styles. Defining distinct ceramic traditions and discovering their distribution centers has presented challenges (and will continue to) for archaeologists working in the Cuzco region. Nevertheless, great strides have been made over the past few decades, and a complex but intelligible picture is beginning to appear.

Besides the Cuzco Basin, two other Killke Period production centers, and their associated styles, have been identified. Recent research indicates that a style named Lucre was being produced in the area of the Pinahua and Mohina ethnic groups east of Cuzco (Barreda Murillo 1973; Gibaja Oviedo 1983; McEwan 1984). To the south, a more distinct style called Colcha was being produced by the Chillque in the village of Araypallpa (Bauer 1992a,

1999, 2002). Reconnaissance work suggests that ceramic production was also occurring in the areas of Chinchero-Maras and the Plain of Anta (Haquehua Huaman and Maqque Azorsa 1996). Furthermore, it seems certain that an additional center was located in the Rachi area, some 130 kilometers southeast of Cuzco in the upper Vilcanota Valley, an area that is the largest pottery production center in the Department of Cuzco today. As archaeological research intensifies, many additional production centers will be identified.

Since the Killke Period ceramic styles from these various centers share many attributes with the better-documented Killke style of the Cuzco Basin, including geometric design elements and some vessel forms, they are frequently referred to as Killke-related styles. It should also be noted that since the various ethnic groups of the Cuzco region shared close contacts, the Killke-related styles not only share stylistic similarity but many of them also have overlapping distribution patterns. It is largely by studying

the regional distribution patterns of sites that contain these ceramic styles, and by conducting programs of excavation at specific Killke Period sites, that we can begin to understand processes of Inca state formation (Covey 2003).

State Formation in the Cuzco Basin

Regional settlement changed radically after about AD 1000 with the decline of the Wari polity and the abandonment of the site of Pikillacta. A regional political vacuum spurred competition between several groups in the Cuzco region, leading to political developments in the Cuzco Basin proper. Population within the basin appears to have increased significantly at this time. A series of new settlements were established in more remote parts of the southern basin, while most of the well-established valley-bottom settlements grew substantially. During this same period the northern side of the basin was transformed dramatically (Map 8.3).

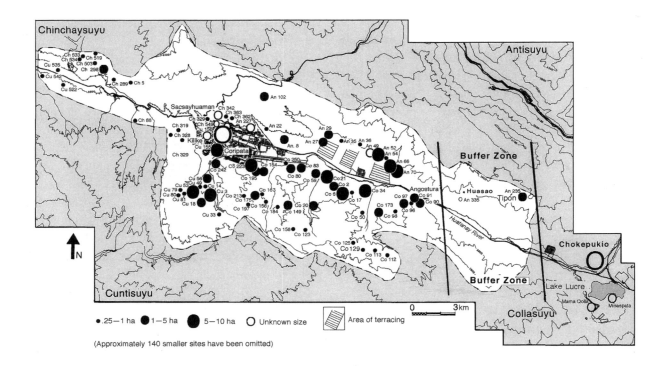

MAP 8.3. Killke Period sites in the Cuzco Valley. After AD 1000, a new system of large villages and agricultural works was developed on the northern side of the Cuzco Basin. Virtually all valley-bottom sites in the Oropesa Basin (the previously densely populated area between the Cuzco and Lucre Basins) were abandoned, creating an empty buffer zone between Inca-controlled villages in the Cuzco Basin and those under the control of the Pinahua and Mohina in the Lucre Basin.

Because streams in this area are entrenched, the northern part of the Cuzco Basin historically had few agricultural settlements. During the Killke Period, however, several large villages were constructed on the lower slopes of the north side of the basin. The agricultural potential of this area was intensified through the construction of terraces and irrigation canals. The canals emerged from ravines near the new villages, supplying water to new agricultural terraces constructed almost all the way to the Huatanay River. These terraces created thousands of hectares of improved agricultural land and rank among the largest agricultural projects to be undertaken within the Cuzco Basin. They would have supplied the developing Cuzco polity with significant agricultural surpluses while also presenting the emerging Inca elite with a means of rewarding supporters in local communities. Just as the Wari most likely used *mit'a* labor to build Pikillacta, it is likely that the Inca built these agricultural works with the use of rotational corvée labor. The ability to organize and construct large public works, and by doing so create new resources for the elite, represents an important element of the state formation process. Although Schaedel (1978: 291) associates the process of resource creation with a slightly later period in Inca history, he aptly sums up the challenges involved:

. . . change was predicated upon the widening of the Cuzco area to encompass an administrative sector that could plan and execute public works through the *mitayo* system of provincially allocated seasonal labor. This was essentially a method of centralizing "dead season" agricultural labor between sowing and harvesting from most of the provinces in Cuzco, then reallocating the manpower to the projects, either in Cuzco itself, or the circum-Cuzco area. The massive corvée work force is alleged to have numbered in the tens of thousands; and these levies were utilized among other objectives in the channeling of the Urubamba River, the building or extension of the longer irrigation systems (particularly in the highlands) and large-scale terracing projects.

Ethnohistoric sources suggest that some of these new agricultural resources (probably lands for the production of maize, a crop requiring constant water supply) were held by important lineage groups of the valley, and others may have been given to groups from outside the main valley that moved onto these lands, either to seek the protection of Cuzco or as a program of forcible resettlement following military defeat. Internal development, resettlement, and colonization were important strategies used by the Inca state not only to increase resources available for regional competition but to reduce redundancy within the developing hierarchy (Flannery 1972). The scale of such processes and their link to dynastic groups indicate political organization beyond the level of prestate societies.

It is difficult to estimate the exact size of the site of Cuzco during the Killke Period. Nevertheless, excavations carried out in the city have revealed that an extensive settlement had developed by this time. Killke pottery was first identified in the very heart of Cuzco, during excavations at the Coricancha (Rowe 1944). A number of excavations conducted in and immediately around the Coricancha by Cuzco archaeologists (Luis Barreda Murillo, Arminda Gibaja Oviedo, Alfredo Valencia Zegarra, and, most recently, Raymundo Béjar Navarro) have yielded exceptionally high-quality Killke ceramics. The recovery of similar high-status materials below the Coricancha demonstrates that the special character of the site extends back to preimperial times.

Killke pottery and building foundations have also been found in the area surrounding the Coricancha (González Corrales 1984; Béjar Navarro, personal communication, 1996), as well as in the adjacent Cusicancha compound (San Román Luna 2003). Excavations conducted in the Jesuit church beside the plaza and within the plaza itself have also yielded abundant Killke materials (Valencia Zegarra, personal communication, 1995; Fernández Carrasco, personal communication, 2000). Furthermore, substantial deposits of Killke ceramics have been found in each of the major suburbs of the city, including Lucrepata (Bustinza, personal communication, 2000), Coripata (Cumpa Palacios, personal communication, 2000), Colcapata (Valencia Zegarra, personal communication, 2000), and Killke (Rowe 1944). Large, deep deposits of Killke ceramics have also been found at Sacsayhuaman (Rowe 1944; Dwyer 1971a), demonstrating a significant occupation throughout the Killke Period and into Inca imperial times (Map 8.4). In other words, current data suggest that the Killke Period occu-

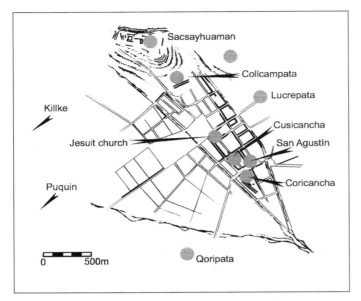

Sacsayhuaman

Collcampata

Lucrepata

Killke

Cusicancha

Jesuit church

San Agustín

Puquin

Coricancha

0   500m

Qoripata

MAP 8.4. Killke ceramics have been recovered in numerous locations in and around Cuzco. (Map from Covey 2003:261)

pation of Cuzco was quite extensive, over time approaching that of the city under the mature Inca Empire.

The Killke Period polity in the Cuzco Basin invested in infrastructure that would create new resources that could be centrally controlled by the Inca elite and used both to attract populations to Cuzco and to compete with groups outside Inca control. Resettled populations enjoyed the use of these resources only through dependent relationships with the Inca elite. They received some benefits from living near productive lands in the well-protected Cuzco Basin, but they would have been obligated to the rulers of the developing state. Internal political consolidation and resource development created settlement buffer zones in the area surrounding much of the main valley as some small groups were brought more closely into Cuzco's orbit. Not all groups were resettled in the Cuzco Valley, however. Several small groups located south of Cuzco came under Inca control early in the Killke Period without experiencing much of the reorganization seen within the main valley.

The Region South of the Cuzco Valley

Historic evidence indicates that during the Killke and Inca Periods the region immediately south of the Cuzco

Valley, now called the Province of Paruro, was inhabited by at least three separate ethnic groups: the Chillque, Masca, and Tambo (Poole 1984; Bauer 1992a). Chillque settlements were clustered around the modern communities of Araypallpa and Paruro, the Masca were concentrated around the town of Yaurisque, and the Tambo were located near the community of Pacariqtambo.[10]

Ethnohistoric research indicates that each of these ethnic groups was organized into a regional moiety system at the time of the Spanish Conquest (Gade and Escobar Moscoso 1982; Poole 1984; Urton 1990). Bauer's regional survey data demonstrate that these systems of dual organization have great antiquity and date to the Killke Period, if not earlier (Bauer 1987; 1992a: 124–139). It is important to note that these ethnic groups were never organized into large polities. During the Inca Period, the smallest group, the Tambo, comprised several hundred individuals, and the larger Masca and Chillque groups each numbered only in the low thousands.[11]

Wari Period populations in Paruro, which appear to have been largely unaffected by the intensive Wari occupation of the Lucre Basin to the northeast, lived primarily within maize-producing elevations (below about 3,500 masl) in a series of scattered hamlets and small villages. Except for the development of the imperial Inca site of Maukallacta (Bauer 1992b), the regional settlement pattern continued relatively unchanged from the Wari Period through the Inca Period. The distribution of Killke pottery (Figure 8.1) at sites in this area indicates that the developing Inca state dominated villages as far south as the Apurímac River, or up to 40 kilometers from Cuzco (Bauer 1992a). Furthermore, systematic surveys in this area recorded no evidence of large Killke Period defensive settlements. The regional settlement system consisted of small, widely scattered, unprotected settlements generally located adjacent to areas of agricultural land. The absence of any clear indication of Killke Period warfare and the continuous occupation of all major Killke Period sites into the Inca Period suggest that this region was absorbed relatively early into the developing Inca state and with little resistance (Bauer 1992a).

The Region West and Northwest of the Cuzco Valley

Several ethnic groups lived to the west and northwest of the Cuzco Valley, including the Limatambo, Quilliscachi,

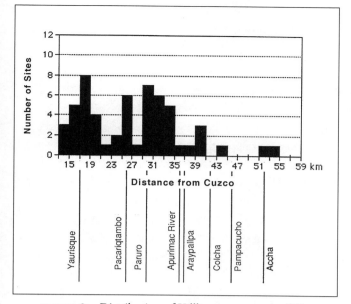

FIGURE 8.1. Distribution of Killke pottery south of Cuzco. The number of sites with Killke pottery decreases as a function of distance from Cuzco, with the presence of Killke materials identified as far as 50 km from the Inca capital.

Mayu, Equeco, Cancu, Conchacalla, Anta, and Ayarmaca.[12] Among the largest and most powerful of these were the Anta and the Ayarmaca. Killke-related pottery produced in this area has a wide distribution throughout the region, and both groups appear to have had large populations. Although there has been no systematic regional survey in this region, reconnaissance work provides some information for preliminary discussion (Rowe

1944; Rostworowski 1970; Kendall 1974, 1976, 1985; Alcina Franch et al. 1976). For example, the Anta were most likely concentrated around the modern town of Anta, which rests above a large prehispanic settlement. This site may well have been the paramount village for the Anta during the Killke Period.

THE AYARMACA ETHNIC GROUP

The Ayarmaca are better known than the Anta (Rostworowski 1970). Their territory extended from the area of Pucyura in the south (where it shared a border with the Anta) to the area of Chinchero in the north (where it shared a border with the Huayllacan). Although the region is largely unexplored archaeologically, the paramount village of the Ayarmaca most likely existed near the modern-day town of Ayarmaca, or perhaps near Chinchero.

Oral histories of the region recorded by the Spaniards tell of long-term conflicts between the Anta, the Ayarmaca, and the Inca (Sarmiento de Gamboa 1906 [1572]; Garcilaso de la Vega 1966 [1609]; Guaman Poma de Ayala 1980 [1615]). These conflicts may finally have subsided after the unification of the groups through a series of strategic elite marriages (Table 8.1).

Sarmiento de Gamboa (1906: 56 [1572: Ch. 24]) notes that Mama Runtucaya, the principal wife of Viracocha Inca (the eighth ruler), was from the Anta ethnic group, and descendants of her family still lived in the Anta area

TABLE 8.1. Inca rulers and their principal wives, according to Sarmiento de Gamboa (1906 [1572])

INCA RULER	PRINCIPAL WIFE	WIFE'S IDENTITY	COMMENTS
Manco Capac	Mama Ocllo	Sister	Culture hero, following imperial marriage pattern
Sinchi Roca	Mama Cuca	Elite woman from Sañu	Intravalley alliance
Lloque Yupanqui	Mama Cava	Elite woman from Uma	Intravalley alliance
Mayta Capac	Mama Tacucaray	Elite woman from Tacucaray	Intravalley alliance
Capac Yupanqui	Curi Hilpay	Elite Ayarmaca woman	Regional alliance
Inca Roca	Mama Micay	Elite woman from Huayllacan	Regional alliance that sparks war with Ayarmaca, leads to alliance with Anta
Yahuar Huacac	Mama Chicya	Elite Ayarmaca woman	Regional alliance
Viracocha Inca	Mama Runtucaya	Elite woman from Anta	Regional alliance
Pachacuti Inca Yupanqui	Mama Anahuarqui	Sister	Establishment of imperial marriage pattern
Topa Inca Yupanqui	Mama Chimpa Ocllo	Sister	
Huayna Capac	Cusi Rimay	Sister	

in colonial times (Toledo 1940: 112–118 [1571]). Similarly, the legitimate wife of Yahuar Huacac (the seventh ruler), Mama Chicya, was the daughter of an Ayarmaca lord, and the wife of Capac Yupanqui (the fifth ruler), Curi Hilpay, may have been an Ayarmaca elite as well (Sarmiento de Gamboa 1906: 48, 54 [1572: Chs. 18, 22]).[13] The marriage of Yahuar Huacac to Mama Chicya is of special interest, since it appears to have involved an exchange of daughters between rival lords. Sarmiento de Gamboa (1906: 54 [1572: Ch. 22]) writes:

> Before Inca Roca died, he made friends with Tocay Capac [Lord of the Ayarmaca], by way of Mama Chicya, daughter of Tocay Capac, who married Yahuar Huacac, and Inca Roca gave a daughter of his, named Curi Ocllo, in marriage to Tocay Capac.[14] (Translation by author)

It was hoped that through such exchanges, regional alliances would be established that would last for generations. This, however, did not always prove to be the case.

THE LIMATAMBO REGION

It is clear that other ethnic groups in this region interacted differently with the emerging Inca state. For example, Kenneth Heffernan (1989) conducted reconnaissance work beyond Anta in the Limatambo area, approximately 50 kilometers west of Cuzco. His field conclusions on the Killke Period settlement patterns in this region are similar to Bauer's for the area south of Cuzco. Heffernan finds that most Killke Period occupations are located near large cultivable areas and that few (if any) of these sites contain clear evidence of fortification. Though there may have been a small shift in population from higher to lower altitudes between the Killke and Inca Periods in the Limatambo region, the overall settlement pattern of the two periods is similar. Comparing his field observations with the information presented in the Spanish chronicles, Heffernan (1989: 413) writes, "The mythico-historic characterization of pre-Inca populations as constantly warring, in light of field evidence, is imbalanced and fails to appreciate stable elements in the socio-economic landscape of Limatambo."

PHOTO 8.2. The Killke Period fortress of Huata, to the northwest of Cuzco

THE QUILLISCACHI ETHNIC GROUP

Research in the region farther northwest of Cuzco, beyond the areas controlled by the Ayarmaca, reveals yet a different scenario. In the area of the Quilliscachi, who lived near the modern town of Huarocondo, we do find fortified Killke Period sites (Map 8.2). The largest of these is Huata, located approximately 40 aerial kilometers northwest of Cuzco on a remote mountain summit, and surrounded by three concentric fortification walls (Photo 8.2).[15] Reconnaissance work conducted by Kendall (1974, 1976, 1985) in the Cusichaca River Valley between Ollantaytambo and Machu Picchu identified other Killke Period sites on extremely steep ridge tops. The presence of ridge-top sites in the Cusichaca region, as well as the fortified site of Huata, indicates that this area was not politically unified during the Killke Period.

The Region North of the Cuzco Valley

Important ethnic groups residing in the region north of Cuzco included the Huayllacan, the Cuyo, the Tambo, the Yucay, and several other unnamed groups, such as those at Ancasmarca and in the Chit'apampa Basin. Until recently, what little we knew about these groups was based largely on the oral histories recorded by Sarmiento de Gamboa. Recent archaeological research by Covey (2003) has provided additional evidence for those of the Chit'apampa Basin as well as the Huayllacan and Cuyo, for whom the chronicle references can now be compared with archaeological data (Map 8.2).

THE CHIT'APAMPA BASIN

The small Chit'apampa Basin connects the Cuzco Basin and the lower Vilcanota Valley (the latter is also called the Sacred Valley and the Urubamba Valley). Wari Period settlement patterns and ceramics indicate that the Chit'apampa Basin had a political and cultural affiliation with the Cuzco Basin (Covey 2003). Small hamlets were dispersed around village sites located near good valley bottom lands with abundant water. Settlement in the basin was restricted to areas closest to the Cuzco Basin. Most Wari Period sites in the Chit'apampa Basin are small, but two discrete clusters of settlements were en-

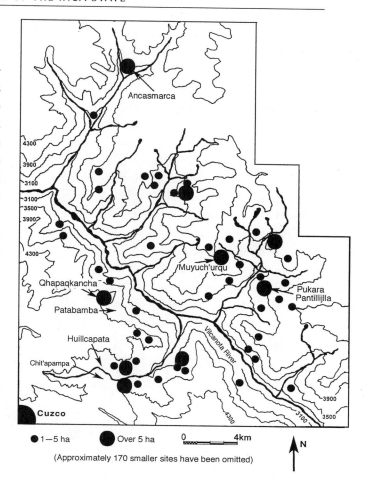

MAP 8.5. Killke Period sites in the lower Vilcanota Valley. Ethnic groups to the south of the river appear to have shared close cultural ties with Cuzco and were incorporated into the developing Inca state earlier than those of thenorth side. The Inca established control over the valleys north of the river throughout this period.

countered near the modern communities of Huillcapata and Patabamba. Occupations in these areas displayed a two-tier settlement hierarchy that included hamlets and dispersed households. In other parts of the Sacred Valley survey region, there is no settlement hierarchy during this period, and the distribution of Wari Period pottery from the Cuzco Basin drops off dramatically at distances greater than 15–20 kilometers from Cuzco.

During the Killke Period, major settlement pattern changes occurred in the Chit'apampa Basin (Map 8.5). In the upper part of the basin (closest to Cuzco), a buffer zone formed as the Wari Period sites of the basin were abandoned. Populations either moved into the Cuzco

Basin or moved farther down into the Chit'apampa Basin into a mosaic environment (near maize, tuber, and pasture lands) that had defensible locations for nucleated settlement. The chronicles mention repeated Inca incursions against their neighbors to the north, and many sites are found in areas with natural (cliffs) and artificial defenses (walls or ditches).

As Cuzco gained direct control over the lower Chit'apampa Basin, parts of the buffer zone were populated with Cuzco allies or newly subjugated local groups, and some sites with almost exclusively Killke pottery were established (Covey 2003). Permanent Inca control of the Chit'apampa Basin involved the development of state infrastructure, including canal and terrace systems, roads, administrative centers, and storage facilities. Under the Inca state, settlement became more dispersed and focused on the valley bottom, particularly in lower elevations where irrigated maize agriculture was possible.

THE HUAYLLACAN ETHNIC GROUP

Although the ethnic identity of the inhabitants of the Chit'apampa Basin is unknown, in some cases the ethnohistory provides specific details on ethnic groups to the north of Cuzco. Chronicles locate one group, the Huayllacan, in the communities of Patahuaillacan (identified as modern Patabamba), Micocancha, Paullu, and Paullupampa (Sarmiento de Gamboa 1906: 51 [1572: Ch. 21]), all of which are located on the southern rim of the lower Vilcanota Valley, approximately 15 kilometers from Cuzco (see also Las Casas 1958 [ca. 1550]; Zuidema 1986). According to Sarmiento de Gamboa (1906: 49 [1572: Ch. 19]), Inca Roca married Mama Micay of Patahuaillacan, who was the daughter of the leader of the Huayllacan, Soma Inca, and may have been a political leader in her own right (also see Murúa 1946: 93 [1590: Bk. 1, Ch. 21]; Cabello de Valboa 1951: 293 [1586: Bk. 3, Ch. 13]; Las Casas 1958 [ca. 1550]; Cobo 1979: 124 [1653: Bk. 12, Ch. 9]; and cf. Gutiérrez de Santa Clara 1963: 81 [ca. 1600: Ch. 49]). Later, their son, Yahuar Huacac, is said to have destroyed this group after they betrayed him during a struggle over dynastic rule in Cuzco. We are told that Yahuar Huacac then took some Huayllacan lands as a personal estate, and that much later his mummy was found by Polo de Ondegardo in Paullu (Sarmiento de

Gamboa 1906: 56 [1572: Ch. 23]; Acosta 1986: 421 [1590: Book 6, Ch. 20]).

The archaeology of the Huayllacan area provides some interesting perspectives on this account. Around AD 1000, local populations moved from the Patabamba area to a large nucleated ridge-top site called Qhapaqkancha (Royal Enclosure). Located more than 4,000 masl, the site comprises over 4 hectares of densely packed semicircular stone structures, many of which have been badly damaged.[16] In addition to this small center, there are about twenty other Killke Period sites nearby, ranging from isolated households to small villages, all situated on the slopes below Qhapaqkancha.

The archaeological survey data suggest that Qhapaqkancha was already the center of a small polity during the early Killke Period. It was located in a defensible area with good views of the main valley, and several subordinate villages were situated below it, 100–200 m above the main valley floor. Additional archaeological data indicate, however, that this center came under the control of Cuzco toward the end of the Killke Period. A large rectangular platform with three early Inca buildings is located just outside the area of nucleated settlement at Qhapaqkancha. This was probably constructed as a royal estate or a small administrative complex.

In sum, the archaeological and ethnohistoric data both suggest how the small Huayllacan polity came under Inca control. Political alliances may have been established initially through marriage exchange, and then transformed through military action, well before the period of Inca imperial expansion. It appears that direct control was established in the area over several generations, and ultimately Huayllacan resources came under the direct administration of Cuzco elites as long-standing kin ties were superseded by state administrative structures. That the Huayllacan were not made Inca of Privilege during the imperial period may be due to their repeated attempts to throw off Inca control. This certainly appears to be the case with their neighbors the Cuyo.

THE CUYO ETHNIC GROUP

The Cuyo ethnic group occupied the Chongo Basin (also referred to as the Cuyo Basin), located in the side valley above the Inca site of Pisaq. Like those related to the

Huayllacan, Pinahua, and Mohina (see below), the oral histories of the Cuyo recorded by Spaniards describe two or more Inca conquests of the region. Several authors suggest that the first Inca territorial expansion from the Cuzco Valley, conducted during the reign of the fifth Inca, Capac Yupanqui, involved the military conquest of the Cuyo (Sarmiento de Gamboa 1906: 48 [1572: Ch. 18]; Cabello de Valboa 1951: 290 [1586: Book 3, Ch. 13]; Santa Cruz Pachacuti Yamqui Salcamayhua 1993: 209 [f. 14]). According to Cobo (1979: 122 [1653: Bk. 12, Ch. 8]), Capac Yupanqui placed Tarco Huaman, a brother and political rival, as governor over the new province. This conquest is linked in the various sources to long-distance exchange (the Inca invaded after the Cuyo ruler refused to send exotic birds from the jungle lowlands to Cuzco) and to religion (the Inca visited the principal shrine of the Cuyo and asserted the superiority of the Inca solar cult over the local deity).

Aside from a possible reconquest of the region by Yahuar Huacac (Sarmiento de Gamboa 1906: 54–55 [1572: Ch. 23]), no mention is made of the Cuyo until the reign of Pachacuti Inca Yupanqui (the ninth ruler). Several authors (Santa Cruz Pachacuti Yamqui Salcamayhua 1993: 226 [f. 22v]; Sarmiento de Gamboa 1906: 71–72 [1572: Ch. 34]) relate that after defeating the Chanka, Pachacuti Inca Yupanqui held a festival at which an attempt on his life was made. The Cuyo were blamed, although Cabello de Valboa (1951: 300 [1586: Bk. 3, Ch. 14]) claims that they were falsely accused. In any case, the Inca reaction was to campaign throughout the region, destroying the Cuyo center and killing many of its inhabitants. Although some authors state that the Cuyo were completely killed off, remnants of this group are mentioned in colonial land documents (Toledo 1940 [1571]; Espinoza Soriano 1977;) and were possibly resettled in the Vilcanota Valley proper or sent to grow coca in the lowlands of Paucartambo.

The archaeological remains from this area seem to substantiate some of the chronicle accounts (Covey 2003). Survey data indicate major population growth during the Killke Period, when the Cuyo Basin was dominated by several large nucleated villages, most of them located on ridge tops at high elevation (above 4,000 masl). Prior to the Inca conquest of the area, the largest of these was the site of Muyuch'urqu, a 6-hectare village protected by cliffs and defensive walls. Muyuch'urqu was the center of a chiefdom and was surrounded by five or six smaller villages. It was positioned to control caravan traffic between the Vilcanota Valley and the Paucartambo lowlands, and it would have commanded a mosaic economy that included agricultural production and herding. Survey work around Muyuch'urqu recorded a ceramic style and mortuary tradition of funerary towers not found in areas to its south, and thus it appears to have been culturally distinct from groups living in the Cuzco Basin. The tradition of mortuary tower construction is absent in the Cuzco Basin, but it has been observed for areas to the north of the Vilcanota River, including Ollantaytambo, Paucartambo, and Ocongate (Franco Inojosa 1937; Isbell 1997: 174–181).

A major settlement shift in the Cuyo Basin during the latter part of the Killke Period indicates that Cuzco was developing indirect control over what had been an independent group. The defensive location of their sites and distinctive pottery and mortuary styles suggest that for much of the Killke Period, the people of the Cuyo Basin did not maintain peaceful contact with the developing Inca state. The largest Killke Period settlement in Cuyo territory is Pukara Pantillijlla, a site located at about 3,950 masl on a ridge across the basin from Muyuch'urqu. At more than 10 hectares, this site is substantially larger than Muyuch'urqu, and it appears to have administered a greater area as well. Pukara Pantillijlla has a mix of semi-circular and rectangular stone structures (Dwyer 1971a; Kendall 1976; Covey 2003). As at Qhapaqkancha, the slopes around the site are heavily terraced and were used for additional settlement and agriculture. Local Killke Period wares and a substantial amount of Killke pottery dominate the dense ceramic scatters that cover the surface of the site. Covey's excavations at Pukara Pantillijlla in 2000 demonstrate that the occupation area expanded between AD 1250 and 1350, when many of the rectangular buildings were constructed (cf. Dwyer 1971a). Inca imperial pottery constitutes a small component of the excavated assemblage at Pukara Pantillijlla, and the abandonment of many of the site's residential structures between AD 1300 and 1500 indicates that the main occupation of the site ended before the florescence of the Inca Period. The archaeological data do not indicate the destruction and complete abandonment of the site around 1450, as described in the chronicles, but rather a steady decline over several generations.

Once the Cuyo Basin was well integrated into the Inca heartland, settlement shifted to the bottom of the Vilcanota Valley (900 meters lower), where it was administered from Pisaq, a site that was the private estate of Pachacuti Inca Yupanqui (Toledo 1940 [1571]; Rostworowski 1970). The construction of Pisaq was associated with massive public works projects to canalize the Vilcanota River and extend irrigated agriculture onto new terrace groups on the lower valley slopes. New Inca state lands were surrounded by small Inca Period villages that were located at elevations where local groups—as well as provincial laborers brought to the valley by the Inca—could work state fields while also having access to other available agricultural lands. In sum, the Cuyo were independent from Cuzco during the early part of the Killke Period. Settlement was then reorganized around Pukara Pantillijlla when the Inca state established control over the region. Before Inca imperial expansion, the occupations in the upper Cuyo Basin were largely abandoned and there was a major settlement shift to the valley bottom, favoring lands associated with intensive maize production. This shift may represent an energetic reaction to state labor tribute demands rather than a systematic program of regional resettlement by the state, and it appears that chronicle descriptions of the destruction of the Cuyo ethnic group are somewhat exaggerated.

The Region East and Southeast of the Cuzco Valley

It is well documented that the Lucre Basin, which lies to the southeast of the Cuzco Basin, contained two separate, but apparently closely related, ethnic groups called the Pinahua (or Pinagua) and the Mohina (or Muyna). Oral histories recorded by the Spaniards suggest that these groups were important rivals when the Inca consolidated their control in the region. Sarmiento de Gamboa (1906: 49, 55, 56 [1572: Chs. 19, 23, 24]) notes that a series of early Inca kings, including Inca Roca, Yahuar Huacac, Viracocha Inca, and Pachacuti Inca Yupanqui, had each staged military incursions against the principal Pinahua and Mohina settlements. For example, Sarmiento de Gamboa (1906: 57–58 [1572: Ch. 25]) writes:

And then he [Viracocha Inca] went against the people of Mohina and Pinahua, Casacancha and Rondocancha, five small leagues from Cuzco. They had already made themselves free, even though Yahuar Huacac had defeated them. And they [the Inca captains] attacked and killed most of the natives and their *cinches* [leaders], who at that time were named Muyna Pongo and Guaman Topa. They suffered this war and cruelties because they said they were free and would not serve or be his subjects.[17] (Translation by authors)

Unlike the major ethnic groups north (Huayllacan) and west (Anta and Ayarmaca) of Cuzco, with whom the Inca practiced some form of elite marriage exchange early in the period of state development, it appears that the Inca became locked in prolonged confrontation with the Mohina and Pinahua, which lasted for much of the Killke Period.

With Inca imperial development under Huascar, many of the Pinahua were removed from their traditional lands and resettled in the lowlands of Paucartambo. Huascar, who was born in a town on the shore of Lake Lucre (Betanzos 1996: 176 [1557: Bk. 1, Ch. 45]), then built a private estate in the basin. Soon after the Spanish Conquest, the Pinahua began petitioning to have their lost lands returned to them (Espinoza Soriano 1974). These early Colonial Period legal proceeding provide important information on the landholding of the Pinahua during prehispanic times.

The Pinahua ethnic group was so decimated by the Inca that today they are not locally well remembered.[18] Nevertheless, documents from the early Colonial Period Pinahua court cases describe their territory in some detail. Before their removal by Huascar, the Pinahua controlled the area on the northern side of the Huatanay River east of the Angostura to its confluence with the Vilcanota River. There is no doubt that the Pinahua once occupied the large site of Chokepukio, since it is specifically and repeatedly mentioned as one of their former towns in the earlier documents of the suit. The site was probably the principal town of the Pinahua, referred to as "Pinagua-Chuquimatero" in the later documents. For example, in 1571 Pedro Lampa, a witness presented by the Pinahua, states: "There was in past times on one side of the narrow drainage of Lake Muyna in some old buildings, a town that was called Pinagua-Chuquimatero" (Espinoza Soriano 1974: 205).[19]

The area and principal city of the Mohina ethnic group is more difficult to define, since no large collection of documents has yet been found to help reconstruct their holdings. The situation is made more complex by the fact that the Spaniards and later travelers refer to the site of Pikillacta as the ruins of Mohina (e.g., Squier 1877: 419–422; Cieza de León 1976: 261 [1553: Pt. 1, Ch. 97]). The Mohina most likely controlled the area to the south of the lake, opposite the Pinahua-controlled region. It is known that the lands of Mohina were awarded to Paullu Topa Inca Yupanqui by Pizarro in 1537, and that his son Carlos Inca continued to hold the land on the basis of his descent from Huayna Capac (Vázquez de Espinosa 1948: 551 [1629: Bk. 4, Ch. 92]; Cook 1975: 131). By the

seventeenth century, some of the Mohina had been removed to the town of Oropesa, located between the Cuzco and Lucre Basins, close to the fortified Killke Period site of Tipón (Stavig 1999: 92).

Exploratory work in the Lucre Basin indicates that Chokepukio is its largest Killke Period settlement, suggesting that the Pinahua quickly filled the power vacuum created by the Wari withdrawal from the region (Photo 8.3). Chokepukio certainly was an impressive site during the Killke Period, with considerable monumental architecture. Dated samples of organic materials (vines) used during the construction of these walls (McEwan 1987: 227; Kendall 1985: 347) suggest that their construction may have begun near the time of the Wari collapse and continued throughout the Killke Period. Although Chokepukio remains one of the best-preserved Killke Period sites in the Cuzco region, it was not unique. Site sizes reported for the nearby sites of Minaspata (Dwyer 1971a: 41) and Coto-

PHOTO 8.3. During the Killke Period, the site of Chokepukio was an impressive settlement with considerable monumental architecture.

PHOTO 8.4. The site of Tipón is surrounded by a large defensive wall.

cotuyoc (Glowacki 2002: 271) are comparable to that of Chokepukio. During the Killke Period, the city of Cuzco was at least as large, and the chronicles describe other nucleated sites in the Anta and Chinchero regions.

The regional settlement data from the eastern end of the Cuzco Valley illustrate the interactions between the Inca and ethnic groups of the Lucre Basin. As early as the Formative Period (ca. 1000 BC), the stretch of valley between the Cuzco Basin and the Lucre Basin, called the Oropesa Basin, contained numerous dispersed settlements located on alluvial terraces and low slopes bordering the rich maize-producing valley bottom. During the Qotakalli Period and the Wari Period, there was an especially large clustering of hamlets and villages around the Huasao area. With the decline of Wari influence in the neighboring Lucre Basin, a major disruption in the settlement pattern of this area occurred. Most strikingly, all valley-bottom settlements were abandoned in the early Killke Period, and a single nucleated settlement, Tipón, was established on a broad ridge 300 to 400 m above the valley floor (Map 8.3). This Killke Period settlement, along with its agricultural lands and water sources, was surrounded by an enormous defensive wall constructed of rough field stones and mud mortar, approximately 5 m

in height (Photo 8.4). In other sections, areas of sheer cliffs blocked access to the site. These defensive features of the site run for more than 6 linear kilometers. The site of Tipón is even more remarkable when one considers that, with the exception of the Inca imperial fortress at Sacsayhuaman, this is the only fortified settlement in the Cuzco Valley.[20]

The complete depopulation of the alluvial terraces and valley floor area between the Cuzco Basin and the Lucre Basin represents the establishment of a well-defined buffer zone between rival polities (Anderson 1994: 39–41; Marcus and Flannery 1996: 124–125). The fact that the only Killke Period settlement in this valley area is within a large, nucleated fortification further supports the argument that the two regions were important rivals (Photo 8.5). From this evidence, it is clear that the ethnic groups of the Lucre Basin were sufficiently large and well organized to resist Inca attempts to expand from the Cuzco Valley to the east until most of the region was already under the sway of their state.

The Tipón area as well as the Lucre Basin did eventually fall under Cuzco domination. According to statements from indigenous informants, recorded in a 1571–1590 land dispute over fields within Tipón, this fortified site fell to

Viracocha Inca (La Lone 1985), who then transformed it into a royal estate (Photo 8.6; Garcilaso de la Vega 1966: 286 [1609: Pt. 1, Bk. 5, Ch. 20]). Our survey data indicate that numerous new Inca sites were established on the low alluvial terraces and valley floor within the buffer zone once it was incorporated under Cuzco control. The nearby Huasao area was resettled with *mitmaes* (colonists) who were given their own land, along with the task of caring for the lands in Tipón assigned to the cults of Viracocha Inca and that of the Sun (La Lone 1985). Other tracts in the region were given to members of important Cuzco-based lineage groups. For example, various documents in the Cuzco archive indicate that several residents of Chocco, as the descendants of Mama Anahuarque, the principal wife of Pachacuti Inca Yupanqui, were awarded land across the valley from Huasao (Rostworowski 1966: 34).

Inca State Formation and Imperial Administrative Strategies

The cases discussed above illuminate how the Inca used diverse strategies to consolidate regional power over allies and rivals of varying ethnicity and organizational complexity. The ethnohistory and archaeology of some areas outside the current Cuzco survey regions suggest that early Inca conquests were often ad hoc affairs, and that the patchwork nature of the linguistic, ethnic, and political landscape favored a pattern of leapfrogging when making conquests (see Mannheim 1991: 31–60 for a description of linguistic diversity). For example, Ollantaytambo (to the northwest) and Huaro (to the southeast) were both separated from Cuzco by regional rivals (the Ayarmaca and the Pinahua, respectively [Rostworowski 1970; Espinoza

PHOTO 8.5. The valley floor area between the Cuzco and Lucre Basins, which had been densely occupied for millennia, was suddenly abandoned during the Killke Period as the region became a buffer zone between the Inca and the ethnic groups of the Lucre Basin.

PHOTO 8.6. Inca terracing at the site of Tipón. The site was developed as an estate by
Viracocha Inca after the conquest of the Pinahua and Mohina polities of the Lucre Basin.

Soriano 1974]), yet they are mentioned as being early allies of the Inca (Cabello de Valboa 1951: 283 [1586: Bk. 3, Ch. 12]; Cobo 1979: 115 [1653: Bk. 12, Ch. 6]; Guaman Poma de Ayala 1980: 71 [1615: f. 89]). The developing Inca polity is likely to have had direct control over, or close alliances with, some groups outside the Cuzco Valley even before it was completely consolidated, a condition documented in other cases of early state formation (Algaze 1992; Marcus 1992; Sidky 1995; Spencer and Redmond 2001). The transition from state to empire is more subtle than suggested in the documents, as alliances and hegemonic control were extended beyond the heartland region prior to the full implementation of direct control. The Inca continued their processes of consolidation throughout the imperial period, developing new estate lands and maintaining the autonomy of remaining local ethnic groups.

The full integration of the Inca heartland was an uneven and unstable process, one whose tempo and duration were influenced by the personalities of elite leadership and the military might that could be mustered. The achievements of one leader's rule did not necessarily continue into a successor's reign, and early territorial conquests were frequently challenged when new Inca rulers came to power. Even intergroup elite marriages whose overall goal was to stabilize cross-generational alliances often broke down, particularly during interregna, a problem that was also common at the provincial level during the imperial period. The numerous rebellions, reconquests, and negotiations that took place between various groups of the region after the death of an Inca leader underscore the importance that individuals played in extending Inca control throughout the heartland (Covey 2003). In certain cases, powerful allies are even said to have played important roles in the promotion of specific Cuzco leaders. Both the Ayarmaca and the Huayllacan are said to have blatantly attempted to manipulate dynamic succession in Cuzco, even to the point of assassinating unwanted contenders to the throne.

Tracing the intermarriages of the elite Inca with women from rival ethnic groups reveals the gradual expansion of Cuzco-based regional alliances over time. Although the earlier Inca rulers are said to have married the daughters of community leaders from within the Cuzco Basin, and the last Inca emperors considered their full sisters as principal wives, several generations of interethnic regional marriage alliances occurred between Cuzco and other powerful groups of the heartland during the period of state formation (Table 8.1). The Inca modified this practice as their empire spread across the Andes, with the Inca ruler and his kin taking only secondary wives (no longer principal wives) from the noble houses of vanquished ethnic groups. This strategy continued well into the Colonial Period, with high-ranking Cuzco elites offering their women to the Spaniards in hopes of building alliances with the newly established power in the Andes.

Internal development accompanied by alliance building, intimidation, and isolation of rivals can be seen as part of the Inca imperial strategy as well. Imperial Inca expansion was based on the opportunistic manipulation of local ethnic and political relationships, and in many cases involved several generations of conquest and reintegration and the establishment of more direct administration of local populations (e.g., the Colla and Lupaqa in the Titicaca Basin [Stanish 1998, 2000, 2003]). Population resettlement (Murra 1985) and the development of natural resources in ways that undercut local identity (Wachtel 1982) are also imperial strategies whose practice is seen in the Killke Period development of the early Inca state. Using the Killke Period settlement patterns and historical sources, we can now discern greater time depth to the development and practice of Inca expansion and administration.

Summary and Discussion

In order to understand incipient state growth in the Cuzco region, we have examined the available documents as well as the archaeological record of the entire region for evidence of the gradual centralization of political, economic, and military control in the hands of a few and the elaboration of social stratification, rather than simply relying on the heroic actions of a single leader as an explanation of state development. Within this perspective, the rise to power of specific kings, such as Pachacuti Inca Yupanqui, and regional conflicts, such as the Chanka War or the hostilities between the Inca of the Cuzco Basin and the ethnic groups of the Lucre Basin, are not viewed as the *causes* of state development, but rather as factors influencing the tempo of processes of state formation that were occurring throughout the entire Cuzco region.

Many of the strategies the Inca used to incorporate and administer new territories and ethnic groups were developed between AD 1000 and 1400, when a state formed in the Cuzco Basin and extended direct territorial control over surrounding regions (Figure 8.2). Within the Cuzco Basin, population numbers and density increased dramatically, and the productive landscape was transformed in a way that created stable state incomes while undercutting local and individual autonomy. The city of Cuzco developed into an urbanized center with a series of large satellite villages surrounding it. During this period, powerful rivals included the Pinahua and Mohina of the Lucre Basin, the Ayarmaca of the Chinchero area, plus many other groups of varying sizes scattered across the Cuzco region. The Paruro area, which was sparsely populated, saw little direct manipulation of local settlement by the Inca, while the Cuyo Basin was reorganized under Inca control during the Killke Period through the site of Pukara Pantillijlla, and then later through the site of Pisaq. The unification, or in a few cases the successful elimination, of these groups over the course of several centuries resulted in the creation of an Inca heartland capable of sustaining rapid Inca imperial expansion.

Early colonial documents provide differing, and frequently contradictory, accounts of how and when various groups within the Cuzco region were incorporated into the emerging Inca state. Nevertheless, the chroniclers all stress that a variety of strategies were undertaken and that numerous social institutions were created during the process. For example, although the ethnic groups to the north and west of Cuzco—including the Anta (west), the Ayarmaca (northwest), and the Huayllacan (north)—appear to have been traditional rivals of the Inca, and frequent conflicts arose between them, these groups were eventually allied through marriage exchanges.

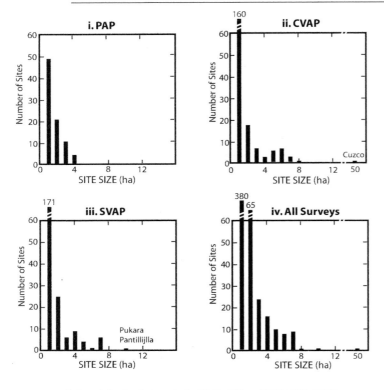

i. Pacariqtambo Archaeological Project (Bauer 1990, 1992, 1999)
ii. Cuzco Valley Archaeological Project (Bauer and Covey 2002)
iii. Sacred Valley Archaeological Project (Covey 2003)
iv. Composite of all surveyed regions

FIGURE 8.2. Settlement hierarchies of the Cuzco region during the Killke Period (AD 1000–1400). The Paruro region (PAP) displays a low population lacking a clear site hierarchy or evidence of a developed administrative center. The Cuzco Valley (CVAP) was dominated by Cuzco and had a dense population with large and small villages, but no secondary administrative center. The Vilcanota Valley (SVAP) has small and large villages, as well as the Inca secondary center at Pukara Pantillijlla.

It is said that the last three Inca kings who ruled before imperial expansion spread beyond the Cuzco region married women from these groups (Sarmiento de Gamboa 1906 [1572]). This includes Inca Roca's marriage to Mama Micay of the Huayllacan, Yahuar Huacac's marriage to Mama Chicya of the Ayarmaca, and Viracocha Inca's marriage to Mama Runtucaya of the Anta.[21] In the case of the Huayllacan, repeated treachery as they attempted to maintain local autonomy ultimately led to their destruction by the Inca, whereas the Ayarmaca and the Anta may have been incorporated more peacefully on the basis of elite kin ties and external threats.

To the southeast of Cuzco, alliance formation failed or was never even attempted, possibly because of ethnic or linguistic differences. The Pinahua remained in a nearly constant struggle with Cuzco until they were defeated militarily and a large proportion of their inhabitants were sent to colonize remote lowland areas. In the less populated regions to the south, where groups had long-standing contact with Cuzco, cultural affiliation with the Inca led to early political incorporation, without evidence of violent conflicts. It is clear that differences in ethnicity and local political complexity had a major influence on the development of the Inca heartland. The end result of these conflicts, marriages, and alliances was the formation of a complex social and political hierarchy across the Cuzco region that reduced ethnic diversity and political competition to create an Inca heartland capable of becoming the largest native empire of the Americas.

Was state consolidation done only through political & economic restructuring? What other social & ideological strategies did the Inca employ? (E.g., huaca capture, taking young elites hostages & re-educating them, other known imperial strategies.)

CHAPTER 9

The Cuzco Valley during Imperial Inca Rule

DURING THE LATE 1300s or early 1400s, the Inca state began to expand beyond the Cuzco region. Over the course of the next several generations, the Inca formed the largest empire of the Americas. During the time of late state development and imperial expansion—here called the Inca Period (ca. AD 1400–1532)—the Cuzco Basin was qualitatively transformed from the power center of a small, emergent state in the south-central Andes to the capital of an empire whose rulers controlled the vast and varied region between Ecuador and Chile. This chapter provides a brief introduction to some of the many Inca sites in the Cuzco Valley. The following chapter will discuss many of the great buildings that existed in the city itself.

Identifying Inca Sites

Inca sites in the Cuzco region are identified through distinct ceramic and architectural styles. The best-known ceramic style from the Cuzco region is Classic Inca (also called Inca, Late Inca, and Cuzco Inca). Although this style is poorly dated, it is generally believed that its production began around AD 1400 and that Classic Inca ceramics continued to be produced until shortly after the Spanish Conquest (AD 1532). Rowe (1946: 246) suggests that the production of Classic Inca ceramics took place within the Cuzco Basin. The most likely loci for imperial ceramic production are the adjacent areas of Larapa and Sañu,[1] between the modern communities of San Sebastián and San Jerónimo. Archival sources indicate that settlements of *olleros* (potters) lived in this area dur-

ing early colonial times (Archivo Agrario: Miscelánea: Hacienda Larapa 1596), and it continues to be exploited for its clay resources today.

Many of the world's major museums obtained substantial collections of Classic Inca ceramics during the nineteenth century (Seler 1893; Valencia Zegarra 1979; Bauer and Stanish 1990). The systematic reporting and analysis of this ceramic style began, however, with the earliest archaeological expeditions into the south-central highlands of Peru in the early twentieth century. Perhaps the most famous collection was made during Hiram Bingham's work at the site of Machu Picchu. Utilizing materials recovered from numerous cave burials surrounding Machu Picchu, and to a lesser extent finds recovered during his excavations, Bingham (1915) developed a vessel typology that is still widely used today. The physician on Bingham's expedition, George Eaton (1916: Plates V–XIV), also provided a large number of illustrations of ceramic vessels found at or near Machu Picchu. There are also several other early reports on Classic Inca ceramics found in the Cuzco region. For example, Luis E. Valcárcel (1934–1935) provides a discussion of the Classic Inca ceramics recovered at Sacsayhuaman, and Luis A. Pardo (1938, 1939, 1957) outlines various museum pieces. In addition, Rowe's landmark work on the archaeology of Cuzco provides a detailed discussion of Classic Inca ceramics, including classifications of different substyles (1944: 47–49).

The post–World War II era has witnessed an increasing number of references to Classic Inca ceramics by researchers working in the Cuzco region. This is not sur-

[handwritten margin note: Typologies of Inca ceramics]

prising, since Classic Inca ceramics are present at most sites in the region. Recent reports that offer significant descriptions and illustrations of Classic Inca ceramics include Ann Kendall's (1976) studies in the Urubamba River Valley. Her work (Kendall 1974; 1985: 347) also provides one of the few radiocarbon dates published for Classic Inca ceramics from Cuzco. Excavations by Kendall at the site of Ancasmarca yielded Inca ceramics within a context dating to 482 ± 91 BP (calibrated 95.4% probability AD 1290–1640).[2] Sara Lunt's (1984, 1987, 1988) study of Inca and Killke ceramics from this same region offers the first detailed examination of late-prehistoric ceramic wares from the Cuzco region. Dean Arnold's 1972–1973 excavations at the site of Qata Casallacta (Liu et al. 1986: 108), on a mountain shelf near the city of Cuzco, yielded examples of Classic Inca storage vessels (Arnold, personal communication, 2001) as well as a radiocarbon date of 370 ± 80 BP (calibrated 95.4% probability AD 1410–1670).[3] A report by José Alcina Franch and colleagues on excavations at Chinchero, a large Inca site north of Cuzco, contains many illustrations of Classic Inca ceramics (Alcina Franch et al. 1976). Heffernan (1989) furnishes numerous examples of this style found in the Limatambo area, located west of Cuzco. Unfortunately, a carbon sample recovered with Classic Inca ceramics near Limatambo provided a radiocarbon date falling within the late Colonial Period,[4] and two carbon samples from the fill of an Inca terrace in the same area provided equally unhelpful dates (Heffernan 1989: 539).[5] Lisbet Bengtsson (1998: 102) reports finding Classic Inca ceramics in the course of her excavations at Ollantaytambo and in the quarry of Kachiqhata. The full spread of her calibrated dates begins as early as AD 1110 and runs as late as AD 1750.[6] Finally, during the course of our test excavations in the Cuzco Basin, carbon recovered at the small site of Pukacancha from a floor containing Classic Inca ceramics (Photo 9.1) provided a date of 440 ± 45 BP (calibrated 95.4% probability AD 1400–1630 [Bauer and Jones 2003]).[7] These scattered references emphasize that there is still a general lack of information concerning the Classic Inca ceramics produced in the Cuzco region. A large, systematic study of Classic Inca ceramics from Cuzco is an important project yet to be done and would be an enormous asset to researchers working in all parts of the former Inca Empire.[8]

PHOTO 9.1. Classic Inca pottery from the site of Pukacancha

NON-INCA CONTEMPORARY CERAMIC STYLES

We know that other styles of ceramics were imported into the Cuzco region during the period of imperial Inca rule. Fine black Chimu ceramics have been found in excavations at the site of Sacsayhuaman (Valcárcel 1946: 181) and in the city of Cuzco itself (Carmen Farfan Delgado, personal communication, 1994). Furthermore, during his excavations at Machu Picchu, Bingham recovered a non-Inca vessel, which, from its stirrup handle, appears to be imported from the north coast (Eaton 1916: Plate XIV, Fig. 1). The recovery of north-coast ceramics in Cuzco is not surprising, however, since the Inca controlled that area for more than a generation.

Other areas of the Inca domain, especially the Lake Titicaca region, are also represented in surface collections from sites in the Cuzco Valley. Fragments of Sillustani- (Tschopik 1946), Urcusuyu- (Rowe 1944: 49; Tschopik 1946), and Pacajes- (Rydén 1957; Albarracín-Jordan and Mathews 1990) style ceramics have been recovered at several sites (Photos 9.2–9.4). The first of these styles, Sillustani, is composed of a white paste, which has been called "kaolin," and was fabricated in the Department of Puno in the Lake Titicaca Basin. Urcusuyu vessels, with their bright orange, red, black, and white designs, are believed to have been produced in the same general region. Pacajes ceramics, known for their dark red background and miniature llama designs, were made in the Tiwanaku region on the southern end of Lake Titicaca. There is no doubt that other imported styles from other parts of the Inca Empire will be recovered as additional research is conducted at sites in the Cuzco region.

PHOTO 9.2. Fragments of Sillustani ceramics recovered in the Cuzco Valley

PHOTO 9.3. Fragments of Urcusuyu ceramics recovered in the Cuzco Valley

PHOTO 9.4. Fragments of Pacajes ceramics recovered in the Cuzco Valley

INCA ARCHITECTURE

Although Inca architecture has impressed visitors to Cuzco for centuries, there is still much to learn (Photo 9.5). Fortunately, significant research progress has been made in recent years. General overviews of Inca architecture have been produced by Kendall (1974), Gasparini and Margolies (1980), Hemming and Ranney (1982), Agurto Calvo (1987), and Protzen (2000). Meanwhile, additional studies have been conducted concerning the construction techniques of the Inca (Protzen 1985, 1986) and intensive studies of specific sites have been undertaken (Niles 1980a, 1980b, 1984, 1987, 1988, 1999; Gibaja 1984; Protzen 1991; Lee 1998, 2000).

Several authors have attempted to associate various styles of architecture with specific rulers, but their models have not been independently tested and confirmed. Jean-Pierre Protzen (2000: 201) writes: "Very few individual buildings are unequivocally attributed to a specific Inca ruler, and sites known to have been established by a given ruler are likely to have been modified over the years. Too few sites have been investigated with a view to their construction history to be certain of which features are associated with which construction phase. When such construction phases have been established, it is generally not known who was responsible for their initiation." Susan Niles (1999) has intensively studied several large sites that the chroniclers state were built by Huayna Capac, the last Inca king to rule over a united empire. Even with this remarkable documentation, it has been difficult to provide a list of clear stylistic traits that can be associated with his period of rule. We are still far from the ultimate goal of correlating architectural styles with reigns of particular Inca royals.

We do have a few carbon dates from Inca buildings in the Cuzco region. One of the few structures to be dated using radiocarbon samples is in Juchuy Cuzco, an Inca site in the Vilcanota River Valley, between the towns of Calca and Lamay. The surprisingly early date, 850 ± 60 BP (calibrated 95.4% probability AD 1030–1280), of a wooden lintel at the site[9] is interpreted by Kendall (1985: 347–348) as evidence for the re-utilization of older building materials by the Inca.

A series of Inca structures north of Cuzco have, however, provided a cluster of dates that fall within the thirteenth and fourteenth centuries (Hollowell 1987).[10] These

PHOTO 9.5. Large ashlar blocks on an Inca wall on the side of the Archbishop's Palace in Cuzco.
Note that at the far left side can be seen the remains of smaller, cellular stones that once covered the older, larger blocks.
(Courtesy of Fototeca Andina–Centro Bartolomé de Las Casas; photograph by Cesar Meza, ca. 1940)

data are noteworthy because they form the earliest cluster of dates from Inca structures and because they come from buildings well outside the Cuzco Valley. A building at the quarry of Kachiqhata, across the river from Ollantaytambo, provides a similar age (Bengtsson 1998: 102).[11] These findings suggest that Inca-style stone architecture in the region of Cuzco may have appeared earlier than previously predicted. If these dates are accurate, then some of the "Inca" structures in the Cuzco region may have been constructed during the Killke Period. They highlight the need for additional research on the relationship between ceramics and architectural styles in the Inca heartland. Recent research, such as that being conducted by Covey (2003) in the nearby Pisaq region and the work of others downstream in the area of Ollantaytambo (Niles 1980b; Hollowell 1987), is making important progress in this direction. We should

soon be able to note differences between Inca state architecture, that which was built in the Cuzco region while the heartland was in formation, and imperial Inca architecture, that which developed during the later period of imperial expansionism.

Distribution of Inca Sites in the Cuzco Valley

During the process of imperial development, the population level of the Cuzco Valley grew rapidly (Map 9.1). Our survey identified more than 850 Inca sites. Since an individual discussion of each of these sites is beyond the confines of this work, I present a brief summary of the settlement pattern found in our survey, and then turn to the question of Inca storage facilities in the valley and at the great site of Sacsayhuaman.

Our survey results indicate that most of the large villages that had emerged on both sides of the Cuzco Basin during the process of Killke Period state formation continued to be occupied during the time of imperial expansion. By the time of Spanish contact, there was a continuous spread of large villages on both sides of the Huatanay River in the Cuzco Basin. References to many of these villages can be found within early colonial documents of the valley. For example, Sites An. 33 (Larapa), An. 49 (Racay Racayniyoc [Andamachay]), An. 102 (Yucaypata), Co. 97 (Kayra), Co. 223 (Wimpillay), Cu. 3 (Chocco), Cu. 53 (Cachona), and Cu. 155 (Coripata [Cayaocache]) are all well documented in archival materials and can be linked to important Inca Period kin groups (Bauer 1998). I believe that with additional archival work, the names of the other prominent archaeological sites in the Cuzco Basin at the time of the conquest can also be determined. Such documentation would then allow new work to be conducted on the land-tenure system of the Inca at the time of European contact and on other important ethnohistoric research themes.

During the period of imperial Inca expansion, a multitude of homesteads and hamlets also sprang up. Most notable is the fact that the Oropesa Basin, which formed a buffer zone between the Lucre Basin and the Cuzco Basin during part of the Killke Period, quickly filled with settlements, and its rich agricultural land began to be fully exploited. All across the Cuzco Valley, from its northwestern end above Sacsayhuaman to its southeast extreme near Lake Lucre, there is a filling in of territory by small hamlets and villages.

We also see the sudden establishment of several new, large sites in the valley, some of which could be the result of natural concentrations of populations. Others represent areas developed by the elite of Cuzco, and still others most likely reflect forced resettlement programs of the state. For example, one of the largest sites in the valley is Muyu Cocha (Ch. 358). This site, which is located within a short walking distance of Sacsayhuaman, shows no evidence of being occupied during the Killke Period. As discussed below, it is likely that this site represents a large village that was established by the state to house

[handwritten margin note: where were the imperial estates? Were they in the Cuzco Valley?]

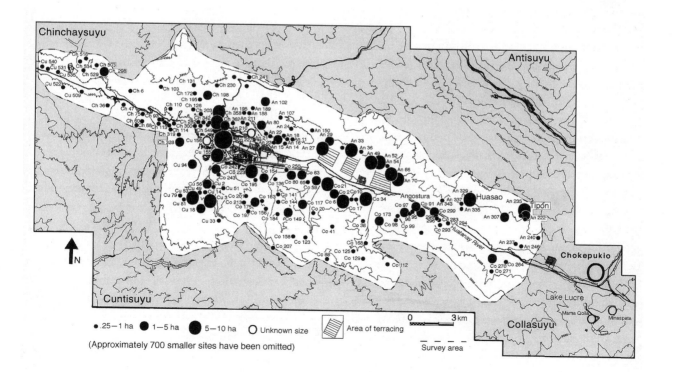

MAP 9.1. One hundred fifty important sites in the Cuzco Valley during the period of imperial development.

hundreds of construction workers who were brought into the valley to participate in public works projects.

Storage Facilities in Cuzco and the Valley

A number of recent studies have focused on the critical roles that various Inca administrative centers played in the collection, storage, and redistribution of state goods.[12] This role is most apparent in the large number of storage houses that surround various regional centers. For example, thousands of storage units were built on the hills surrounding the Inca provincial centers of Hatun Xauxa (Peru), Cotapachi (Bolivia), and Campo del Pucara (Argentina; Snead 1992). Hundreds of other storage units were built surrounding other secondary and tertiary sites of Inca administration (D'Altroy and Earle 1992; Snead 1992). These buildings generally held agricultural materials, including maize, quinoa, and potatoes (D'Altroy and Hastorf 1992).

The tributary demands placed on the inhabitants of the provinces required them to produce large quantities of agricultural surplus as well as to collect other important resources for the empire. Terry LeVine (1987) has outlined the labor services that one ethnic group, the Chupachu of the central Andes, gave to the Inca, as recorded in two early documents dating to 1549 and 1562. It is an astonishing list that includes labor services ranging from the collection of lowland bird feathers to providing guards for the mummies of the dead Inca rulers in Cuzco. When one considers that the Chupachu were a rather small group among the many controlled by Cuzco, the enormous amount of tribute service paid each year to the Inca begins to be revealed.

Heavy, bulky, and in need of cooler conditions for long-term storage, the agricultural surplus paid to the state was placed in storage units constructed near to, but above, the provincial Inca administrative centers. Smaller and more valuable resources, such as wool, feathers, leather, and special woods, were placed in storage units within the centers where they could then be converted into goods by means of rotational labor. For example, Xerez (1985: 116 [1534]) mentions the extensive storehouses that existed within the city of Cajamarca:

> In this town of Cajamarca they found certain houses filled with clothes packed in bales that reached to

the ceilings of the houses. They say that it was a depot to supply the army. The Christians took what they wanted, and still the houses remained so full that what was taken seemed not to be missed. The cloth is the best that has been seen in the Indias. The greater part of it is very fine and elegant wool, and the rest is cotton of various colors and rich hues.[13] (Translation by author)

Although much of what was produced for the state in the provinces remained in the control of regional lords, the finest objects were transported to Cuzco. In the words of Santillán (1950: 68 [1564]), "The richest and choicest clothes were carried to Cuzco, and the others were put in the storerooms, and from these they dressed the people that fulfilled the mentioned services of the Inca."[14] Year after year, the tribute, as well as spoils of war, poured into Cuzco, and its storage facilities came to hold the premier objects of the realm. Like many of the Spaniards who arrived in the Inca capital in 1533, Pedro Sancho de la Hoz was astonished at its unparalleled wealth:

> There are houses where the tribute is kept which the vassals bring to the caciques; and there is a house where are kept more than a hundred thousand dried birds because they make garments of their feathers, which are of many colors, and there are many [storage]houses for this. There are bucklers, oval shields made of leather, copper sheets for repairing the walls of houses, knives and other tools, sandals and breastplates for the warriors and everything in such great quantity that the mind does not cease to wonder how so great a tribute of so many kinds of things can have been given. (Sancho 1917: 158–159)[15]

Likewise, Pedro Pizarro was surprised by the range of items found within the storage rooms in Cuzco. He mentions that the rooms held an enormous amount of highly valued goods, which ranged from rooms filled with emerald green hummingbird feathers to bars of copper and plates of silver and gold:

> I shall now give an account of what was in this city of Cuzco when we entered it, for there were many storehouses which had very fine clothing as well as other

coarser garments, and there were stores of grain, of food, of coca. There were deposits of turnsole feathers, which looked like very fine gold, and other turnsole feathers were of a golden green colour. It was a very slender feather grown by some little birds hardly larger than a cigar, and because they are so small, they call them comine birds. These little birds grow this feather already called turnsole only upon their breast, and the place where they grow is scarcely larger than a fingernail. [These Indians] had many of these feathers twisted into a thin cord closely wound about a framework of maguey in such a fashion as to form pieces more than a palm wide, and the whole was fastened upon certain chests [which they had]. Of this feather they made garments which caused the beholders to wonder how so many turnsole feathers could have been gathered together. There were likewise many other plumes of diverse colours for the purpose of making clothing with which the Lords and Ladies delight themselves at the time of the festivals. There were also mantles made with very delicate little spangles of mother-of-pearl, gold and silver in such wise as to cause astonishment at the dexterity of the work, for the whole was so covered with these spangles that nothing of the closely woven network [which formed the basis of the garment] was visible. These garments were likewise for the Ladies. There were stores of sandals with the soles made of cabuya, and above the toes they were made of very fine wool of many colours . . . I shall not be able to describe the deposits which I saw of all the varieties of apparel which they made and used in this kingdom, for time would be lacking for seeing it all and understanding [and] comprehending such a great thing. There were many stores of small bars of copper [from] the mines, of sacks and ropes, of wooden vessels, of plates of gold and silver [so that] all that was found here was a thing causing astonishment . . . (Pedro Pizarro 1921: 265–267 [1571])[16]

Besides being housed within the immense warehouses of the state, it is also clear that goods and elite objects were stored within the confines of the specific state institutions. For example, Garcilaso de la Vega (1966: 249 [1609: Pt. 1, Bk. 5, Ch. 5]) describes extensive maize stor-

age bins within a compound called the Acllahuaci (House of Chosen [Women]) in Cuzco, in which lived hundreds of women who had dedicated their lives to serving the state. Cieza de León (1976: 145–146 [1553: Pt. 1, Ch. 92]) describes other maize storage bins within the Coricancha, the most important religious compound within Cuzco. The fact that both the Acllahuaci and the Coricancha contained large food storage facilities is not surprising, since both of these institutions were required to host large numbers of people on special occasions.

The individual *panacas* (royal descent groups) of Cuzco also controlled storage facilities in and near the city. Much of each former king's wealth was retained by his descendants after his death and stored in central Cuzco. For example, we know that although the first three Spaniards to arrive in Cuzco were allowed to sack the Temple of the Sun, they were asked by Atahualpa not to touch the treasures of his father, Huayna Capac, which were still held in the city.

The *panacas* were also given control of the lands and country estates that were owned by the king during his lifetime. Much of the agricultural yields from those lands was then used to support the cult of the founding ancestor. This is best documented in the case of Amaru Topa Inca, Topa Inca Yupanqui's elder brother. Santa Cruz Pachacuti Yamqui Salcamayhua (1950: 245–247 [ca. 1613]) writes:

. . . And thus Pachacuti Inca Yupanqui renounced the kingdom to his son Amaru Topa Inca, who did not accept it, instead applying himself to his fields and buildings. Seeing this, Pachacuti Inca Yupanqui offered the kingdom to his second son Topa Inca Yupanqui . . .

And at this time there began a great famine which lasted seven years, in those seven years no seed that was sown produced fruit . . . During this time, they say that Amaru Topa Inca always, in those seven years of famine, grew much food in his field at Callachaca and Lucriocchullo. And they say more, that his fields were always covered by clouds, raining on them in the evening, and thus they say that the frosts never fell, but . . . He had filled the *collcas* (granaries) and storage houses with food a long time before.[17] (Translation by author)

The remains of the storage houses can still be seen in the area of Callachaca on the slopes of the Cuzco Valley above the town of San Sebastián. Although now poorly preserved and spread over a large area, more than thirty storage houses may once have been located in this area of the valley. The state also controlled various storage houses outside the city. We were able to identify some of these sites through their architectural remains and others by the great quantity of storage vessels found at them (Map 9.2). With the exception of Sacsayhuaman, discussed in detail below, we believe these storage houses, because they are located outside the city on the valley slopes, held agricultural surplus.

Although more than a dozen sites with storage houses are now known in the Cuzco Valley, the total volume of materials contained in these was relatively small, compared to the thousands of units found around the largest provincial centers. Craig Morris (1992: 169), the first researcher in the Andes to conduct a series of investigations on Inca storage houses, notes, ". . . we might be incorrect in assuming that simply because Cuzco was the capital and most important center in the realm that it would automatically have the largest food stores." Cuzco, like other Inca centers, did receive a great amount of goods, but as the capital, it received the finest luxury goods, while the other centers received more of the agricultural surplus (Morris 1967, 1992; LeVine 1992).

The largest set of Inca storage buildings in the Cuzco Valley can be found at the site of Qata Casallacta, situated on the south side of the valley, not far from the city (Rowe 1944, 1967; Morris 1992). Dean Arnold conducted test excavations at Qata Casallacta in 1972–1973, and he found evidence of a large number of Inca storage vessels and many rectangular buildings at the site. More recent excavations there have recovered examples of Killke pottery, suggesting that this facility was established during the period of state development (Candía Gómez 1992). Although the site (Cu. 96) is now nearly destroyed by urban growth, we estimate that it once held more than one hundred storage units.[18]

The Site of Sacsayhuaman

The most important site outside the city but within the Cuzco Basin is the massive site of Sacsayhuaman (Photo 9.6). It is located on a steep hill that overlooks the city

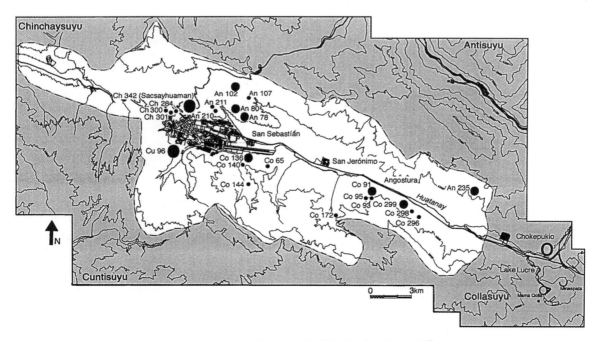

MAP 9.2. Location of storage facilities in the Cuzco Valley

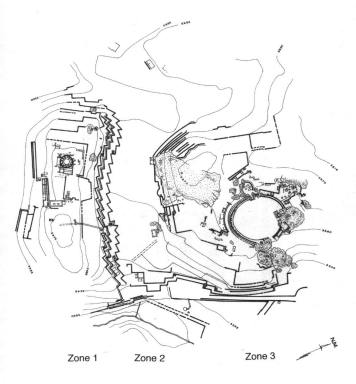

Zone 1   Zone 2   Zone 3

MAP 9.3. Map of the site of Sacsayhuaman
(Courtesy of Instituto Nacional de Cultura, Peru)

and provides an impressive view of the valley to the south-east. Surface collections at Sacsayhuaman indicate that the site dates back to at least the Qotakalli Period, and excavations have revealed that a substantial occupation existed there during Killke times (Rowe 1944; Dwyer 1971a). The complex was, however, greatly expanded during the period of Inca imperial rule and now is one of the most famous archaeological sites in the Americas.

The site of Sacsayhuaman can be divided into three zones (Map 9.3). To the north is a large circular reservoir with a small adjacent complex of finely made buildings. The architectural features of this zone were unknown until the late 1980s, when work by the National Institute of Cuzco exposed the reservoir and the network of water channels that filled it. This area most certainly represents what the Inca called Calispuquio (Spring of Good Health), which is described as being near Sacsayhuaman (Bauer 1998: 55). Calispuquio played an important role in a number of Inca rituals (Betanzos 1996: 63 [1557: Pt. 1, Ch. 14]), and it was near this pool that Topa Inca Yupanqui had an estate (Cobo 1990: 55–56 [1653: Bk. 13, Ch. 13]).

The second zone lies near the middle of the site. It con-

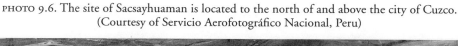

PHOTO 9.6. The site of Sacsayhuaman is located to the north of and above the city of Cuzco.
(Courtesy of Servicio Aerofotográfico Nacional, Peru)

PHOTO 9.7. The famous carved stone known as "the throne of the Incas"

tains many smooth outcrops and the faint remains of various building foundations. The most notable feature of this area is the famous carved stone, referred to as "the throne of the Incas" (Photo 9.7). This carving was a shrine of the Cuzco *ceque* system and may have held an important role in the Inca rituals that took place in the complex (Cobo 1990: 57 [1653: Bk. 13, Ch. 13]; Bauer 1998: 61).

The third and best-known zone of Sacsayhuaman includes its great plaza as well as its three massive terrace walls. The stones of these terrace walls are among the largest used in any building in prehispanic America, and they display a precision of fitting that is unmatched in the Americas (Figure 9.1). Because of its location high above Cuzco and its immense terrace walls, this area of Sacsayhuaman is frequently referred to as a fortress. The importance of its military functions was highlighted in 1556 when Manco Inca lay siege to Cuzco. Much of the fighting occurred in and around Sacsayhuaman, as it was seen as critical for maintaining control over the city. We know from descriptions of the siege, as well as from excavations at the site, that there were towers on its summit and a series of other buildings (Valcárcel 1934, 1935, 1946). Sancho, who visited the complex before the siege, writes the following:

Upon the hill which, towards the city, is rounded and very steep, there is a very beautiful fortress of earth and stone. Its large windows which look over the city make it appear still more beautiful. Within, there are many dwellings, and a chief tower in the centre, built square, and having four or five terraces one above the other. The rooms inside are small and the stones of which it is built are very well worked and so well adjusted to one another that it does not appear that they have any mortar and they are so smooth that they look like polished slabs with the joinings in regular order and alternating with one another after the usage in Spain. There are so many rooms and

FIGURE 9.1. The massive terrace walls of Sacsayhuaman (Squier 1877: 477)

towers that a person could not see them all in one day; and many Spaniards who have been in Lombardy and in other foreign kingdoms say that they have never seen any other fortress like this one nor a stronger castle. Five thousand Spaniards might well be within it, nor could it be given a broadside or be mined, because it is on a rocky mountain. On the side towards the city, which is a very steep slope, there is no more than one wall; on the other side, which is less steep, there are three, one above the other. The most beautiful thing which can be seen in the edifices of that land are these walls, because they are of stones so large that anyone who sees them would not say that they had been put in place by human hands, for they are as large as chunks of mountains and huge rocks, and they have a height of thirty palms and a length of as many more, and others have twenty and twenty-five, and others fifteen, but there is none so small that three carts could carry it. These are not smooth stones, but rather well joined and matched one with another, . . . These walls twist in such a way that if they are attacked it is not possible to do so from directly in front, but only obliquely. These walls are of the same stone, and between wall and wall there is enough earth to permit three carts to go along the top at one time. They are made after the fashion of steps, so that one begins where another leaves off. The whole fortress was a deposit of arms, clubs, lances, bows, axes, shields, doublets thickly padded with cotton and other arms of various sorts, and clothes for the soldiers collected here from all parts of the land subject to the lords of Cuzco. They had many colors, blue, yellow, brown and many others for painting, much tin and lead with other metals, and much silver and some gold, many mantles and quilted doublets for the warriors. . . . (Sancho 1917: 155–157 [1534])[19]

In the above quote, Sancho mentions the labyrinth-like quality of the complex and the fact that it held a great number of storage rooms filled with a wide variety of items. He also notes that there were buildings with large windows that overlooked the city. These structures, like so much of the site, have long since been destroyed (Hyslop 1990: 54).

Other early accounts of Cuzco (Cieza de León 1976: 154 [1554: Pt. 2, Ch. 51]) indicate that Sacsayhuaman included a Sun Temple, which suggests that the complex was the focus of ritual activities as well (Map 9.4). The large plaza area, capable of holding thousands of people, is well designed for ceremonial activities, and several of the large structures at the site may also have been used during rituals. It is also clear from early accounts that the complex held a great number of storage rooms. Pedro Pizarro, whose cousin Juan Pizarro was killed while trying to take control of Sacsayhuaman during the 1556 siege, describes the storage rooms within the complex and that were filled with military equipment.

To return to the matter of Cuzco, [I will say that] on top of a hill they had a very strong fort surrounded with masonry walls of stone and having two very high round towers. And in the lower part of this wall there were stones so large and thick that it seemed impossible that human hands could have set them in place . . . And they were so close together, and so well fitted, that the point of a pin could not have been inserted in one of the joints. The whole [fortress was built up in] terraces and flat spaces. There were so many rooms that ten thousand Indians could get within them. All these rooms were occupied by and filled with arms, lances, arrows, darts, clubs, bucklers, and large oblong shields under which a hundred Indians could go, as though under a mantle, in order to capture forts. There were many morions made of certain canes very well woven together and so strong that no stone nor blow could penetrate them and harm the head which wore the morion. There were also, here in this fortress, certain stretchers in which the Lords

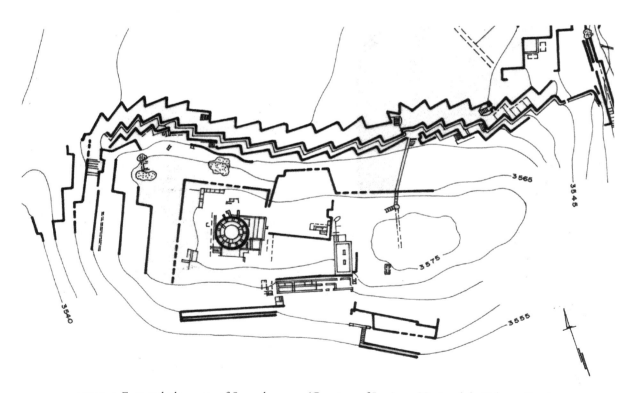

MAP 9.4. Fort and plaza area of Sacsayhuaman (Courtesy of Instituto Nacional de Cultura, Peru)

traveled, as in litters. There were here many Indians who guarded these stores and who saw to it that these terraces and rooms were kept in repair if it rained in the winter-time. This fortress would have been impregnably strong had it been provided with water and [it had] great labyrinths and rooms which I never saw completely and never understood.
(Pedro Pizarro 1921: 272–273 [1571])[20]

As noted by Hyslop (1990: 53), the earliest accounts of Sacsayhuaman stress two aspects above all others. First, everyone marveled at the great stonework of the terrace walls. Second, it is emphasized that the complex contained a great number of storage rooms that held an array of military items. Among the more interesting items mentioned are a wide range of weapons, cotton armor, siege equipment, and litters for the Inca. Recent excavations by the National Institute of Culture on an expanse immediately west of its circular tower has exposed a maze of small rooms, many of which could have functioned as storage rooms, as described by both Pizarro and Sancho.

BUILDING SACSAYHUAMAN

The Inca used similar construction techniques in building Sacsayhuaman as they used on all their stonework, albeit on a far more massive scale. The stones were rough-cut to the approximate shape in the quarries using river cobbles (Protzen 1986, 1991). They were then dragged by rope to the construction site, a feat that at times required hundreds of men (Gutiérrez de Santa Clara 1963: 252 [ca. 1600]). The ropes were so impressive that they warranted mention by Diego de Trujillo (1948: 63 [1571]) as he inspected a room filled with building materials.

The stones were shaped into their final form at the building site and then laid in place (Lee 1986). The work, though supervised by Inca architects, was largely carried out by groups of individuals fulfilling their labor obligations to the state. In this system of *mit'a* or "turn" labor, each village or ethnic group provided a certain number of individuals to participate in public works projects.

Although multiple regions might provide labor for a single, large-scale state project, the ethnic composition of the work-gangs remained intact, as different groups were assigned different tasks. Cieza de León, who visited

Sacsayhuaman at least two times in the late 1540s, provides an account of its construction in which he mentions the quarrying of the stones, their transportation to the site, and the digging of foundation trenches—all of which was conducted by rotational labor under the close supervision of imperial architects.[21]

He [Pachacuti Inca Yupanqui] ordered twenty thousand men sent in from the provinces, and that the villages supply them with the necessary food, and if one of them took sick, that another should be sent in his place and he could return to his home. These Indians were not permanently engaged in this work, but only for a limited time, and then others came and they left, so the work did not become onerous. Four thousand of them quarried and cut stones; six thousand hauled them with great cables of leather and hemp; the others dug the ditch and laid the foundations, while still others cut poles and beams for the timbers. So that they would be contented, these people lived in separate groups, each with those of his own region, near the site where the building was to be erected. Even today most of the walls of the houses they occupied can still be seen. Overseers went around watching what they did, and masters who were highly skilled in their work.
(Cieza de León 1976: 153–154 [1554: Pt. 2, Ch. 51])[22]

Protzen (1991) has shown how the Inca built long and complex ramps within the stone quarries near Ollantaytambo, and how additional ramps were built to drag the blocks to the construction above the village. Cobo offers additional information on the construction techniques of the Inca. Specifically, he describes how, by building large ramps, they were able to place the stone blocks on the upper tiers of their tall walls:

Thinking about this truly does cause one to marvel, and it makes one realize what a vast number of people were necessary to make these structures. In fact, we see stones of such enormous size that a hundred men could not work even one of them in a month. Therefore, what they say becomes believable, and it is that when the fortress [Sacsayhuaman] of Cuzco was under construction, there

PHOTO 9.8. At the site of Sillustani near Lake Titicaca, a possible construction ramp can still be seen beside a large funerary tower.

were normally thirty thousand people working on it. This is not surprising since the lack of implements, apparatus, and ingenuity necessarily increased the amount of work, and thus they did everything by sheer manpower.

The implements that they had to cut the stones and work them were hard, black cobblestones from the rivers, with which they worked more by pounding than cutting. The stones were taken to the work site by dragging them, and since they had no cranes, wheels, or apparatus for lifting them, they made a ramp of earth next to the construction site, and they rolled the stones up the ramp. As the structure went up higher, they kept building up the ramp to the same height. I saw this method used for the Cathedral of Cuzco which is under construction. Since the laborers who work on this job are Indians, the Spanish masons and architects let them use their own methods of doing the work, and in order to raise up the stones, they made the ramps mentioned above, piling earth next to the wall until the ramp was as high as the wall (Cobo 1990: 229–230 [1653: Bk. 14, Ch. 12]).[23]

The Inca removed the construction ramps used to make the great walls at Sacsayhuaman at the end of the building phase. Nevertheless, evidence for such ramps can be seen at other Inca sites. For example, at the site of Sillustani near Lake Titicaca, a possible ramp can still be seen beside a large, unfinished funerary tower (Photo 9.8).

Much of the stone used in the construction of Sacsayhuaman may have been quarried from the outcrops to the north of the site (Kalafatovich 1970). This area continues to serve as an important source of cobblestones and other construction materials for Cuzco. Many of the laborers that worked on Sacsayhuaman lived near it. Cieza de León indicates that in his time, "most of the walls of the houses they occupied can still be seen."[24] Our survey identified a large Inca site that may have functioned as the temporary living facility for the *mit'a* laborers that built Sacsayhuaman. The site, Muyu Cocha (Ch. 358), is only a few minutes' walk from Sacsayhuaman and it contains more than 5 hectares of dense domestic remains.[25] It is clearly visible today, and it is even more notable on photographs dating to the early 1930s (Photo 9.9).

Unlike most other large domestic Inca sites in the Cuzco Valley, Muyu Cocha does not contain evidence of earlier occupations. In other words, the site was both founded and abandoned during the relatively short period during which Classic Inca pottery was being manufactured. Furthermore, our surface collections from the site recovered an unusually large number of Lake Titicaca ceramic styles, including Sillustani, Urcusuyu, and Pacajes—all of which are known to have been produced in the Lake Titicaca region during the Inca Period.[26] The presence of these ceramic styles at the site of Muyu Cocha suggests that many of the workers who lived there were from the southern lake territory of the empire.

Following the siege of Cuzco, the Spaniards began to use Sacsayhuaman as a source of stones for building Spanish Cuzco, and within less than a year, much of the complex was demolished (Betanzos 1996: 157–158 [1557: Pt. 1, Bk. 37]). The site was destroyed block by block to build the new governmental and religious buildings of the city,

as well as the houses of the wealthiest Spaniards. In the words of Garcilaso de la Vega (1966: 471 [1609: Pt. 1, Bk. 7, Ch. 29]): "to save themselves the expense, effort and delay with which the Indians worked the stone, they pulled down all the smooth masonry in the walls. There is indeed not a house in the city that has not been made of this stone, or at least the houses built by the Spaniards."[27] Today, tragically, only the stones that were too large to be easily moved remain at the site.[28]

Summary and Discussion

The Cuzco Valley was transformed during the period of imperial development. Not only did the number and size of settlements dramatically increase, but many began to take on the character of the newly emergent empire. State-

PHOTO 9.9. The large site of Muyu Cocha can be seen in the upper center of this photograph.
An Inca road divides the site into two parts, and irregular vegetation marks the area of domestic structures.
Also note the many quarried rock outcrops that may have provided stone for the nearby site of Sacsayhuaman.
(Neg. no. 334794, photo courtesy the Library, American Museum of Natural History)

sponsored construction projects rose to an unprecedented level, as palaces, estates, temples, storage facilities, and other state installations were constructed. The rivers of the valley were canalized, and major tracts of land continued to be terraced. The finest agricultural areas were set aside for the many religious cults of the city or as the private holdings of the Cuzco elite. Craft production, especially in ceramics, textiles, and metals, rose to an unparalleled scale to meet the increased consumption as well as the sacrificial demands of the growing empire. At the same time, immense amounts of exotic materials were being brought to the city as tribute payment by conquered peoples. To accommodate the great numbers of people who came and went from the city each day, the numerous roads that had always led to the valley were expanded and widened. Pedro Sancho (1898: 137 [1534]) describes the thriving valley as seen from the northwest end, near the fortress of Sacsayhuaman, as he entered with Pizarro's forces in 1534:

> From this fort, looking around, one sees the houses of the city extending a quarter, a half and a league away. In the valley that is surrounded by hills, there are more than five thousand houses. Many of these are houses of pleasure and recreation of past lords. Others are those of foreign *caciques* who reside permanently in the city. There are also some that are houses or storehouses full of mantles, wool, arms, metals, clothes and everything else that is grown or made in this land.[29] (Translation by author)

Within the city, spectacular elite and religious buildings expanded to fill the entire area between the two rivers, and a large plaza capable of holding thousands of people was built. The numerous villages that surrounded the city also underwent impressive growth as they provided support personnel for many institutions in the city center (Garcilaso de la Vega 1966: 417–430 [1609: Pt. 1, Bk. 7, Chs. 8–11]).

The provincial populations under Inca rule across the Andes produced vast amounts of goods, the finest of which were sent to the imperial capital. As tribute demands brought boundless amounts of wealth into the capital, Cuzco became a cosmopolitan center, and people from diverse areas of the empire came to live there. Some of these foreigners were nobility, sent to represent their ethnic groups in the imperial capital. Others came to Cuzco on pilgrimage to see and to make offerings at the great temples of the city. Still others had been forcibly removed from rebellious regions and were resettled in the Cuzco Valley as part of the massive pacification policies of the Inca. For example, it is well documented that large numbers of Cañari (from the central area of Ecuador) and Chachapoyas (from the northeastern highlands of Peru) were resettled in Cuzco in an attempt to depopulate and thus pacify these rebellious, newly conquered territories. Yet others had been sent by their village leaders to fulfill labor obligations, which reshaped the valley and its principal city in ways that still, a half-millennium later, astound visitors to the region.

Cuzco Valley in Inca Period:

1) huge pop. increase, spreading throughout the valley

2) establishment of many new sites, public & agricultural works, all in Inca imperial style

3) huge architectural projects (e.g., Sacsayhuaman), built using mit'a labor.

4) expansion of storage complexes, but not largest in the empire

5) incredible scale of craft production, esp. ceramics, textiles, precious metals

6) just as many imported exotic goods, tribute from provincial subjects

7) roadways expanded & widened to accomodate increased traffic

8) Cosmopolitan, occupied by provincial caciques, resettled rebels, temp. mitayos, Inca elites

CHAPTER 10

Inca Cuzco

VISITORS TO MODERN CUZCO frequently marvel at the exquisite workmanship of its many Inca walls. The prevailing impression is that a great deal of Inca Cuzco has survived and that the layout of the central plaza and the surrounding sectors of the city have remained largely unchanged since Inca times. Although this is true in the most general sense, it is important to note that the majority of the architectural features that adorned central Cuzco during the rule of the Inca were long ago destroyed. New streets have been created, ancient ones lost, and the bulk of the city's former palaces, halls, temples, and shrines have been demolished.

Although the loss of Inca Cuzco has for the most part been gradual, several early events did profoundly alter the central core area.[1] Spanish influence on the city began as early as 1533 with the arrival of an advance party sent by Francisco Pizarro to extract precious metals from its temples. Foreign control of Cuzco was established in 1534 with the founding of what can be called "Spanish" Cuzco (*Libro Primero del Cabildo de la Ciudad del Cuzco* 1965 [1534]). This involved the division of central Cuzco into house lots for the conquistadors and the establishment of various major Spanish institutions, including the first Christian church on the plaza and the Municipal Council (Cabildo).

Two years later, in 1536, Manco Inca burned much of central Cuzco as he fought against Hernando Pizarro for control of the city. The razing of Cuzco, the full retreat of Manco Inca, and the subsequent establishment of un-contested Spanish domination of the city was followed by a prolonged period of construction in the central district (1536–1650), during which numerous formally sacred places were transformed to commercial uses or destroyed. Various regal buildings were either pulled down or greatly altered to accommodate shops and new houses for the Spaniards. Even the size and shape of the central plaza was dramatically altered as new buildings were built in the city center and Inca monuments removed.

Finally, there was the devastating earthquake of March 31, 1650, that leveled much of Cuzco (Photo 10.1). Hundreds of buildings were damaged and scores of people were killed (Esquivel y Navia 1980 [1749]; Julien 1995). As Cuzco was slowly rebuilt, construction followed the canons of European architecture rather than those established by the Inca for the city. The Inca Empire had fallen more than a century earlier, and the importance of Cuzco had already been eclipsed by the new Spanish capital of Lima (Ciudad de los Reyes) on the coast.

This chapter examines the city of Cuzco and its many different elite and religious compounds as they stood at the height of the empire, just before contact with Pizarro occurred. Using the Inca structures that have survived into the present, and various accounts of Cuzco written between the arrival of the first Spaniards in 1533 and the 1650 earthquake, I discuss many of the royal palaces, temples, and other major monuments that existed in the center of Cuzco during Inca times.[2]

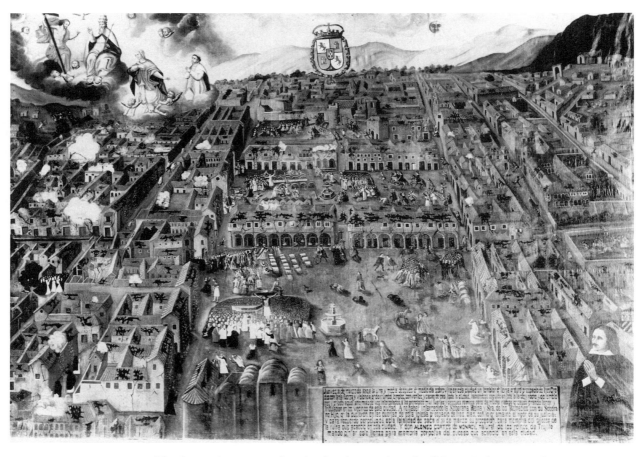

PHOTO 10.1. The devastating 1650 earthquake that destroyed much of Cuzco is documented in a painting ordered by Alonso Cortés de Monroy. Known as the Monroy Panorama, it currently hangs in the Triunfo, in Cuzco. (Courtesy of the Latin American Library, Tulane University)

Important Documents

Any attempt to reconstruct Inca Cuzco must begin with a map of the urban center and copies of the earliest descriptions of the city.[3] Although many historic sources describe parts of Inca Cuzco, several documents stand out for their details and accuracy. Among these is the *Libro Primero del Cabildo de la Ciudad del Cuzco* (First Book of the City Council of Cuzco, 1965 [1534]) in which were recorded the Cuzco house lots that were awarded by Francisco Pizarro to his men. This document provides a lot-by-lot account of the division of Cuzco among the first Spaniards, and it contains various references to the important Inca buildings they came to own. Another important document is the chronicle of Pedro Pizarro. Cousin to the older and more famous Pizarro bothers (Francisco, Hernando, and Gonzalo), Pedro Pizarro was

one of the few early conquistadors to write an account of the full conquest. He was present in Cuzco during its Spanish founding and spent much of his life there. Other notable eyewitness accounts of Cuzco at the time of the Spanish invasion are those written by Pedro Sancho (1917 [1534]), Cristóbal Mena (1929 [1534]), Miguel de Estete (1985 [1534]), and Francisco Xerez (1985 [1534]).

Also critical in understanding the layout of the Inca capital is the work of Garcilaso de la Vega. In his old age, Garcilaso de la Vega wrote a general history of Peru that includes many of his memories of growing up in Cuzco between 1539 and 1560. He provides especially detailed information on the destruction of various Inca buildings that surrounded the plaza and the locations of the most important royal compounds of the city.

Another important source on Inca Cuzco, although

one that is more difficult to use, is a long list of Inca shrines (*huacas*) preserved within the work of Bernabé Cobo (1990 [1653]). Cobo, who gained his information from a now lost 1559 manuscript written by Polo de Ondegardo, provides a detailed account of several hundred shrines located in and around the city of Cuzco (Bauer 1998). Since the shrines were organized along lines, or *ceques,* the shrine system as a whole is frequently referred to as the "Cuzco *ceque* system." Although Cobo provides only brief descriptions of each of the shrines, his list does include many details that are not recorded in other historical sources.[4]

The Arrival of the First Europeans in Cuzco

Francisco Pizarro captured the ruling Inca, Atahualpa, in November of 1532 in the city of Cajamarca. Pizarro held the Inca king hostage for over eight months while enormous amounts of gold and silver were transferred to Cajamarca from across the empire in exchange for the king's release. During this period of captivity, the invading Spanish forces had free rein to explore the vast unknown world they had only recently entered. Pizarro took advantage of this time and sent small groups of men on different expeditions.

One team traveled across the central Andean mountains to the imperial city of Cuzco. The round-trip journey took over four months, although just eight days were spent in Cuzco itself.[5] The expedition was composed of three Spaniards[6] and a high-ranking Inca official,[7] all of whom were carried in royal litters.[8]

This small expedition was the second invading force to enter Cuzco within a short period. A few months earlier, one of Atahualpa's armies under the command of Chalcochima and Quizquiz had fought and won a decisive victory over Huascar's men and had invaded the imperial capital. Atahualpa's generals assembled and executed as many of Huascar's family, and members of other opposed kin groups, as they could find. They were still in control of Cuzco when the three Spaniards entered it for the first time. Yet with Atahualpa held hostage, there was little that Chalcochima or Quizquiz could do but watch the Spaniards as they searched the city for treasure.

The Spaniards wandered through Cuzco, astonished by its large size, paved streets, and the fine stone construc-

tions of its many palaces and temples. Xerez (1985: 149 [1534]) records the impression of Juan de Zárate of Cuzco:

> He said that the city of Cuzco is as large as has been described, and that it is located on a hillside near a plain. The streets are very well organized and paved, and in the eight days that they were there they could not see everything.[9]

Nevertheless, they soon turned to the business at hand: stripping the Inca capital of its wealth. The Spaniards removed the fine gold plates from the walls of one building within the Coricancha as well as those of a second building that contained less valuable gold alloy (see Chapter 11). Among their greatest finds was a large golden bench (altar)[10] and a large gold fountain (Mena 1929: 37 [1534]). In another building, they discovered a room that contained so many silver vessels that they could not transport them all back to Cajamarca. Sealing the room and placing guards at its door, the Spaniards claimed this hoard in the name of King Charles I and Francisco Pizarro (Mena 1929: 37 [1534]).

The Spaniards were surprised to find that the palaces of the former Inca rulers continued to be maintained in royal splendor long after the death of the king. Even more shocking to the Europeans was that each of the former rulers of Cuzco was embalmed at the time of his death, and that these mummies continued to be seen in public and to be served by royal attendants. On entering one building, they found Huayna Capac, the father of Atahualpa, who had died about eight years earlier. Mena records this first encounter between the Spaniards and the royal mummies of the Inca:

> In another very large building they found many very heavy earthenware pitchers covered with gold leaf. They did not wish to break these for fear of angering the Indians. In this temple were many women and there were the embalmed bodies of two men and with them was a live woman with a mask of gold on her face dusting (and chasing) out flies and they [the mummies] had in their hands a very rich cane of gold. The woman would not allow them to enter the temple till they had removed their shoes, and when this was done they went to see the

mummies and took from them many rich pieces. And they did not succeed in taking all the pieces because the cacique Atahualpa had begged them not to take them saying that one was his father Cuzco. And on account of this they did not dare take off more. (Mena 1929: 37 [1534])[11]

After a little more than a week, the three Spaniards left Cuzco and began the long journey back to Cajamarca. Following them was a line of more than seven hundred men carrying the treasure that had been robbed from the city (Xerez 1985: 149 [1534]). In less than six months, Cuzco had been ravaged in the civil war between Atahualpa and Huascar and its finest buildings stripped of their wealth by the newly arrived European strangers.

The Fall of Inca Cuzco (1533–1536)

In November of 1553, five months after the first three Spaniards visited Cuzco, Pizarro's small army arrived at the imperial city. Sancho (1917: 153–154 [1534]), who arrived with the army, describes his impressions of the city:

The city of Cuzco is the principal one of all those where the lords of this land have their residence; it is so large and so beautiful that it would be worthy of admiration even in Spain; and it is full of the palaces of the lords, because no poor people live there, and each lord builds there his house, and all the caciques do likewise, although the latter do not dwell there continuously. The greater part of these houses are of stone, and others have half the façade of stone. There are many houses of adobe, and they are all arranged in very good order. The streets are laid out at right angles, they are very straight, and are paved, and down the middle runs a gutter for water lined with stone. The chief defect which the streets have is that of being narrow, so that only one horse and rider can go on one side of the gutter and another upon the opposite side. (Sancho 1917: 153–154 [1534])[12]

Pizarro and his men entered the central plaza and immediately occupied the various royal compounds that surrounded it. After installing Manco Inca as the new ruler of the Inca Empire, the Spaniards began a more

systematic looting of the city than had been conducted during the rushed visit of the advance party. The recovered wealth from this second looting of Cuzco was even greater than that assembled in Cajamarca. Sancho (1917: 128–129 [1534]) provides the best description of the wealth that resulted from this monumental event:

Truly it was a thing worthy to be seen, this house where the melting took place, all full of so much gold in plates of eight and ten pounds each, and in vessels, and vases and pieces of various forms with which the lords of that land were served, and among other very slightly things were four sheep in fine gold and very large, and ten or twelve figures of women of the size of the women of that land, all of fine gold and as beautiful and well made as if they were alive. . . . The Governor divided and distributed all this treasure among all the Spaniards who were at Cuzco and those who remained in the city of Xauxa . . . (Sancho 1917: 128–129 [1534])[13]

The following March, Francisco Pizarro took formal control of the imperial city of the Inca, claiming it as a Spanish town. In doing so, he divided the most important compounds of the central city into house lots and distributed them among his men according to their rank. Sancho describes this event:

In the month of March 1534, the Governor ordered that the greater part of the Spaniards he had with him should be assembled in this city, and he made an act of foundation and settlement of the town saying that he placed it and founded it in his own authority, and he took possession of it in the middle of the plaza. . . . And continuing the settlement, he appointed the site for the church which was to be built, its boundaries, limits and jurisdiction, and immediately afterwards he proclaimed that all who might come to settle here would be received as citizens . . . (Sancho 1917: 130–131 [1534])[14]

The looting of Cuzco by the Spaniards, its division into house lots, and the abusive treatment of Manco Inca by Pizarro and his men led to a native revolt. Manco Inca escaped from Spanish control and organized a massive attack on Cuzco. During this siege, which lasted for several months, much of the city was burned to the ground. The siege came to an unsuccessful end when Diego de Almagro returned from Chile and reinforced the troops of Hernando Pizarro. Reluctantly, Manco Inca pulled his army from the area and retreated into the mountains to the northwest.

As the Spaniards slowly rebuilt Cuzco following the siege, it was transformed. European institutions were established and new architectural styles were introduced. Most of the temples and palaces of the city center were destroyed, and churches, governmental buildings, and commercial districts were constructed on their foundations. It was a slow process that continues to this day. Although much of Inca Cuzco has now been lost, by combining information contained within various historical sources with the surviving architectural remains in the city, we can gain some idea of its ancient form and what it was like at the time of contact.

The Plazas of Central Cuzco

Cuzco developed between two small rivers, the Saphy and Tullumayu (Map 10.1 and Photo 10.2). Within the city, and for some distance outside, the banks of these rivers were walled and canalized (Photo 10.3) and the water flowed over flat paving stones (Sancho 1917: 153 [1534]). Numerous bridges crossed the two rivers (Figure 10.1), and offerings were made each year at their confluence (Bauer 1998: 118–119). These features of Cuzco remained visible until the 1930s, when the rivers were covered over to create modern streets.

One of the most imposing features of Inca Cuzco was the great plaza that stood near its center (Hyslop 1990: 37). The plaza, spanning both sides of the Saphy River, was composed of two sacred spaces. The area to the west of the river was called Cusipata,[15] and the area to the east was referred to as Haucaypata.[16] These two areas played distinctly different roles within the life of the city.[17]

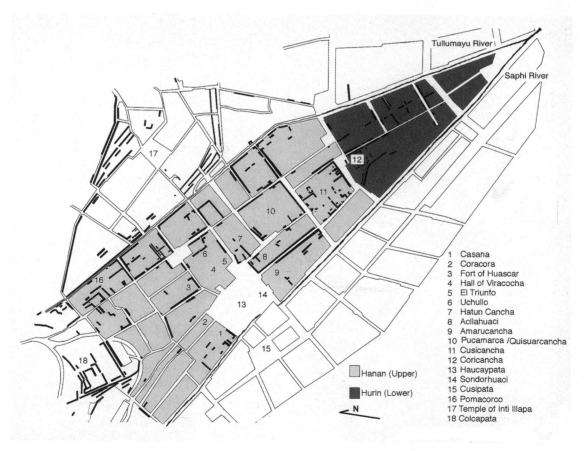

1 Casana
2 Coracora
3 Fort of Huascar
4 Hall of Viracocha
5 El Triunfo
6 Uchullo
7 Hatun Cancha
8 Acllahuaci
9 Amarucancha
10 Pucamarca /Quisuarcancha
11 Cusicancha
12 Coricancha
13 Haucaypata
14 Sondorhuaci
15 Cusipata
16 Pomacorco
17 Temple of Inti Illapa
18 Colcapata

Hanan (Upper)

Hurin (Lower)

N

MAP 10.1. Map of Inca Cuzco

PHOTO 10.2. The city of Cuzco in the 1930s (Courtesy of the Latin American Library,
Tulane University; photograph by Emilio Harth-Terré)

FIGURE 10.1. Stone bridge in Cuzco (Squier 1877: 432)

THE PLAZA OF HAUCAYPATA

Haucaypata, or what is now called the Plaza de Armas, was of great importance to the Inca. Thousands of people gathered in it several times a year to attend the elaborate festivals of the city and to see the ruling Inca (Map 10.2 and Photo 10.4). These festivals included, among others, the June and December solstices as well as the August (planting) and May (harvest) celebrations for maize. At these times, the mummified remains of the previous Cuzco rulers were taken from their own palaces and set, in order of their rule, in the plaza. The palaces of these ancient kings were among the many important compounds that surrounded the plaza of Haucaypata on three sides.

Polo de Ondegardo reduced the size of Haucaypata in 1559 by approximately 30 percent as he began building the Cuzco cathedral. During this construction project, he discovered that the plaza contained a thick layer of coastal sand. This sand was of great interest to him, not only because it contained numerous offerings, but also

PHOTO 10.3. In Inca times, the rivers within Cuzco were walled and canalized. Many of these constructions lasted until the 1930s, when the rivers were covered over to create modern streets. (Courtesy of Fototeca Andina–Centro Bartolomé de Las Casas; photograph by Hermanos Cabrera, ca. 1920)

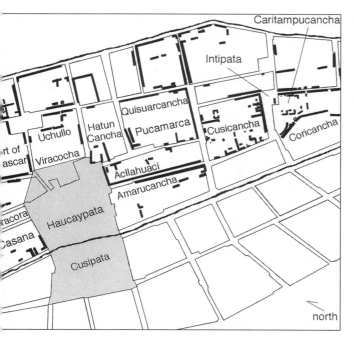

MAP 10.2. Central Cuzco in Inca times

because by extracting and reusing the sand he could reduce the cost of the cathedral construction and diminish the sanctity of the Inca plaza. His observations on the plaza are worth quoting at length:

And thus they stated that all of the plaza of Cuzco had its own earth removed from it, and it was taken to other places because it was greatly esteemed, and they covered it over with sand from the seacoast to a depth of two palms and a half, and in some places more. They planted in every part of it many gold and silver vases and tiny sheep and men of the same materials, of which a great quantity have been removed, which we have all seen. The entire plaza was of this sand when I went to govern that city, and, if it is true that that sand was brought from where they say and have in their records, it seems to me that it would be so much that the entire country as a whole had to know about it, because the plaza is

PHOTO 10.4. The Plaza de Armas in 1994. In Inca times, the entire plaza area was covered with a thick layer of sand.

large and the number of loads brought into it was countless, and the coast at the nearest point is more than 90 leagues, as I think it to be. I satisfied myself as to that, because everyone says that that type of sand does not exist short of the coast. I made all the inquiries possible, both among Indians and among Spaniards, inquiring about the reason for which it was brought, and they said that it must have been out of reverence for Tizibriacocha, [Titi Viracocha] to whom they mainly offer their sacrifices . . .

And it is thus, that, breaking the ground for the principal church of Cuzco, the sand which was found thereabouts being poor and distant, the masons said that if that of the plaza were not taken the cost would be very great, because what was found was poor and difficult to get. I thus had all of it removed, which was a great quantity, and we leveled it with other soil, which the Indians there regretted much in their opinions and would not pay poorly if

we would include in the price leaving the plaza as it had been, which, after I had learned of it, I gave it with the best will to the church, and there is no doubt but that it was worth more than 4000 *castellanos,* because it would have cost much more to bring it and would not have been profitable and with it I built four masonry bridges in the same river of the city, in which much labor was saved, and much expense because it was a great quantity, and other works which were usefully built there. And the main thing was that it took away from them the great reverence which they had for that plaza . . . (Polo de Ondegardo 1965: 118–119 [1571])[18]

Polo de Ondegardo notes that there were many miniature figurines buried in the plaza beneath the sand. They are also mentioned by Betanzos (1996: 48–49 [1557: Ch. 11]). In 1996, during a renovation of the central fountain of the Plaza de Armas, a set of three miniature llamas[19] was recovered by INC archaeologists (Fernández Carrasco, personal communication, 1998).

Near the center of Haucaypata was a standing stone called an *ushnu* (platform). *Ushnus* were built by the Inca in the plazas of many Inca installations, such as Huánuco Pampa, Vilcashuamán, and Curamba, to name only a few. Generally, *ushnus* were square, multitiered platforms, with a staircase leading up one side. They functioned as viewing platforms on which the Inca and other elites conducted important rituals. The Cuzco *ushnu* seems, however, to have taken a very different form.[20] It is described by a number of individuals as a standing stone, or pillar, covered with gold.[21] For example, Albornoz (1984: 205 [ca. 1582]) writes, "Usno was a pillar of gold where they drank to the Sun in the plaza."[22] At the foot of this stone was a basin into which liquid offerings, especially corn beer, were poured. This basin must have been impressive, since it is described by Pedro Pizarro (1921: 252 [1571]), Betanzos (1987: 48–49 [1557: Pt. 1, Ch. 11]), and Molina (1989: 74, 79 [ca. 1575]). It is widely believed that acts of ritual pouring took place in the center of most Inca plazas, and evidence of a similar basin has recently been found in an Inca plaza on the Island of the Sun (Bauer and Stanish 2001).

THE PLAZA OF CUSIPATA

Across the river from the plaza of Haucaypata was the plaza of Cusipata. Although indigenous writers, such as Guaman Poma de Ayala, continued calling the plaza area on the west side of the Saphy River "Cusipata" well into the seventeenth century, the Spaniards soon began to refer to it using the central Mexican Nahuatl word for market, "Tianquez" (see *Libro Primero del Cabildo de la Ciudad del Cuzco* 1965 [1534]; Betanzos 1996: 13 [1557: Bk. 1, Ch. 3]; Dean 1999: 225). This suggests that part of the plaza was dedicated to a market during Inca times, such as was seen in the plaza of Xauxa when the Spaniards marched through it in 1533 (Photo 10.5; Estete 1985: 144 [1534]).

Of the original Cusipata, now called the Plaza de Regocijo, only a small percentage survives (Photo 10.6

PHOTO 10.5. Northeast corner of the Plaza de Armas during a market day, ca. 1900 (Courtesy of the Maxwell Museum of Anthropology, University of New Mexico, photographer unknown, Negative 96 25 3)

PHOTO 10.6. The Plaza de Regocijo. Compare this photograph with the etching shown in Figure 10.2. (Courtesy of the Latin American Library, Tulane University; photograph by E. George Squier, 1865)

FIGURE 10.2. Squier's (1877:450) etching of the Plaza de Regocijo

and Figure 10.2). In 1548 the Municipal Council granted permission for houses and shops to be constructed along the Saphy River that separated the two open areas (Dean 1999: 30). A few years later, in 1556, when the father of the famous writer Garcilaso de la Vega (1966: 545 [1609: Pt. 1, Bk. 9, Ch. 1]) was the Chief Magistrate of Cuzco, additional buildings were placed along the river. During the Colonial Period, the Royal Treasury (now the Hotel Cuzco) was built on the eastern half of the plaza, reducing its dimensions even more.

The Casana Compound

Perhaps the most splendid palace on the central plaza of Cuzco was the Casana. Francisco Pizarro stayed in this royal compound when he first arrived in the imperial city, and he selected it as his architectural prize during the division of Cuzco among the Spaniards a little more than a year later. The Casana stood at the northwest corner of Haucaypata, beside the Saphy River (Photo 10.7). Although Garcilaso de la Vega suggests that it was the palace of Pachacuti Inca Yupanqui, a host of other writers indicate that it was built for Huayna Capac.[23] For example, Cobo (1979: 161 [1653: Bk. 11, Ch. 17]) specifically mentions that the mummy of Huayna Capac was held in the Casana.

As Niles (1999: 232) notes, the Casana consisted of a number of impressive structures encircled by a large wall. Garcilaso de la Vega (1966: 321 [1609: Pt. 1, Bk. 6, Ch. 40]) indicates that the Casana held the largest festival hall in Cuzco, one that was capable of holding some three thousand persons. He states that this was one of four great halls that still stood around the plaza when he was a boy living in Cuzco.

In many of the Inca's houses there were large halls some two hundred paces in length and fifty to sixty in breadth. They were unpartitioned and served as places of assembly for festivals and dances when the weather was too rainy to permit them to hold these in the open air. In the city of Cuzco I saw four of these halls, which were still standing when I was a

PHOTO 10.7. The northwest corner of the Plaza de Armas where the Casana once stood

boy. One was in Amarucancha, among the houses that belonged to Hernando Pizarro, where the college of the Holy Society of Jesus now is. The second was at Cassana, where my old schoolmate Juan de Cellorico now has his shops. The third was at Collcampata in the house formerly belonging to the Inca Paullu and his son Don Carlos, who was also a schoolfellow of mine. This was the smallest of the four halls, and the largest was that of Cassana, which was capable of holding three thousand persons. It seems incredible that timber could have been found to cover such vast halls. The fourth is that which now serves as the cathedral church. (Garcilaso de la Vega 1966: 320–321 [1609: Pt. 1, Bk. 6, Ch. 4])[24]

Later in his chronicle, Garcilaso de la Vega provides an even more detailed account of the great hall in the Casana. He states that it was large enough to hold a jousting match and that he witnessed both its brief use as a convent (around AD 1555) and its final destruction as shops were built on the plaza.

The other royal palace, to the west of Coracora, was called Cassana, "something to freeze." The name was applied to it out of wonder, implying that the buildings in it were so large and splendid that anyone who gazed on them attentively would be frozen with astonishment. . . . I saw in my time a great part of the walls of the building called Cassana, which were of finely worked masonry, showing that it had been a royal dwelling, as also a splendid hall which the Incas used for festivals and dances in rainy weather. It was so large that sixty mounted men could easily joust with canes in it.

I saw the convent to St. Francis established in this hall, for it was moved from the ward of Totocachi, where it had formerly been, owing to the great distance of the latter from the houses of the Spaniards. A large section of the hall, big enough to hold many people, was set apart as a church; then there were the cells, the dormitory and the refectory and remaining dependencies of the convent, and if the inside had not been roofed, a cloister could have been made too. The hall and all the necessary space was presented to the friars by Juan de Pancorvo, one of the first con-

querors, to whom the royal mansion fell in the distribution of the houses.[25] Many other Spaniards had shares in them, but Juan de Pancorvo bought them all at the very first, when they were given away for a song. . . . I also saw the hall destroyed, and the modern shops with doorways for merchants and craftsmen built in the ward of Cassana. (Garcilaso de la Vega 1966: 425–426 [1609: Pt. 1, Bk. 7, Ch. 10])[26]

Pedro Pizarro offers additional information on the great hall within Casana as he describes the seizure of Cuzco from Hernando Pizarro by Almagro in April of 1537:

Hernando Pizarro had with him some friends in a galpón[27] where he was living, a very large one with an entrance at one end of the room from which could be seen the whole interior, for the doorway is so wide that it extends from one wall to the other, and it is open up to the roof. These Indians have these galpones for their orgies. They have others with the ends closed up and provided with many doors in the middle or to one side. These galpones are very large, without any partitions, being instead open and clear. While Hernando Pizarro was in this galpón, in the midst of the houses where he lived . . . Almagro and his men, arrived at this door with the intention of taking him prisoner . . . and seeing that Hernando Pizarro did not intend to surrender, he ordered that [the roof of] this galpón where Hernando Pizarro was, be set on fire, for it was of straw, and until it began to fall in flames, never would Hernando Pizarro have wished to give himself up. (Pedro Pizarro 1921: 353–354 [1571])[28]

This passage indicates that the assembly hall in the Casana had a large doorway at one end.[29] Guaman Poma de Ayala (1980: 303 [1615: 331 (332)]) depicts such a hall on the left-hand side of his illustration of royal Inca houses (Figure 10.3). He labels it as Cuyus Mango and shows a hunchbacked individual guarding the entrance. Given the form of the hall, a long rectangle with a large entrance at one end, it is easy to understand why the Franciscans would select it as a temporary location for their church.

329

FIGURE 10.3. Illustration of royal Inca houses by Guaman Poma de Ayala (1980: 303 [1615: 331 (332)]). The caption reads: "Royal palaces [,] House of the Inca [called] Cusimanco." Below the caption are a variety of structures. In the background is a series of buildings with corbel arches labeled "Storehouses (*churacona uaci*)," midframe is a structure with a pointed roof labeled "Canopy House (*carpa uaci*)" and a ∪-shaped structure labeled "Curved House (*quenco uaci*)." To the left is a large assembly hall with a single entrance at one end labeled "Cuyus Mango." In the doorway sits a hunchbacked guard (*cumo, punco camayoc*). In the foreground, a round tower (*suntor uaci*) is also shown.

Besides containing a great hall, the Casana also featured two round towers, which stood on either side of the main entrance at the interior corners of a courtyard. In the early years of the Spanish occupation of the city, these towers were favored places for imprisoning leaders. For example, Almagro placed Hernando, Gonzalo, and Pedro Pizarro in the towers during the brief period in 1537 that he controlled Cuzco. In turn, Hernando Pizarro locked Almagro in one of the towers once he had regained control of the city (Pedro Pizarro 1921: 359, 366, 369, 382 [1571]).

It is within the contexts of these descriptions of alternating Spaniards' imprisonments that we gain our most detailed information on the towers.[30] For example, Pedro Pizarro, who himself was held in one of the towers, describes the capture of Hernando Pizarro by Almagro:

. . . where they [Almagro's men] kept him [Hernando Pizarro] some days until a round tower was made ready in Caxana, houses where the Marquis Don Francisco Pizarro was and where Hernando Pizarro was when they took him prisoner. Then, having fortified this tower by closing up the windows and door, leaving a small hole through which a man could crawl, they put him there, walled up, as I say. This Caxana had two round towers, one on one side of the door and the other upon the other side, I mean almost at the corners of this square. These towers were of well made masonry and very strong. They were round, covered with straw very strangely placed thus. The straw eaves stood out beyond the wall more than a *braza,* so that the shelter of this eave favored the horsemen around the tower when it rained. The houses and rooms belonged to Guaina Capac.
The Indians burned [the roofs of] these towers when they laid siege [to Cuzco] with burning arrows or stones. So thick was the thatch that it took eight days or more for it to be entirely burned, or, I should say, before the wooden framework fell. They had closed these towers [at the top] with thick beams of wood with earth above like *azoteas* [ornamental tiles]. In one of these they held Hernando Pizarro. (Pedro Pizarro 1921: 355–356 [1571])[31]

Circular towers are rare features of Inca architecture. Though a round tower is known to have existed in Sacsayhuaman, and there may have been another round tower on the southern side of the Haucaypata plaza in central Cuzco, there do not seem to have been similar structures in Inca provincial centers. However, more recent constructions can provide us with a general idea of what the Casana towers might have looked like. Perhaps the best-known example is that of the Sondorhuaci recorded by Squier in the town of Azángaro in the Lake Titicaca Basin. This was a large multistory tower built in an interior corner of a large courtyard, like those described

PHOTO 10.8. The circular tower (Sondorhuaci) in the town of Azángaro in the Lake Titicaca Basin in 1865 (Courtesy of the Latin American Library, Tulane University; photograph by E. George Squier)

FIGURE 10.5. Anonymous field sketch of Sondorhuaci, n.d. (Denver Art Museum Collection: Gift of Fred A. Rosenstock, 1984.203.8; © Denver Art Museum 2004)

FIGURE 10.4. The Sondorhuaci in Azángaro (Squier 1877: 394). Compare this etching with Photo 10.8.

FIGURE 10.6. Anonymous field sketch of the interior ceiling of the Sondorhuaci, n.d. (Denver Art Museum Collection: Gift of Fred A. Rosenstock, 1984.203.8; © Denver Art Museum 2004)

in the Casana. Squier's photograph and etching of the structure (Photo 10.8 and Figure 10.4) show the outside of the tower. An anonymous artist, who was most likely traveling with Squier, also produced two watercolors of the Sondorhuaci, one of the exterior (Figure 10.5) and one of the interior (Figure 10.6).[32] The latter is especially dramatic, showing the high ceiling and the interior framework of the thickly thatched roof. Unfortunately, the building no longer exists.

In addition to its great hall and its two round towers, the entrance to the Casana also commanded the attention of the Spaniards. Estete (1924: 45 [1534]) notes:

> The plaza of the city was almost square, not large nor small. The house of Atahualpa (*sic* Huayna Capac) that is in it had two fine towers [and] a fine entranceway richly faced with pieces of silver and other metals.[33] (Translation by author)

Sancho, who was in Cuzco at the same time as Estete, was equally impressed with the entrance to the Casana, although he describes it differently:

> The plaza is rectangular, and the greater part of it is flat and paved with small stones. Around the plaza are four houses of noblemen, who are the chief men of the city; [the houses] are of stone, painted and carved, and the best of them is the house of Huayna Capac, a former chief, and the door of it is of marble [colored] white and red and of other colors; and there are other very sightly buildings with flat roofs. (Sancho 1917: 154 [1534])[34]

The entrance to the Casana must have been very distinct, since Cobo includes it as a shrine within the *ceque* system. He also notes that the following shrine within the *ceque* system was a "lake" called Ticcicocha that was within the compound.

> [Ch-6:4] The fourth *guaca* had the name of Guayra and was in the doorway of Cajana. At it sacrifice was made to the wind so that it would not do damage, and a pit had been made there in which the sacrifices were buried.
> [Ch-6:5] The fifth *guaca* was the palace of

Guayna Capac named Cajana, within which was a lake named Ticcicocha which was an important shrine and at which great sacrifices were made (Cobo 1990: 58 [1653: Bk. 13, Ch. 13])[35]

Today, true to Garcilaso de la Vega's description, the punctured walls of the Casana still stand on the northwest corner of the Plaza de Armas and serve as entrances to restaurants and shops (Photo 10.9).

PHOTO 10.9. The punctured walls of the Casana still stand on the northwest corner of the Plaza de Armas and serve as entrances to restaurants and shops.

The Coracora Compound

A lesser-known compound called the Coracora was located beside the Casana. It was in this building that the first three Spaniards to see Cuzco stayed during their short time in the imperial capital (Betanzos 1996: 269 [1557: Ch. 25]). The Coracora is included in the Cuzco *ceque* system, where it is associated with Pachacuti Inca Yupanqui:[36]

[Ch-5:5] The fifth *guaca* was a *buhio* [hut] named Coracora, in which Inca Yupanqui used to sleep, which is where the *cabildo* [municipal council] houses are now. This said Inca ordered worship of that place and burning of clothing and sheep in it, and so it was done. (Cobo 1990: 57 [1654: Bk. 13, Ch. 13])[37]

We know the approximate location of the Coracora on the plaza and its destruction date (1548) through the writings of Garcilaso de la Vega and the *Libro Primero del Cabildo* . . . (1965 [1534]). In the latter, we learn that Gonzalo Pizarro was given a lot on the plaza between that of Francisco Pizarro (the Casana) and the "fort of Huascar."[38] Garcilaso de la Vega confirms that the Casana and the Coracora stood side by side on the plaza and that the Coracora was granted to Gonzalo Pizarro. Garcilaso de la Vega, however, associates the Coracora with Inca Roca, rather than Pachacuti Inca Yupanqui:

Moving southward from the ward of the schools, we come to two others containing two royal palaces giving on to the main square. They filled the whole side of the square: one of them, to the east of the other, was called Coracora, "the pastures," for the place used to be pasture and the square in front of it was a swamp or marsh until the Incas had it transformed to its present state. Cieza de León confirms this in his ch. xcii. In this pasture King Inca Roca established his royal palace to favor and assist the schools, where he often went to hear the masters. I saw nothing of the house called Coracora, for it had been razed by my time. When the city was divided among the Spaniards it fell to Gonzalo Pizarro, the brother of the marquis Don Francisco Pizarro. He

was one of its conquerors. I knew this gentleman in Cuzco after the battle of Huarina [October 21, 1547] and before that of Sacsahuana [Jaquijahuana, April 9, 1548], and he treated me as if I were his own son. I was then about eight or nine. (Garcilaso de la Vega 1966: 425 [1609: Pt. 1, Bk. 7, Ch. 10])[39]

Elsewhere, Garcilaso de la Vega states that he witnessed the demolition of the Coracora after Gonzalo Pizarro's failed revolt against the king of Spain. The revolt ended with Gonzalo's defeat at Jaquijahuana and his immediate execution:

They sentenced Pizarro to be beheaded as a traitor; his houses in Cuzco were pulled down and the site sown with salt, and a stone pillar was erected with an inscription reading: "This is the house of the traitor Gonzalo Pizarro," etc.

I saw all this carried out. The houses were those granted to him in the allocations of Cuzco, when he and his brothers conquered the city. The place is called Coracora, or "meadow" in the Indian tongue. (Garcilaso de la Vega 1966: 1202 [1609: Pt. 2, Bk. 5, Ch. 39])[40]

Zárate (1995: 374 [1555]) also notes the destruction of Gonzalo's houses in Cuzco and the inscription that was then placed on the salted land.[41] Because of this Carthaginian act, nothing remains of the Coracora today.

East Side of the Plaza

When the Spaniards arrived in Cuzco, there were several important structures on the east side of the plaza. At the northeast corner were a series of steep terraces on which various Spaniards made their homes (*Libro Primero del Cabildo* . . . 1965 [1534]). Above them was the palace of Huascar for which, unfortunately, we have no detailed information. The palace must have been impressive, since Diego de Almagro, second in command after Francisco Pizarro, took it as his prize during the establishment of Spanish Cuzco. It is possible that this palace was located on the spot where the Casa de la Admiral (now the Archaeological Museum) was later founded.

A structure near the southeast corner of the plaza was

PHOTO 10.10. After the siege, a permanent chapel called "El Triunfo" (The Triumph) was constructed on the southeast corner of the plaza. (Courtesy of Fototeca Andina–Centro Bartolomé de Las Casas; photograph by Miguel Chani, ca. 1920)

selected by Pizarro to serve as a temporary church. Some writers suggest that this location was selected for the church following the siege of Cuzco, during which it was spared from burning by the divine intervention of either Santiago or the Virgin Mary. The *Libro Primero del Cabildo . . .* (1965: 33 [1534]) indicates, however, that the spot had already been selected by Pizarro as the site of the church before the fighting between the Spaniards and the local

population began. After the siege, a permanent chapel called El Triunfo (The Triumph),[42] which still stands today, was constructed on this location (Photo 10.10).

In the area near the church was another structure for which we have little information. The *Libro Primero del Cabildo . . .* (1965 [1534]) indicates that this building was called Uchullo and that it was granted to the first Chief Magistrate of Cuzco, Beltrán de Castro. From Murúa

PHOTO 10.11. The Cuzco cathedral was built on the location of one of the great halls that bordered the central plaza of Cuzco.

(1962: 77 [ca. 1615: Vol. 1, Ch. 26]), we learn that the Uchullo was the palace of Huayna Capac before the construction of the Casana. There appear to be no other references to this once important building.

Near the center of the east side of the plaza stood a large hall. Almagro and numerous other Spaniards were housed in this hall when they first entered Cuzco (Pedro Pizarro 1921: 250 [1571]), and it later became the site of the first municipal council house. In the *Libro Primero del Cabildo* . . . (1965: 33 [1534]) we read, "Chosen for the municipal council house and foundry is the large hall that is on the terrace above the plaza."[43] The hall was destroyed in 1559 when the construction of the Cuzco cathedral was begun under the direction of Polo de Ondegardo. To gain additional space for the cathedral, the front half of it was built extending out into the plaza. It was during this process that Polo de Ondegardo discovered that the plaza was covered with a layer of sand.

Blas Valera (1950: 144 [ca. 1585]) states that the large hall on the east side of the plaza was a temple for the Creator god, Titi Viracocha. Several other sources, however, indicate that the temple of Titi Viracocha was located farther to the south, in the area of Pucamarca.[44] Garcilaso de la Vega helps to resolve the confusion by indicating that the hall was the palace of Viracocha Inca

(the eighth Inca), a name that could have been confused by Blas Valera with Titi Viracocha. When describing the siege of Cuzco, Garcilaso de la Vega writes:

> The bravest Indians, who had been picked to burn the house of Inca Viracocha where the Spaniards were lodged, attacked it vigorously and set fire to it from a distance with their incendiary arrows: it was burnt down and not a trace of it remains. The great hall inside it, where the cathedral now is, and where the Christians then had a chapel to hear mass, was saved by our Lord from the flames. . . . (Garcilaso de la Vega 1966: 799 [1609: Pt. 2, Bk. 2, Ch. 24])[45]

Given the available historical data, it seems likely that the palace of Inca Viracocha stood on the east side of the plaza. This compound was partially burned during the siege of Cuzco and was completely pulled down by Polo de Ondegardo with the construction of the Cuzco cathedral (Photo 10.11).[46]

The Amarucancha Compound

On the southwest corner of the plaza, near the Saphy River, stood the Amarucancha (Enclosure of the Serpent).

Several writers suggest that Huascar built this complex during his short period of rule (ca. 1528–1532).[47] If this is the case, then the Amarucancha was the last royal palace to be constructed in the imperial city. The structure must have been of considerable importance, because it was awarded to Hernando de Soto, one of the highest-ranking members of Pizarro's expedition, during the division of central Cuzco. In this respect, it is worth noting that in the *Libro Primero del Cabildo . . .* (1965: 35 [1534]) we find that a soldier named Pedro de Ulloa was granted a lot adjacent to where the *palla* (noblewoman) of Hernando de Soto was staying.[48] This *palla* was Huascar's daughter, Cori Cuillor (Golden Star), with whom de Soto would have a daughter named Leonor de Soto.

Despite the fact that much of the Amarucancha survived the fires of the siege, we know little about this complex. Pedro Pizarro (1921: 250–251 [1571]) reports that it was where de Soto first stayed when he arrived in Cuzco, and at that time some of its rooms were used for the ancient kings. Garcilaso de la Vega provides a more detailed description of the complex and indicates that there was a round tower in front of it:

At the end of the square to its south, there were two other royal houses, one that was near the stream, and opposite it, called Amarucancha, "ward of the great snakes." It faced Cassana and was the palace of Huaina Capac; it now belongs to the holy Society of Jesus.[49] I remember seeing still a great hall, though not so large as that of Cassana. I also saw a very fine round tower which stood in the square before the house. Elsewhere we shall speak of this tower, which was the first lodging of the Spaniards in the city, and for this reason, apart from its great beauty, it would have been well if the conquerors had preserved it. I saw no other remains of this palace: all the rest was razed. In the first division the main part of this palace, giving on to the square, fell to Hernando Pizarro, the brother of the marquis Don Francisco Pizarro, who was also one of the first conquerors of the city. I saw this gentleman in the court of Madrid in 1562. Another part fell to Mancio Serra de Leguiçamo,[50] one of the first conquerors.[51] A further part was awarded to Antonio Altamirano, who had two houses when I knew him: he must have bought one of them.[52] A further part was set aside as the prison for Spaniards. Still another part was given to Alonso Mazuela, one of the first conquerors, and later passed to Martín Dolmos. Other sections fell to others whom I do not recall. (Garcilaso de la Vega 1966: 426–427 [1609: Pt. 1, Bk. 7, Ch. 10])[53]

Garcilaso de la Vega commits an understandable mistake in suggesting that the Amarucancha was awarded to Hernando Pizarro, and not to Hernando de Soto, during the founding of Spanish Cuzco. Hernando Pizarro did not receive any land when central Cuzco was divided up by the Spaniards because he was then in route to Spain to present King Charles the crown's portion of Atahualpa's ransom. De Soto's holdings at Amarucancha were, however, later taken by Hernando Pizarro in 1536 after de Soto had left Peru and Hernando Pizarro had returned to take charge of Cuzco. The legality of this seizure became the focus of a suit filed by his daughter, Leonor de Soto, against Hernando Pizarro (see below).

Garcilaso de la Vega is correct in stating that various Spaniards received land in the Amarucancha during the founding of Spanish Cuzco. His assertion that Antonio Altamirano settled in this part of Cuzco is supported by the *Libro Primero del Cabildo . . .* (1965 [1534]).[54] Elsewhere in his chronicle, Garcilaso de la Vega provides two additional passages that contain information on the Amarucancha and Antonio Altamirano. When discussing the idolatry of the Inca, he states that the Inca worshiped objects and locations that had been struck by lighting. In this context, Garcilaso de la Vega notes:

All this I saw in Cuzco, for in the royal house that had belonged to the Inca Huaina Cápac (*sic* Huascar), in the part of it that fell to Antonio Altamirano when the city was divided among the conquerors, there was a room where a thunderbolt had fallen in the days of Huaina Cápac. The Indians shut the doors with stone and mud and took it as an ill omen upon their king, . . . I beheld the closed room. The Spaniards later rebuilt it, and within three years another bolt struck the same room and burnt it all up. (Garcilaso de la Vega 1966: 69 [1609: Pt. 1, Bk. 2, Ch. 1])[55]

PHOTO 10.12. With the construction of the Jesuit church, most of the Amarucancha was destroyed.

Garcilaso de la Vega also mentions that a hoard of gold and silver objects were accidentally found in the Amarucancha:

> When the houses in the city were shared out among the Spaniards, it happened that in one of them, a royal palace called Amarucancha which fell to Antonio Altamirano, a horseman was galloping in the yard, when his horse sank its foot into a hole, which had not previously been there. When they went to look at the hole to see if it was the bed of some former stream passing under the house, they found that it was the mouth of a golden jar holding eight or nine arrobas. These jars are made in various sizes by the Indians to serve as vats for brewing their drink. It was accompanied by many silver and gold vessels to a value of over 80,000 ducats. (Garcilaso de la Vega 1966: 749 [1609: Pt. 2, Bk. 2, Ch. 7])[56]

Hernando Pizarro still held de Soto's original property at Amarucancha when Pizarro was released from prison in Spain in 1561. It was at this time that Garcilaso de la Vega met him. Knowing that he would not be returning to Peru, Hernando Pizarro began selling many of his holdings in Peru. In 1572, de Soto's daughter, Leonor de Soto, unsuccessfully sued to recover her father's portion of the palace that she believed to have been seized illegally (Hemming 1970: 564, 571). In the end, Hernando Pizarro sold his portion of Amarucancha to the Jesuits. With the construction of the Jesuit church, the great hall and all of the other interior buildings of Amarucancha were destroyed (Photo 10.12). Today, only parts of its massive enclosure walls have survived (Photo 10.13).

The Sondorhuaci Tower

Garcilaso de la Vega states that there was a tower in front of the Amarucancha. Although no other writer mentions this tower, Garcilaso de la Vega provides a detailed description of it:

> There was a very fine round tower, standing alone before the entrance to the house [Amarucancha]. I saw it in my time, and its walls were about four times the

height of a man; but its roof, made of excellent timber they used for their royal palaces, was so high that I might say without exaggeration that it equaled any tower I have seen in Spain in height, with the exception of the one at Seville. Its roof was rounded like the walls, and above it, in place of a weathervane—for the Indians did not observe the wind—it had a very tall and thick pole that enhanced its height and beauty. It was more than sixty feet in height inside, and was known as *sunturhuasi,* "excellent house or room." There was no other building touching it. In my time it was pulled down so as to clear the square, as it now is; the tower projected into it, though the appearance of the square was not spoiled by having the building on one side, especially as it took up very little of its space. The colossal building of the Holy Society of Jesus now stands on the site, as we have already remarked. (Garcilaso de la Vega 1966: 701 [1609: Pt. 2, Bk. 1, Ch. 32])[57]

This account of the Sondorhuaci is interesting for a number of reasons. As noted in the discussion of the Casana, round buildings are rare features in Inca architecture. Guaman Poma de Ayala (1980: 302, 303 [1615: 329 (330), 331 (332)]), however, provides a drawing of a "Suntor Uaci" to illustrate his list of royal palaces of the Inca (see Figure 10.3). In the drawing, the round tower appears to be standing in a large plaza. Since Garcilaso de la Vega states that the Cuzco tower was pulled down before he left Cuzco in 1560, it is possible that Guaman Poma de Ayala saw it or was told about it.[58] On the other hand, if this structure was as impressive as Garcilaso de la Vega suggests, one must wonder why it is not mentioned by other writers, and question if there is not some confusion between the Sondorhuaci and the two towers of the Casana. Nevertheless, since Garcilaso de la Vega does provide such a clear and detailed eyewitness account of the building, it is possible that such a structure did exist in Inca Cuzco.[59]

PHOTO 10.13. Today, only a few sections of the massive enclosure walls of the Amarucancha have survived.

The Acllahuaci Compound

A paved street, now called Loreto, separated the Amarucancha from the next compound on the plaza, the Acllahuaci (House of Chosen [Women]).[60] It was within this complex that the *mamaconas,* women who were selected at a young age to serve the state, lived. Garcilaso de la Vega provides the most detailed description of the Acllahuaci complex. He indicates that the street that separates this compound from the Amarucancha was called the "Street of the Sun"[61] and that Francisco Mejía was given the area of the Acllahuaci that bordered the plaza:

> East of Amarucancha across the Street of the Sun is the suburb called Acllahuasi, "the house of the chosen virgins," where stood the convent of the maidens dedicated to the Sun, . . . The part of the building that still existed in my time was divided between Francisco Mejía[62]—who was given the part giving onto the square, which also is filled with merchant shops—Pedro del Barco, Licentiate de la Gama, and others whose names I do not remember. (Garcilaso de la Vega 1966: 427 [1609: Pt. 1, Bk. 7, Ch. 10])[63]

Elsewhere Garcilaso de la Vega describes the boundaries of the Acllahuaci, and he provides hints of what was once contained within its great walls:

> A quarter of the city of Cuzco was called Acllahuasi, "house of the chosen women." The quarter is between two streets that run from the main square to the convent of St. Dominic, which used to be the house of the Sun. One of those streets goes out of the corner of the square to the left of the cathedral and runs north and south. When I left Cuzco in 1560 this was the main shopping street. The other leaves the middle of the square, where the prison was, and runs parallel towards the same Dominican convent. The front of the house faced the square between these two streets, and its back gave onto a street running across them east and west, so that it occupied an island site between the square and these three streets. Between it and the temple of the Sun there was a large block of houses and a big square

> which is in front of the temple. (Garcilaso de la Vega 1966: 195 [1609: Pt. 1, Bk. 4, Ch. 1])[64]

A few pages later, Garcilaso de la Vega provides additional details concerning the interior of the Acllahuaci. He emphasizes the fact that the complex contained a large number of rooms:

> I saw this house intact, for only its quarter and that of the temple of the Sun, and four other buildings that had been royal palaces of the Incas were respected by the Indians in their general rebellion against the Spaniards. Because they had been the house of the Sun, their god, and of his women, and of their kings, they did not burn them down as they burnt the rest of the city. Among other notable features of this building there was a narrow passage wide enough for two persons that ran the whole length of the building. The passage had many cells on either side which were used as offices where women worked. At each door were trusted portresses, and in the last apartment at the end of the passage where no one entered were the women of the Sun. The house had a main door as convents do in Spain, but it was only opened to admit the queen or to receive women who were going to be nuns. . . . In the division the Spaniards made of the royal houses of Cuzco to supply themselves with dwellings, half of this convent fell to Pedro del Barco, whom we shall mention later. This was the part of the offices. The other half went to Licentiate de la Gama, whom I met as a child, and after passed to Diego Ortiz de Guzmán, a gentleman from Seville whom I knew. He was still alive when I came to Spain. (Garcilaso de la Vega 1966: 197 [1609: Pt. 1, Bk. 4, Ch. 2])[65]

While describing the burning of the city during Manco Capac's siege, Garcilaso de la Vega repeats the claim that there were numerous structures within the Acllahuaci as well as four alleyways:

> They shot these [flaming arrows] at all the houses in the city in general without respect for the royal palaces, but only sparing the house and temple of the

Sun and all the apartments it contained, and the house of the chosen virgins, and the workshops in the four streets inside the house. (Garcilaso de la Vega 1966: 798 [1609: Pt. 2, Bk. 2, Ch. 24])[66]

He also recalls an elaborate set of storage bins for maize that were contained in the Acllahuaci:

The bins are called *pirua.* They are made of trodden clay mixed with plenty of straw. In Inca times they were very skillfully constructed. Their size varied in proportion to the height of the walls of the buildings in which they were placed. They were narrow, square, and of one piece, and had to be made with moulds of different sizes. They were of various capacities, some bigger than others, some of thirty *fanegas,* or fifty, one hundred or two hundred, more or less as they were required. Each size of bin was kept in a special building, which it had been made to fit. They were placed against the four walls, and also in the middle of the building. An alley was left between the rows of bins so that they could be emptied and filled in turn. Once erected they were not moved. In order to empty a bin little holes about an *ochava* in size were made in the front of it. They were made so that it was possible to tell how many fanegas had been taken out and how many were left without measuring them. In this way it could easily be reckoned from the size of the bins how much maize there was in each barn and each granary, and the small holes showed what had been extracted and what remained in each bin. I have seen some of these bins which survived from Inca times, and they were some of the first, since they were in the house of the chosen virgins, the wives of the Sun, and were made for the use of these women. When I saw them, the house belonged to the children of Pedro del Barco, who were schoolfellows of mine. (Garcilaso de la Vega 1966: 249 [1609: Pt. 1, Bk. 5, Ch. 5])[67]

It is not surprising that the Acllahuaci contained such a granary, since one of the principal tasks of the Chosen Women was to make enormous amounts of *chicha* for festivals.

Garcilaso de la Vega mentions that Pedro del Barco,[68] who was one of the founders of Spanish Cuzco, owned part of the Acllahuaci.[69] He states this several times and indicates that a treasure was found in Barco's house lot by the next owner:

And in the part of the house of the chosen women which fell to Pedro del Barco and was later owned by an apothecary, one Hernando de Segovia whom I knew, this Segovia[70] happened to dig part of a foundation and found a treasure of 72,000 ducats. (Garcilaso de la Vega 1966: 749 [1609: Pt. 2, Bk. 2, Ch. 7])[71]

Part of the Acllahuaci was destroyed during the siege of Cuzco, and the rest was largely leveled in 1605 when Dominican nuns founded the convent of Santa Catalina (Burns 1999).[72] Intriguingly, this convent, the second to be built in the city, was constructed near to, and perhaps even over, part of the former Acllahuaci. Cobo, who was in Cuzco while Santa Catalina was being built, describes the destruction of the Inca walls within this area in his account of Inca stone masonry:

[One example] is an entire section of a wall that still remains in the city of Cuzco, in the Convent of Santa Catalina. These walls were not made vertical, but slightly inclined inward. The stones are perfectly squared, but in such a way that they come to have the same shape and workmanship as a stone for a ring of the sort that jewelers call "faceted." The stones have two sets of faces and corners, so that a groove is formed between the lesser faces of the fitted stones, separating the faces in relief. Another skillfully made feature of this work is that all of the stones are not of the same size, but the stones of each course are uniform in size, and the stones are progressively smaller as they get higher. Thus the stones of the second course are smaller than those of the first, and the stones of the third course are also smaller than those of the second, and in this way the size of the stones diminishes proportionately as the wall becomes higher. Thus the above-mentioned wall of the structure, which remains standing to this day, has a lower course of ashlar blocks of more than one cubit in diameter, while the stones of the upper course are the size of *azulejos* [ornamental tile]. This wall is two or three *estados* high. It is the most skillfully made of all the Inca structures that I have seen. We said that the Indians did not use mortar in these buildings, that all of them were made of dry stone. . . . But this does not mean that the stones were not joined together on the inside with some type of mortar; in fact it was used to fill up space and made the stones fit. What they put in the empty space was a certain type of sticky, red clay that they call *llanca,* which is quite abundant in the whole Cuzco region. I was able to see this for myself while watching as part of that wall of the Convent of Santa Catalina was being torn down for the construction of the church that is there now. (Cobo 1990: 228–229 [1653: Bk. 14, Ch. 12])[73]

The west side of the Acllahuaci is still well preserved and can be seen along Loreto Street (formerly called the Street of the Sun; Photo 10.14). The north side, which faces the plaza and was once owned by Mejía, remains, but it has been severely altered by the creation of shops (Photo 10.15). The east side is poorly preserved, although the magnificent exterior corner described by Cobo can be seen beside Santa Catalina (Photos 10.16 and 10.17, Figure 10.7). Almost nothing has survived of the numerous rooms and buildings that once filled the compound. Today only a few small segments of Inca walls remain within the convent itself.

The Hatuncancha Compound

The earliest chroniclers of Cuzco wrote of a large enclosed compound near the southwest corner of the plaza called

PHOTO 10.14. The Street of the Sun, now called Loreto, divided the Acllahuaci (right) from the Amarucancha (left). It is the best-preserved Inca street in Cuzco.

PHOTO 10.15. The plaza side of the Acllahuaci remains, but it has been severely altered by the creation of shops.

PHOTO 10.16. The southeast corner of the Acllahuaci has long held visitors' attention. It is described in detail by Cobo and centuries later was photographed by Squier. (Courtesy of the Latin American Library, Tulane University; photograph by E. George Squier, 1865)

PHOTO 10.17. The southeast corner of the Acllahuaci today

FIGURE 10.7. The southeast corner of the Acllahuaci (Squier 1877: 446). Compare this etching to Photo 10.16.

the Hatuncancha (Great Enclosure) that had a single large entrance. Pedro Pizarro indicates that the Hatuncancha was beside the Acllahuaci, and he states that a number of Spaniards lodged in it when they first entered the imperial city:

And the rest of the soldiers were quartered in a large galpón which was near the plaza, and in Atun Cancha which was a huge enclosed area, with but one entrance. On the plaza side this enclosure was [a house of] mamaconas, and there were in it many rooms. In these [buildings] which I mention were lodged all the Spaniards. (Pedro Pizarro 1921: 250 [1571])[74]

The substantial size of this compound is also highlighted in Pedro Pizarro's account of the siege of Cuzco:

Hernando Pizarro and his captains assembled many times to discuss what they should do, and some said that we ought to desert the town and leave it in flight; others said that we ought to establish ourselves in Hatuncancha, which was a great enclosure where we might all be, and which, as I have already said, had but one doorway and a very high wall of stone masonry. (Pedro Pizarro 1921: 306–307 [1571])[75]

Estete (1924: 45 [ca. 1535]) also mentions the complex and emphasizes the fact that the Hatuncancha was near to, and perhaps even included, the Acllahuaci with its *mamacona*:

In the plaza there was a door where there was a monastery that was called Atuncancha, totally enclosed by a very beautiful stone wall, within which there were a little more than a hundred houses, where resided the priests and ministers of the temple and the women who lived in chastity, according to their religion, who were called by name *mamaconas,* of which there were a great many.[76] (Translation by author)

Garcilaso de la Vega provides additional information on the area of the Hatuncancha. He indicates that it was across the street from the cathedral and that Diego Maldonado owned much of it.[77] Garcilaso de la Vega also

suggests that the Hatuncancha contained the palace of Pachacuti Inca Yupanqui:

To the south of the cathedral, and across the street, stand the main shops of the wealthier merchants. . . . Behind the chief shops are the houses that used to belong to Diego Maldonado, called "the rich," for he was wealthier than anyone else in Peru: he was one of the first conquerors. In Inca times the place was called Hatuncancha, "big ward." It had been the site of the palace of one of the kings called Inca Yupanqui. (Garcilaso de la Vega 1966: 424 [1609: Pt. 1, Bk. 7, Ch. 9])[78]

This reference to the house of Diego Maldonado as being within the confines of the Hatuncancha is important, because Maldonado's house is used as a landmark by Cobo as he describes the former locations of various shrines in Inca Cuzco. For example, Cobo indicates that there were two sacred springs, one inside and one outside Maldonado's house:

[Ch-3:2] The second *guaca* was called Canchapacha. It was a fountain which was in the street of Diego Maldonado, to which they made sacrifice on account of certain stories that the Indians tell.
[Ch-3:3] The third *guaca* was another fountain named Ticicocha, which is inside the house that belonged to the said Diego Maldonado. This fountain belonged to the *coya* or queen, Mama Ocllo.[79] In it were made very great and ordinary sacrifices, especially when they wanted to ask something of the said Mama Ocllo, who was the most venerated woman there was among these Indians. (Cobo 1990: 55 [1653: Bk. 13, Ch. 13])[80]

A nearby shrine related to sleep was also worshiped by the Inca. Cobo writes:

[Ch-4:2] The second *guaca* was named Puñui; it was in a small flat place next to the house of Diego Maldonado. It was a very solemn shrine because it was held to be the cause of sleep; they offered every kind of sacrifice to it. They went to it with two petitions, one to pray for those who were unable to

PHOTO 10.18. The small plaza area in front of Santa Catalina may have been
a shrine of the Cuzco *ceque* system during Inca times.

sleep, and the other that they might not die in their
sleep. (Cobo 1990: 56 [1653: Bk. 13, Ch. 13])[81]

This flat place may be the small plaza that separated the
Hatuncancha, the Acllahuaci, and the Pucamarca and is
now called the Plaza of Santa Catalina (Photo 10.18).

Polo de Ondegardo also provides information on what
seems to have been the discovery of a shaft tomb within
the house of Maldonado.

Similarly they relate that the Inca would order, when
some woman whom he had loved greatly would die in
Cuzco, that earth from her homeland be brought for
the burial. I also satisfied myself that this was the case,
because they declared that in the houses of Captain
Diego Maldonado there was a grave made of masonry
below the ground, where a wife of the Inca, one of the
Yungas, was buried, which we found to be quite deep
and all worked of three courses of very fine masonry
and about twelve feet square, and they asserted that

that sand was from the sea coast, and, when the sand
was removed, there was found below only a corpse in
a certain hollow which there was at one side of the
sepulcher, which seems to prove what had been said,
. . . (Polo de Ondegardo 1965: 121 [1571])[82]

The unnamed noblewoman in the shaft tomb was from
the Yungas (lowlands), a fact that is emphasized by the
presence of coastal sand in her burial. Since the Hatuncancha appears to have been associated with Pachacuti
Inca Yupanqui, perhaps the shaft tomb contained one of
his secondary wives.

Maldonado's house was badly damaged in the 1650
earthquake. Today little of it, or the Hatuncancha in general, remains. A small section of the exterior wall of the
compound, which so impressed the Spaniards when they
first arrived in the city, still stands across the street from
the cathedral. Within the original area of the Hatuncancha there is also a magnificent, but badly damaged Inca wall that must have been part of a large hall

PHOTO 10.19. A high interior niche and one side of a doorway of what was once a great hall within Hatuncancha can be seen along Avenida Santa Catalina Angosta.

(Photo 10.19). The destruction of the Hatuncancha is emphasized by the fact that one end of this wall juts out into, and is cut by, the Avenida Santa Catalina Angosta.

The Pucamarca Compound

Another large compound to the south of the plaza was called Pucamarca.[83] Garcilaso de la Vega (1966: 424 [1609:

Pt. 1, Bk. 7, Ch. 9]) suggests that this ward was associated with Topa Inca Yupanqui; however, he may have been confused with the adjacent compound, Cusicancha, in which Topa Inca Yupanqui was born. The area of Pucamarca is also briefly mentioned by Guaman Poma de Ayala (1980: 310 [1615: 337 (339)]).

Little additional information is available on this sector of Cuzco other than scattered, and partially contradictory, references to the locations of two temples within it.[84] Cobo (1990: 58 [1653: Bk. 13, Ch. 13]), while describing the shrines of Cuzco, states that Pucamarca was "a house or temple designated for the sacrifices of the Pachayachachic [Creator] in which children were sacrificed and everything else."[85] Elsewhere he notes that there was a temple named Pucamarca "in the houses which belonged to the Licentiate [Antonio] de la Gama;[86] in it was an idol of the Thunder called Chucuylla" (Cobo 1990: 57 [1653: Bk. 13, Ch. 13]).[87] These two temples are also mentioned by Albornoz, who writes, "Pucamarca quisuarcancha, which was the house of the Creator and of the Thunders."[88]

Molina, when writing of the works of Pachacuti Inca Yupanqui, provides a few additional details on these temples and the ward of Pucamarca:[89]

> . . . he ordered built the houses and temple of Quisuarcancha, which are above the houses of Diego Hortiz de Guzmán,[90] coming from the plaza of Cuzco, where Hernando López de Segovia[91] now lives. There he put the gold statue of the Creator, the size of a ten-year-old boy. It was in the shape of a man standing, the right arm raised high with his hand almost closed and his fingers raised, like a person who was ordering.[92] (Translation by author)

In a later section of his account, Molina offers supporting, yet slightly contradictory information, suggesting that the temple of Quisuarcancha was located in Pucamarca, but in the house lot owned by Isabel de Bobadilla (not Hernando López de Segovia):

> . . . they carried to the Temple of the Sun the figures called Chuquilla and Wiracocha, which had their own temple in Pucamarca and Quisuarcancha which are now the houses of Doña Isabel de Bobadilla.[93] (Translation by author)

Loarte (1882: 230 [1572]), writing in Cuzco at the same time as Molina,[94] confirms the fact that Isabel de Bobadilla owned a house in Pucamarca.

In sum, although our information is fragmentary at best, it seems likely that the area of Pucamarca was located in the large city block to the west of the Acllahuaci and south of the Hatuncancha. If this is the case, then the impressive Inca wall that remains on Maruri Street may have belonged to Pucamarca (Photo 10.20). Within this sector of Cuzco were two temples, one dedicated to the Creator god and the other to Thunder.[95]

Cusicancha

Another compound was situated between Pucamarca and the Temple of the Sun. Garcilaso de la Vega (1966: 424

[1609: Pt. 1, Bk. 7, Ch. 9]) notes the existence of this ward, but he states that he had forgotten its name. Fortunately, both Albornoz and Cobo identify it as Cusicancha (Happy Enclosure) in their descriptions of the shrines of Cuzco.[96] Albornoz writes of a shrine called "Cusicancha pachamama [Happy Enclosure, Earth Mother], which was the house where Topa Inca Yupangui was born."[97] Similarly, Cobo (1990: 57 [1653: Bk. 13, Ch. 13]) notes that Cusicancha ". . . was the place where Inca Yupanqui was born, opposite the temple of Coricancha; for this reason the members of the *ayllo* Inacapanaca[98] sacrificed there."[99]

Other Important Buildings in Cuzco

There were various other important buildings within Cuzco for which we have little information. For example,

PHOTO 10.20. The impressive Inca wall that remains on Maruri Street may have belonged to Pucamarca. (Courtesy of the Latin American Library, Tulane University; photograph by E. George Squier, 1865)

PHOTO 10.21. The Church of San Blas may mark the former location of the Temple of Thunder.

near the ward of Cusicancha was a prison.[100] Furthermore, a house called Condorcancha, in which Pachacuti Inca Yupanqui lived, may have been within Hatuncancha (Cobo 1990: 55 [1653: Bk. 13, Ch. 13]), and a palace of Topa Inca Yupanqui may have been located where the convent of San Agustín was built (Santa Cruz Pachacuti Yamqui Salcamayhua 1950 [ca. 1613]).

On the north side of central Cuzco, on a street that still displays finely made Inca walls, was a house belonging to Huayna Capac called Pomacorco (Bauer 1998: 55). Farther up the hill was the famous Palace of Colcapata,

which housed the Conquest Period Kings of Cuzco: Manco Inca, Paullu Inca, and Carlos Inca. Nearby, in the area formerly known as Totocachi (now called San Blas), was another temple for Thunder. Cobo writes,

The Thunder also had a separate temple in the Totocachi district. Inside the temple there was a gold statue of the Thunder placed on a litter of the same metal. This statue was made by the Inca Pachacuti in honor of the Thunder, and he called the statue Inti Illapa. Pachacuti took this statue as a brother, and during his lifetime he carried it with him whenever he went to war. This idol was greatly venerated, and it was served in a very stately and ceremonious fashion. (Cobo 1990: 33 [1653: Bk. 14, Ch. 7])[101]

It was within this temple that the mummified body of Pachacuti Inca Yupanqui was found by Polo de Ondegardo in 1559 (Acosta 1986 [1590: Ch. 21]; Cobo 1990: 54 [1653: Bk. 13, Ch. 13]). It seems likely that this temple was located where the Church of San Blas was later constructed (Photo 10.21).

Finally, it should be noted that even Atahualpa, whose captains sacked Cuzco on the eve of his encounter with Pizarro in Cajamarca, had a large hall in Cuzco. In the *Libro Primero del Cabildo . . .* (1965 [1534]) we find that Antonio de Espinoza, Pedro de la Carrera, and Juan de Andagoya each had lands associated with the *galpón* of Atahualpa. Its precise location, however, remains to be identified.

Summary and Discussion

The city of Cuzco was the imperial capital of the Inca. Rebuilt and expanded by a series of successful kings, the city held some of the greatest architectural works of the Americas. Around its great central plaza stood several palaces and at least four large halls. The major temples of the empire, including those of the Sun, Moon, Thunder/Lighting, and the Creator god, were also located near the plaza, along with the impressive facilities that housed an elite class of women who helped support the temples.

At the height of its Inca architectural splendor, the city of Cuzco was built on a loose grid system of large compounds divided by narrow streets. The compound walls were substantial, with some reaching 4 or 5 meters in height and made of superbly crafted stones. A few of these exterior walls have survived and can still be seen. Within the compounds, however, were hundreds of smaller buildings, many of them also built of stone. Almost all of these smaller buildings were destroyed after the Spaniards divided the compounds among themselves in 1536 and began to rebuild the city along European conventions.

At this time, not only were the interiors of the royal compounds of the city completely gutted and transformed, but new sacred spaces were created by the Europeans with the construction of several immense religious structures. These included the Cuzco Cathedral; the Franciscan, Jesuit, and Dominican churches; and the convents of Santa Clara and Santa Catalina, to name only a few. Acosta, writing in 1580, describes how the work was organized as the stones from the Inca buildings were taken to build the new structures of Spanish Cuzco:

> For the foundation [the Indians] have brought ancient cut stones in such quantities that even if the church were to be twice as large, there would be a surplus. They take these stones from old buildings . . . of the time of the Incas. Organizing themselves by ayllus, or kin groups, to carry the stones to our church, and dressing as for a festival with their feather ornaments and adornments, they come through the city singing in their language . . . Even women transport stones and do their work while singing. (Acosta 1954 [1580]; translation by Sabine MacCormack 1991: 252)

In other words, not only were the new Spanish structures built on top of important Inca buildings and plazas, but their construction required vast amounts of stone, much of which was acquired through the demolition of nearby royal palaces and temples. With this destruction, the character of Cuzco was forever changed.

CHAPTER 11

The Coricancha

THE MOST FAMOUS SANCTUARY in the Inca Empire was the Coricancha, called "Templo del Sol" (Temple of the Sun) by the Spaniards. Coricancha translates as "Golden Enclosure," a name that derives from the gold sheets that were attached to its walls. This great sanctuary was located on a slight rise in the heart of Cuzco, near the confluence of the two small, canalized rivers that flow through the city. It was built out of the exquisitely cut stone blocks for which the Inca are justifiably famous (Photos 11.1 and 11.2). Soon after the Spaniards took control of Cuzco, the sanctuary was taken over by the Dominican order and construction was begun on a church and adjacent monastery. Today, nearly five centuries later, the Dominicans continue to control the sanctuary.

The Coricancha was actually a series of buildings and courtyards surrounded by a large exterior wall. Within the complex were a series of temples dedicated to various deities, as well as various rooms for the support personnel and offering materials (Photo 11.3 and Figure 11.1). Together, these formed an impressive architectural complex that dominated the center of the city and was visible from a great distance. Cobo offers the following description of the Coricancha:

The most important and most sumptuous temple of this kingdom was the one located in the city of Cuzco; this temple was held to be the chief center or capital of their false religion and the most venerated sanctuary that these Indians had, and for this reason,

it was visited by all of the people of the Inca Empire, who came to it out of devotion on pilgrimages. This temple was called Coricancha, which means "house of gold," because of the incomparable wealth of this metal which was embedded in the temple's chapels and walls, its ceilings and altars.

Although this temple was dedicated to the Sun, statues of Viracocha, the Thunder, the Moon, and other important idols were placed there. (Cobo 1990: 48–49 [1653: Bk. 13, Ch. 12])[1]

Unlike many other features of Inca Cuzco, the Coricancha has been the subject of substantial research, beginning with Squier's visit in 1865. He lived for a short period with the monks of Santo Domingo and took two photographs of the Coricancha's interior courtyard (Photos 11.4 and 11.5). Elements of both of these photographs were later combined in a single engraving (Figure 11.2). Squier (1877: 441) also produced the first map of the interior of the Coricancha and an engraving of its famous curved wall (Figure 11.3).[2]

Notable early-twentieth-century studies include those of Uhle (1930 [1905]) and Lehmann-Nitsche (1928), as well as that of a local Dominican priest named Rosario Zárate (1921), each of which provides descriptions and plans of the complex. These accounts pale, however, in comparison to John H. Rowe's (1944) extensive discussion of the Coricancha. Although Rowe's observations have been recently updated by Gasparini and Margolies

PHOTO 11.1. The famous curved Inca wall of the Coricancha rests under the belvedere of Santo Domingo. (Courtesy of the Maxwell Museum of Anthropology, University of New Mexico; photograph by Edgar Lee Hewett, 1935, Negative 92 23.236)

PHOTO 11.2. Outside wall of the Coricancha along Avenida Ahuacpinta
(Courtesy of Fototeca Andina–Centro Bartolomé de Las Casas; photograph by Cesar Meza, ca. 1940)

FIGURE 11.1. Santo Domingo stands above the remains of the Coricancha. (Squier 1877: 430)

PHOTO 11.3. Early photograph of Santo Domingo and the Coricancha. This photograph was taken from the far side of the Saphy River that is now covered with the Avenida del Sol in central Cuzco. This photograph was used to make the etching shown in Figure 11.1. (Courtesy of the Latin American Library, Tulane University; photograph by E. George Squier, 1865)

PHOTO 11.4. Monks in the courtyard of Santo Domingo
(Courtesy of the Latin American Library, Tulane University; photograph by E. George Squier, 1865)

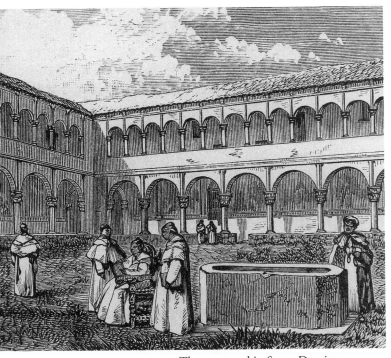

FIGURE 11.2. The courtyard in Santo Domingo.
Compare this etching with Photos 11.4 and 11.5.
Note that the locations of trees, the fountain, and various
monks have been altered. (Squier 1877: 440)

PHOTO 11.5. Monks and stone fountain in the courtyard of
Santo Domingo (Courtesy of the Latin American Library,
Tulane University; photograph by E. George Squier, 1865)

(1980), Béjar Navarro (1990), and Hyslop (1990), his report on the Coricancha remains the definitive study of this Inca temple.

Atahualpa's Ransom and the Gold of the Coricancha (1533–1534)

The Coricancha contained many of the finest gold and silver objects of the empire and was partially sacked in 1533 as part of Atahualpa's ransom. Accounts of the gold-covered walls of this complex were included in the initial reports of Francisco Pizarro's stunning achievements, which were published a year later in Spain, and they helped to fire the public's imagination of the great riches of Peru. The earliest description was written by Cristóbal de Mena, who returned to Spain on one of the first ships to arrive from Peru carrying both news of, and treasure from, the newly won Inca Empire. Mena, who had been in Cajamarca to hear the accounts of the first three Chris-

FIGURE 11.3. The curved wall of the Temple of the Sun (Coricancha) (Squier 1877: 443)

tians to see Cuzco, provides the following narrative of the stripping of the Coricancha:

> Then he [Quizquiz] sent them to some buildings of the Sun in which they worshipped. These buildings were sheathed with gold, in large plates, on the side where the sun rises, and on the part that was more shaded from the sun the gold in them was more debased. The Christians went to the buildings and, with no aid from the Indians, who did not want to help, saying that it was a building of the Sun and they would die, the Christians decided to remove the ornament from these buildings with some copper crowbars; and so they did, as they related it themselves.[3] (Translation by John H. Rowe; 1944: 37–38)

The men found several different chambers and courtyards within the Coricancha that also contained items of gold and silver. In the central courtyard they found a large gold fountain. In one room they recovered a great altar of gold, and in another they found the mummified remains of Atahualpa's father (Huayna Capac) and those of another lord surrounded by many gold and silver objects (Mena 1929: 37 [1534]). Though the Spaniards took the fountain and the altar to Cajamarca, much of Huayna Capac's wealth remained in Cuzco until Pizarro's full expeditionary force arrived there several months later (Ruiz de Arce 1933: 371, 372 [ca. 1545]).

Francisco de Xerez, secretary to Francisco Pizarro, returned to Spain with part of Atahualpa's ransom a few months after Mena. Like Mena, Xerez had been in Cajamarca to hear the accounts of the imperial city given by the returning three Christians. Xerez (1985: 152 [1534]) states that there were two buildings in Cuzco that were covered with gold.[4] He also tells of the stripping of the gold plates from these buildings as well as their arrival in Cajamarca:

> [They saw] a house in Cuzco plated with gold. The house is very well made and square and measures three hundred and fifty paces from corner to corner. They removed seven hundred of these gold plates from the house that in all weighed five hundred *pesos*. And from another house the Indians removed a total of two hundred thousand *pesos,* but because it

was of very low (quality), having (only) seven or eight karats, they did not accept it. They did not see more than these two plated houses, because the Indians did not allow them to see the whole city. . . .

All this gold arrived in one hundred and seventy-eight loads, with four Indians carrying each load in a litter. They brought very little silver. The gold was brought to the Christians little by little, very slowly, because they needed many Indians, and they collected them in each town [they passed]. It was believed that it would arrive in Cajamarca in one month. However, the gold that came from Cuzco arrived in the town of Cajamarca on the thirteenth of June of that year. Two hundred loads of gold and twenty-five of silver came. The gold appeared to be more than one hundred and thirty carats. And after this had arrived, another sixty loads of lower [-quality] gold arrived, most of which was in plates, like the boards of a box, each three and four *palmos* long. This had been removed from the walls of the houses, and they had holes in them that seem to have been for nails.[5] (Translation by author)

Pedro Sancho became secretary to Francisco Pizarro after the departure of Xerez for Spain. Sancho's (1898: 310 [1534]) account of the conquest of Peru begins with a description of the gold arriving in Cajamarca from Cuzco.

The two Spaniards that brought the gold from Cuzco arrived and immediately part of the gold was melted because they were small and very fine pieces. It added up to five hundred (plates) of gold pulled from some walls of the house of Cuzco.[6] The smallest plates weighed four or five pounds each and other sheets (weighed) ten to twelve pounds. The walls of the temple were covered with these. They also brought a seat of very fine gold, worked into the form of a footstool that weighed eighteen thousand *pesos*. They also brought a fountain of pure gold, very subtly worked, which was something to see, not only for the quality of its work but also for the shape in which it was made. And many other vessels, pots, and plates were also brought.[7] (Translation by the author)

To these descriptions we can add that of Pedro Pizarro, who also saw the treasure from Cuzco arrive in Cajamarca. Like the other writers, he was impressed with the sheets of gold that had been taken from the Coricancha.

Then there was collected a great deal of gold which Quizquiz assembled by means of causing certain plates to be taken from the House of the Sun, for they were laid on over the stones of the wall and covered the whole front of the house. (Pedro Pizarro 1921: 212 [1571])[8]

These four descriptions are all developed from eye-witness accounts of the Coricancha itself or from people who saw the materials that were stripped from it and shipped to Cajamarca. They each emphasize the fact that several walls, if not complete buildings, within the complex were covered with sheets of gold. It seems, however, that the gold varied in quality depending on the location of the walls. According to Xerez, more than seven hundred plates of fine gold were removed from the Coricancha and sent to Cajamarca.[9] We are told that these covered the walls where the sun shone. A much larger number of sheets of lesser-quality gold, perhaps as many as 2,800, covered other parts of the complex.[10] Some of these sheets of lesser-quality gold had also been shipped to Cuzco and arrived several days after the men carrying the finer gold items entered Cajamarca.[11]

According to Xerez, the planks from the Coricancha were 3–4 *palmos* (2–2.5 feet) long and had an average weight of 4.5 pounds (Hemming 1970: 64). Because the Spaniards describe prying the planks from the walls with copper crowbars, and sheets were later seen in Cajamarca with what seem to have been nail holes, we can suggest that some of them were attached to the walls of the buildings. Although most of the planks were melted down, there is evidence that some examples were sent to the king in their original form. Las Casas (1958: 193 [ca. 1550: Ch. 58]) may have seen these sheets while they were en route to Spain. He writes:

These plates or pieces of gold were of the size and shape of the leather back pieces which the backs of chairs we use have; they were a little less than a finger in thickness, and I saw plenty of them.[12] (Translation by John Rowe; 1944: 38)

It is also worth noting that the earliest accounts of the Coricancha do not describe precious stones as being embedded within the walls of the complex. This more romantic image of the Temple of the Sun was developed later by Garcilaso de la Vega, after much of the complex had been destroyed.

Several other items in the Coricancha, besides its impressive gold-covered walls, attracted the attention of the early Spaniards. There was an altar of gold, referred to as a bench by the chroniclers, on which the principal idol of the Sun stood while it was in the courtyard. This altar was taken to Cajamarca as part of Atahualpa's ransom and was claimed by Francisco Pizarro as part of his personal share of the loot. There was also a gold fountain that arrived in Cajamarca in pieces (Pedro Pizarro 1921: 212 [1571]; Mena 1929: 37 [1534]; Ruiz de Arce 1933: 371

[ca. 1545]; Xerez 1985: 152 [1534]; Zárate 1995: 59 [1555: Bk. 2, Ch. 14]).[13] In addition, there was also an idol of the Sun within the Coricancha called the Punchao. This statue was not taken during the first visit and soon disappeared from Cuzco. However, it was captured some forty years later along with Tupac Amaru Inca (Toledo 1924 [1572]). After the death of Tupac Amaru Inca, it was sent by Toledo to the king of Spain (Julien 1999).

Perhaps the most remarkable of all the features of the Coricancha was the so-called Garden of the Sun, which included various life-size figures made in gold and silver. Pedro Pizarro was the first of the writers to mention the famous garden. His description, even though it was written years later in 1571, is critical because it is the only surviving description of the garden by an actual eyewitness. Pizarro writes:

Away from the room where the Sun was wont to sleep, they made a small field, which was much like a

PHOTO 11.6. Gold stalk with cobs. Sculptures like this once filled the famous garden of the Coricancha. (Courtesy of Staatliche Museen zu Berlin–Preussischer Kulturbesitz Ethnologisches Museum, Berlin; inventory number VA 64430)

PHOTO 11.7. Maize stalk of hammered copper, Inca, fifteenth century (Denver Art Museum Collection: Museum exchange, 1960.64; © Denver Art Museum 2004)

large one, where, at the proper season, they sowed maize. They sprinkled it by hand with water brought on purpose for the Sun. And at the time when they celebrated their festivals, which was three times a year, that is: when they sowed the crops, when they harvested them, and when they made orejones [i.e., male initiation rites], they filled this garden with cornstalks made of gold having their ears and leaves very much like natural maize, all made of very fine gold, which they had kept in order to place them here at these times. (Pedro Pizarro 1921: 255 [1571])[14]

Although the size and complexity of this garden would grow and grow with each retelling, until in Garcilaso de la Vega's account it reaches fantastic proportions, there is no doubt that it existed in some form. Evidence of this can be found in the inventory of Atahualpa's ransom, which included "A gold stalk of maize, of 24 karats, with three leaves and two cobs of gold, which weighed ten marcs, six ounces and four-eighths" (Fernández de Alfaro 1904: 168 [1533]).[15] A surviving example of this artistic tradition can be seen in Berlin at the Ethnologisches Museum (Photo 11.6). A second example, albeit of less noble material, is housed in the Denver Art Museum (Photo 11.7).

Other Early Descriptions of the Coricancha

The Coricancha was one of the first places to be plundered by the Spaniards when they took over the city. Unfortunately, few of the men who stripped the complex of its remaining wealth left a written record of what they saw. A foot soldier named Diego Trujillo was one of the first to arrive at the Coricancha. As he approached the complex, the head priest (called the Villac Uma), ran up and tried to block his entrance. Trujillo (1948: 64 [1571]) describes this encounter:

> We entered the Houses of the Sun and the Villac Uma, who was like a priest in their religion, said, "How did you enter; anyone who enters must fast for a year first and must carry a load and be barefoot." But paying no attention to what he said, we entered.[16] (Translation by author)

Even though much of the Coricancha's gold had been

taken to Cajamarca months earlier, what remained in the complex astounded the Spaniards. Juan Ruiz de Arce (1933: 372 [ca. 1545]), a horsemen with Pizarro's forces, tells of the sacking of the Coricancha:

> We found many sheep [i.e., llamas] of gold and women and pitchers and jars and other objects. We found a lot in the chambers of the monastery. There was a band of gold as wide as a *palmo* around the buildings at roof level. This was found in all the chambers of the monastery . . .[17] (Translation by author)

Ruiz de Arce is not alone in mentioning that a band of gold once decorated various buildings in the Coricancha.[18] For example, Pedro Pizarro (1986: 91–92 [1571]), who had a chance to visit the temple before it was completely sacked, states the following:

> They had for this Sun certain very large houses, all of very well made masonry . . . On the front of it there was a band of gold plates more than a *palmo* wide, fastened upon the stones [of the wall].[19] (Translation by author)

Other men who came to Cuzco later were told of the band. Although he never saw it, Betanzos provides the most detailed account, indicating that the gold band was high up on the wall, just under the overhang of the roof. He also suggests that it was a relatively late addition to the temple, having been placed there by Topa Inca Yupanqui.

> With this done, Topa Inca Yupanque ordered that a strip two and a half spans wide, very thin, and the thickness of a small tin plate be made from the gold that had been brought. This strip was to be as long as the distance around the lodging where the Sun was. After it was made, the strip was put around that lodging of the Sun. It was placed on the outside, from where the straw roof reaches up to the masonry of the house, which makes the strip of gold as wide as the distance from the straw roof to the masonry. (Betanzos 1996: 127 [1557: Pt. 1, Ch. 28])[20]

A similar description of the band is also given by

PHOTO II.8. After the 1950 earthquake, a series of unusual marks were revealed on the upper tiers of the structures in the Coricancha. These carvings may once have helped hold the gold band on the exterior face of the buildings. (Courtesy of Fototeca Andina–Centro Bartolomé de Las Casas; photograph by Oscar Ladrón de Guevara, ca. 1958)

Sarmiento de Gamboa (1906: 74–75 [1572: Ch. 36]), who was in Cuzco in 1572, long after it had been taken down and melted. Until the 1950 earthquake that destroyed much of the Dominican monastery in Cuzco, it was not known how such a band could have been attached to the otherwise smooth and flawless stone exteriors of the buildings. However, with the clearance of the colonial architecture damaged in the earthquake, a series of unusual marks were revealed on the upper tiers of the structures (Ladrón de Guevara 1967; Béjar Navarro 1990). These carvings may once have helped hold the gold band on the exterior face of the buildings within the Coricancha (Photos II.8 and II.9).[21]

There are several other accounts of the Coricancha by writers who saw the complex during the Colonial Period. As the descriptions become increasingly sensational through time, it is important to determine what the witnesses actually saw, compared to their interpretations of what was once there. Among the most careful of the early writers in Peru was Cieza de León. He was in Cuzco in 1550 and took keen interest in visiting the Temple of the Sun. Cieza de León (1976: 255 [1555: Pt. 1, Ch. 94]) had, after all, been lured to the Americas after seeing the treasures sent by Pizarro to the king of Spain, much of which had come from the Coricancha.

PHOTO II.9. Building shown in Photo II.8 after the reconstruction of the Coricancha. Note the unusual carvings on the uppermost tier of stonework along the front of the building.

Cieza de León states that a finely made wall surrounded a large complex of buildings. Within the complex were four structures of central importance. The gateways and doors as well as many other parts of these structures were covered with sheets of gold. Furthermore, he suggests that many support personnel lived within the complex and that certain ritual supplies were stored there as well. He also indicates that there were two benches (or niches) along an east-facing wall, upon which the light of the rising sun fell (Cieza de León 1976: 145–146 [1553: Pt. 1, Ch. 92]).

Garcilaso de la Vega, like Cieza de León, describes special niches within the Coricancha in detail.[22] Calling them tabernacles, he writes:

> They had moldings round the edges and in the hollows of the tabernacles, and as these moldings were worked in the stone they were inlaid with gold plates not only at the top and sides, but also the floors of the tabernacles. . . .
>
> In two of these tabernacles in a wall facing east, I remember noticing many holes in the moldings made in the stonework. Those in the edges passed right through while the rest were merely marks on the walls. I heard the Indians and the religious of the temple say that those were the places in which the precious stones were set in pagan times. (Garcilaso de la Vega 1966: 184 [1609: Pt. 1, Bk. 3, Ch. 22])[23]

Part of one of these niches has survived into modern times (Photo 11.10). True to Cieza de León's and Garcilaso de la Vega's accounts, it is on an east-facing wall in the courtyard of the complex. Rather than being used to hold "precious stones," the drillings in this niche were most likely used to hold plates of gold against the fine stonework. Rowe (1944) suggests that the adjacent building, now also partially destroyed, held the second niche mentioned by both Cieza de León and Garcilaso de la Vega. Together, these buildings with their elaborate exterior gold-plated niches may be the buildings referred to by Mena (i.e., "these buildings were sheathed with gold, in large plates, on the side where the sun rises") and may be the areas from which the Spaniards pried the planks of finest gold.

It is clear that Garcilaso de la Vega had read Cieza de León's account of the Coricancha before writing his own description of it. Nevertheless, though Garcilaso de la Vega does present a highly romantic vision of the riches of the complex, he also provides other useful details not mentioned by Cieza de León. For example, he notes that there was a large northward-facing gateway into the complex (Garcilaso de la Vega 1966: 181, 185, 359 [1609: Pt. 1., Bk. 3, Ch. 20, Ch. 23; Bk. 6, Ch. 21]). He also suggests that there were a total of twelve doorways opening onto an interior patio (Garcilaso de la Vega 1966: 184 [1609:

PHOTO 11.10. An elaborate, east-facing niche within the Coricancha. The right side of the niche and its adjacent wall are original, but the left side of the niche and its adjacent wall have been reconstructed. Note also the small window that was located in the upper back wall of the niche. The holes and grooves cut into the stone were used to attach plates of gold.

PHOTO 11.11. The Christian religious orders of Peru frequently established their first churches in large Inca buildings. An Inca temple in the town of Huaytara continues to be used as a church today.

Pt. 1, Bk. 3, Ch. 22]). Most importantly, however, he states that there was a large building within the complex that he specifically calls the "house of the Sun":

Coming therefore to the plan of the temple, we should say that the house of the Sun was what is now the church of the divine St. Dominic. I do not give the exact length and breadth because I have not got them, but as far as size is concerned, it exists today. It is built of smooth masonry, very level and smooth. The high altar (I use the term to make myself clear, though the Indians did not, of course, have altars) was at the east end. The roof was of wood and very lofty so that there would be plenty of air. It was covered with thatch: they had no tiles. (Garcilaso de la Vega 1966: 180 [1609: Pt. 1., Bk. 3, Ch. 20])[24]

Apparently this large building was still standing, and being used as a church for the Dominicans, when

Garcilaso de la Vega left Cuzco in 1560. As noted in the previous chapter, it was not uncommon during early colonial times for the Spaniards to use the long rectangular halls of the Inca as churches. For example, one of the great halls of the Casana was used by the Franciscans as a chapel (Garcilaso de la Vega 1966: 425–426 [1609: Pt. 1, Bk. 7, Ch. 10]), and another hall on the plaza was used as the first church of Cuzco (*Libro Primero del Cabildo . . . 1965*: 33 [1534]). Another example can be seen in the Department of Huancavelica in the town of Huaytara, where an Inca temple continues to be used as a church today (Photo 11.11).

The so-called House of the Sun in Cuzco was destroyed sometime after Garcilaso de la Vega's departure. The timing of its destruction can be estimated from data provided by two separate chroniclers. Cobo notes that when he was in Cuzco in 1610 he saw a thin sheet of silver between two stones in a wall of the House of the Sun. He writes that at that time "many walls of this edifice were still standing, and on one corner that was still in-

PHOTO 11.12. Corner of the Plaza de Armas and Avenida Santa Catalina Angosta after the 1950 earthquake
(Courtesy of Fototeca Andina–Centro Bartolomé de Las Casas; photograph by Antonio Mendoza, 1950)

tact part of a thin sheet of silver could be seen in the joint between two stones. I saw it myself on numerous occasions" (Cobo 1990: 49 [1653: Bk. 13, Ch. 12]).[25] In contrast, Calancha, writing in 1638, mentions that he personally witnessed the destruction of the building containing the sheet of silver while he was in Cuzco some years earlier (Rowe 1944: 62). This suggests that one of the principal buildings of the Coricancha survived until sometime between 1610 and 1638, when it was demolished in a remodeling of the Dominican church. Perhaps it was during this remodeling episode that the large, formal entrance to the Coricancha was also destroyed. Nevertheless, the new church building that was constructed on this site did not last long, since the Santo Domingo complex suffered badly during the earthquake that struck Cuzco in 1650 (Esquivel y Navia 1980: 93 [1749]; Julien 1995: 313–314).

Garcilaso de la Vega also indicates that directly behind the large House of the Sun was a small courtyard surrounded by five buildings:

Beyond the temple, there was a cloister with four sides, one of which was the temple wall. All round the upper part of the cloister there ran a cornice of gold plates more than a vara wide, which crowned the cloister. In its place the Spaniards had a white plaster cornice made of the same width as the golden one, in order to preserve its memory. I saw it before I left on the walls which were still standing and had not been pulled down. Round the cloister there were five halls or large square rooms, each built separately and not joined to the others, covered in the form of a pyramid, and forming the other three sides of the cloister. (Garcilaso de la Vega 1966: 181 [1609: Pt. 1, Bk. 3, Ch. 21])[26]

Although in the above account Garcilaso de la Vega states that there were five buildings around the courtyard, he notes later in his work that only three of them remained in good condition: "Of the five halls, I saw the three that were still standing with their ancient walls and roofs. Only the plates of gold and silver were missing" (Garcilaso de

PHOTO 11.13. The pre-1950 interior of the Coricancha. The large arch was one of the many colonial features of the compound that were removed after the 1950 earthquake to expose more of the Inca remains. (Courtesy of Library of Congress, photograph number 4720 H)

PHOTO 11.15. Collapsed end of Dominican church above the famous curved Inca wall after the 1950 earthquake (Courtesy of Fototeca Andina–Centro Bartolomé de Las Casas; photograph by Antonio Mendoza, 1950)

PHOTO 11.16. The rebuilt end of the Dominican church in 1998

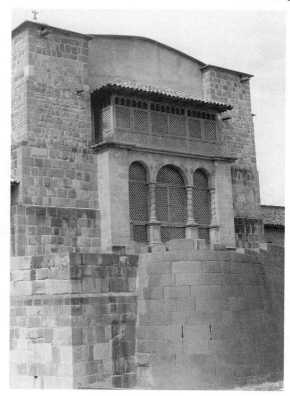

PHOTO 11.14. The Dominican church above the famous curved Inca wall before the 1950 earthquake (Courtesy of Library of Congress, photograph number 2424; gift of Carroll Greenough)

PHOTO 11.17. Interior structures of the Coricancha during reconstruction. During the course of this restoration project, priority was given to exposing and reconstructing the Inca remains at the site. (Courtesy of Fototeca Andina–Centro Bartolomé de Las Casas; photograph by Oscar Ladrón de Guevara, 1958)

la Vega 1966: 184 [1609: Pt. 1, Bk. 3, Ch. 22]).[27] Because this courtyard corresponded closely with the European notion of a monastic cloister, it was not destroyed by the Dominicans. The courtyard was preserved and portions of four of the rooms, two on the east side and two on the west, were incorporated into the monastery both before and after the 1650 earthquake.

On May 21, 1950, Cuzco was again hit by a devastating earthquake (Photo 11.12), and this one flattened much of the city and caused parts of the Dominican church and monastery to collapse (Photos 11.13–11.17). UNESCO conducted a survey of the city to evaluate the damage done to its colonial and Inca monuments (Kubler 1952). The reconstruction of the badly damaged Santo Domingo monastery started in 1956. During the course of this restoration project, priority was given to exposing and reconstructing the Inca remains at the site. As a result of the controversial project, much of the colonial monastery was removed and various parts of the Inca complex were restored.[28]

Archaeological excavations within the plaza of the monastery and in the triangular terrace area beside the church were also conducted following the 1950 earthquake. Small patches of a cobblestone floor were found within the courtyard area (Ladrón de Guevara 1967). The excavations also revealed the wall foundations of the buildings that once stood on the southern and northern sides of the courtyard (Béjar Navarro 1990). Based on these findings, Rowe's 1944 map, and their own extensive research at the site, Gasparini and Margolies illustrate what the Coricancha might have looked like during Inca times (Map 11.1 and Figure 11.4).[29]

The Coricancha and Inca Astronomy

Because the Coricancha was the central sanctuary of the solar cult in Cuzco, it has long been speculated that solar observations were made from it. Particular interest has been placed on the east-facing wall of the courtyard, since the earliest accounts of the complex suggest that parts of its façade were covered with gold. Nevertheless, no clear solar alignments have been found there. It is possible that most of the important public solar observations were made, instead, from a plaza such as the Haucaypata (Bauer and Dearborn 1995; Dearborn et al. 1998).

Anthony Aveni and Tom Zuidema have found, however, that the walkway between the two eastward-facing structures in the Coricancha (Buildings A and B on Map 11.1) has an azimuth of 66°44' or slightly more than 20' north of the position where the Pleiades rose in AD 1500. From this, Zuidema (1982: 214) suggests that the heliacal rise of the Pleiades was observed from this area. This is not an unreasonable suggestion, as it is widely noted that the Inca were interested in the Pleiades (Duviols 1986: 151; Cobo 1990: 30 [1653: Bk. 13, Ch. 6]; Bauer and Dearborn 1995) and that they held an important feast related to the Pleiades near the time of Corpus Christi (Avendaño 1904: 381 [1617]; Arriaga 1968: 213 [1621: Ch. 5]).

The Coricancha as the Center of the Empire

The city of Cuzco was conceptually divided by the Inca into two halves, or moieties. Like other moiety systems worldwide, Andean moieties are expressed in terms of ranked pairs such as male:female or right:left (Bauer 1992a: 124–139; Gelles 1995). In the Quechua-speaking sectors of the Andes, these pairs are most frequently called Hanansaya (upper division) and Hurinsaya (lower division). For example, Cobo writes:

> The Incas made the same division throughout all of their kingdom that they had made in dividing Cuzco into Hanan Cuzco and Hurin Cuzco. Thus they divided each town and *cacicazgo* [ethnic group] into two parts, known as the upper district and the lower district, or the superior part or faction and the inferior; and even though these names denote inequality between these two groups, nevertheless, there was none, . . . (Cobo 1979: 195 [1653: Bk. 12, Ch. 24])[30]

In the case of Cuzco, the Coricancha was at the junction of the two parts. Downstream from the Coricancha was Hurin Cuzco, and the area upstream was called Hanan Cuzco.

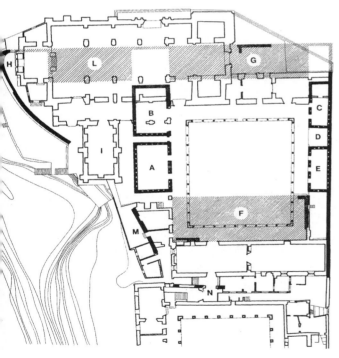

MAP 11.1. Map of the Coricancha (Gasparini and Margolies 1980: 224; courtesy of Luise Margolies and Graziano Gasparini)

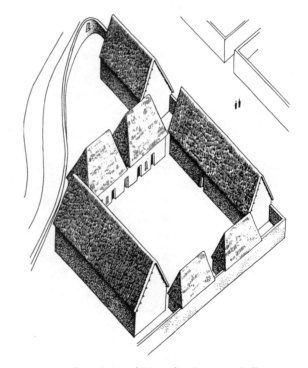

FIGURE 11.4. Gasparini and Margolies (1980: 229) illustrate what the Coricancha might have looked like during Inca times. (Courtesy of Luise Margolies and Graziano Gasparini)

Both of the Cuzco moieties were, in turn, further divided in half. These four quarters, or *suyus* (divisions), radiated from the Coricancha as the center of the Inca world (Cobo 1990: 51 [1653: Bk. 12, Ch. 13]; Betanzos 1996: 71 [1557: Pt. 1, Ch. 16]; Bauer 1998). The indigenous name for the Inca Empire, Tawantinsuyu (the four parts together), was derived from the four great spatial divisions that together made up the realm. The Hanansaya quarters, consisting of the regions to the northwest and northeast of Cuzco, were called Chinchaysuyu and Antisuyu respectively. The Hurinsaya division included the two southern quarters: Collasuyu to the southeast and Cuntisuyu to the southwest. The Inca Empire was seen as the sum of these four parts, and for the Inca, the Coricancha marked its center.

The Coricancha and the Shrines of the *Cuzco* Ceque *System*

The spatial organization of Cuzco and the Inca Empire is discussed in a number of chronicles, and there is general agreement on its broadest moiety and *suyu* divisions. However, Cobo's work goes further and describes a related but vastly more complex Inca partitioning system (Cobo 1990: 51–84 [1653: Bk. 13, Chs. 13–16]). In addition to the moieties of Cuzco (Hanansaya and Hurinsaya) and the quarters of the valley (Chinchaysuyu, Antisuyu, Collasuyu, and Cuntisuyu), Cobo states that the Cuzco region was further partitioned by forty-two abstract lines, or *ceques,* that radiated out, like spokes of a wheel, from the Coricancha (Zuidema 1964; Bauer 1998). The course of these lines was defined by the location of hundreds of sacred objects, or *huacas,* situated in and around the city of Cuzco:

> From the Temple of the Sun, as from the center, there went out certain lines which the Indians call *ceques;* they formed four parts corresponding to the four royal roads which went out from Cuzco. On each one of those *ceques* were arranged in order the *guacas* and shrines which there were in Cuzco and its region, like stations of holy places, the veneration of which was common to all. (Cobo 1990: 51 [1653: Bk. 13, Ch. 13])[31]

In the course of his account, which was taken from a lost

1559 manuscript written by Polo de Ondegardo, Cobo describes the *ceques* contained in each of the four *suyus,* as well as the individual shrines that formed the organizational lines (Bauer 1998: 13–22).

Cobo's description of the Cuzco *ceque* system is divided into four chapters; each characterizing the *ceques* and the *huacas* in a specific *suyu.* The shrines along each *ceque* are presented according to their relative distance from the Temple of the Sun. The first shrine of a *ceque* is generally within the city of Cuzco, often in or near the Coricancha. The last shrine of a *ceque* is always outside the city, frequently near or just beyond the border of the Cuzco Valley. A second, much abbreviated list of the shrines in the area of Chinchaysuyu was recorded by Albornoz (1984 [ca. 1582]). Albornoz's account provides additional information on some of the shrines described by Cobo and introduces several additional ones as well (Bauer 1998: 135–142).

Because of the large-scale destruction that has occurred in the area of the Coricancha, the precise location of most of the shrines that were once in or near it cannot be determined (Table 11.1 and Table 11.2). Nevertheless, the position of a few of the shrines *can* be identified and are worthy of commentary. For example, a large and important stone called Sabaraura, which was thought to be a petrified warrior, was situated where the belvedere of Santo Domingo was constructed, and just below it, at the base of the complex, was a spring called Pilcopuquio.

Furthermore, there were several plazas in or near the complex that held important shrines. One shrine called Guaracince[32] was located near the Coricancha and was dedicated to the prevention of earthquakes. Cobo writes:

> [Ch-2:1] The first *guaca* was called Guaracince, which was in the square of the Temple of the Sun; this square was called Chuquipampa (it means "plain of gold"). It was a bit of flat ground which was there, where they said that the earthquake was formed. At it they made sacrifices so that it would not quake, and they were very solemn ones, because when the earth quaked children were killed, and ordinarily sheep and clothing were burned and gold and silver were buried. (Cobo 1990: 54 [1654: Bk. 13, Ch. 13])[33]

The plaza in which this shrine was located may well have

been the small open area north of the Coricancha.[34] Garcilaso de la Vega (1966: 424 [1609: Pt. 1, Bk. 7, Ch. 9]) calls this plaza Intipata, which he translates as "square of the Sun"[35] and suggests that only those who were Inca of Royal Blood could cross it and enter the Coricancha (see Map 10.2).

A second plaza area described by Cobo was the court-yard that still survives within the Dominican monastery:

[Cu-5: 1] The first they named Caritampucancha. It was a small square which is now inside the monastery of Santo Domingo, which they held to be the first place where Manco Capac settled on the site of Cuzco when he came out of Tampu. Children were offered to it along with everything else. (Cobo 1990: 80 [1653: Bk. 13, Ch. 16])[36]

Near the Coricancha there was also a stone brazier[37] in which offerings to the Sun were burned.

[Ch. 3: 1] The first was named Nina, which was a brazier made of a stone where the fire for sacrifices was lit, and they could not take it from anywhere

else. It was next to the Temple of the Sun; it was held in great veneration, and solemn sacrifices were made to it. (Cobo 1990: 55 [1654: Bk. 13, Ch. 13])[38]

It is worth noting that elsewhere in his chronicle Cobo describes the use of the stone brazier during the offering of food to the Sun:

The women who resided in the temple of Cuzco were in charge of lighting and stirring the fire that burned in the temple for the sacrifices. This fire was not fed with ordinary wood but with a very special kind of carefully carved and painted wood. The cook got up early every day to cook the food for the Sun and his attendants. As the Sun appeared on the horizon and struck with its rays at the Punchao, which was a golden image of the Sun placed so that as the Sun came up its light would bathe the image, the women offered the Sun this food that they had prepared, burning it with special solemnity and songs. (Cobo 1990: 174 [1653: Bk. 13, Ch. 37])[39]

This brazier must have been a prominent feature of

PHOTO 11.18. Santo Domingo and the curved wall of the Coricancha in 1998

TABLE II.I. Shrines listed by Cobo (1990 [1653]) as located in or near the Coricancha

[Ch-2:1] The first *guaca* was called Guaracince, which was in the square of the Temple of the Sun; this square was called Chuquipampa (it means "plain of gold"). It was a bit of flat ground which was there, where they said that the earthquake was formed. At it they made sacrifices so that it would not quake, and they were very solemn ones, because when the earth quaked children were killed, and ordinarily sheep and clothing were burned and gold and silver were buried.

[Ch-3:1] The first was named Nina, which was a brazier made of a stone where the fire for sacrifices was lit, and they could not take it from anywhere else. It was next to the Temple of the Sun; it was held in great veneration, and solemn sacrifices were made to it.

[Ch-6:1] The first was called Catonge and was a stone of the *pururaucas*, which was in a window next to the Temple of the Sun.

[Ch-8:1] The first was a small house next to the Temple of the Sun named Illanguarque in which were kept certain weapons which they said the Sun had given to Inca Yupanqui; with them he conquered his enemies. Universal sacrifice was made to this *guaca*.

[An-1:1] The first *guaca* of it was called Chiquinapampa. It was an enclosure next to the Temple of the Sun in which the sacrifice for the universal health of the Indians was made.

[An-1:2] The second *guaca* was called Turuca. It was an almost round stone, which was next to the said Temple of the Sun in a window; this stone was said to be the *guauque* of Ticci Viracocha. Universal sacrifice was made to it for all the needs that arose.

[An-6:1] The first was called Auriauca; it was a sort of portico or arbor which was next to the Temple of the Sun, where the Inca and the lords took their places.

[Co-9:1] The first was a seat named Tampucancha, where they said that Mayta Capac used to sit, and that while he was sitting here he arranged to give battle to the Acabicas [*sic*; Alcabiças]. Because he defeated them in the battle, they regarded the said seat as a place to be venerated. It was next to the Temple of the Sun.

[Cu-1:1] The first was a stone called Sabaraura, which was where the belvedere of Santo Domingo is now; they believed that it was an officer of the *pururaucas*.

[Cu-1:2] The second *guaca* was another stone like this one, named Quingil, which was in a wall next to Coricancha.

[Cu-4:1] The first was called Pururauca. It was one of those stones into which they said that the *pururaucas* had changed, and it was on a stone bench next to the Temple of the Sun.

[Cu-5:1] The first they named Caritampucancha. It was a small square which is now inside the monastery of Santo Domingo, which they held to be the first place where Manco Capac settled on the site of Cuzco when he came out of Tampu. Children were offered to it along with everything else.

[Cu-6:1] The name of the first was Apian. It was a round stone of the *pururaucas* which was on the site which Santo Domingo has today.

[Cu-7:1] The first was a small house called Inticancha, in which they held the opinion that the sisters of the first Inca, who came out of the window [cave] of Pacaritampu with him, dwelt. They sacrificed children to it.

[Cu-7:2] The second *guaca* was named Rocromuca. It was a large stone which was next to the Temple of the Sun.

[Cu-10:1] The first was a fountain called Pilcopuquiu, which is in the garden of Santo Domingo.

TABLE II.2. Shrines listed by Albornoz (1984 [CA. 1582]) as located in or near the Coricancha

(#1) "The first huaca was Coricancha, which means 'House of Gold' and was house of the Sun."

(#2) "Quillcai cancha, which was on the plaza which now is the plaza of Santo Domingo."

(#3) "Yllanguaiqui [Wavy Lightning], which was another house on the said plaza where the Raymi festival was celebrated." (See Cobo, Ch-8:1)

(#32) "Nina [Flame] was a brazier that always burned." (See Cobo, Ch-3:1)

(#33) "Guaracinci, a worked stone in the door of the sun."

Inca Cuzco, since it is further described by Murúa, Montesinos, and Polo de Ondegardo. From the latter of these writers we learn that a special red wood that was carved and at times painted was placed in this fire, and that the wood was brought from hundreds of kilometers away by the Chincha, who were located on the coast of Peru (Polo de Ondegardo 1990: 100–101 [1571]).[40]

Summary and Discussion

The importance of the Coricancha cannot be underestimated. The Inca Empire was seen as being composed of four great geopolitical quarters that radiated out from this complex. For the Inca, the Coricancha marked the central and most sacred spot in the universe (Photo 11.18).

Excavations by Rowe (1944) in the patio of the Dominican theological school to the southeast of the Dominican monastery found large quantities of Killke pottery. These findings are supported by a number of separate archaeological excavations that have been conducted in and around the Coricancha over the past several decades by Cuzco archaeologists, including Luis Barreda Murillo, Arminda Gibaja Oviedo, Alfredo Valencia Zegarra, and most recently, Raymundo Béjar Navarro. These researchers have each recovered exceptionally high quality Killke ceramics, further documenting that the special character of the site extends back before the establishment of the Inca Empire. Furthermore, excavations in the areas surrounding the complex have revealed Killke Period architectural remains, indicating that even during that time the shrine area was surrounded by buildings and plazas (González Corrales 1984; San Román Luna 2003).

Because of its great wealth, the Coricancha was sacked by the Spaniards even before they had established a secure rule over the Andes. Nevertheless, we know something about the organization of the complex and the activities that occurred within its confines from the various Spaniards who saw it during or just after the conquest. The Coricancha comprised a group of buildings dedicated to various deities. The stones for much of the complex were brought from the quarry of Rumicolca, some 35 kilometers from the city, just beyond the site of Pikillacta (Hunt 1990).

By far the most important idol held within the complex was the highly venerated gold image of the Sun called Punchao (sunlight), which by the end of the empire had become almost synonymous with Inca rule. Various early colonial writers state that the image was in the shape of a man (Molina 1989 [ca. 1575]; Sarmiento de Gamboa 1906 [1572]). Likewise, we are told that the Coricancha housed the silver image of the Moon, which was in the form of a woman (Molina 1989 [ca. 1575]; Garcilaso de la Vega 1966 [1609]). These were, without a doubt, among the most sacred idols of the late prehispanic Andean world.

In the division of Spanish Cuzco, Juan Pizarro gained control of the Coricancha (Rowe 1944: 40; Hemming and Ranney 1982: 82). After his death during the siege of Cuzco, it was bequeathed to the Dominicans, who immediately established the first Christian order within Cuzco. The Coricancha, which like so much of Cuzco was damaged in the siege, was then slowly transformed from the center of the Inca world to the focal point of a powerful Christian institution. By the time of the 1650 earthquake, many of its buildings had been destroyed and new colonial edifices had been erected. In the years following the earthquake, the monastery was again remodeled, and it reached its height of power during the eighteenth century. But by the mid-nineteenth century, like most of Cuzco's religious institutions, the Dominican order had fallen on hard times (Burns 1999).

Squier lived for a week in the complex in 1865. His study has been followed by many others, most notably that by Rowe (1944), who spent several months studying the Coricancha and who produced the definitive work on its history. A few years after Rowe concluded his fieldwork another earthquake racked Cuzco, and parts of the complex collapsed again. In the reconstruction that followed, many of its colonial features were demolished in an effort to expose the underlying Inca buildings at the site. Today one sees an uneasy combination of Inca buildings, reduced colonial architecture, and modern scaffoldings.

Although much of the Inca complex has been lost, including what was the original House of the Sun, what remains still astonishes visitors. The great exterior walls and curved western corner of the Coricancha are world famous for their craftsmanship. Inside, the remains of four buildings constructed with superb stonework can be seen on either side of a plaza. One can only wonder what the complex would have looked like at the height of the Inca Empire, when it was complete and parts of its façades were covered with gold.

CHAPTER 12

The Mummies of the Royal Inca

THE INCA MUMMIFIED their dead kings, and several times a year these mummies were assembled, in order of their reigns, in the plaza of Cuzco for all to see. During the rest of the year, they gave and sought private audiences in their Cuzco palaces or in nearby royal estates. In the words of one early eyewitness, "it was customary for the dead to visit one another, and they held great dances and debaucheries, and sometimes the dead went to the house of the living, and sometimes the living came to the house of the dead."[1] Speaking through oracles and attended by servants, the ancient kings of Cuzco counseled the living and attempted to protect and extend the resources of their descendants. In this chapter, we turn from discussions of the development of the Inca state and the physical organization of Cuzco to explore this unusual worldview in which deceased rulers continued to play critical roles in the social and political organization of the capital generations after their death.[2]

Polo de Ondegardo and the Inca Mummies

In 1558, Juan Polo de Ondegardo, was appointed corregidor (chief magistrate) of Cuzco by Viceroy Andrés Hurtado de Mendoza, Marqués de Cañete.[3] He soon received orders from the viceroy and the archbishop of Lima, Jerónimo de Loaysa, to investigate the history and ritual practices of the Inca. To this end, Polo de Ondegardo brought together various officials and priests who had held offices in the empire at its height, a little more than thirty years earlier. They were questioned about their own experiences in Cuzco as well as about the empire as a whole (Cobo 1979: 99 [1653: Bk. 12, Ch. 2]). Polo de Ondegardo's findings were sent to Lima, accompanied by several of the royal Inca mummies.

Although various Spaniards had already conducted inquiries into the history and religion of the Inca, and there would be many more to follow, Polo de Ondegardo's investigation was one of the largest and best organized.[4] Cobo hints at the massiveness of Polo de Ondegardo's investigation when describing the "sorcerers" of the Inca:

. . . in his account the Licentiate Polo de Ondegardo tells that on the basis of the inquiry made by the Indian mayors in the city of Cuzco on his orders, just from among the inhabitants of that city there were four hundred seventy-five men and women who had no other occupation. Each of them was brought before him with the instruments that they used. (Cobo 1990: 161–162 [1653: Bk. 13, Ch. 34])[5]

Polo de Ondegardo's report circulated widely and had a significant impact on various governmental and religious leaders. Unfortunately, his report, one of the most important documents produced during the early Colonial Period, is now lost. We do, however, know some of the information that it contained, because several later writers incorporated parts of it into their own reports. Cobo, who came to possess a signed copy of the report some ninety years after it was sent to the archbishop of Lima, tells of its importance and impact:

For these reasons, the report, based on the inquiry at that meeting, that was made by Licentiate Polo has always been considered authoritative; in the provincial councils that have been held in this kingdom, everything in it was adopted. It was used for the instruction that is given to the priests assigned to Indians concerning their ancient rites and superstitions so that the utmost diligence and care could be taken in eradicating these practices, as well as for resolving the doubts and difficulties that often came up in the beginning concerning the marriages of those who were converted over to our Holy Faith. I have this report in my possession; it is the same one that, with his own signature, Licentiate Polo sent to Archbishop Jerónimo de Loaysa. (Cobo 1979: 99–100 [1653: Bk. 12, Ch. 2])[6]

Cobo quotes a great deal from the 1559 report, although he does not always credit it as the source of his information.

Pedro Sarmiento de Gamboa (1906 [1572]), who was in Cuzco during Polo de Ondegardo's second term as corregidor (1571–1572), is another important source of information on the 1559 inquiry. Like Polo de Ondegardo, Sarmiento de Gamboa ordered the leaders of Cuzco to assemble and to tell their histories. In Sarmiento de Gamboa's record of the meeting, there are various references to Polo de Ondegardo's earlier inquiry, especially within the discussions of the royal mummies.

Additional information on Polo de Ondegardo's now lost 1559 report is provided in the works of José de Acosta. In 1585 Acosta published a summary of Polo de Ondegardo's report as part of the proceedings of the Third Provincial Council of Lima under the title of *Tratado sobre los errores y supersticiones de los indios* (Treaties on the errors and superstitions of the Indians). Five years later, Acosta also relied heavily on the report while writing his own overview of the history of the Americas, titled *Historia natural y moral de las Indias* (The natural and moral history of the Indies; 1590).

When Polo de Ondegardo began his investigation of the history and ritual practices of the Inca, the royal mummies were still being kept and worshiped by their respective Cuzco-based lineages. In an effort to end these idolatrous practices, he began to hunt down the royal mummies. Within a relatively short time, Polo de

Ondegardo found the mummies of all the Inca kings who had ruled Cuzco. Along with each royal mummy, Polo de Ondegardo also recovered specific ritual and historic items associated with their reign. Most importantly, he discovered their *huauques* (brothers): statues that stood as proxy for a ruler when he was unable to attend a meeting or function. Polo de Ondegardo also found the mummified remains of several of the Inca *qoyas* (queens). The discovery of these highly revered individuals and objects dealt a crippling blow to the already weakened nobility of the imperial city. Before I summarize where each of the royal mummies was found and what became of them, it is important to place the role of the deceased kings within the broader context of Andean ancestor worship.

Ancestor Worship in the Andes

Elaborate preservation of the dead and associated ancestor worship is a tradition that extends back millennia in the Andes. On the coast, hunting-and-gathering bands were mummifying their dead as early as 6000 BC (Moseley 2001). At a much later date, in the first centuries of the first millennium AD, burial towers began to be built in the northern Andes of Peru (Isbell 1997). It is argued that these early towers were used for ancestor worship because they accommodated the leaving of offerings and the visitation of the dead. By Inca times, a great variety of burial-tower traditions had developed across the highlands (Figure 12.1).

Early Spanish writers provide numerous descriptions of native Andeans visiting the burial chambers of the dead and of natives bringing the mummified remains of important leaders into the center of their villages during annual festivals. These visits to and by the dead were widespread practices in the Andes at the time of the European invasion. In an effort to stop the adoration of the dead, the Catholic authorities soon required that all natives be buried in church cemeteries. This, however, did little to stop the practice, as many bodies were later exhumed at night and placed in traditional burial chambers where they could be visited (Polo de Ondegardo 1916 [1567]; Acosta 1986: 325 [1590: Bk. 5, Ch. 7]). Pablo Joseph de Arriaga, a relentless agent in the anti-idolatry movement, describes the situation in 1621:

In many places, in fact wherever they have managed to do so, they have removed the bodies of their dead from the church and taken them out to the fields to their *machays* [caves], or burial places of their ancestors. The reason they give for this is expressed by the word *cuyaspa*, or the love they bear them. In conclusion, to demonstrate their wretched condition, their extreme need for a remedy, and the ease with which they receive it, no proof is needed beside that of seeing them on one of their exhibition days, when they bring out all the accessories of their idolatry. They are grouped about the plaza by clans and factions and bring out the mummified bodies of their ancestors, called *munaos*, in the lowlands and *malquis* in the sierra, together with the bodies taken from the church, and it looks like the living and the dead come to judgment. (Arriaga 1968: 18–19 [1621])[7]

FIGURE 12.1. Guaman Poma de Ayala (1980: 264 [1615: 289]) shows the remains of an important individual being carried to a burial tower. To the right, his widow and a child grieve. To the left is the burial tower of his ancestors. The caption reads "Entiero de Chincaisuios" [Burial in Chinchaysuyu].

Try as they might, it proved extremely difficult for the Spaniards to stop these practices from occurring. For example, in just one anti-idolatry campaign, which lasted from February of 1617 to July of 1618, Arriaga (1968: 20 [1621: Ch. 1]) reports that some 477 bodies were returned to the church for reburial.

The worship of mummified leaders was particularly confrontational to the Spaniards and was interpreted as both a religious and political threat to their tenuous control of the Andes. In the end, the Spaniards found that burning the mummified bodies of past leaders was the best way to discourage the practice. This is illustrated in the case of Hernando de Avendaño's anti-idolatry work in the Province of Chancay. There he discovered the mummified remains of an important lord and a lower-level official. These remains were so respected in former times that a gold diadem and many finely woven textiles (*cumbi*) had been sent to them by the Inca. The remains were transported by Avendaño to Lima for the viceroy and archbishop to see, and then they were publicly burned:

He [Hernando de Avendaño] visited still other towns and discovered in them much idolatry and many *huacas* [shrines], among them one famous among the Indians and venerated even in remote villages. This was the mummy of a very ancient *curaca* [lord], named Libiacancharco, located about a league and a half from the town of San Cristóbal de Rapaz in a shelter below a cave in a very steep mountain. It had its *huama*, or diadem of gold, on its head and was dressed in seven fine shirts of *cumbi* (fine cloth). These, the Indians said, had been sent to them as a present by the ancient Inca kings. This mummy, and that of a majordomo of his called Chuchu Michuy, located in a different place and much venerated by the Indians, were brought to Lima just as they were for the Lord Viceroy and the Lord Archbishop to see. They were paraded publicly and then a solemn auto-da-fé was held to which all the inhabitants of the province were invited, and the mummies were burned together with a great many *huacas*, to the great consternation and fear of the Indians. (Arriaga 1968: 15–16 [1621: Ch. 1])[8]

Hundreds, if not thousands, of similar burnings took

place across the Andes as the Spaniards sought to destroy the roots of the autochthonous religions within their newly won territories.

Yet even the burning of the corpses did not always end the indigenous practice of ancestor worship. The enduring nature of this religious practice is perhaps best illustrated in the cases of Viracocha Inca's (the eighth Inca) and Topa Inca Yupanqui's (the tenth Inca) mummies. The body of Topa Inca Yupanqui was burned in 1533 by Atahualpa's forces when they captured Cuzco, because his descent group had allied themselves with Huascar. However, the ashes of Topa Inca Yupanqui were placed in a small jar and continued to be worshiped by surviving family members (Sarmiento de Gamboa 1906: 102, 122–123 [1572: Ch. 54, Ch. 66]; Cobo 1979: 151 [1653: Bk. 12, Ch. 15]). Likewise, Viracocha Inca's mummy was hunted down and burned by Gonzalo Pizarro as he searched the Cuzco region for treasure. The ashes of Viracocha Inca were also placed in a small jar and worshiped until Polo de Ondegardo discovered them (Sarmiento de Gamboa 1906: 59 [1572: Ch. 25]; Cobo 1979: 132 [1653: Bk. 12, Ch. 11]; Acosta 1986: 421, 429–430 [1590: Bk. 6, Ch. 20]).

The Royal Panacas of Cuzco

The practice of mummification and ancestor worship in the Andes reached its most complex form within the city of Cuzco. At the time of the European invasion, the royal Inca of Cuzco traced their ancestry back some eleven generations from the last undisputed ruler of the empire, Huayna Capac, to the mythical founder of Cuzco, Manco Capac (Table 1.1). It is widely recognized that the Inca subdivided this dynastic list into two groups: rulers associated with Hurin (lower) Cuzco and those associated with Hanan (upper) Cuzco. The first five Inca kings, Manco Capac through Capac Yupanqui, were affiliated with Hurin Cuzco, and the last five, Inca Roca through Topa Inca Yupanqui, were associated with Hanan Cuzco.

The social elite of Cuzco, or what Garcilaso de la Vega classifies as the Inca of Royal Blood, was composed of the ruling Inca and his sister/wife, as well as the direct descendants of all previous Inca rulers. Generally, at the death of an Inca king, his eldest son inherited the position of Inca, and the other male descendants of the dead

Inca formed a royal descent group called a *panaca* (or *panaca ayllu*) dedicated to supporting the cult, lands, and prestige of their deceased father. Cobo summarizes the *panaca* system of Cuzco:[9]

> Furthermore, upon the death of the king, the prince did not inherit his house and treasure, but it was handed over along with the body of the deceased king to the family that he had founded. This entire treasure was used for the cult of his body and the sustenance of his family. After having the body of their father the king embalmed, they kept it with all of his dishes and jewelry; the king's family and all of his descendants adored the body as a god. The body was handed down to the most prominent members of the family, and they did not make use of the dead king's dishes, except when the town or place where the body was deposited held an important fiesta. And the successor to the crown set up his house anew, accumulating for it a treasure to leave to those of his ayllo and lineage. (Cobo 1979: 111 [1653: Bk. 12, Ch. 4])[10]

Thus at the death of an Inca king a cult was established by his descendants that was then maintained through time with the wealth that the king had accumulated during his reign. Each of the dead kings continued to own his central palace in Cuzco as well as various estates, agricultural land, and camelid herds in the Cuzco region. This system grew to such an extreme that Huascar, frustrated by the fact that some of the richest lands of the Cuzco region were held by the royal *panacas*, once declared that "the dead had the best of everything in his kingdom"[11] (Pedro Pizarro 1921: 205–206 [1571]).[12]

Care for the Mummies

Some of the royal mummies appear to have been maintained in their estates or palaces, and others spent much of their time in the Coricancha. Regardless of where they were generally kept, *panaca* members carried the Inca mummies to the central plaza of Cuzco for the public to see on the most important ritual days of the year. Those former Inca kings associated with Hurin Cuzco were arranged in order of their rule on the left side of the plaza; those of Hanan Cuzco were placed on the right.

During the important rituals of Cuzco, each of the mummies was accompanied by an entourage of servants who provided food and drink for the deceased kings as well as for the living persons who attended the celebrations. Pedro Pizarro offers an especially detailed description of the mummified Inca kings being fed while sitting near the center of the plaza. Because Pedro Pizarro arrived in Cuzco in 1534, when the mummies were still being openly displayed and worshiped, there is little doubt that he was an actual eyewitness to these extraordinary events:[13]

. . . they took them all out into the plaza and sat them down in a row, each one according to his antiquity, and there the men and women servitors ate and drank. And for the dead they made fires before

them with a piece of very dry wood which they had worked into a very even shape. Having set this piece of wood on fire, they burned here every thing which they had placed before the dead in order that he might eat of the things which they eat, and here in this fire they consumed it. Likewise before these dead people they had certain large pitchers, which they call *verquis,* made of gold, silver or pottery, each one according to his wish, and into [these vessels] they poured the *chicha* which they gave to the dead man with much display, and the dead pledged one another as well as the living, and the living pledged the dead. When these *verquis* were filled, they emptied them into a round stone in the middle of the plaza, which they held to be an idol, and it

FIGURE 12.2. The ruling Inca and his wife make liquid offerings to a previous Inca king and queen. The mummified Inca king sits on a low stool, and the mummified queen kneels on the ground to the right of him. In the background is an open burial chamber. The caption reads "Capítulo Primero, Entiero del Inga/inca illapa aia/defunto" [First Chapter, Burial of an Inca, lightening Inca corpse, deceased]. (Guaman Poma de Ayala 1980: 262 [1615: 287])

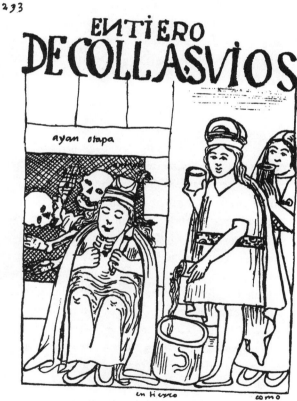

FIGURE 12.3. A high-ranking leader and his wife make offerings to the well-preserved mummy of an ancestor in Collasuyu. Both the man and woman drink corn beer while the man simultaneously pours a cup of the same liquid into a large vessel on the ground. Behind the mummy is a burial tower in which the remains of older individuals can be seen. The caption reads "Entiero de Colla Suios" [Burial in Collasuyu]. (Guaman Poma de Ayala 1980: 268 [1615: 293])

was made around a small opening by which it [the chicha] drained itself off though some pipes which they had made underground. (Pedro Pizarro 1921: 251–252 [1571])[14]

The indigenous chronicler Guaman Poma de Ayala (1980: 262, 268 [1616: 287, 293]) depicts two scenes similar to the one described by Pedro Pizarro. In the first drawing, he shows the ruling Inca toasting the mummies of the previous king and queen while pouring the contents of a second cup into a large ceramic vessel (Figure 12.2). In the second drawing, he illustrates a nearly identical scene occurring in the area of Collasuyu (Figure 12.3).

Betanzos, who saw several of the royal mummies in Cuzco just before Polo de Ondegardo found them, provides an especially elaborate description of Huayna Capac visiting each of the palaces of the former kings. Betanzos emphasizes the fact that there were special servants of the kings who would sing epic songs about the dead king's achievements.

[Huayna Capac] ordered that, since he was looking into the things of these lords, the *mamaconas* and servants of each lord should sing his history and past deeds. Thus as he was inspecting the images and their houses, whenever he noticed anything lacking, he would provide it for them. When he reached the house of Inca Yupanque, hearing the song of his history, the great deeds and livestock of this lord, the Inca stayed for one month holding great feasts and making sacrifices to the image of Inca Yupanque, his grandfather. To this image he gave great gifts, a great number of *mamacona* maidens, as well as many *yanacona* youths. He ordered them to settle in the valleys near Cuzco and that from there to bring what they cultivated and raised to the house of Inca Yupanque. Thus they brought fruit, fresh maize, and birds. These were placed before the image of Inca Yupanque as if he were alive and with the same show of reverence as when he was alive. Moreover, he ordered the Soras, the Lucanas, and the Chankas of Andahuaylas put in the service of this image because they were the first provinces that this lord Inca Yupanque conquered and subjugated in his life.

After this the Inca went into the house where the image of his uncle, Yamque Yupanque, was kept. Then he heard his story in his song of praise. Remaining there ten days and with great reverence to him, the Inca made sacrifices, left provisions, and gave him great gifts. He gave him a certain repartimiento in Vilcas. From there he went into the house of his father, and in his story and song of praise he heard and learned of his great deeds and of the lord who was fond of subjugating lands and provinces. (Betanzos 1996: 166–167 [1557: Pt. 1, Ch. 41])[15]

In the above, Betanzos indicates that each of the Inca kings continued to control important estates after his death and that the produce from these holdings were used to support the cult of that particular king and his retainers.

Cobo, building on information provided by Polo de Ondegardo and Pedro Pizarro, also stresses that the descent groups of the deceased kings supported themselves on his lands for generations after his death.

The relatives of the deceased would look after these dead bodies, and they kept them adorned and carefully preserved. The bodies were wrapped in a large amount of cotton with the face covered. The bodies were not brought out except for major festivals. No ordinary people saw the bodies except for those responsible for dressing them, watching over them, and caring for their preservation. These attendants sustained themselves on the farmland that the descendants of the deceased had designated for this purpose. The embalmed bodies were greatly venerated, and sacrifices were made to each one according to their resources. . . . The lords and chiefs of their family units always looked after them, and the whole family devoted itself to paying tribute to their deceased. The bodies were brought out with a large retinue for all solemn festivals, and for less solemn occasions, in place of the bodies, their *guauques* were brought out. (Cobo 1990 39–40 [1653: Bk. 13, Ch. 10])[16]

After the Spanish Conquest and the fall of the *panaca* system in Cuzco, a series of legal battles developed over the control of the former kings' estates. For example, by the early 1550s multiple disputes had arisen concerning the rights to various fields in the Yucay Valley. These included some of the finest maize-growing lands in the Andes, which, prior to the conquest, had been held by the *panacas* of Huayna Capac and Topa Inca Yupanqui (Villanueva 1971).

Most early colonial accounts of the royal mummies emphasize the fact that, as in life, these elite individuals had limited contact with the lower classes, except during the large ceremonies that were held in the center of Cuzco. It was during these rituals that the mummies were placed in the central plaza for all to see. Ceremonies involving the Inca mummies did not, however, last long after the Spaniards arrived in the imperial city. Yet there was a brief period of time, between when the Spaniards first entered Cuzco (November 1533) and when they consolidated their control after the siege (May 1536), that the royal mummy cults were practiced in the open. Thus, a few eyewitness descriptions of the mummies during this period are critical to review, since they provide details of how the ancestor cults functioned in the final moments of the empire.

When the Spanish forces first reached Cuzco, they were unaccustomed to the fact that its deceased kings played a central role in Inca society or that the dead held influence over the actions of the living. The importance of the mummy cults in everyday life in Cuzco was made clear to Pedro Pizarro as he accompanied a native captain who wished to marry a woman from one of the noble houses. Pedro Pizarro believed that he was requesting permission from one of the woman's living guardians. But to his surprise, Pedro Pizarro found himself in an audience with one of the dead rulers of Cuzco. He writes:

I came to understand this when we first entered Cuzco for the first time . . . and just before setting out a captain of Mango Inca's who was to go with him came to the Marquis to ask him to send and ask it of one of these dead men that a relative of his who was in his service be given to him [the captain] for wife. The Marquis sent me [with orders to] go with Don Martín, the interpreter, to speak to this dead man and ask on his [Pizarro's] behalf that the Indian woman be given to this captain. Then I, who believed that I was going to speak to some living In-

dian, was taken to a bundle, [like] those of these dead folk, which was seated in a litter, which held him and on one side was the Indian spokesman who spoke for him, and on the other was the Indian woman, both sitting close to the dead man. Then, when we were arrived before the dead one, the interpreter gave the message, and being thus for a short while in suspense and in silence, the Indian man looked at the Indian woman (as I understand it, to find out her wish). Then, after having been thus as I relate it for some time, both the Indians replied to me that it was the will of the Lord the dead one that she go, and so the captain already mentioned carried off the Indian woman, since the Apoo, for thus they called the Marquis, wished it. (Pedro Pizarro 1921: 204–205 [1571])[17]

It is clear from this early description that each mummy had an oracle: an individual who spoke for and received things on behalf of the dead king. In this case, the oracle did not enter into a trance or become possessed in any way, but instead simply sat quietly beside the mummy bundle and spoke for it. Pedro Pizarro repeats this information elsewhere in his chronicle where he describes the busy day-to-day activities of the dead kings:

Each dead man had allotted to him an important Indian, and likewise an Indian woman, and whatever these wanted they declared it to be the will of the dead one. Whenever they wished to eat, to drink, they said that the dead ones wished to do that same thing. If they wished to go and divert themselves in the houses of other dead folk, they said the same, for it was customary for the dead to visit one another, and they held great dances and orgies, and sometimes they went to the house of the living, and sometimes the living came to them. (Pedro Pizarro 1921: 203 [1571])[18]

Molina, in his description of the major rituals of Cuzco, also provides an account of the dead kings being taken into the plaza and served their favorite foods and drink. Molina (1989: 111 [ca. 1575]) emphasizes that the kings from Hanan Cuzco were placed on one side of the plaza and the kings from Hurin Cuzco were placed on the other:

For this festival they took to the square all the said *huacas* [shrines] and the bodies of the dead Inca Lords and Ladies, to drink with them, placing those who had been Lords of Hanan Cuzco in it, and those of Hurin Cuzco in their place. Thus they brought food and drink to the dead as though they were living, saying, "When you were alive you used to eat and drink this: may your soul now receive and eat it wherever you may be."[19] (Translation by author)

Cieza de Leon, who interviewed many of the original conquistadors in Cuzco, provides a similar account of the royal mummies in the plaza. He clearly indicates that the mummies of the royal Inca were brought out for viewing in the plaza during the coronation of Manco Inca (December 1533), shortly after Pizarro and his men arrived in Cuzco:

To this end they made a statue in the form they chose to give it, which they called by the name of the dead Inca. These statues were set up in the square of Cuzco when they held their celebrations, and around each statue of these Incas their wives and servants gathered, and they all came, setting out their food and drink there, for the devil probably spoke to them through those statues, as they were used for this purpose. Each statue had its buffoons, or jesters, who amused the people with merry words, and all the treasure the Inca had possessed when he was alive was in the custody of his servants and kinfolk, and was brought forth on such occasions with great display. In addition to this, they had their *chararas* [fields], which is the name they give their plantations, where they raised corn and other victuals to maintain the wives and all the other members of the family of these lords who had statues and memorials, even though they were already dead. And beyond doubt it was this custom that was in large part responsible for the vast treasures beheld by our own eyes in this kingdom. I have heard from Spanish conquistadors that when they were discovering the provinces of the kingdom, these statues still existed in Cuzco, which would seem to be true, for when shortly afterwards Manco Inca Yupanqui [son of Huayna Capac] aspired to the royal fringe, they were brought out into the square of Cuzco before the Spaniards and Indians who were there at the time. (Cieza de León 1976: 189 [1554: Pt. 2, Bk. 11])[20]

Betanzos also provides a vivid description of the care of the mummies by a large number of retainers and of the songs that they would sing:

He [Pachacuti Inca Yupanqui] picked out and named a certain number of *yanaconas* and *mamaconas* to serve these statues and gave them land on which to sow and harvest for the services of these statues. He also designated much livestock for the sacrifices that were to be made to the statues. These servants, lands, and livestock were given out to each one of the statues for itself. He ordered that great care be taken to give food and drink to these statues every evening and morning and to make sacrifices to them. For this purpose, he had a steward put in charge of the servants he had designated for each one of the statues. He also ordered each one of these stewards to make up songs which the *mamaconas* and *yanaconas* would sing in praise of the deeds of each one of these lords in his day. These songs were ordinarily to be sung by the servants of those statues whenever there were fiestas starting first with the song, story, and praise of Manco Capac, and these *mamaconas* and servants would sing about each lord as they had succeeded one another up to that time. And that was the order that was followed from then on. Thus they preserved the memory of them and their times. . . . When Inca Yupanque had these statues put on the benches, he ordered that, on their heads, there be placed some diadems with very attractive feathers. Gold earplugs were hanging from the diadems. After this was in place, he ordered that some gold disks also be placed on the foreheads of each one of the statues. The *mamacona* women were always to have in their hands some long red feathers attached to some rods. With these they were to shoo away any flies that might light on the statues. The service articles for these statues were to be kept very clean, and every time the *mamacona* women and *yanacona* servants appeared before these statues to serve or revere them, or others, whoever they might be, they came very clean and well dressed. With cleanliness, reverence, and obeisance they appeared before these statues. (Betanzos 1996: 79–80 [1557: Pt. 1, Ch. 17])[21]

In sum, the mummified kings played a number of important roles within the imperial capital. On one level, they served to legitimate the current king. During the large public ceremonies of Cuzco, the ruling Inca was physically seen as the direct descendant of the long line of divine leaders that had been assembled in the plaza and that stretched back into the mythical times of the first Inca, Manco Capac (Bauer 1996). The mummies and their oracles also served the king in an advisory capacity. The ruling Inca was expected to seek advice from the ancestors on issues of importance, and it was carefully observed which oracles provided sound advice and which did not. The most trusted mummies and their spokespersons were also used as ambassadors for the Inca. For example, a rebellion in Ecuador was averted when Huayna Capac sent an image of his mother, Mama Ocllo, and its accompanying female Cañari oracle to negotiate with the rebel leaders (Cabello de Valboa 1951: 374 [1586: Pt. 3, Ch. 22]; Murúa 1962: 92 [ca. 1615: Ch. 34]).

Furthermore, the mummies provided a way for the noble houses of Cuzco to actively influence and gain power in the internal affairs of the state without directly or publicly challenging the divine ruler. In the words of Peter Gose (1996: 16), "Through the voice of their mummified ancestors, these groups could assert their own perspective and interest without questioning the nominally absolute power of the current sovereign." It was not, however, unusual for the *panacas* to become embroiled in the politics of the day. Their power and wealth could rise or fall as a result of these actions. For example, in one case, a contender to the kingship is said to have had his mother marry the mummy of one of the dead kings so that he would be seen as a more legitimate candidate (Santa Cruz Pachacuti Yamqui Salcamayhua 1950 [ca. 1613]). The decimation of Topa Inca Yupanqui's bloodline provides another illustrative case. Atahualpa's generals burned the mummy of Topa Inca Yupanqui and killed many of his descendants because they had openly sided with Huascar during the civil war. It was a mistake from which the *panaca* never recovered.

Representations of the Inca Kings and Their Huauques and Bultos

Closely related to the concept that dead rulers could continue to hold influence over the living through their mummies was the ruling Inca's practice of creating statues that could represent him at times of need. These figures were called *huauques* (brothers) of the Inca king.[22] Using information gathered from Polo de Ondegardo's 1559 investigation of the Inca mummies, Sarmiento de Gamboa describes two of these "brothers."[23] Within the account of the life of Sinchi Roca, the second Inca, Sarmiento de Gamboa (1906: 44 [1572: Ch. 15]) writes:

[Sinchi Roca] left a stone idol in the form of a fish, call Huanachiri Amaru, that was in his life his *huauque* idol. This idol was found with the body of Sinchi Roca among some copper bars by the lawyer Polo [de Ondegardo], who was then the Chief Magistrate of Cuzco, in the town of Bimbilla [Wimpillay]. The idol had servants and cultivable lands for its service.[24] (Translation by author)

Within Sarmiento de Gamboa's (1906: 94 [1572: Ch. 48]) discussion of Pachacuti Inca Yupanqui's reign, we find this description of his *huauque*:

The lawyer Polo [de Ondegardo] found the body of this Inca in Totocachi, where the Parish of San Blas of the city of Cuzco is now, well adorned and guarded, and he sent it to Lima by order of the Marquis of Cañete, the viceroy of this kingdom. The *huauque* idol of this Inca was called Inti Illapa. It was very large and of gold. It was carried in pieces to Cajamarca. The said lawyer Polo found the house, estates, servants, and women of this *huauque* idol.[25] (Translation by author)

Cobo provides the most detailed description of the brother-idols and the various roles that they held. Although long, it is worth quoting at length, since it is no doubt based on information gained from the now lost 1559 work of Polo de Ondegardo:

During their lifetimes, all of the kings and lords of the

Inca class were in the habit of each making a statue that depicted its owner, and with a certain solemnity and ceremonies they would take the statue for their brother, calling it *guauque,* which means brother. Some made the statue large; others made it small; still others made it the same size and shape as themselves. Some of the statues were made of gold, others of silver, wood, stone, or other materials. The kings gave their *guauques* a house and servants. They also assigned some farmland to support those who were in charge of each statue. From the day that they made their *guauques* their brothers, the Inca kings would order the people, especially those of their lineage and family unit, to treat the *guauques* with the same reverence as the king himself. These idols were greatly venerated during the lifetime of the lords whom they represented. After the death of the lords, the idols were kept with their bodies, and both the bodies and the idols were always respected and served equally. The idols were kept very well dressed, and during the less solemn festivals, when the occasion did not warrant bringing out the bodies of the lords, their *guauques* or images were brought out. This custom was so ancient that if it was not a fabrication of theirs, it must date from the time of their earliest recollections. Although initially it was only the practice of the kings and great lords, as time passed the custom was extended so much that any important man might have a *guauque.* During his lifetime he would have a statue made or designate a stone or idol, made of whatever material struck his fancy, and he would take it for his *guauque.* He would order the members of his family to treat the *guauque* as if it were him during his lifetime, and after his death his family was to continue to venerate the *guauque* in the same way. As a result, before long there were a great number of these idols in Cuzco and the surrounding area. And there would have been many more if it had not been for the custom of the majority to forsake the less important ones; the people would forget these after a time. However, the *guauques* of the Inca kings lasted up to the arrival of the Spaniards, and at that time the *guauques* were venerated as much as when this practice started. This veneration was so great that in all their times of need, the descendants of the deceased's family unit would entrust themselves to

these *guauques,* and these idols were carried by the armies with all of the authority that they could muster because they thought that this was a great help to them in their victories and that it made the enemies fearful. At least, there is no doubt that the warriors felt very confident about their success with the patronage of the *guauques,* and according to what the elders say, this patronage fired the imagination of the warriors. The sacrifices made to these statues of the *guauques* were noteworthy and extensive, and the people thought that as long as these *guauques* endured, they had the same powers as the bodies of their owners when they were still alive. During the time when they had them in the city the *guauques* were placed in the company of the bodies, and whenever the kinship units and families carried them, they honored the *guauques* as much as when their owner was alive. Thus they contributed offerings to the people who looked after the *guauques.* (Cobo 1990: 37–38 [1653: Bk. 13, Ch. 9])[26]

From these passages, we learn that the *huauques* of the Inca kings, like so many of the important shrines of the empire, had estates and attendants to help maintain them.[27] It seems, however, that "brothers" of the Inca were "retired" at the end of the king's life and kept with the mummy. Thus, as Polo de Ondegardo systematically hunted down and found the dead kings of Cuzco, he also found their *huauques* at their sides (Table 12.1).

Other early writers of Peru also describe *bultos* (bundles) that represented and spoke for the Inca. The term *bultos* implies that these figures may have taken a more human form than the *huauques,* perhaps appearing like the mummy bundles. The *bultos* were given a special status and were seen to hold intimate connections with a ruler, since they contained bits of his hair or fingernails, or small pieces of his flesh.[28] Huayna Capac's *bultos* were seen by the first Spaniards who visited Cuzco:

There are other images of plaster or clay which have only the hair and nails which were cut off in life and the clothes that were worn, and these images are as much venerated by those people as if they were their gods. (Sancho 1917: 170 [1534: Ch. 19])[29]

TABLE 12.1. The Inca and their *huauques*

MALE RULERS	*Huauques* (BROTHER IDOLS)	NOTES ON MUMMIES	REPORTED BY
1. Manco Capac	A bird called Inti	Found in Wimpillay	Sarmiento de Gamboa (1906: 42 [1572: Ch. 14]) Cobo (1979: 111–112 [1653: Bk. 12, Ch. 4])
2. Sinchi Roca	A fish-shaped stone called Huanachiri Amaru	Found in Wimpillay with copper bars in a house called Acoywasi	Sarmiento de Gamboa (1906: 44 [1572: Ch. 15]) Cobo (1979: 114 [1653: Bk. 12, Ch. 5]) Cobo (1990: 74 [1653: Bk. 12, Ch. 15])
3. Lloque Yupanqui	Called Apu Mayta	Found with the rest	Sarmiento de Gamboa (1906: 45 [1572: Ch. 16]) Cobo (1979: 117 [1653: Bk. 12, Ch. 6])
4. Mayta Capac	An idol	Found with the rest	Sarmiento de Gamboa (1906: 48 [1572: Ch. 17]) Cobo (1979: 120 [1653: Bk. 12, Ch. 7])
5. Capac Yupanqui	Called Apu Mayta	Found with the rest in a town near Cuzco	Sarmiento de Gamboa (1906: 49 [1572: Ch. 18]) Cobo (1979: 123 [1653: Bk. 12, Ch. 8])
6. Inca Roca	A stone idol called Vicaquirao	Found in Larapa Body produced rain	Sarmiento de Gamboa (1906: 50 [1572: Ch. 19]) Cobo (1979: 125 [1653: Bk. 12, Ch. 9]) Cobo (1979: 125 [1653: Bk. 12, Ch. 9])
7. Yahuar Huacac	Unknown	Found in Paullu	Sarmiento de Gamboa (1906: 55–56 [1572: Ch. 23]) Acosta (1986: 421 [1590: Bk. 6, Ch. 20]) Cobo (1979: 129 [1653: Bk. 12, Ch. 10])
8. Viracocha Inca	Called Inca Amaru	Kept in Caquia Jaquijaguana Burned by Gonzalo Pizarro Jar with ashes sent to Lima Misidentified in Cuzco	Betanzos (1996: 79 [1557: Pt. 1, Ch. 17]) Sarmiento de Gamboa (1906: 59 [1572: Ch. 25]) Acosta (1986: 429–430 [1590: Bk. 6, Ch. 21]) Cobo (1979: 132 [1653: Bk. 12, Ch. 11]) Ruiz de Navamuel (1882: 256–257 [1572]) Calancha (1981: 219 [1638: Bk. 1, Ch. 15]) Garcilaso de la Vega (1966: 306–307 [1609: Pt. 1, Bk. 5, Ch. 28])
9. Pachacuti Inca Yupanqui	Gold image called Inti Illapa	Housed in Patallacta but found in Totocachi	Betanzos (1996: 139 [1557: Pt. 1, Ch. 32]) Sarmiento de Gamboa (1906: 92 [1572: Ch. 47]) Acosta (1986: 423 [1590: Bk. 6, Ch. 21]) Cobo (1990: 51 [1653: Bk. 13, Ch. 13])

TABLE 12.1. *continued*

MALE RULERS	*Huauques* (BROTHER IDOLS)	NOTES ON MUMMIES	REPORTED BY
		Andahuaylas idol found with mummy	Polo de Ondegardo (1990: 86 [1571])
		Mummy sent to Lima	Polo de Ondegardo (1990: 86 [1571])
			Ruiz de Navamuel (1882: 256–257 [1572])
			Acosta (1986: 423 [1590: Bk. 6, Ch. 21])
			Calancha (1981: 212 [1638: Bk. 1, Ch. 15])
10.1 Topa Inca Yupanqui	Called Cusichuri	Kept at Calispuquio	Sarmiento de Gamboa (1906: 102 [1572: Ch. 54])
			Cobo (1979: 151 [1653: Bk. 12, Ch. 15])
		Burned during civil war	Sarmiento de Gamboa (1906: 122–123 [1572: Ch. 66])
		Misidentified in Cuzco	Garcilaso de la Vega (1966: 306–307 [1609: Pt. 1, Bk. 5, Ch. 28])
10.2 Amaru Topa Inca (brother of Topa Inca Yupanqui)		Sent to Lima	Ruiz de Navamuel (1882: 256–257 [1572])
11. Huayna Capac	Gold image called Inca Huaraqui	Died in Quito	Xerez (1985: 119 [1534])
			Betanzos (1996: 185 [1557: Pt. 1, Ch. 48])
			Acosta (1986: 422 [1590: Bk. 6, Ch. 22])
		Seen in Cuzco	Sancho (1917: 170 [1534: Ch. 19])
			Mena (1929: 37 [1534])
			Sarmiento de Gamboa (1906: 112 [1572: Ch. 62])
		Found in Cuzco	Polo de Ondegardo (1990: 128 [1571])
			Cobo (1979: 161–162 [1653: Bk. 12, Ch. 19])
			Garcilaso de la Vega (1966: 306–307 [1609: Pt. 1, Bk. 5, Ch. 28])
			Acosta (1986: 424 [1590: Bk. 6, Ch. 22])
		Sent to Lima	Ruiz de Navamuel (1882: 256–257 [1572])

FEMALE RULERS		NOTES	REPORTED BY
8. Mama Runtu		Seen in Cuzco	Garcilaso de la Vega (1966: 307 [1609: Pt. 1, Bk. 5, Ch. 28])
9. Mama Anaguarque		Kept in Pumamarca	Cobo (1990: 67 [1653: Bk. 13, Ch. 14])
10. Mama Ocllo		Kept in Picchu	Betanzos (1996: 172–173 [1557: Pt. 1, Ch. 44])
			Cobo (1990: 61 [1653: Bk. 13, Ch. 13])
			Acosta (1986: 422 [1590: Bk. 6, Ch. 22])
		Sent to Lima	Ruiz de Navamuel (1882: 256–257 [1572])
			Garcilaso de la Vega (1966: 307 [1609: Pt. 1, Bk. 5, Ch. 28])

Not surprisingly, many descriptions are ambiguous, and it is at times unclear if the Spaniards were describing an Inca mummy, a *huauque*, or a *bulto*. Nevertheless, several accounts provide detailed descriptions of *bultos* and the important role they played in the Inca kingdom. For example, the role of the *bulto* as a physical representation of the Inca king is clearly expressed in Betanzos's account of Atahualpa's actions soon after the death of his father.

With this information and finding himself lord, he [Atahualpa] ordered that a statue be prepared of his own nail clippings and hair, which was a representation of his person. He ordered that this statue be called Incap Guauquin, which means the brother of the Inca.

Once this statue was completed, he had it placed on a litter and charged one of his servants named Chima with guarding and watching over it. Giving this statue many other young men as servants, he ordered that it be taken and carried on its litter by the messengers to where his captains Chalcochima and Quizquiz were so that the peoples of the subjugated provinces could render obedience to that statue in place of his person. Thus this statue was carried and given to the captains, who received it and were very pleased with it. They performed many and great sacrifices and served and respected this statue as if the very person of Atahualpa were there. (Betanzos 1996: 205 [1557: Pt. 2, Bk. 6]).[30]

Although Atahualpa made a *bulto* once he became king, it is also clear that *bultos* could be made when an Inca died. Betanzos, who was especially concerned with chronicling the achievements of Pachacuti Inca Yupanqui, records the making of a *bulto* at the time of this Inca's death:

After he [Pachacuti Inca Yupanqui] was dead, he was taken to a town named Patallacta, where he had ordered some houses built in which his body was to be entombed. He was buried by putting his body in the earth in a large new clay urn, with him very well dressed. Inca Yupanque ordered that a golden image made to resemble him be placed on top of his tomb. And it was to be worshiped in place of him by the

people who went there. Soon it was placed there. He ordered that a statue be made of his fingernails and hair that had been cut in his lifetime. It was made in that town where his body was kept. They very ceremoniously brought this statue on a litter to the city of Cuzco for the fiestas in the city. This statue was placed in the houses of Topa Inca Yupanque. When there were fiestas in the city, they brought it out for them with the rest of the statues. . . .

When the statue was in the city, Topa Inca Yupanque ordered those of his own lineage to bring this statue out for the feasts that were held in Cuzco. When they brought it out like this, they sang about the things that the Inca did in his life, both in the wars and in his city. Thus they served and revered him, changing its garments as he used to do, and serving it as he was served when he was alive. All of which was done thus.

This statue, along with the gold image that was on top of his tomb, was taken by Manco Inca from the city when he revolted. On the advice that Doña Angelina Yupanque[31] gave to the Marquis Don Francisco Pizarro, he got it and the rest of the wealth with it. (Betanzos 1996: 138–139 [1557: Pt. 1, Ch. 32])[32]

Multiple representations of a ruler are especially important in societies with divine kingships, since in these cultures the king is seen to exist in a nearly separate sphere from all other humans. Gose (1996: 21) writes: "By working through the multiple embodiments of 'substitutes,' statues, and mediums, a ruler extended his influence in space and time and delegated enough power to govern effectively. At the same time, he demonstrated his divinity by 'animating' these far-flung subdivisions of himself, thereby making an ideological virtue out of administrative necessity." Thus, the *huauques* and *bultos* of the royal Inca can be seen as highly effective tools of imperial rule in the Andes. They could be sent to convey the ruling Inca's wishes to lower-level administrators or generals. They could also accompany an official as he traveled across the countryside, emphasizing the fact that the official spoke on behalf of the ruler. These representations could also attend the major celebrations and rituals of Cuzco when the living Inca was otherwise occupied. Finally, through their oracles, the *huauques* and *bultos* of the royal Inca provided advice to the ruling Inca on running the empire as well as navigating the complex web of political relations within the social hierarchy of the imperial city.

Discovery and Destruction of the Royal Inca Mummies

Soon after Polo de Ondegardo accepted the position of chief magistrate of Cuzco, he was instructed by the viceroy to conduct a massive campaign against the idolatrous activities of the natives. Part of his anti-idolatry efforts focused on finding the mummies of the Inca kings. These mummies, which had been publicly viewed during the great festivals of Inca Cuzco, had been on the run since the Europeans gained control of the city in 1536. Juan Betanzos, who saw some of the mummies before Polo de Ondegardo began his investigation in Cuzco, writes:

> Inca Yupanque ordered that the *yanaconas* and servants [of the deceased kings] should have houses, towns, and farmland in the valleys and towns around the city of Cuzco and that these servants and their descendants should always take care to serve those statues which he had designated for them, all of which was done from then until today. Now it is done in secret and sometimes in public because the Spaniards do not understand what it is. They keep these statues in *orones,* which are storage bins used here for maize and other foods and others in large jars and in niches in the walls, and in this way the statues cannot be found. (Betanzos 1996: 79–80 [1557: Pt. 1, Ch. 17])[33]

Although the exact order in which Polo de Ondegardo found the mummies is not known, it is clear that he conducted a search that yielded fantastic results for the Spaniards. Using information provided from Polo de Ondegardo's few remaining works, and accounts based on his lost 1559 report (as recorded by Sarmiento de Gamboa [1572], Acosta [1590], and Cobo [1653]), as well as information provided by several other independent sources, it is possible to provide summaries of what happened to each of the Inca mummies as well as the mummies of several of their principal wives.

THE REMAINS OF THE INCA KINGS

The first mythical Inca, Manco Capac, was represented by a stone statue that stood about 1.5 meters high (Sarmiento de Gamboa 1906: 42 [1572: Ch. 14]; Cobo 1979: 111–112 [1653: Bk. 12, Ch. 4]). Later Inca kings carried this figure to war as well as to the shrine of Huanacauri during the male initiation ritual of Cuzco.[34] We are also told that Huayna Capac took the stone with him to Quito and Cayambis, and that it was returned to the imperial city with Huayna Capac's mummy after his death. The stone was found by Polo de Ondegardo in 1559, "all dressed and properly adorned"[35] along with its *huauque,* a bird called Inti,[36] in the village of Wimpillay just south of Cuzco (Cobo 1979: 112 [1653: Bk. 11, Ch. 4]). Years earlier, when the Spaniards first entered the city of Cuzco, a golden statue of Manco Capac was also found in a cave outside the city (Pedro Pizarro 1921: 268 [1571]).

The body of Sinchi Roca, the second Inca, was kept in a house named Acoywasi[37] in the town of Wimpillay, outside Cuzco (Cobo 1990: 74 [1653: Bk. 13, Ch. 15]). At the time of its discovery by Polo de Ondegardo, the mummy bundle was sewn together with maguey fiber. Beside it was Sinchi Roca's *huauque,* a stone fish called Huanachiri Amaru, as well as various copper bars (Sarmiento de Gamboa 1906: 44 [1572: Ch. 15]; Cobo 1979: 114 [1653: Bk. 12, Ch. 5]).

Very little information is available about the mummies of the third Inca, Lloqui Yupanqui; the fourth Inca, Mayta Capac; or the fifth Inca, Capac Yupanqui.[38] We are only told that Polo de Ondegardo found the bodies of these kings, along with their associated idols, "with the rest," suggesting that in 1559 all the mummies of Hurin Cuzco were held in a single place (Sarmiento de Gamboa 1906: 45, 48–49 [1572: Chs. 16–18]; Cobo 1979: 117, 120, 123 [1653: Bk. 12, Chs. 6–8]). If this is the case, then the most likely location would have been with body of Sinchi Roca, in the Acoywasi in the town of Wimpillay.[39]

We have considerably more information on the mummies of the kings of Hanan Cuzco. For example, the body of Inca Roca, the sixth Inca, was found a few kilometers east of Cuzco in the town of Larapa. Inca legends associate Inca Roca with the establishment of the two major irrigation canals that flowed into Hanan Cuzco (Cieza de León 1976: 202–203 [1554: Pt. 2, Ch. 35]; Sarmiento de Gamboa 1906: 49 [1572: Ch. 19]; Cobo 1990: 143 [1653: Bk. 13, Ch. 28]). Accordingly, his mummy was used to promote rain. Cobo notes:

His body was found well adorned and with much authority in a small town of the Cuzco region called Rarapa, along with a stone idol that represented him, of the same name as his *ayllo,* Vicaquirao, and this body was much honored by those of the aforesaid *ayllo* and family; in addition to the ordinary adoration and sacrifices made for it, when there was a need for water for the cultivated fields, they usually brought out his body, richly dressed, with his face covered, carrying it in a procession through the fields and punas, and they were convinced that this was largely responsible for bringing rain. (Cobo 1979: 125 [1653: Bk. 12, Ch. 9])[40]

The mummy of the seventh Inca, Yahuar Huacac, and his idol were found in the village of Paullu, in the Vilcanota Valley (Sarmiento de Gamboa 1906: 55–56 [1572: Ch. 23]; Acosta 1986: 421 [1590: Bk. 6, Ch. 20]; Covey 2003). The mummy may have been kept at Paullu, because his mother was from that area.

It is said that Viracocha Inca, the eighth ruler of Cuzco, died in self-imposed exile in the town of Caquia Jaquijahuana (now called Juchuy Cuzco), where his body was later kept (Betanzos 1996: 79 [1557: Pt. 1, Ch. 17]). Soon after the Spaniards arrived in Cuzco, Gonzalo Pizarro began searching for the body of Viracocha and for his great wealth. Gonzalo Pizarro found the mummy in Jaquijahuana and burned it. However, members of Viracocha Inca's *panaca* collected his ashes and placed them in a small ceramic vessel. This vessel and its contents were then worshiped until Polo de Ondegardo recovered them (Sarmiento de Gamboa 1906: 59 [1572: Ch. 25]; Acosta 1986: 429–430 [1590: Bk. 6, Ch. 20]). Cobo provides a full description of these events:

The body of this king was deposited in Jaquijaguana, and having some information and indications of its whereabouts, Gonzalo Pizarro searched a long time for it in order to get the great treasure that was widely thought to be buried with it; in order to discover it, he burned some Indians, men and

women. At last he found it and a large amount of wealth was given to him by the Indians who looked after it. Pizarro had the body burned, but the Indians of the Inca's *ayllo* collected the ashes, and, with a certain concoction, they put them in a very small earthenware jar along with the idol, which, since it was a stone, was left by Gonzalo Pizarro's men, who paid no attention to it. Later, at the time when Licentiate Polo was in the process of discovering the bodies and idols of the Incas, he got word of the ashes and idol of Viracocha; so the Indians moved it from where it was before, hiding it in many places because, after Gonzalo Pizarro burned it, they held it in higher esteem than before. Finally, so much care was taken in searching that it was found and taken from the possession of the Inca's descendants. (Cobo 1979: 132 [1653: Bk. 12, Ch. 11])[41]

The site of Juchuy Cuzco is well preserved, and a square, especially well constructed structure near the center of the ruins may have served as the funerary chamber for Viracocha Inca (Photos 12.1 and 12.2).

Perhaps the greatest of all Inca kings was Pachacuti Inca Yupanqui, the ninth ruler. The fate of his remains is well documented. Immediately after his death, Pachacuti Inca Yupanqui's mummy was placed in Patallacta, one of his estates, a few kilometers to the northwest of Cuzco (Sarmiento de Gamboa 1906: 92 [1572: Ch. 47]; Cobo 1990: 51 [1653: Bk. 13, Ch. 13]; Bauer 1998: 50).[42] His body remained at Patallacta for a long time after the Spanish Conquest and was seen there by Betanzos in 1557, two years before Polo de Ondegardo came to Cuzco. Betanzos writes:

Only the body [of Pachacuti Inca Yupanqui] is in Patallacta at this time, and, judging by it, in his lifetime he seems to have been a tall man. (Betanzos 1996: 139 [1557: Pt. 1, Ch. 32])[43]

Perhaps in response to Polo de Ondegardo's investigation, the body of Pachacuti Inca Yupanqui was moved from Patallacta soon after Betanzos saw it. The effort to hide the mummy from the Spaniards proved futile, since it was later discovered in a neighborhood of Cuzco called Totocachi (now San Blas) within the temple of his

PHOTO 12.1. This square structure at Juchuy Cuzco may once have held the mummy of Viracocha Inca. (Courtesy of Fototeca Andina–Centro Bartolomé de Las Casas; photograph by Cesar Meza, ca. 1940)

PHOTO 12.2. The square structure at Juchuy Cuzco today

huauque (Acosta 1986: 423 [1590: Bk. 6, Ch. 21]; Cobo 1990: 55 [1653: Bk. 13, Ch. 13]).

In regard to the discovery of Pachacuti Inca Yupanqui's mummy, it is worth mentioning that when the Inca conquered a rival ethnic group, the principal shrines of the vanquished group (which frequently included the mummified remains of their former leaders) were taken to Cuzco. This explains why, after Pachacuti Inca Yupanqui's defeat of the Chanka, their central idol, which represented the mummy of the first Chanka "king," was kept as a prize by Pachacuti Inca Yupanqui, remaining with him even after his death, when it was found next to his own mummified body. In telling of the discovery of Pachacuti Inca Yupanqui's remains, Polo de Ondegardo (1990: 86 [1571]) writes:

I learned of this system when I discovered the body of Pachacuti Inca Yupanqui Inca, who was one of those that I sent to the Marquis in the City of the Kings [i.e., Lima]. He was embalmed and well preserved, as were all those that I saw. I found with him the principal idol of the Province of Andahuaylas, because he conquered it and placed it under the domination of the Inca when he defeated Valcuvilca, the principal lord of them, and killed him.[44] (Translation by author)

In the above, Polo de Ondegardo indicates that he found the principal idol of the Chanka with the mummy of Pachacuti Inca Yupanqui. He also notes that he sent this mummy, along with several others, to Viceroy Hurtado de Mendoza (Marqués de Cañete) in Lima. There has been much interest and debate over which mummies were sent and what happened to them after they were sent to the viceroy (Hampe 1982). These issues are addressed in detail later in this chapter.

There is also some information on the postmortem worship of the tenth Inca, Topa Inca Yupanqui (Pachacuti Inca Yupanqui's son). For example, we know that after his death, the mummified body of Topa Inca Yupanqui was placed in his estate called Calispuquio, which stood on the edge of Sacsayhuaman just outside of Cuzco (Sarmiento de Gamboa 1906: 103–104 [1572: Ch. 57]; Cobo 1964: 171 [1653: Bk. 13, Ch. 13]; Bauer 1998: 55).

The remains of Topa Inca Yupanqui did not, however, remain safe for long. In 1533, during the civil war between his grandsons, Atahualpa's generals (Chalcochima and Quizquiz) invaded Cuzco and searched the city for Huascar loyalists. In a series of acts that stress the importance the noble houses of past Inca kings continued to hold in the affairs of the empire, Atahualpa's forces questioned each of the Cuzco *panacas* to determine their alliances. During this process, it was revealed that the descendants of Topa Inca Yupanqui were sympathetic to, if not directly allied with, Huascar. Sarmiento de Gamboa (1906: 122–123 [1572: Ch. 66]) tells of the events that followed Chalcochima's and Quizquiz's arrival in Cuzco:

The lords and ladies of Cuzco who were found to be friends of Huascar were taken prisoner, and they were also hung on poles. Then they examined all the houses of the dead Inca, determining which had been on the side of Huascar and the enemies of Atahualpa. They found that the house of Topa Inca Yupanqui had been with Huascar. Cusi Yupanqui assigned the punishment of the house to Chalcochima and Quizquiz, who then apprehended the steward of the house and the *bulto* of Topa Inca Yupanqui, and those of the house, and they hung them all, and they burned the body of Topa Inca outside of town and reduced it to ashes. And to burn it, they killed many *mamaconas* and servants, so that almost no one was left of the house except a few of no consequence.[45] (Translation by author)

The ashes of Topa Inca Yupanqui were collected by the few remaining members of his family and placed in a jar. This jar, along with Topa Inca Yupanqui's *huauque*, called Cusichuri, continued to be worshiped until Polo de Ondegardo discovered them some twenty-five years later still being kept at his estate at Calispuquio near Sacsayhuaman (Sarmiento de Gamboa 1906: 102 [1572: Ch. 54]; Cobo 1979: 151 [1653: Bk. 12, Ch. 15]).

It is also worth noting that a *bulto* of Topa Inca Yupanqui was also made. Betanzos states that one year after Topa Inca Yupanqui's death, at the end of the official mourning period, those of his kin group made a *bulto* with some of his remains:

After the fiesta they made the statue of his fingernails and hair, which was worshiped and adored as a lord.

They made the sacrifices to this statue that were customarily made to the dead lords of the past. With solemnity and a show of respect as if it were alive, they would give food and drink to it as a sacrifice at the same times that the Inca ate and drank during his lifetime. (Betanzos 1996: 162 [1557: Pt. 1, Ch. 39])[46]

Although we do not know what exactly happened to this *bulto,* it would not be surprising if it was destroyed by Chalcochima and Quizquiz at the same time that they burned the mummy of Topa Inca Yupanqui.

Huayna Capac was the last Inca king to rule over a unified kingdom. He died in Quito, around the year 1528. It was there, far from Cuzco, that the mummification process took place. As Betanzos writes:

When he [Huayna Capac] died, the nobles who were with him had him opened and took out all his entrails, preparing him so that no damage would be done to him and without breaking any bone. They prepared and dried him in the Sun and the air. After he was dried and cured, they dressed him in costly clothes and placed him on an ornate litter well adorned with feathers and gold.

When the body was prepared, they sent it to Cuzco. (Betanzos 1996: 185 [1557: Pt. 1, Ch. 48])[47]

Some writers suggest that various parts of Huayna Capac's body were sent to different locations after his death. For example, Xerez (1985: 119 [1534]) states that the body of Huayna Capac remained in an elaborate palace in Quito, but his head was sent to Cuzco.[48] From eyewitness accounts of Huayna Capac's mummy in Cuzco, this certainly was *not* the case.

Acosta (1986: 422 [1590: Bk. 6, Ch. 22]) states that Huayna Capac's heart and entrails were left in Quito, whereas the body was carried to Cuzco.[49] This also seems unlikely, since it is reported that after their deaths, the hearts of the Inca kings were placed in a special container in the center of the Punchao, the golden image of the Sun in Cuzco (Salazar 1867: 280 [1596]; Toledo 1924: 344–345 [1572]; Cobo 1990: 26 [1653: Bk. 13, Ch. 5]).

In death, as in life, Huayna Capac divided his time between his royal estate in Yucay and his palace on the

central plaza of Cuzco (Betanzos 1996: 190 [1557: Pt. 2, Ch. 1]). It was in Cuzco that the first three Spaniards to visit the city saw Huayna Capac's embalmed body in audience with a second mummy (Mena 1929: 37 [1534]). Sancho describes Huayna Capac as he was seen in Cuzco at the time of the conquest:

[Huayna Capac's] body is in the city of Cuzco, quite whole, enveloped in rich cloths and lacking only the tip of the nose. There are other images of plaster or clay which have only the hair and nails which were cut off in life and the clothes that were worn, and these images are as much venerated by those people as if they were their gods. Frequently they take the [body] out into the plaza with music and dancing, and they always stay close to it, day and night, driving away flies. When some important lords come to see the *cacique,* they go first to salute these figures, and they then go to the cacique and hold, with him, so many ceremonies that it would be a great prolixity to describe them. (Sancho 1917: 170 [1534: Ch. 19])[50]

The body of Huayna Capac disappeared from view some time after the conquest. Betanzos (1996: 190 [1557: Pt. 2, Ch. 1]), writing in 1557, specifically states that it had not been seen for many years. Sarmiento de Gamboa (1906: 112 [1572: Ch. 62]) indicates, however, that Huayna Capac's mummy was found in a house somewhere between the center of Cuzco and Sacsayhuaman, guarded by two servants named Hualpa Titu and Sumac Yupanqui. Cobo describes the events that led to the discovery of Huayna Capac's remains in even greater detail:

After the Spaniards entered this land, they made every effort to discover his body, and they even resorted to violence many times, because it was widely believed that he had a great treasure and that it would be buried with his body or in the places he frequented the most during his lifetime, since this was an ancient custom among them. At last, owing to the great diligence that was taken, it was found, at the same time as the bodies of the other Incas, on the road to the fortress, in a house where the body seems to have been taken the night before; since the Spaniards were on the right track and catching up with it, the Indians who took care of it would move it to many different places; and although they took it in such a rush, unexpectedly moving it from one place to another, they always took it in the company of five or six idols, for which they showed great veneration, because they were convinced that these idols helped guard the body of the Inca. (Cobo 1979: 161–162 [1653: Bk. 12, Ch. 17])[51]

Thus, like the bodies of all the other kings of Cuzco, the mummy of Huayna Capac was hunted down and found in 1559 through the tireless efforts of Polo de Ondegardo (1990: 128 [1571]).

The Contact Period Inca Kings

The civil war between the Inca kings Atahualpa and Huascar, and the arrival of the Spaniards, disrupted the long-term practice of Inca mummification in Cuzco. Nevertheless, the fate of the bodies of the contact period Inca kings can also be traced. Huascar was captured and killed by forces loyal to Atahualpa while the latter was being held prisoner in Cajamarca. Huascar's body may have been cut up and thrown into the Yanamayu River (Sarmiento de Gamboa 1906: 125 [1572: Ch. 68]), or it may have been burned (Acosta 1986: 424 [1590: Bk. 6, Ch. 22]). If it was burned, the ashes may have been collected by people from Cuzco and worshiped, as was the case for Viracocha Inca and Topa Inca Yupanqui (Cobo 1979: 171 [1653: Bk. 12, Ch. 17]).

Atahualpa was killed by Francisco Pizarro shortly after the death of Huascar. All eyewitnesses to the dramatic events at Cajamarca indicate that after Atahualpa was garroted in the plaza, his body was buried in a nearby building that the Spaniards were using as a church (Sancho 1917: 18–20 [1534: Ch. 1]; Mena 1929: 42 [1534]; Xerez 1985: 155 [1534]; Pizarro 1986: 63–64 [1571]). It is reported that Atahualpa's body was later secretly removed from Cajamarca and carried back to Quito in a litter (Betanzos 1996: 274 [1557: Pt. 2, Ch. 26]). There are unsubstantiated reports that his skull was obtained by a French research mission (Mission de E. Senéchal de la Grange) in 1906 in Antofagasta (Chervin 1902: 700–704; 1908).

Early Colonial Period Inca Kings

During the period of early Spanish rule in the Andes (1531–1572), two separate lines of Inca kings developed. Paullu Inca and his son Carlos represented one line. They lived in Cuzco and cooperated with the Europeans in controlling the former Inca capital. The other line was represented by Manco Inca, who fled Cuzco in 1536 after the failed siege. Manco Inca and his three sons (Sayri Topa, Titu Cusi Yupanqui, and Tupac Amaru) conducted a forty-year campaign against the imposition of Spanish rule in the Andes.

Although Paullu Inca died a Christian in Cuzco, members of his family took pieces of his fingernails and hair and made a *bulto* to worship (Cobo 1979: 176 [1653: Bk. 12, Ch. 20]). Sayri Topa also converted during his short stay in the Cuzco region after emerging from the Vilcabamba area. He left funds in his will for a chapel to be constructed on the spot of the former Coricancha (Morales 1944; Hemming 1970: 297; Hemming and Ranney 1982: 82). After his death, however, his remains were taken to Vilcabamba before they could be buried. The bodies of Manco Inca and Sayri Topa were captured in the final Spanish raid into Vilcabamba (Salazar 1867: 276–277 [1596]; Oviedo 1908: 406 [1573]; Cobo 1979: 176 [1653: Bk. 12, Ch. 20]). These mummies were buried, perhaps with Paullu, in Santo Domingo (Morales 1944; Hemming and Ranney 1982: 82). Tupac Amaru was beheaded in the plaza of Cuzco. His body was buried either in Santo Domingo or the cathedral, and his head was displayed on a pole in the city center. Since the head immediately began to attract large crowds, it was buried with the body the next day (Ocampo Conejeros 1907: 228 [1610]; Oviedo 1908: 406 [1573]; Vasco de Contreras y Valverde 1982: 174 [1649]).

THE REMAINS OF THE QOYAS

It is clear that the royal *qoyas* were also mummified at the time of their deaths, yet we know far less about them. We have specific information on only three of the Inca queens: Mama Runtucaya, Mama Anaguarque, and Mama Ocllo.

Mama Runtucaya was the wife of Inca Viracocha. Garcilaso de la Vega (1966: 307 [1609: Pt. 1, Bk. 5, Ch.

PHOTO 12.3. The elegant Inca estate called Pumamarca once held the mummy of Mama Anaguarque.

28]) states that he saw her body in Cuzco in 1560 after it was discovered by Polo de Ondegardo. Mama Anaguarque was the principal wife of Pachacuti Inca Yupanqui. Though she is said to have been from the village of Chocco, just southwest of Cuzco, her mummy was kept in a small but elegant estate called Pumamarca, located a few kilometers northeast of the city (Cobo 1990: 67 [1653: Bk. 13, Ch. 14]; Bauer 1998: 89–90). The remains of this complex, with its fine Inca structures and adjacent garden, can still be seen today (Photo 12.3).

Mama Ocllo was the wife of Topa Inca Yupanqui and the mother of Huayna Capac. After her death, a statue of Mama Ocllo was placed in her house in Cuzco (Betanzos 1996: 172–173 [1557: Pt. 1, Ch. 44]), which was located near the current Hacienda of Picchu (Cobo 1990: 61 [1653: Bk. 13, Ch. 13]; Bauer 1998: 133). She was also associated with a spring in central Cuzco, and a large cornfield (near the current Cuzco airport) was dedicated to her cult (Cobo 1990: 55, 72 [1653: Bk. 13, Chs. 13 and 15]; Bauer 1998: 55, 103). Polo de Ondegardo found the body of this queen and sent it, along with the mummies of several Inca kings, to Lima (Garcilaso de la Vega 1966: 307 [1609: Pt. 1, Bk. 5, Ch. 28]; Acosta 1986: 422 [1590: Bk. 6, Ch. 22]).

We also know that a figure of Mama Ocllo was made of gold, and that it was taken by her son, Huayna Capac, into Ecuador during his northern campaigns. Cobo reports:

The Inca traveled with his army, not halting until he reached Tumibamba; . . . he commanded that a magnificent palace be constructed for himself and a temple for his gods, and in the temple he put a golden statue of his mother, a large number of silver dishes, and servants, both men and women. The Cañares Indians served the statue of Mama Ocllo willingly because she had given birth in that place to Guayna Capac. (Cobo 1979: 155 [1653: Bk. 12, Ch. 16])[52]

This figure of Mama Ocllo held considerable influence in the region. In a famous event, Huayna Capac sent this statue of his dead mother, along with its Cañari oracle, to speak with the leaders of a nearby area. A revolt was averted when, after extensive negotiations, the statue offered the leaders additional food and supplies (Cabello de Valboa 1951: 374 [1586: Pt. 3, Ch. 22]; Murúa 1962: 92 [ca. 1615: Ch. 34]). This golden figure, as well as the figures of many other *qoyas,* may have met their final fate in the Spanish forges as Pizarro and his men took control of Cuzco. Sancho visited the house where much of the Cuzco gold was stored before it was melted down. He provides the following description:

> . . . among other very sightly things were four sheep in fine gold and very large, *and ten or twelve figures of women of the size of the women of that land, all of fine gold and as beautiful and well made as if they were alive.* These they held in as much veneration as if they had been the rulers of all the world, and alive [as well], and they dressed them in beautiful and very fine clothing, and they adored them as Goddesses, and gave them food and talked with them as if they were women of flesh. (Sancho 1917: 128–129 [1534]; emphasis added)[53]

Since there are no additional eyewitness accounts of the statues of the *qoyas* after the Spaniards entered Cuzco, it is possible that the ten to twelve statues that Sancho saw represented the various Inca queens who ruled the empire before the arrival of the Europeans.

Polo de Ondegardo, Viceroy Hurtado de Mendoza, and the Fate of the Inca Mummies

As noted above, when Polo de Ondegardo became corregidor of Cuzco, he immediately began a systematic search for the mummified remains of the Inca kings that were hidden in the region (Hampe 1982). With astonishing success, Polo de Ondegardo soon found in Cuzco the mummies (or representations) of all eleven Inca kings said to have ruled Cuzco before the arrival of the Spaniards, and an unknown number of Inca queens.

Polo de Ondegardo saved several individuals for the viceroy to see. Garcilaso de la Vega, who was himself a descendant of royal blood from Topa Inca Yupanqui, provides a remarkable description of these mummies.[54] Just before he left Peru for Spain, in the year 1560, Garcilaso de la Vega visited the house of Polo de Ondegardo, where he was shown a group of embalmed Inca kings and queens. He describes in vivid detail this encounter with his mummified ancestors:

When I was to come to Spain, I visited the house of Licentiate Polo Ondegardo, a native of Salamanca who was corregidor of the city, to kiss his hand and take leave of him before departing. Among other favors he showed me, he said: "As you are going to Spain, come into this room, and you shall see some of your ancestors whom I have exhumed: that will give you something to talk about when you get there." In the room I found five bodies of Inca rulers, three males and two females. The Indians said that one of them was this Inca Viracocha: it certainly corresponded to his great age and had hair as white as snow. The second was said to be the great Túpac Inca Yupanqui, the great-grandson of Viracocha Inca. The third was Huaina Cápac, the son of Túpac Inca Yupanqui and great-great-grandson of Viracocha. The last two bodies could be seen to be of younger men: they had white hairs but fewer than those of Viracocha. One of the women was Queen Mama Runtu, the wife of Inca Viracocha. The other was Coya Mama Ocllo, mother of Huaina Cápac, and it seems probable that the Indians buried husband and wife together as they had lived. The bodies were perfectly preserved without the loss of a hair of the head or brow or an eyelash. They were dressed as they had been in life, with *llautus* on their heads but no other ornaments or royal insignia. They were buried in a sitting position, in a posture often assumed by Indian men and women: their hands were crossed across their breast, the left over the right, and their eyes lowered, as if looking at the ground. . . .

I remember having touched one of the fingers of Huaina Cápac, which seemed like that of a wooden statue, it was so hard and stiff. The bodies weighed so little that any Indian could carry them in his arms or his back from house to house, wherever gentlemen asked to see them. They were carried wrapped in white sheets, and the Indians knelt in the streets and squares and bowed with tears and groans as they passed. Many Spaniards took off their caps, since they were royal bodies, and the Indians were more grateful than they could express for this attention. (Garcilaso de la Vega 1966: 306–308 [1609: Pt. 1, Bk. 5, Ch. 29])[55]

In the above, Garcilaso de la Vega states that he saw five mummies in Cuzco in the house of Polo de Ondegardo: three males and two females. He indicates that the eldest male, who is described as having "hair as white as snow," was Viracocha Inca, and that the two younger men were Topa Inca Yupanqui and Huayna Capac. The women are reported to be Mama Runtu and Mama Ocllo.

Unfortunately, given information provided by other writers concerning the fates of the royal mummies, Garcilaso de la Vega's recounting of the kings that he saw in Cuzco is problematic. For example, although various sources indicate that Gonzalo Pizarro burned the mummy of Viracocha Inca, Garcilaso de la Vega claims that the mummy of Viracocha Inca was among those that Polo de Ondegardo showed him.[56] Likewise, it is widely believed that Atahualpa's generals burned Topa Inca Yupanqui's mummy when they invaded Cuzco in 1533.[57] Yet Garcilaso de la Vega states he saw Topa Inca Yupanqui's mummy in Polo de Ondegardo's house. These contradictions suggest that at the time of his writing, Garcilaso de la Vega did not remember correctly the individuals he saw so long ago in his native land.[58]

Soon after Garcilaso de la Vega visited the house of Polo de Ondegardo, the mummies were sent to Viceroy Hurtado de Mendoza in Lima. They were then placed on public display within the confines of the Hospital of San Andrés (Hampe 1982). Although a large number of people must have seen the deceased kings in Lima, only two write about them. In 1590, nearly twenty years after the mummies were confiscated, Acosta provides a short account of the deceased kings and their condition in Lima. Contrary to Garcilaso de la Vega, Acosta (1986: 423 [1590: Bk. 6, Ch. 21]) suggests that one of the bodies was that of Pachacuti Inca Yupanqui:[59]

> The body [of Pachacuti Inca Yupanqui] was so complete and well preserved with certain rosin, that it seemed to be alive. His eyes were made of gold cloth, so well set, that one did not miss the natural ones, and he had on his head a blow that he gained in a certain war. He was gray and had a full head of hair, as if he died the same day, although it was more than sixty or eighty years since he had died. This body, with those of other Inca, was sent by the above mentioned Polo to the city of Lima, on the command of the Viceroy Marquis of Cañete. This was very necessary in order to eradicate the idolatry of Cuzco. Many Spaniards have seen his body, with the other ones, in the Hospital of San Andrés, although they are now poorly preserved and in decay.[60] (Translation by author)

The gray-haired mummy that Acosta identified as being Pachacuti Inca Yupanqui is in all certainty the same mummy that Garcilaso de la Vega suggests was Viracocha Inca. Acosta provides an intriguing observation that supports his identification of this mummy as being that of Pachacuti Inca Yupanqui. Acosta notes that the gray-haired mummy had a scar on his head that he received during a war. This wound may have been the result of a battle with the Acos (Sarmiento de Gamboa 1906: 74 [1572: Ch. 35]) or an assassination attempt (Sarmiento de Gamboa 1906: 71–72 [1572: Ch. 34]; Santa Cruz Pachacuti Yamqui Salcamayhua 1950 [ca. 1613]; Cabello de Valboa 1951: 300 [1586: Bk. 3, Ch. 14]; Rostworowski 1999: 33). It lends support to the belief that the gray-haired mummy seen by Acosta in the Hospital of San Andrés was that of the famous ninth Inca, Pachacuti Inca Yupanqui, and not that of his father, Viracocha Inca, as suggested by Garcilaso de la Vega.

Acosta (1986: 424 [1590: Bk. 5, Ch. 22]) also indicates that one of the other male mummies that he saw in Lima was that of Huayna Capac and a female mummy was that of his mother, Mama Ocllo:[61]

> His [Huayna Capac's] mother was much esteemed. She was called Mama Ocllo. Polo sent her corpus and that of Huayna Capac, well embalmed and cured, to Lima . . .[62]

It is logical that Viceroy Hurtado de Mendoza placed the mummies of the Inca kings in the Hospital of San Andrés, because he was a major benefactor of it (Hampe 1982: 412). In addition, since the hospital was for the Spanish citizens of Lima, the mummies would have been placed on "public" display for the Spanish citizenry while at the same time kept out of sight of the native population.

Antonio de la Calancha (1981: 219 [1638: Bk. 1, Ch. 15]), writing in Lima almost eighty years after the royal mummies were found by Polo de Ondegardo, confirms that several of the Inca were sent to the Hospital of San Andrés (Hampe 1982). He also notes that the jar that contained the ashes of Viracocha Inca, who had been burned by Gonzalo Pizarro, was also sent to Lima.

> . . . and seizing the treasure, he [Gonzalo Pizarro] burned the body [of Viracocha Inca]. The Indians collected the ashes and put them in a small jar that they worshiped. Licenciado Polo sent those ashes and other bodies to Lima in the time of the first Marquis de Cañete. They are in a corral in the Hospital of San Andrés.[63] (Translation by author)

A few pages further on, Calancha (1981: 212 [1638: Bk. 1, Ch. 15]), like Acosta, indicates that the body of Pachacuti Inca Yupanqui was among those that Polo de Ondegardo sent to San Andrés.

From the writings of Acosta and Calancha, it seems likely that the bodies of Pachacuti Inca Yupanqui, Huayna Capac, and Mama Ocllo were among those sent to Lima. But were there others, and if so, who were they? A little-known document provides additional information on the names of the royal mummies who were on display in the Hospital of San Andrés. In January 1572, during Polo de Ondegardo's second term as corregidor of Cuzco, Viceroy Toledo ordered the production of four large cloths on which the history of the Inca kings was painted. Upon completion, these cloths were shown to a group of individuals who represented the eleven *panacas* of Cuzco for verification. Afterward the cloths were also shown to a small group of highly respected Spaniards for their approval. Within the documents produced during these extraordinary meetings, the royal secretary, Alvaro Ruiz de Navamuel (1882: 256–257 [1572]), notes the fact that years earlier Polo de Ondegardo had found the royal mummies:

> Twelve or thirteen years ago, he [Polo de Ondegardo] offered with much diligence and by various means, to discover the bodies [of the Inca kings] to end the damage [of idolatry]. And indeed he found most of them, those of the *ayllu* of Hanan Cuzco as well as those of Hurin Cuzco. Some of them were embalmed and as fresh as when they died. Four of

them were Huayna Capac and Amaru Topa Inca and Pachacuti Inca Yupanqui Inca[64] and the mother of Huayna Capac, who is called Mama Ocllo. The other ones he found enclosed in some copper boxes.[65] These he secretly buried. With them he discovered the ashes of the body of Topa Inca Yupanqui [*sic* Viracocha Inca], conserved in a small jar wrapped in rich clothes and with his insignias, because Juan [*sic* Gonzalo] Pizarro had burned this body . . . he also found with the bodies the *guacas* and main idols of the countries that each one had conquered, which were also notable nuisances in the conversion of these natives.[66] (Translation by author)

Although Ruiz de Navamuel wrote the above statement, the information that it contains should be given special attention, since Polo de Ondegardo was one of the signatories of the document. Ruiz de Navamuel documents for the first time that Polo de Ondegardo secretly buried the majority of the royal mummies. Secrecy was needed to dispose of the bodies so that they would not be exhumed and worshiped by the natives of the region. However, it is almost certain that Polo de Ondegardo sent the four mummies that were "embalmed and as fresh as when they died" to Lima. Supporting the observations recorded by Acosta, Ruiz de Navamuel indicates that among the best-preserved royal mummies were those of Huayna Capac, Pachacuti Inca Yupanqui, and Mama Ocllo. Furthermore, like Calancha, Ruiz de Navamuel records the fact that a jar containing the burned remains of an Inca, most likely those of Viracocha Inca, was recovered. However, unlike other information sources on the royal mummies, the 1572 document states that Polo de Ondegardo also found the mummy of Amaru Topa Inca, a well-known person in Inca history. Amaru Topa Inca was the eldest son of Pachacuti Inca Yupanqui, who was passed over as crown prince in favor of his younger brother, Topa Inca Yupanqui.[67] Although he did not succeed his father as ruler, Amaru Topa Inca did retain considerable power. For example, it is believed that Amaru Topa Inca was in charge of Cuzco when his brother, Topa Inca Yupanqui, was away on military campaigns.[68] Although he may never have been the principal ruler of the Inca Empire, Amaru Topa Inca's high social position in imperial Cuzco is un-

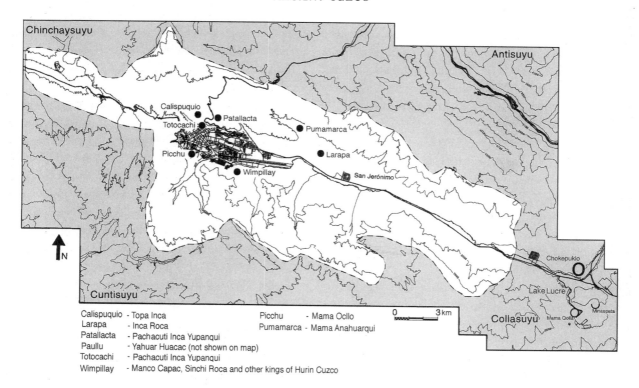

Calispuquio - Topa Inca
Larapa - Inca Roca
Patallacta - Pachacuti Inca Yupanqui
Paullu - Yahuar Huacac (not shown on map)
Totocachi - Pachacuti Inca Yupanqui
Wimpillay - Manco Capac, Sinchi Roca and other kings of Hurin Cuzco

Picchu - Mama Ocllo
Pumamarca - Mama Anahuarqui

MAP 12.1. Locations where the royal Inca mummies were discovered by Polo de Ondegardo in 1559

questionable, and there is every reason to believe he would have been mummified at the time of his death.[69]

Summary and Discussion

Ancestor worship was a religious tradition going back thousands of years in the Andes. It reached its most elaborate form, however, in the city of Cuzco at the height of the Inca Empire. When the Spaniards entered the city, they were amazed to see the mummies of previous kings and queens playing an active role in the politics of the day. The mummies were accompanied by oracles who spoke for them as well as by various attendants who served them. Because the king's wealth was passed down from one generation to another, the descendants of each ruler were able to maintain elaborate mummy cults for generations.

The ruling Inca visited the mummies of previous kings to seek advice, develop alliances, and form consensus among the royal lineages of the city. The ruling Inca could also "animate" a wide range of objects with his persona.

Representations of a ruling Inca could be created with bits of his hair or fingernails, or sculpted from other materials into his likeness. These figures could be sent on missions to represent the ruler and to speak on his behalf.

The Spaniards saw the mummies and their cults as both religious and political threats to Christian rule of the Andes. Seeking to destroy the foundations of the indigenous religions in their newly won territories, the Spaniards began a series of campaigns against idolatry. In Cuzco this task fell to the newly appointed chief magistrate, Polo de Ondegardo. He was ordered in 1559 to find and destroy the mummified Inca kings and to expose the idolatrous rituals that surrounded the mummy cults (Map 12.1). Although Polo de Ondegardo's report on his activities has been lost, it is clear from the writing of his contemporaries that the investigation achieved stunning success. Within a relatively short time, all the mummies of the deceased Inca kings were discovered and confiscated. Polo de Ondegardo found several, if not all, of the kings of Lower Cuzco in a house in the village of Wimpillay, a few kilometers south

PHOTO 12.4. Parts of the old Hospital of San Andrés still exist in downtown Lima. Most recently, it has been called Colegio Nacional de Mujeres "Oscar Miró Quesada de la Guerra."

begun to decay after being shipped from the dry, cool climate of Cuzco to the warm and moist conditions of Lima. The last recorded eyewitness report of the royal mummies in Lima is that of Calancha, who states that in 1638 several Inca mummies, along with the jar containing the ashes of Viracocha Inca, were still in the hospital.

The old hospital of San Andrés still exists just over the Rimac River from downtown Lima (Photo 12.4).[70] It continued to serve as a hospital until 1875, when the health authorities of the Republic of Peru opened the newly constructed Dos de Mayo Hospital in Lima (Hampe 2000). The former royal hospital housed two Catholic convents over the course of the next century. In more recent times, after having been declared a national historical monument in 1972, the San Andrés building has been used for instructional purposes, hosting the Colegio Nacional de Mujeres "Oscar Miró Quesada de la Guerra" (Hampe 2000). Although much of the hospital grounds, which once covered an entire city block, have been lost to urban growth,

of Cuzco. In contrast, the kings of Upper Cuzco were recovered in different locations. Inca Roca was located in the village of Larapa and Yahuar Huacac, near the town of Paullu. The ashes of Viracocha Inca were found after they were moved from Caquia Jaquijahuana (Juchuy Cuzco), and Pachacuti Inca Yupanqui's remains were identified in a suburb of Cuzco. Topa Inca Yupanqui's ashes were recovered in Calispuquio near Sacsayhuaman, and Huayna Capac's mummy was seized while it was being moved between hiding places in Cuzco.

Historic sources also indicate that Polo de Ondegardo sent several of the royal Inca mummies to Lima, where they were placed on public display within the confines of the San Andrés Hospital (Hampe 1982). Although the accounts vary, it is most likely that these included the mummies of Huayna Capac, Pachacuti Inca Yupanqui, and Mama Ocllo as well as that of Amaru Topa Inca and the ashes of Viracocha Inca. Acosta, writing in 1590, provides the best account of the royal mummies in Lima. From his description, it seems that the mummies had

PHOTO 12.5. Several royal Inca mummies may be buried on the grounds of the old Hospital of San Andrés.

approximately 80 percent of the original hospital building and its adjacent enclosures have survived.

Researchers became interested in finding the Inca mummies in Lima during the late nineteenth century. In 1876 José Toribio Polo (1877: 378) opened a large crypt in the hospital looking for the mummies but found no evidence of them (Hampe 1982). Some sixty years later, in 1937, José de la Riva-Agüero conducted limited excavations within the hospital grounds but again found noth-

ing related to the royal mummies (Hampe 1982). Since that time, it has largely been assumed that the location of the mummies will never be known. Nevertheless, a renewed effort to find them was started in 2001 by Teodoro Hampe Martínez and myself.[71] Using nondestructive Ground Penetrating Radar technology, we surveyed the surviving hospital grounds, testing for anomalies below the current ground surface (Photo 12.5). The results of that investigation are still being analyzed.

CHAPTER 13

Overview of the Inca Heartland

FOR ANTHROPOLOGICAL ARCHAEOLOGISTS, the topic of state development is one of the major theoretical issues of our time. Surprisingly, the Inca have been largely excluded from these discussions, because relatively little archaeological research has been conducted in the Cuzco region. Although over sixty years have passed since Rowe's initial work on the Inca and pre-Inca remains in the Cuzco Valley, archaeological studies of the Inca are still just beginning. What theories have been presented concerning the development of the Inca state are largely derived from readings of the Spanish chronicles, and we know little of the cultures that occupied the Cuzco region before the Inca. In short, despite the critical role that the Inca played in South American history, their heartland remains largely unexplored and the cultural processes that led to their development remain to be investigated.

One of the greatest limitations to understanding the long-term development of societies in the Cuzco region has been the lack of regional surveys in the area. Without a regional perspective of the Inca heartland, the development of models of culture change through time has not been possible. Archaeological work in the Cuzco region has traditionally focused on single sites, especially those that contain monumental architecture. Thus, although important contributions have been made to the study of several of the largest and best-preserved Inca sites in the region, we know little about the system of settlements that surrounded them. Furthermore, although researchers investigating the pre-Inca occupations of the Cuzco region have dramatically increased our knowledge of the

early villages of the area, including Marcavalle and Chanapata, as well as a few of the large sites occupied during the period of Wari influence (Pikillacta and Huaro), there has not been a tradition of archaeological survey that would provide data to place these single sites within the regional contexts of their times.

The present investigation begins to address the need for more thorough regional archaeological research in the Inca heartland through a synthesis of survey data from the Cuzco Valley. An important benefit of conducting a systematic archaeological survey is that it allows researchers to document the locations of all significant archaeological sites in the region, regardless of their age, during the course of the fieldwork. This complete coverage of all sites of all ages permits archaeologists to simultaneously address a number of different research questions within a single problem-oriented research program.

The overall goal of this book is to document the settlement patterns for each major time period in the history of the Cuzco Valley and to examine how those patterns changed over time. Although the major database for the project was a systematic archaeological survey conducted between 1994 and 1999, the project also included two field seasons of excavations to gain additional information on two of the least-understood time periods of the valley: the Archaic Period (9500–2200 BC) and the Qotakalli Period (AD 200–600). Furthermore, I have tried to include the most recent ethnohistoric data when appropriate and to enhance the study with current findings of other researchers working in the region.

Until this research began, it was believed that the Cuzco Valley was first occupied around 1000 BC by small groups of farmers. However, our survey work has identified the remains of much earlier hunter-gatherers who may have arrived as early as 7000 BC during what is here called the Early Archaic Phase (9500–7000 BC). The discovery of preceramic remains necessitates rewriting the cultural history of the valley, and further investigations are needed to better understand these early band societies. Unfortunately, the small population levels, highly mobile lifestyles, and light impact these groups had on the environment makes their campsites extremely difficult to locate. Currently, the earliest people in the valley are represented by only a few projectile points. These points, the remains of hunting activities on the valley slopes, are all made from extremely high quality, nonlocal materials, suggesting that the earliest peoples were traveling widely and curating the finest lithic materials they encountered.

Elsewhere in the Andean highlands it has been documented that hunter-gatherer groups began to settle down and develop larger occupations during the Middle Archaic Phase (7000–5000 BC). This may well have been the case in the Cuzco Valley, since our survey has identified the remains of at least two Middle Archaic occupations. The Late Archaic Phase (5000–2200 BC) marks a time of important shifts in food-procurement strategies. The period begins with most peoples of the sierra still organized in bands and supporting themselves through hunting and the collection of wild plants. Yet by the end of the phase, many of the Late Archaic groups had grown relatively large and semi-sedentary and had begun to experiment with horticulture. Excavations at the site of Kasapata have helped to highlight how and when these gradual processes occurred in the Cuzco Valley. Our excavations identified a dense strata of cultural materials dating to around 4400 BC that contained evidence of a circular hut with a possible hearth, as well as various small pits, projectile points, bone tools, and other domestic debris. The later preceramic occupations at the site presented evidence of remarkably altered subsistence activities. By around 3000 BC, groups at the site were much larger, lived in more permanent dwellings, and were presumably well on the path to animal husbandry and incipient agriculture.

The Formative Period (2200 BC–AD 200) in the Cuzco Valley is marked by the development of ceramics and the concomitant establishment of the permanent villages and agriculture. For analytical purposes, the period is currently subdivided into three phases. The Early Formative Phase (2200 BC–1500 BC) represents the final transition from a mobile lifestyle to a fully sedentary one based largely on domesticated food resources. Our systematic survey found several sites that contained dense lithic debris as well as scattered fragments of sand-tempered ceramics. Additional research is needed at these and other possible Early Formative Phase sites to better understand this critical era of developmental change.

The Middle Formative Phase (1500–500 BC) is best illustrated at the site of Marcavalle, located between Cuzco and San Sebastián. Marcavalle was a small egalitarian village that was occupied for hundreds of years. Numerous other nearly identical villages were located in the valley and adjacent regions. Although supplementing their diets through the hunting of deer and small game, the occupants of these small villages were increasingly dependent on domestic camelids (llamas and alpacas) as well as their own grown foods (corn, beans, quinoa, and potatoes).

Through time, a select few sites grew to occupy disproportionately important roles within the regional settlement patterns. In the Cuzco Basin, it appears that the site of Wimpillay emerged as the center of a small chiefdom-level society during the Late Formative Phase (500 BC–AD 200). The site is the largest Late Formative Phase occupation known in the valley and contains the finest Formative ceramics. Adjacent to Wimpillay is the distinctly round hill of Muyu Orco, the top of which contains a ceremonial sunken court dating to the Late Formative. The emergent leaders of Wimpillay may have controlled the other settlements within a few hours' walk, and toward the end of the period, perhaps the entire valley came to be united under a single elite clan located in this village.

There is evidence of strong population growth and a shift in settlement locations from knoll and ridge tops to the large alluvial terraces of the valley during the little-studied Qotakalli Period (AD 200–600). This change in settlement pattern is suggestive of a shift from a mixed economy to one based on more intensive agriculture, perhaps focusing on the production of maize. At this time, a series of large villages developed on the south side of the Cuzco Basin, and the Oropesa Basin area filled with numerous scattered hamlets. The greatest concentration of population, however, was at the western end of the Cuzco Basin, where, it is currently believed, the chiefly society of the basin, begun in the Formative Period, continued to grow. The site of Wimpillay no longer dominated the local political landscape as it did in the Late Formative Phase; instead, a concentration of equally successful villages developed. Most of these villages would continue to be occupied over the next millennium and would play important roles in the Inca Period. It is also documented that Cuzco was well connected with other regions of the Andes during this period. For example, obsidian was imported into the region from a number of different sources (Burger et al. 2000). But there seem to have been especially close interactions with the Altiplano region to the southeast, where certain polities (such as those centered at Pucara and Tiwanaku) were reaching levels of social complexity far beyond those developed in the Cuzco region.

The character of the Altiplano-Cuzco interactions changed when the Cuzco region came under the influence of the Wari. Expanding from its heartland in the area of Ayacucho sometime around AD 600, the Wari Empire was to maintain a dominant position in the Cuzco region for several centuries. The Wari presence in the Cuzco region was strongest in a short stretch of the Vilcanota River Valley between the Lucre and Huaro Basins. In the Lucre Basin, the Wari built what was perhaps the largest installation yet constructed in the Andes, the site of Pikillacta. From their position in the Lucre Basin, the Wari had both direct and indirect access to large areas of maize production. They also gained access to the traditional trade routes that brought coca from lowlands beyond Paucartambo into the southern highlands. Furthermore, they were able to establish a boundary and develop a major administrative center close to but still outside the region controlled by Tiwanaku.

The immense site of Pikillacta appears to have been planned in large sections, several of which were still not completed three to four hundred years later when the complex was abandoned. The facility was built with rotational labor provided by the various ethnic groups of the Cuzco region. Although the use of rotational labor to build public works projects was an ancient tradition in the Andes, it was used on an unprecedented local scale to build Pikillacta. The site functioned as the political center for Wari influence in the south-central Andes and most certainly helped to define a frontier with the similarly expanding Tiwanaku Empire of the Lake Titicaca region. The fact that the site of Pikillacta was never completed or occupied on the scale that its planners had originally intended indicates that the Wari did not establish the kind of control over the region that they had hoped for when the construction project was begun.

The level and impact of Wari influence over local groups varied widely across the Cuzco region. For example, the Wari established direct control over those groups living in the Lucre and Huaro Basins and initiated major changes in the social and political organizations of these areas. Other regions and peoples were brought into the orbit of Wari influence through more subtle means. Survey data indicate that Wari administration did not significantly disrupt the local settlement pattern in the Cuzco Basin. Both before and throughout the Middle Horizon, a network of villages was concentrated along the southern side of the Cuzco Basin, where large transverse streams drained into the Huatanay River, and where low alluvial terraces provided excellent locations for villages close to valley bottom lands. Likewise, the Wari appear to have had little effect on the settlement patterns of the lower Vilcanota River Valley, and they did not establish a secondary center in either region. The peoples located in the Cuzco Basin and those found in the lower Vilcanota River Valley were most likely brought into compliance through the co-option of local leaders and a combination of political intimidation and military threats. The Wari impact on the more remote populations that lived to the south of the Cuzco Valley was substantially less. They would have been aware of the political and social changes that were occurring in the Lucre Basin, but their daily lives continued relatively unchanged.

The Wari were certainly interested in the maize of the Cuzco region and most likely gathered large quantities of it through taxation on various local groups. It is worth repeating, however, that we currently know of no secondary Wari centers in the Cuzco Basin nor in the lower

Vilcanota River Valley, both of which contain some of the finest maize-producing lands of the Andean highlands. This suggests that the Wari were content to establish some kind of negotiated relations with the elites of the groups that lived in the most important regions of maize production, rather than take direct control over these resources. On the other hand, the areas of the Lucre and Huaro Basins were completely transformed by the construction of the site of Pikillacta as well as a wide range of support facilities, including massive terraces and canal systems.

Sometime after AD 900 the site of Pikillacta was abandoned and then burned. The collapse of Wari influence in the Cuzco region is mirrored at two other critical Wari centers. In the Wari heartland, the capital city of Wari itself appears to have been abandoned in mid-construction (Isbell et al. 1991). Likewise in the north, the site of Viracochapampa was abandoned soon after its construction was initiated. Perhaps the tributary demands of the empire, combined with generally degrading economic and environmental conditions, brought about and galvanized local resistance to state demands.

As Wari influence declined in the Cuzco region, the balkanized political landscape filled with rival polities of various sizes and diverse ethnic identities. In the Cuzco Basin, some time between AD 1000 and 1400, a state developed and then extended its direct administrative control over numerous neighboring groups. It was during this period that the Inca were successfully able to consolidate their rule over the various and diverse ethnic groups of the Cuzco region to form a united heartland.

The Inca's largest and most powerful rivals were the Pinahua and Mohina of the Lucre Basin and the Ayarmaca of the Chinchero area, but a host of other ethnic groups of varying sizes were scattered across the region. The unification or, in a few cases, the successful elimination of these ethnic groups over the course of several centuries resulted in the creation of an Inca state and a heartland capable of sustaining rapid Inca imperial expansion. Less powerful neighboring ethnic groups accepted Inca administration early on, perhaps even initiating Inca patronage. This is most certainly the case with the small ethnic groups that lived to the south of the Cuzco Valley who were absorbed into the developing state early in the process. Strong rivals to Inca control maintained their independence, at

times depopulating areas and settling in defensive sites to protect settlements and resources. This is clearly shown with the Pinahua and Cuyo, who lived, until their military defeat by the Inca, to the southeast and north of the Cuzco Valley respectively. Finally, groups of intermediate complexity used alliances and violence to align themselves with the strongest regional competitors. In many cases, marriages between elite families of different ethnic groups helped to promote stable, cross-generation coalitions. In time, most of the groups within the area came to see themselves as "Inca." The ethnic integration of the greater Cuzco region was a critical phase in the cultural development of the region, and it later enabled these groups to expand into neighboring non-Inca regions. In other words, the processes of state development ran concurrent with the course of heartland formation.

During the late 1300s or early 1400s, the Inca expanded beyond the Cuzco heartland. At this time of imperial development, the character of the Cuzco Valley was transformed as Cuzco became the capital of the largest empire of the Americas. A new pottery style developed that would form a time horizon across several thousand kilometers of the Andes, and a new imperial architectural style spread with the construction of provincial centers and other state facilities. Agricultural storehouses were built in the valley and other warehouses were constructed within the city to house the tribute items that were brought from all corners of the empire.

At this time, the population of the Cuzco Valley dramatically increased as people were drawn to the capital from the provinces. Others were resettled in the valley as part of a massive pacification system of the Inca. Still others were brought to the valley as representatives of their ethnic groups, and they worked in the large public works projects that began to change the face of the local geography. Immense terrace systems were established, royal estates built, and numerous other new state facilities were constructed throughout the region. Among the greatest projects devised by the Inca in the Cuzco Valley was the construction of Sacsayhuaman. Although the site had been occupied in earlier times, during the imperial period it was greatly expanded. Thousands of workers toiled for decades to construct what is now one of the most impressive archaeological sites in the Americas.

Within the city of Cuzco stood some of the most important buildings of the Inca Empire. They were largely clustered around the central plaza of the city. The most outstanding of these included the palaces of the last four Inca kings, the House of the Chosen Women, and a number of temples built to honor important deities. The central plaza area, once much larger than it is today, held a monolith and an offering basin near its center. It may also have contained a large round tower. The precise boundaries of the largest compounds in Cuzco, such as the Hatuncancha and Pucamarca, are still open to debate, since the available descriptions of Inca Cuzco are incomplete and contain many ambiguities. Additional archival research in Cuzco tracing the ownership of various Colonial Period houses and landholdings may lend some clarity to this situation.

Of central importance to Cuzco was the Coricancha compound. From this compound radiated the four parts that made up the Inca Empire. The Coricancha contained a group of buildings set within large enclosure walls. The compound was among the first to be sacked by the Spaniards, and it provided much of the gold that was included in the ransom of Atahualpa. Although much of the Coricancha has been destroyed, a few of its buildings and walls have survived to mark what was certainly the most important compound within the Inca Empire.

With the arrival of the Spaniards, followed by a series of wars between the Inca and the Europeans and then between the Europeans themselves, the character of Cuzco rapidly changed. Tragically, only five years after the Spaniards first entered the imperial city, Vicente de Valverde wrote to the king of Spain suggesting that much of the glory that was Cuzco had already been lost:

. . . the organization of this valley was so beautiful in buildings and population, that it was a thing to be admired, because although the city had but only three or four thousand houses,[1] [the valley] held more than twenty thousand people. The fort that was above the city was like the great forts of Spain. But now the greater part of the city is all demolished and burned. Nothing of the fort is intact.[2] (Translation by author)

The most notable Inca architectural features that remain in central Cuzco, and that so impress the visitors of our times, are the great compound walls that border many of the streets. Most of the interior buildings, which once numbered in the hundreds, were destroyed even before the devastating earthquake of 1650.

The Cuzco Valley is one of the great centers of cultural development in the Americas. In this work I have attempted to provide a general outline of the long and complex social developments that occurred in and around the valley from the time of its first inhabitants to the fall of the Inca Empire. By necessity, parts of this work are speculative, and there is still much to be learned. A better-defined ceramic sequence and large-scale excavations are urgently needed to test and refine many of the suggestions put forth in this book. Unfortunately, with the rapid population growth and urban expansion of Cuzco, dozens of archaeological sites in the valley are being destroyed each year. There is little time left to collect information on the heartland of the Inca. Once the sites of the Cuzco Valley are destroyed, much of the history of the Inca, like their empire, will be lost forever.

APPENDIX
Radiocarbon Dates from the Cuzco Region

SITE	LAB NO.	ASSOCIATED CERAMICS	RADIOCARBON AGE	CALENDAR	SOURCE		CALIBRATED DATE
Juchuy Cuzco	UCLA 1676F	none**	modern	modern	Kendall 1985		modern
Pisaq	UCLA 1676Q	none**	modern	modern	Kendall 1985		modern
Pisaq	UCLA 1676R	none**	modern	modern	Kendall 1985		modern
Pisaq	UCLA 1676S	none**	modern	modern	Kendall 1985		modern
Urco	UCLA 1676I	none**	160 BP	AD 1790	Kendall 1985		modern
Patallacta	BM 926	none**	168 ± 73 BP	AD 1782 ± 73	Kendall 1985	68.2%	AD 1660 (11.9%) AD 1700 AD 1720 (31.8%) AD 1820 AD 1830 (13.1%) AD 1880 AD 1910 (11.4%) AD 1950
						95.4%	AD 1630 (95.4%) AD 1960
Queswawayqo	ANU 5838	Inca*	200 ± 80 BP	AD 1750 ± 80	Heffernan 1989	68.2%	AD 1640 (17.6%) AD 1700 AD 1720 (30.2%) AD 1820 AD 1830 (10.2%) AD 1880 AD 1910 (10.3%) AD 1950 AD 1510 (9.4%) AD 1600
						95.4%	AD 1620 (86.0%) AD 1960
Urco I	BM 928	none**	209 ± 65 BP	AD 1741 ± 65	Kendall 1985	68.2%	AD 1630 (20.9%) AD 1700 AD 1720 (34.6%) AD 1820 AD 1850 (1.9%) AD 1870 AD 1910 (10.7%) AD 1950
						95.4%	AD 1520 (8.4%) AD 1600 AD 1620 (87.0%) AD 1960
Canabamba	BM 927	none**	227 ± 69 BP	AD 1723 ± 69	Kendall 1985	68.2%	AD 1520 (8.8%) AD 1570 AD 1620 (22.0%) AD 1690 AD 1720 (29.1%) AD 1820 AD 1920 (8.2%) AD 1950
						95.4%	AD 1490 (85.5%) AD 1890 AD 1910 (9.9%) AD 1960
Pumamarca	AA 5353	none**	260 ± 35 BP	AD 1690 ± 35	Kendall 1996	68.2%	AD 1520 (17.8%) AD 1560 AD 1630 (41.6%) AD 1670 AD 1780 (8.8%) AD 1800
						95.4%	AD 1490 (32.6%) AD 1600 AD 1610 (48.0%) AD 1680 AD 1760 (12.6%) AD 1810 AD 1930 (2.2%) AD 1950
Pumamarca	AA 5354	none**	260 ± 40 BP	AD 1690 ± 40	Kendall 1996	68.2%	AD 1520 (17.8%) AD 1560 AD 1630 (41.6%) AD 1670 AD 1780 (8.8%) AD 1800

SITE	LAB NO.	ASSOCIATED CERAMICS	RADIOCARBON AGE	CALENDAR	SOURCE		CALIBRATED DATE
Fortaleza Ollantay	BM 931	none**	295 ± 54 BP	AD 1655 ± 54	Kendall 1985	95.4%	AD 1490 (32.6%) AD 1600 / AD 1610 (48.0%) AD 1660 / AD 1760 (12.6%) AD 1810 / AD 1930 (2.2%) AD 1950
Urco J	BM 929	Inca*	307 ± 41 BP	AD 1643 ± 41	Kendall 1985	68.2%	AD 1510 (46.6%) AD 1600 / AD 1610 (21.16) AD 1660
						95.4%	AD 1450 (91.9%) AD 1680 / AD 1770 (3.5%) AD 1800
Queswawayqo	ANU 5840	Inca?*	310 ± 80 BP	AD 1640 ± 80	Heffernan 1989	68.2%	AD 1510 (52.5%) AD 1600 / AD 1620 (15.7%) AD 1650
						95.4%	AD 1480 (95.4%) AD 1660
Ollantaytambo	AA 1530	Inca?**	320 ± 60 BP	AD 1630 ± 60	Bengtsson 1998	68.2%	AD 1480 (68.2%) AD 1660
						95.4%	AD 1400 (93.4%) AD 1850 / AD 1900 (2.0%) AD 1950
Ollantaytambo	AA 1528	none**	320 ± 70 BP	AD 1630 ± 70	Bengtsson 1998	68.2%	AD 1490 (68.2%) AD 1650
						95.4%	AD 1440 (95.4%) AD 1670
Queswawayqo	ANU 5839	Inca?*	320 ± 110 BP	AD 1630 ± 110	Heffernan 1989:539	68.2%	AD 1480 (68.2%) AD 1650
						95.4%	AD 1400 (92.4%) AD 1700 / AD 1750 (3.0%) AD 1850
Yucay	UCLA 1676K	Inca**	365 ± 60 BP	AD 1585 ± 60	Kendall 1985	68.2%	AD 1440 (68.2%) AD 1670
						95.4%	AD 1400 (95.4%) AD 2000
Patallacta	UCLA 1676A	Inca*	365 ± 60 BP	AD 1585 ± 60	Kendall 1985	68.2%	AD 1450 (33.8%) AD 1520 / AD 1560 (34.4%) AD 1630
						95.4%	AD 1430 (95.4%) AD 1650
Qata Casallacta	ISGS 545	Inca*	370 ± 80 BP	AD 1580 ± 80	Liu et al 1986	68.2%	AD 1450 (33.8%) AD 1530 / AD 1560 (34.4%) AD 1630
						95.4%	AD 1430 (95.4%) AD 1650
Pumamarca	AA 5352	none**	380 ± 35 BP	AD 1570 ± 35	Kendall 1996	68.2%	AD 1440 (35.5%) AD 1530 / AD 1550 (32.7%) AD 1640
						95.4%	AD 1410 (95.4) AD 1670
Fortaleza Ollantay	SI 6991B	none**	390 ± 00 BP	AD 1560 ± 100	Hollowell 1987	68.2%	AD 1430 (36.7%) AD 1530 / AD 1540 (31.5%) AD 1640
						95.4%	AD 1300 (95.4%) AD 1850

SITE	LAB NO.	ASSOCIATED CERAMICS	RADIOCARBON AGE	CALENDAR	SOURCE		CALIBRATED DATE
Ollantaytambo	AA 2217	none**	409 ± 66 BP	AD 1541 ± 66	Bengtsson 1998	68.2%	AD 1430 (50.9%) AD 1530 AD 1580 (17.3%) AD 1630
						95.4%	AD 1410 (95.4%) AD 1640
Tunasmocco	UCLA 1676B	none**	415 ± 60 BP	AD 1535 ± 60	Kendall 1974, 1985	68.2%	AD 1430 (55.5%) AD 1520 AD 1590 (12.7%) AD 1630
						95.4%	AD 1410 (95.4%) AD 1640
Canaraccay	BM 925	none**	425 ± 67 BP	AD 1525 ± 67	Kendall 1974, 1985	68.2%	AD 1420 (59.1%) AD 1520 AD 1590 (9.1%) AD 1620
						95.4%	AD 1400 (95.4%) AD 1640
Pukacancha	AA 34936	Inca*	440 ± 45 BP	AD 1510 ± 45	Bauer and Jones 2003	68.2%	AD 1420 (68.2%) AD 1485
						95.4%	AD 1400 (85.3%) AD 1530 AD 1570 (10.1%) AD 1630
Kachiqhata	AA 2218	none**	454 ± 49 BP	AD 1496 ± 49	Bengtsson 1998	68.2%	AD 1415 (68.2%) AD 1480
						95.4%	AD 1330 (1.0%) AD 1350 AD 1390 (87.0%) AD 1530 AD 1580 (7.4%) AD 1630
Fortaleza Ollantay	SI 6991A	none**	470 ± 70 BP	AD 1480 ± 70	Hollowell 1987	68.2%	AD 1330 (3.9%) AD 1350 AD 1390 (61.0%) AD 1500 AD 1600 (3.3%) AD 1620
						95.4%	AD 1300 (10.1%) AD 1370 AD 1380 (71.5%) AD 1530 AD 1550 (13.9%) AD 1640
Pumamarca	AA 5058	none**	475 ± 50 BP	AD 1475 ± 50	Kendall 1996	68.2%	AD 1405 (68.2%) AD 1470
						95.4%	AD 1320 (4.8%) AD 1350 AD 1390 (88.2%) AD 1520 AD 1590 (2.5%) AD 1620
Canamarca	UCLA 1676D	none**	475 ± 60 BP	AD 1475 ± 60	Kendall 1985	68.2%	AD 1400 (68.2%) AD 1490
						95.4%	AD 1300 (8.7%) AD 1360 AD 1380 (79.4%) AD 1530 AD 1570 (7.3%) AD 1630
Ancasmarca A	BM 930	Inca*	482 ± 91 BP	AD 1468 ± 91	Kendall 1985	68.2%	AD 1320 (9.4%) AD 1360 AD 1380 (54.3%) AD 1520 AD 1590 (4.4%) AD 1620
						95.4%	AD 1290 (95.4%) AD 1640
Kachiqhata	Ua 1711	none**	485 ± 60 BP	AD 1465 ± 60	Bengtsson 1998	68.2%	AD 1330 (3.1%) AD 1340 AD 1390 (65.1%) AD 1480
						95.4%	AD 1300 (13.5%) AD 1370 AD 1380 (78.1%) AD 1530 AD 1590 (3.8%) AD 1630

SITE	LAB NO.	ASSOCIATED CERAMICS	RADIOCARBON AGE	CALENDAR	SOURCE		CALIBRATED DATE
Kachiqhata	Ua 1710	Inca**	485 ± 60 BP	AD 1465 ± 60	Bengtsson 1998	68.2%	AD 1330 (3.1%) AD 1340 / AD 1390 (65.1%) AD 1480
						95.4%	AD 1300 (13.5%) AD 1370 / AD 1380 (78.1%) AD 1530 / AD 1590 (3.8%) AD 1630
Palacio de Sayri Tupac		Inca**	500 ± 100	AD 1450 ± 100	Gibaja 1982:90	68.2%	AD 1300 (22.0%) AD 1370 / AD 1380 (46.2%) AD 1490
						95.4%	AD 1290 (95.4%) AD 1640
Intihuatana	SI 6989	none**	515 ± 50 BP	AD 1435 ± 50	Hollowell 1987	68.2%	AD 1330 (8.0%) AD 1350 / AD 1390 (60.2%) AD 1450
						95.4%	AD 1300 (24.4%) AD 1370 / AD 1380 (71.0%) AD 1470
Ollantaytambo	AA 2215	Inca*	540 ± 49 BP	AD 1494 ± 49	Bengtsson 1998	68.2%	AD 1320 (20.7%) AD 1350 / AD 1390 (47.5%) AD 1440
						95.4%	AD 1300 (39.8%) AD 1370 / AD 1380 (55.6%) AD 1450
Tankarpata	AA 34940	disturbed	640 ± 50 BP	AD 1310 ± 50	Bauer and Jones 2003	68.2%	AD 1295 (26.6%) AD 1330 / AD 1345 (41.6%) AD 1395
						95.4%	AD 1280 (95.4%) AD 1410
Ccorpina	AA 35005	Colcha*	640 ± 50 BP	AD 1310 ± 50	Bauer 1999, 2002	68.2%	AD 1295 (26.6%) AD 1330 / AD 1345 (41.6%) AD 1395
						95.4%	AD 1280 (95.4%) AD 1410
Kachiqhata	SI 6990	none**	640 ± 55 BP	AD 1310 ± 55	Hollowell 1987	68.2%	AD 1295 (26.8%) AD 1330 / AD 1345 (41.4%) AD 1395
						95.4%	AD 1280 (95.4%) AD 1410
Pumamarca	SI 6988B	none**	645 ± 45 BP	AD 1305 ± 45	Hollowell 1987	68.2%	AD 1295 (27.1%) AD 1325 / AD 1345 (41.1%) AD 1395
						95.4%	AD 1280 (95.4%) AD 1410
Pumamarca	SI 6988A	none**	660 ± 50 BP	AD 1290 ± 50	Hollowell 1987	68.5%	AD 1280 (30.2%) AD 1330 / AD 1350 (38.0%) AD 1390
						95.4%	AD 1270 (95.4%) AD 1410
Ancasmarca B	UCLA 1676M	Killke*	660 ± 60 BP	AD 1290 ± 60	Kendall 1985	68.2%	AD 1280 (31.7%) AD 1330 / AD 1340 (36.5%) AD 1400
						95.4%	AD 1260 (95.4 %) AD 1410
Chokepukio	BM 924[1]	none**	695 ± 59 BP	AD 1255 ± 59	Kendall 1985	68.2%	AD 1260 (41.2%) AD 1320 / AD 1350 (27.0%) AD 1390
						95.4%	AD 1220 (95.4%) AD 1400

SITE	LAB NO.	ASSOCIATED CERAMICS	RADIOCARBON AGE	CALENDAR	SOURCE		CALIBRATED DATE
Kachiqhata	Ua 1709	Inca**	700 ± 65 BP	AD 1250 ± 64	Bengtsson 1998	68.2%	AD 1260 (43.3%) AD 1320 / AD 1350 (24.9%) AD 1390
						95.4%	AD 1210 (95.4%) AD 1410
Pumamarca	SI 6987	none**	710 ± 55 BP	AD 1240 ± 55	Hollowell 1987	68.2%	AD 1250 (47.1%) AD 1310 / AD 1350 (21.1%) AD 1390
						95.4%	AD 1210 (68.8%) AD 1330 / AD 1340 (26.6) AD 1400
Rokeccasa	AA 8936	Ccoipa*	730 ± 55 BP	AD 1220 ± 55	Bauer 1989	68.2%	AD 1220 (63.1%) AD 1310 / AD 1370 (5.1%) AD 1380
						95.4%	AD 1190 (79.9%) AD 1330 / AD 1340 (15.5%) AD 1400
Sacsayhuaman	GaK 2958	Killke*	770 ± 140 BP	AD 1180 ± 140	Dwyer 1971	68.5%	AD 1040 (6.7%) AD 1090 / AD 1120 (3.7%) AD 1140 / AD 1150 (49.6%) AD 1320 / AD 1350 (8.3%) AD 1390
						95.4%	AD 990 (95.4%) AD 1430
Huillca Raccay	OXA 3958	LIP(Killke)*	850 ± 55 BP	AD 1100 ± 55	Kendall 1996	68.2%	AD 1066 (4.6%) AD 1090 / AD 1120 (4.5%) AD 1140 / AD 1150 (59.0%) AD 1270
						95.4%	AD 1030 (95.4%) AD 1280
Juchuy Cuzco	UCLA 1676G	none**	850 ± 60 BP	AD 1100 ± 60	Kendall 1985	68.2%	AD 1060 (6.0%) AD 1090 / AD 1120 (5.3%) AD 1140 / AD 1150 (56.8%) AD 1270
						95.4%	AD 1030 (95.4%) AD 1280
Llactallactayoc	Q 3090	LIP (Killke)***	915 ± 50 BP	AD 1035 ± 50	Kendall 1996	68.2%	AD 1030 (68.2%) AD 1190
						95.4%	AD 1020 (95.4%) AD 1220
Pumamarca	SI 6986²	none**	940 ± 40 BP	AD 1010 ± 40	Hollowell 1987	68.2%	AD 1020 (25.1%) AD 1070 / AD 1080 (43.1%) AD 1160
						95.4%	AD 1010 (95.4%) AD 1190
Tejahuaci	B 27494	Killke and Colcha*	940 ± 140 BP	AD 1010 ± 140	Bauer 1992	68.2%	AD 980 (68.2%) AD 1250
						95.4%	AD 750 (95.5%) AD 1300
Pikillacta	Beta 43233	Wari**	1060 ± 50 BP	AD 890 ± 50	McEwan 1996	68.2%	AD 890 (14.5%) AD 920 / AD 950 (53.7%) AD 1030
						95.4%	AD 880 (92.0%) AD 1050 / AD 1090 (1.9%) AD 1120 / AD 1140 (1.5%) AD 1160
Chokepukio	TX 4748	none**	1090 ± 60 BP	AD 860 ± 60	McEwan 1984, 1987	68.2%	AD 890 (68.2%) AD 1020
						95.4%	AD 770 (95.4%) AD 1040

SITE	LAB NO.	ASSOCIATED CERAMICS	RADIOCARBON AGE	CALENDAR	SOURCE		CALIBRATED DATE
Pukacancha	AA 34937	Arahuay*, Qotakalli (b/c³)	1100 ± 45 BP	AD 850 ± 45	Bauer and Jones 2003	68.2% 95.4%	AD 890 (25.2%) AD 930 AD 935 (43.0%) AD 995 AD 780 (1.3%) AD 800 AD 820 (94.1%) AD 1030
Pikillacta	TX 3996	Wari**	1100 ± 60 BP	AD 850 ± 60	McEwan 1984, 1987	68.2% 95.4%	AD 880 (68.2%) AD 1020 AD 770 (95.4%) AD 1030
Tankarpata	AA 39786	Arahuay*, Qotakalli (b/c)	1127 ± 40 BP	AD 823 ± 40	Bauer and Jones 2003	68.2% 95.4%	AD 885 (68.2%) AD 985 AD 780 (95.4%) AD 1000
Muyu Roco	AA 35003	Arahuay*** Wari (Viñaque) Black-incised	1135 ± 50 BP	AD 815 ± 50	Bauer 2002	68.2% 95.4%	AD 780 (2.6%) AD 790 AD 850 (3.1%) AD 840 AD 870 (62.5%) AD 990 AD 770 (95.4%) AD 1000
Pikillacta	TX 4247	Wari*	1140 ± 60 BP	AD 810 ± 60	McEwan 1984, 1987	68.2% 95.4%	AD 780 (3.5%) AD 800 AD 820 (6.1%) AD 850 AD 860 (58.6%) AD 990 AD 720 (1.1%) AD 740 AD 770 (94.3%) AD 1020
Tankarpata	AA 39785	Qotakalli*	1148 ± 39 BP	AD 802 ± 39	Bauer and Jones 2003	68.2% 95.4%	AD 780 (3.6%) AD 790 AD 820 (4.8%) AD 840 AD 860 (59.8%) AD 980 AD 770 (95.4%) AD 990
Kachiqhata	AA 1407B	Inca**	1150 ± 60 BP	AD 800 ± 60	Bengtsson 1998:102[4]	68.2% 95.4%	AD 780 (4.1%) AD 800 AD 810 (64.1%) AD 980 AD 720 (2.9%) AD 750 AD 760 (92.5%) AD 1020
Pikillacta	Beta 43230	Wari*	1150 ± 80 BP	AD 800 ± 80	McEwan 1996	68.2% 95.4%	AD 780 (68.2%) AD 980 AD 680 (95.4%) AD 1030
Pukacancha	AA 39793	Arahuay*, Black Incised Qotakalli (b/c)	1167 ± 39 BP	AD 783 ± 39	Bauer and Jones 2003	68.2% 95.4%	AD 780 (56.7%) AD 900 AD 920 (11.5%) AD 950 AD 770 (95.4%) AD 980
Pikillacta	Beta 43232	Wari**	1180 ± 60 BP	AD 770 ± 60	McEwan 1996	68.2% 95.4%	AD 770 (55.6%) AD 900 AD 920 (12.6%) AD 960 AD 680 (95.4%) AD 990
Tankarpata	AA 39790	Qotakalli (b/c)***	1189 ± 40 BP	AD 761 ± 40	Bauer and Jones 2003	68.2% 95.4%	AD 770 (68.2%) AD 890 AD 710 (5.2%) AD 750 AD 760 (90.2%) AD 980
Tankarpata	AA 39788	Arahuay*	1192 ± 40 BP	AD 758 ± 40	Bauer and Jones 2003	68.2% 95.4%	AD 770 (66.8%) AD 890 AD 710 (6.0%) AD 750 AD 760 (89.4%) AD 980

SITE	LAB NO.	ASSOCIATED CERAMICS	RADIOCARBON AGE	CALENDAR	SOURCE		CALIBRATED DATE
Pukacancha	AA 34935	Arahuay*, Wari (Huamanga)	1210 ± 45 BP	AD 740 ± 45	Bauer and Jones 2003	68.2%	AD 730 (1.4%) AD 740 AD 770 (66.8%) AD 890
						95.4%	AD 680 (89.7%) AD 900 AD 920 (5.7%) AD 960
Rokeccasa	AA 35004	Ccoipa**	1230 ± 50 BP	AD 720 ± 50	Bauer 2002	68.2%	AD 710 (14.2%) AD 750 AD 760 (54.0%) AD 890
						95.4%	AD 670 (93.1%) AD 900 AD 920 (2.3%) AD 940
Tankarpata	AA 34941	disturbed*	1250 ± 45 BP	AD 700 ± 45	Bauer and Jones 2003	68.2%	AD 680 (62.9%) AD 820 AD 840 (5.3%) AD 860
						95.4%	AD 670 (95.4%) AD 890
Tankarpata	AA 34939	disturbed*	1275 ± 50 BP	AD 675 ± 50	Bauer and Jones 2003	68.2%	AD 670 (68.2%) AD 780
						95.4%	AD 660 (95.4%) AD 890
Tankarpata	AA 34938	Arahuay*, Wari (Viñaque), Qotakalli	1290 ± 50 BP	AD 660 ± 50 (b/c)	Bauer and Jones 2003	68.2%	AD 675 (68.2%) AD 775
						95.4%	AD 650 (95.4%) AD 880
Pikillacta	Beta 43231	Wari**	1290 ± 60 BP	AD 660 ± 60	McEwan 1996	68.2%	AD 660 (68.2%) AD 780
						95.4%	AD 650 (95.4%) AD 890
Pukacancha	AA 39791	Arahuay*, Qotakalli (b/c)	1322 ± 40 BP	AD 628 ± 40	Bauer and Jones 2003	68.2%	AD 660 (52.4%) AD 720 AD 740 (15.8%) AD 770
						95.4%	AD 650 (95.4%) AD 780
Pikillacta	Beta 43234	Wari**	1330 ± 60 BP	AD 620 ± 60	McEwan 1996	68.2%	AD 650 (49.2%) AD 730 AD 740 (19.0%) AD 780
						95.4%	AD 600 (95.4%) AD 870
Tankarpata	AA 39789	Qotakalli (b/c)***	1345 ± 49 BP	AD 605 ± 49	Bauer and Jones 2003	68.2%	AD 640 (57.6%) AD 720 AD 740 (10.6%) AD 770
						95.4%	AD 600 (95.4%) AD 780
Pikillacta	TX 4750	Wari*	1350 ± 60 BP	AD 600 ± 60	McEwan 1984, 1987	68.2%	AD 640 (55.2%) AD 720 AD 740 (13.0%) AD 770
						95.4%	AD 560 (95.4%) AD 810
Tankarpata	AA 39787	Qotakalli*	1404 ± 47 BP	AD 546 ± 47	Bauer and Jones 2003	68.2%	AD 600 (68.2%) AD 670
						95.4%	AD 540 (95.4%) AD 710
Peqokaypata	AA 39784	Incised incensarios*, Qotakalli	1422 ± 51 BP	AD 528 ± 51	Bauer and Jones 2003	68.2%	AD 565 (2.3%) AD 570 AD 580 (2.7%) AD 590 AD 595 (63.2%) AD 665
						95.4%	AD 530 (95.2%) AD 700
Pikillacta	TX 4751	Wari*	1430 ± 90 BP	AD 520 ± 90	McEwan 1984, 1987	68.2%	AD 470 (1.2%) AD 480

SITE	LAB NO.	ASSOCIATED CERAMICS	RADIOCARBON AGE	CALENDAR	SOURCE		CALIBRATED DATE
Pikillacta	TX 4747	Wari*	1430 ± 370 BP	AD 520 ± 370	McEwan 1984, 1987	95.4%	AD 530 (67.0%) AD 690 AD 420 (95.4%) AD 780
Pukacancha	AA 34934	Qotakalli (b/c)*	1435 ± 65 BP	AD 515 ± 65	Bauer and Jones 2003	68.2% 95.4%	AD 200 (68.2%) AD 1000 400 BC (95.4%) AD 1300
Peqokaypata	AA 39781	Qotakalli*	1439 ± 39 BP	AD 511 ± 39	Bauer and Jones 2003	68.2% 95.4%	AD 560 (68.2%) AD 665 AD 430 (95.4%) AD 720
Peqokaypata	AA 39783	Qotakalli*	1527 ± 40 BP	AD 423 ± 40	Bauer and Jones 2003	68.2% 95.4%	AD 595 (68.2%) AD 660 AD 540 (95.4%) AD 670
Huillca Raccay	Q 3091	Qotakalle***	1580 ± 60 BP	AD 370 ± 60	Kendall 1996:153	68.2% 95.4%	AD 430 (22.9%) AD 520 AD 530 (45.3%) AD 610 AD 430 (95.4%) AD 620
Peqokaypata	AA 34931	Unknown[5]	1615 ± 50 BP	AD 335 ± 50	Bauer and Jones 2003	68.2% 95.4%	AD 410 (68.2%) AD 560 AD 340 (95.4%) AD 620ß
Peqokaypata	AA 39792	Derived Chanapata*	1881 ± 42 BP	AD 69 ± 42	Bauer and Jones 2003	68.2% 95.4%	AD 400 (68.2%) AD 540 AD 260 (2.0%) AD 280 AD 320 (93.4%) AD 570
Peqokaypata	AA 39782	Derived Chanapata*	1985 ± 43 BP	35 ± 43 BC	Bauer and Jones 2003	68.2% 95.4%	AD 70 (56.7%) AD 180 AD 190 (11.5%) AD 220 AD 20 (2.1%) AD 40 AD 50 (93.3%) AD 240
Batan Orco	Hd 17619-17089	Derived Chanapata*	2073 ± 29 BP	105 ± 35 BC	Zapata 1998:333	68.2% 95.4%	50 BC (68.2%) AD 70 100 BC (95.4%) AD 130
Marcavalle	P 1561	Derived Chanapata*	2096 ± 51 BP	146 ± 51 BC	Lawn 1971:373	68.2% 95.4%	160 BC (9.9%) 130 BC 120 BC (58.3%) 40 BC 180 BC (95.4%) AD 10
Chokepukio	Beta 81424	Chanapata*	2130 ± 70 BP	180 ± 70 BC	McEwan et al. 1995:15	68.2% 95.4%	180 BC (68.2%) 40 BC 360 BC (5.8%) 290 BC 240 BC (89.6%) 30 AD
Marcavalle	P 1560	Derived Chanapata*	2131 ± 55 BP	181 ± 55 BC	Lawn 1971:373	68.2% 95.4%	360 BC (10.1%) 310 BC 230 BC (58.1%) 40 BC 380 BC (95.4%) 10 AD
Chokepukio	Beta 81425	Chanapata*	2190 ± 60 BP	240 ± 70 BC	McEwan et al. 1995:15	68.2% 95.4%	360 BC (36.2%) 270 BC 260 BC (32.0%) 170 BC 390 BC (95.4%) 90 BC 360 BC (34.9%) 270 BC 260 BC (33.3%) 170 BC 390 BC (95.4%) 90 BC

SITE	LAB NO.	ASSOCIATED CERAMICS	RADIOCARBON AGE	CALENDAR	SOURCE		CALIBRATED DATE
Chanapata	N 90	Chanapata*	2360 ± 760 BP	410 ± 760 BC	Yamasaki et al. 1966:33	68.2%	1400 BC (68.2%) AD 500
						95.4%	2300 BC (95.4%) AD 1200
Huillca Raccay	BM 1633	Chanapata*	2380 ± 70 BP	414 ± 70 BC	Burleigh et al. 1983	68.2%	760 BC (15.7%) 690 BC
							550 BC (52.5%) 380 BC
						95.4%	800 BC (93.1%) 350 BC
							300 BC (2.3%) 200 BC
Chanapata	N 89	Chanapata*	2520 ± 150 BP	570 ± 150 BC	Yamasaki et al. 1966:337	68.2%	800 BC (61.1%) 480 BC
							470 BC (7.1%) 410 BC
						95.4%	1000 BC (95.4%) 200 BC
Marcavalle	P 1562	Marcavalle*	2571 ± 45 BP	621 ± 45 BC	Lawn 1971:373	68.2%	810 BC (39.8%) 750 BC
							690 BC 8.4%) 660 BC
							630 BC (13.9%) 590 BC
							580 BC (6.1%) 560 BC
						95.4%	830 BC (44.3%) 740 BC
							730 BC (51.1%) 520 BC
Chanapata	Gak ?	Chanapata*	2600 ± 150 BP	650 ± 150 BC	Patterson 1967:143	68.2%	910 BC (68.2%) 510 BC
						95.4%	1150 BC (95.4%) 350 BC
Marcavalle	Gak 0453	Marcavalle*	2645 ± 115 BP	695 ± 115 BC	Patterson 1967:143	68.2%	980 BC (1.9%) 950 BC
							940 BC (46.7%) 750 BC
							690 BC (3.9%) 660 BC
							650 BC (17.7%) 540 BC
						95.4%	1050 BC (95.4%) 400 BC
Marcavalle	P 1563	Marcavalle*	2661 ± 46 BP	711 ± 46 BC	Lawn 1971:373	68.2%	895 BC (11.4%) 875 BC
							840 BC (56.8%) 795 BC
						95.4%	920 BC (95.4%) 780 BC
Marcavalle	P 1564	Marcavalle*	2685 ± 49 BP	735 ± 49 BC	Lawn 1971:373	68.2%	900 BC (18.5%) 875 BC
							860 BC (6.8%) 850 BC
							845 BC (42.8%) 800 BC
							970 BC (1.1%) 960 BC
						95.4%	930 BC (94.3%) 790 BC
Marcavalle	P 1566	Marcavalle*	2860 ± 47 BP	910 ± 47 BC	Lawn 1971:373	68.2%	1130 BC (58.8%) 970 BC
							960 BC (9.4%) 930 BC
						95.4%	1220 BC (95.4%) 890 BC
Marcavalle	P 1567	Marcavalle*	2916 ± 55 BP	966 ± 55 BC	Lawn 1971:373	68.2%	1220 BC (68.2%) 1000 BC
						95.4%	1300 BC (95.4%) 920 BC
Chanapata	GX 203	Chanapata or Marcavalle*	3330 ± 240 BP	1380 ± 240 BC	Krueger & Weeks 1966	68.2%	1950 BC (68.2%) 1300 BC
						95.4%	2300 BC (95.4%) 900 BC

SITE	LAB NO.	ASSOCIATED CERAMICS	RADIOCARBON AGE	CALENDAR	SOURCE		CALIBRATED DATE
Peqokaypata	AA 34932	disturbed*	3395 ± 55 BP	1445 ± 55 BC	Bauer and Jones 2003	68.2%	1770 BC (68.2%) 1600 BC
						95.4%	1880 BC (6.5%) 1840 BC 1830 BC (2.8%) 1790 BC 1780 BC (86.1%) 1520 BC
Kasapata	AA 39776	none*	4428 ± 37 BP	2478 ± 37 BC		68.2%	3270 BC (7.3%) 3230 BC 3100 BC (42.8%) 3010 BC 2990 BC (18.0%) 2920 BC
						95.4%	3330 BC (21.7%) 3220 BC 3180 BC (3.2%) 3150 BC 3120 BC (70.5%) 2910 BC
Kasapata	AA 39777	none*	5464 ± 53 BP	3514 ± 53 BC		68.2%	4360 BC (68.2%) 4240 BC
						95.4%	4460 BC (91.7%) 4220 BC 4190 BC (3.7%) 4160 BC
Kasapata	AA 39780	none*	5507 ± 61 BP	3557 ± 61 BC		68.2%	4450 BC (15.6%) 4420 BC 4400 BC (39.4%) 4320 BC 4290 BC (13.2%) 4250 BC
						95.4%	4460 BC (95.4%) 4220 BC
Kasapata	AA 39779B	none*	5567 ± 38 BP	3617 ± 38 BC		68.2%	4450 BC (28.7%) 4415 BC 4405 BC (39.5%) 4355 BC
						95.4%	4460 BC (95.4%) 4330 BC
Kasapata	AA 39779A	none*	5645 ± 76 BP	3695 ± 76 BC		68.2%	4550 BC (68.2%) 4360 BC
						95.4%	4690 BC (95.4%) 4340 BC

* = excavation, carbon
** = architectural sample: wooden lintel, wall vine, or *ichu* grass
*** = excavation, bone

1. Note that there are two widely different dates (Samples TX 4748 and BM 924) from wall vines at the site of Chokepukio.
2. Given the other dates from lintels at Pumamarca (SI 6988A, SI 6988B, and SI 6987), this date seems too early.
3. b/c = black-on-cream
4. Bengtsson believes this to be a poor date and defers to Sample Ua 1709, which is from the sample structure.
5. Sample collected from a feature with examples of an unknown orange-on-buff ceramic style.

NOTES

1. Introduction to the Inca

1. The lack of archaeological research in the Cuzco Valley has been noted by various authors, including Niles (1984: 205), Murra (1984: 77), Conrad and Demarest (1984: 96), Burger (1989: 56), and Hyslop (1990: 29).

2. The Quechua terms, toponyms, and personal names contained in this work are written according to their Hispanicized spelling as found in the Spanish chronicles and on modern maps. The English and Spanish plural *s* form is generally used in this text rather than the Quechua form (*kuna* or *cuna*). For example, I discuss *huacas* rather than *huacakuna*.

3. The first geographic study of the Cuzco Valley was conducted by Herbert Gregory (1916) under the direction of Hiram Bingham. For additional information on the ecology of the valley, see K. Chávez (1977).

4. "Conocí el valle del Cuzco adornado de innumerables árboles de estos tan provechosos, y en pocos años le vi casi sin ninguno; la causa fué que se hace de ellos muy lindo carbón para los braseros" (Garcilaso de la Vega 1960: 309 [1609: Pt. 1, Bk. 8, Ch. 12]).

5. The best single source for seventeenth- and eighteenth-century events in Cuzco is Diego de Esquivel y Navia 1980 [1749]. For a summary of other early accounts of Cuzco, see Porras Barrenechea (1992).

6. The Bibliothèque Nationale in Paris holds a collection of his drawings.

7. Other noteworthy early reports on the city of Cuzco include Hill (1850), Marcoy (1875), and Middendorf (1895).

8. For additional information on Squier's photographs, see McElroy (1986). Some of Squier's photographs are currently housed in the Latin American Library of Tulane University.

9. For a more complete review of early archaeological research in the Cuzco region, see Rowe (1944: 8–9).

10. For a summary of the publications produced by Bingham and his colleagues, see Bingham (1922: 347–351).

11. For a detailed summary of research that took place in the Cuzco region between 1940 and 1968, see K. Chávez (1982: 207–214).

12. Since the very first archaeological reports about the Cuzco region were published, researchers have struggled to define the ceramic sequence for the area (Uhle 1912; Bingham 1915; Jijón y Caamaño 1934). Not surprisingly, the earliest reports focused largely on Inca pottery. However, in the 1940s John H. Rowe began to develop a pre-Inca ceramic sequence for the area with test excavations at several sites in and near the city of Cuzco and exploratory visits to many other sites in the region. Building upon this work and on excavated data generated by the Cuzco archaeologist Manuel Chávez Ballón, in 1956 Rowe presented a prehispanic ceramic sequence for the region that included seven broad temporal-ceramic classifications. These classifications span, from latest to earliest: Classic Inca, Killke, Wari (Huari) and contemporary regional styles, Huaro, Derived Chanapata, Chanapata, and Marcavalle.

2. The Inca Heartland

1. As a prelude to the emergence of the four brothers and four sisters from the cave of Tamputoco, Guaman Poma first describes Manco Capac and Mama Huaco leaving Lake Titicaca and walking to Tamputoco (Guaman Poma de Ayala 1980: 63–65 [1615: 80–85]).

2. *Capac* = royal.

3. *Capac apu* = royal lord.

4. "Que todo los que tienen orexas se llaman yngas, pero no son perfetos, cino son yndios pobres y gente uaja ni son caualleros, cino picheros. Destos dichos que tienen orexas, sólo uno fue rrey Ynga primero, Mango Capac. Por

eso le nombró capac [poderoso]; que dezir ynga es común, no es rrey, cino capac apo quiere dezir rrey. Y así fue primero el Ynga Mango Capac, el segundo, Anta ynga, Caca Guaroc ynga, Quiuar ynga, Masca ynga, Tambo ynga, Lari ynga, Equeco, Xaxa Uana ynga, Uaro Conde ynga, Acos ynga, Chillque ynga, Mayo ynga, Yana Uara ynga, Cauina ynga, Quichiua ynga" (Guaman Poma de Ayala 1980: 66 [1615: 84–85]).

5. *Millma rinre* = term unknown.

6. "En la ley de los Yngas se ordenaua para ser rrey, Capac Apo Ynga. Ynga no dezir rrey cino que ynga ay gente uaja como Chillque ynga ollero; Acos ynga enbustero; Uaroc ynga Llulla Uaroc mentiroso; Mayo ynga falzo testimoniero; Quillis Cachi, Equeco ynga lleua chismes y mentiras; poquis colla millma rinre; estos son yngas. Y así no es señor ni rrey ni duque ni conde ni marqués ni caualleros yngas cino son gente uaja ynga y pecheros" [Guaman Poma de Ayala 1980: 96 (1615: 117–118)].

7. Capac Apu Inca = Royal Lord Inca.

8. Auquiconas = Nobles.

9. *Milma rinri* = term unknown.

10. "Cómo tenía sus uicios y horadamientos y costumbres antigos de los Yngas Capac Apo Ynga y de los otros yngas auquiconas y comunes yngas, Hanan Cuzco, Hurin Cuzco, Anta ynga, Tambo ynga, Queuar ynga, Uaroc ynga, Quillis Cachi ynga, Uaro Condo ynga, Lari ynga, Masca ynga, Acos ynga, Chillque ynga, Cauina ynga, Quichiua ynga, Yana Uara ynga, Chilpaca Yunga, Uro Collo, puquis colla, milma rinri. Cada uno conforme a su calidad se ahoradauan las orexas en su ley y serimonia que usuaron en tiempo del Ynga" [Guaman Poma de Ayala 1980: 310 (1615: 337)].

11. For additional discussions concerning hierarchical kinship models for the Cuzco region, see Zuidema (1983).

12. Guaman Poma de Ayala incorrectly places the Masca, Tambo, and Chillque groups in Collasuyu. There is, however, ample evidence to suggest that they were located directly south of Cuzco in Cuntisuyu (Zuidema 1983: 14; Poole 1984: 462; also see Bauer 1992a).

13. "Auqui capac churi, príncipes deste rreyno, hijos y nietos y bisnietos de los rreys Yngas destos rreynos: don Melchor Carlos Paullo Topa Ynga, don Cristóbal Suna, don Juan Ninancuro, don Felepe Cari Topa . . . Son casta y generación y sangre rreal deste rreyno.

Ingaconas señores caualleros Hanan Cuzco, Lurin Cuzco Yngas, tartarnietos y sobrinos y sobrinas, ñustas, prensesas: Casta rreal deste rreyno.

Haua ynga, Uaccha ynga, Chinchay Suyo ynga, Anta ynga, Sacsa Uana ynga, Quilis Cachi ynga, Mayu ynga, Quichiua ynga, y sus mugeres, palla, aui: Son yndios tributarios.

Anti Suyo ynga, Tambo ynga, Lare ynga y sus mugeres, palla, aui: Son yndios tributarios

Colla Suyo ynga, Queuar ynga, Uaroc ynga, Cauina ynga, Masca ynga, Tambo ynga, Acos ynga, Chillque ynga, Papri ynga y sus mugeres, palla, aui: Son yndios tributarios.

Conde Suyo ynga, Yana Uara ynga y sus mugeres se llaman ynaca aui y son yndios tributarios" [Guaman Poma de Ayala 1980: 690 (1615: 740)].

14. "Y es así que al oriente de la ciudad, de la gente que por aquella banda [Manco Capac] atrajo, en el espacio que hay hasta el río llamado Paucartampu, mandó poblar a una y a otra banda del camino real de Antisuyu, trece pueblos, y no los nombramos por excusar prolijidad; casi todos o todos son de la nación llamada Poques. Al poniente de la ciudad, en espacio de ocho leguas de largo y nueve o diez de ancho, mandó poblar treinta pueblos, que se derraman a una mano y otra del camino real de Cuntisuyu. Fueron estos pueblos de tres naciones de diferentes apellidos; conviene a saber: Masca, Chillqui, Pap'ri. Al norte de la ciudad se poblaron veinte pueblos, de cuatro apellidos, que son: Mayu, Zancu, Chichapucyu, Rimactampu . . . El pueblo más alejado de éstos está a siete leguas de la ciudad, y los demás se derraman a una mano y a otra del camino real de Chinchasuyu. Al mediodía de la ciudad se poblaron treinta y ocho o cuarenta pueblos; los diez y ocho de la nación Ayarmaca, los cuales se derramaban a una mano y a otra del camino real de Collasuyu por espacio de tres leguas de largo, empezando del paraje de las salinas, que están una legua pequeña de la ciudad . . . los demás pueblos son de gentes de cinco o seis apellidos, que son: Quespicancha, Muyna, Urcos, Quehuar, Huaruc, Cauiña . . .

. . . Ahora en nuestros tiempos, de poco más de veinte años a esta parte, aquellos pueblos que el Inca Manco Capac mandó poblar, y casi todos los demás que en el Perú había, no están en sus sitios antiguos, sino en otros muy diferentes, porque un visorey, como se dirá en su lugar, los hizo reducir a pueblos grandes, juntando cinco y seis en uno y siete y ocho en otro, y más y menos como acertaban a ser los poblezuelos que se reducían . . ." [Garcilaso de la Vega 1960: 32–33 (1609, Pt. 1, Bk. I, Ch. 20)].

15. "Mas también fué con limitación del tamaño del horado de la oreja, que no llegase a la mitad de como los traía el Inca, sino de medio atrás, y que trajesen cosas diferentes por orejeras, según la diferencia de los apellidos y provincias. A unos dió que trajesen por divisa un palillo del grueso del dedo merguerite, como fué a la nación llamada Mayu y Zancu. A otros mandó que trajesen una vedijita de lana blanca, que por una parte y otra de la oreja asomase tanto como la cabeza del dedo pulgar, y éstos fueron la nación llamada Poques. A las naciones Muina, Huaruc, Chillqui mandó que trajesen orejeras hechas del junco común que los indios llaman *tutura*. A la nación Rimactampu y a sus circunvecinas mandó que las trajesen de un palo que en las islas de Barlovento llaman *Maguey* y en la lengua general del Perú se llama *chuchau*, que

quitada la corteza el meollo es fofo, blando y muy liviano. A los tres apellidos, Urcos, Y'ucay, Tampu, que todas son el río abajo de Y'ucay, mandó por particular favor y merced que trajesen las orejas más abiertas que todas las otras naciones, mas que no llegasen a la mitad del tamaño que el Inca las traía, . . ." [Garcilaso de la Vega 1960: 35–36 (1609: Pt. 1, Bk. 1, Ch. 23)].

16. *Apocuracas* = Lord Chiefs.

17. *Mancopchurincuzco* = Cuzco Sons of Manco [Capac].

18. *Acacacuzcos* = term unknown (see Zuidema 1977: 278, 279).

19. *Aylloncuzcos* = Cuzco ayllus.

20. "Y assi parte del Cuzco, lleuandole en su compañia á todos los apocuracas y auquiconas por su soldado, y por alabarderos de su persona, á todos los orejones de mancopchurincuzco, que son caballeros, y acacacuzcos y aylloncuzcos, que son caballeros particulares; y por delanteros trae á los Quiguares y Collasuyos, y Tambos, Mascas, Chillques, Papres, y Quicchguas, Mayos Tancos, Quilliscches, y por alabarderos destos trae á los Chachapoyas y Cañares en lugar de ybanguardia ó retaguardia, todos con buena horden" (Santa Cruz Pachacuti Yamqui Salcamayhua 1950: 273 [ca. 1613]).

21. The baptism took place on Epiphany Sunday (Three Kings Day), January 6, so the child was named Melchior, after one of the three Magi who brought gifts to the infant Jesus.

3. Human Impact and Environmental History of the Cuzco Region

1. It should be noted, however, that since most of the precipitation that falls on the Quelccaya glacier derives from Atlantic sources, its use in inferring a detailed Late Holocene climatic history for the Andean highland region is somewhat contentious (e.g., Ortlieb and Macharé 1993; Gartner 1996).

2. Several other lakes in the Cuzco region have been cored, and their samples are currently undergoing analyses (Chepstow-Lusty et al. 1998).

3. Further upstream the name of the Urubamba River changes to the Vilcanota River.

4. For detailed discussions of the research methodology, see Chepstow-Lusty et al. (1996, 1997, 1998).

5. However, they can also be sensitive to regional factors, yet separating the climatic signal from the anthropogenic response is not always simple.

6. The lowest organic deposits at Marcacocha date to around 2200 BC, and the ice cores at Quelccaya begin at about AD 500.

7. The presence of arboreal species, such as *Alnus*

acuminata, Escallonia resinosa, and *Myrsine pseudocrenata,* in protected areas of the Patacancha Valley suggest that humid montane forest would have naturally occurred there before human impact. In addition, there are several fragments of *Polylepis* forest surviving nearby, which would have been the original vegetation of much of the Andes from 3,500 m (Chepstow-Lusty et al. 1998). These are found at Lake Cunacocha (4,000 m), 6 kilometers southeast of Marcacocha, and at Lakes Yanacocha (4,000 m) and Quellococha (4,200 m), northeast of Urubamba.

8. These plants are generally considered to be adapted to cold, seasonally dry conditions (Chepstow-Lusty et al. 1996, 1998).

9. It is also used to stabilize soils to some extent today.

10. From AD 1500 to 1720, the accumulation in the ice core was 20 percent higher than the average of the whole ice core, which spans 1,500 years.

4. The Archaic Period and the First People of the Cuzco Valley

1. For recent reviews of the Archaic Period in the central highlands, see Rick (1988), Aldenderfer (1989a, 1998), and Lynch (1999).

2. Sample AA 39779A.

3. Sample AA 39779B. The mean of these two dates is 5532 ± 49 BP (calibrated 95.4% probability: 4460 BC [88%] 4330 BC; 4290 BC [7.4%] 4250 BC).

4. Sample AA 39776. The calibrated 95.4 percent probability curve provides an uneven spread: 3330 BC (21.7%) 3220 BC; 3180 BC (3.2%) 3150 BC; 3120 BC (70.5%) 2910 BC.

5. We are currently attempting to identify the source of these obsidian flakes.

6. A few petroglyphs have been reported from the Sacred Valley area (Taca Chunga 1990), from quarries in the Lucre Basin (Protzen 1985), as well as from the areas of Ccorca, Yauri, and Canchis (Barreda 1973, 1991) south of Cuzco. Others can be seen just north of Maras.

5. The Formative Period and the Emergence of Ranked Societies

1. In earlier works, much of this era encompassed what has been called the Early Horizon, a time that is associated with the spread of the Chavin material culture across parts of northern and central Peru. This alternative temporal classification is used because no Chavin artifacts have been found in the Cuzco region and because we are becoming more concerned with local developments in the Cuzco region per se than with their possible contact with Chavin cultures to the far north.

2. Like the subdivisions within the Archaic Period, the

Formative Period subdivisions (Early, Middle, and Late) are currently based on largely arbitrary dates. They are useful, nevertheless, because they divide these very long periods into shorter time units and can be used heuristically to divide and discuss the general process of cultural development that occurred during these long periods. As additional data become available, the lengths and subdivisions of these periods can be better defined.

3. Sample GX 0453. K. Chávez (1980: 214) also reports that two additional dates (I-3093 and I-3094) were obtained by Engel at the site in 1966.

4. Sample P 1562: 2571 ± 45 BP (calibrated 95.4% probability 830 BC [44.3%] 740 BC; 730 BC [51%] 520 BC).

Sample P 1563: 2661 ± 46 BP (calibrated 95.4% probability 920–780 BC).

Sample P 1564: 2685 ± 49 BP (calibrated 95.4% probability 970 BC [1.1%] 960 BC; 930 [94.3%] 790 BC).

Sample P 1566: 2860 ± 47 BP (calibrated 95.4% probability 1220–890 BC).

Sample P 1567: 2916 ± 55 BP (calibrated 95.4% probability 1300–920 BC).

5. Sample GX 203.

6. Also see Burger et al. (1998) and Burger and Asaro (1979).

7. As one of the earliest sites of the Cuzco Valley, Chanapata has received considerable archaeological attention. In 1960, Chávez Ballón excavated there with members of the Tokyo University Scientific Expedition to the Andes. Additional studies at Chanapata have been conducted by Jorge Yábar Moreno (1959, 1972, 1982), Frederick Engel, Luis Barreda Murillo, and various other faculty and students of the Universidad San Antonio Abad del Cuzco. Unfortunately, the site has been destroyed by Cuzco's expansion.

8. Derived Chanapata is at times called Pacallamocco (Patterson 1967: 143).

9. Sample N 89.

10. Sample N 90.

11. Sample GX 203.

12. Sample BM 1633. The calibrated 95.4 percent probability curve provides an uneven spread: 800 BC (93.1%) 350 BC; 300 BC (2.3%) 200 BC.

13. Sample Beta 81424.

14. Sample Beta 81425.

15. Sample P 1560.

16. Sample P 1561. The calibrated 95.4 percent probability curve provides an uneven spread: 360 BC (5.8%) 290 BC; 240 BC (89.6%) AD 30.

17. Sample Hd 17619–17089.

18. Sample AA 39792. The calibrated 95.4 percent probability curve provides an uneven spread: AD 20 (2.1%) AD 40; AD 50 (93.3%) AD 240).

19. Sample AA 39782. A third Formative date, 3,395 ± 55 BP (Sample AA 34932), also comes from Peqokaypata, but its context is far less secure (Bauer and Jones 2003).

20. During colonial times, the area of Wimpillay was referred to as Membilla, and the large settlement that existed there is mentioned in numerous colonial documents. It is best known in the chronicles as the village where Polo de Ondegardo discovered several of the royal Inca mummies, including that of Sinchi Roca and a stone image of Manco Capac. Wimpillay was also associated with a number of sacred places, or *huacas,* during Inca times (Bauer 1998).

21. Quechua: Muyu = round; Orco = hill.

22. It is worth noting that five small gold items believed to have been found in a tomb in the Cuzco area most likely date to the Late Formative Phase. First reported in 1853 in the possession of the president of Peru, José Rufino Echenique, the collection includes a small inscribed disk (approximately 13.5 cm in diameter), an inscribed "plum" (approximately 13 cm long), a narrow band (56 cm long), and three small plain disks (averaging about 6 cm in diameter). The fact that a second stylistically similar inscribed disk made of copper or bronze was more recently recovered in the Cuzco region by Italo Oberti Rodríguez supports the proposition that these items were actually found in the Cuzco area. Rowe convincingly argues that the figures engraved on these items reflect the Paracas tradition of the south-central coast (Rowe 1976). The importation of such exotic items into the Cuzco region during a period of chiefdom development is consistent with well-documented patterns of elite-class formation (Earle 1997). Their probable inclusion in a grave supports the notion that a group of individuals were beginning to gain sufficient power, prestige, and wealth to form a distinct elite class.

23. Sites 201 and 467 respectively (Bauer 1999, 2002).

6. The Qotakalli Period

1. Some scholars have suggested that the appearance of Qotakalli ceramics in the Cuzco sequence may record early contact with, and influence from, the Ayacucho region (Glowacki 1996). If this is the case, it seems an example of peer interaction rather than a situation of early Ayacucho dominance.

2. Because of this, Qotakalli has also been called a Wari Period style (Bauer 1999). Recent research indicates, however, that most Qotakalli production took place during the Early Intermediate Period (Bauer 2002; Bauer and Jones 2003).

3. Sample number Q 3091.

4. Sample number AA 34934.

5. Sample number AA 39791.

6. Sample number AA 39787.

7. Sample number AA 34937. The calibrated 95.4 percent probability curve provides an uneven spread: AD 780 (1.3%) AD 800; AD 820 (94.1%) AD 1030. Additional contexts in Tankarpata with Qotakalli ceramics yielded dates of 1127 ± 40 BP (sample AA 39786), 1148 ± 39 BP (sample AA 39785), 1189 ± 40 BP (sample AA 39790), 1290 ± 50 BP (sample AA 14938), 1345 ± 49 BP (sample AA 39789).

8. Sample number AA 39783.

9. Sample number AA 39781.

10. Sample number AA 34931. The calibrated 95.4 percent probability curve provides an uneven spread: AD 260 (2.0%) AD 280; AD 320 (93.4%) AD 570.

11. Neutron activation work suggests that some of the Qotakalli workshops began to produce Wari-style vessels during the Wari Period (Montoya et al. 2000).

12. Muyu Orco (Round Hill) is a common Quechua toponym. This ceramic style is named for a site near the town of Yaurisque in the Province of Paruro (Bauer 1989; 1999; 2002).

13. For other examples of Muyu Orco ceramics found in the Cuzco Valley, see Espinoza Martínez (1983) and Torres Poblete (1989).

14. It was proposed that Muyu Orco ceramics reflected a Tiwanaku influence in the Cuzco region (Bauer 1989). With the further development of the Tiwanaku sequence (Janusek 1994) and excavations at the site of Peqokaypata in the Cuzco Valley, it is now suggested that Muyu Orco represents a more generalized Altiplano influence (Bauer 2002).

15. K. Chávez (1985) suggests that incised *incensarios* were produced during the period of early Tiwanaku development (or Tiwanaku III [AD 100–400; Kolata 1993: 78]). Nevertheless, based on her study of their wares, vessel shapes, and motifs, she concludes that these incised *incensarios* do not represent imports from the Tiwanaku heartland but instead reflect a stylistic influence that spread northward from the Lake Titicaca region.

16. For a detailed description of these vessels, see K. Chávez (1985).

17. Sample AA 39784.

18. In an earlier report, I suggested that Muyu Orco ceramics post-dated incised *incensarios* (Bauer 1999). Based on the excavation data from Peqokaypata, I now believe that they were both produced during the late Qotakalli Period (Bauer 2002; Bauer and Jones 2003).

19. Surface collections suggest that the adjacent ceremonial site of Muyu Orco was abandoned at the end of the Late Formative. This conclusion is supported by recent excavations that uncovered no Qotakalli Period remains on the hill (Zapata 1998).

20. Among the most important destroyed sites are: Colcapata [An. 361] (Valencia Zegarra 1984), Coripata [Cu. 155] (Cumpa Palacios 1988), and Aqomoqo [An. 227] (Espinoza Martínez 1983).

7. The Wari Period in the Cuzco Region

1. This is a slightly different terminology than has been used in earlier works discussing the ceramic styles of the Cuzco region (Bauer 1999, 2002). The refinement is based on our increased understanding of the local and imported ceramics of the Cuzco region over several additional years of research.

2. Sample AA 34938.

3. Sample AA 34935. The calibrated 95.4 percent probability curve provides an uneven spread: AD 680 (89.7%) AD 900; AD 920 (5.7%) AD 960.

4. The level of Wari influence on the central coastal areas of Peru is still a topic of many debates, but it is clear that the Wari controlled the core area of Ayacucho as well as several other regions in the highland.

5. Both Cieza de León and Squier called Pikillacta "Muyna." Squier (1877: 419–422) referred to the Inca gateway of the Cuzco Valley, currently known as Rumi Colcha, as "Piquillacta." Cieza de León (1976: 261 [1551: Pt. 1, Ch. 97]) mentions Rumi Colcha but does not give it a name.

6. "Hubo en este mohína grandes edificios: ya están todos perdidos y deshechos. Y cuando al gobernador don Francisco Pizarro entró en el Cuzco con los Españoles, dicen que hallaron cerca destos edificios, y en ellos mismos mucha cantidad de plata y de oro y mayor de ropa de la preciada y rica que otras veces he notado. Y a algunos Españoles he oydo decir, que hubo en este lugar un bulto de piedras, conforme al talle de un hombre, con manera de vestidura larga y cuentas en la mano: y otras figuras y bultos" (Cieza de León 1995: 267 [1553: Pt. 1, Ch. 97]).

7. For modern examples of the use of *ayllu* labor to build public monuments, see Urton (1984).

8. Sample AA 34937. The calibrated 95.4 percent probability curve provides an uneven spread: AD 780 (1.3%) AD 800; AD 820 (94.2%) AD 1030.

9. Sample AA 35003.

10. In Late Prehistoric and Early Colonial times, the area of Coripata was called Cayaocache. This large village is mentioned by a number of different writers (see Bauer 1998: 124).

11. For a discussion of Wari dates from across the Andes, see Williams (2001).

12. See samples TX 4750 and TX 4751 in the Appendix.

13. See samples Beta-43233, Beta-43230, and Beta-43232 in the Appendix.

14. See samples AA 34938 and AA 39791 in the Appendix.

15. Sample AA 39784.

8. The Development of the Inca State

1. Sections of this chapter have appeared in Bauer (1992a) and Bauer and Covey (2002). They are reproduced here with permission of the University of Texas Press and the American Anthropological Association.

2. The Pacariqtambo Archaeological Project.

3. The Cuzco Valley Archaeological Project.

4. The Sacred Valley Archaeological Project.

5. Each of the survey projects followed essentially the same methodology, as described in Chapter 1 of this book.

6. For additional examples of Killke and Killke-related ceramics in the Cuzco region, see Rivera Dorado (1971a, 1971b, 1972, 1973), Barreda Murillo (1973), Kendall (1974, 1976, 1985), González Corrales (1984), and Lunt (1984, 1987).

7. Sample number GaK 2958.

8. Sample number B 277494.

9. An additional Killke Period carbon sample has been recorded by Kendall (1985: 347) at Ancasmarca. The sample yielded a date of 660 ± 60 BP (calibration 94.5% probability AD 1260–1410 [sample UCLA 1676M]).

10. For a more detailed reporting of these findings, see Bauer (1992a).

11. The large-scale complexity of settlement in the Cuzco Basin and the relatively small-scale organization to its south during the Killke Period demonstrate the historical inaccuracy of migration accounts present in Inca origin myths (Bauer 1991; 1992a: 120–123).

12. The Mayu, Equero, Cancu Conchacalla, and Anta all lived on or around the Plain of Anta (Bauer and Barrionuevo Orosco 1998).

13. It is also worth noting that a lord of Anta gave his daughter, Chimbo Orma, to the Lord of the Ayarmaca (Tocay Capac) as a secondary wife (Sarmiento 1906: 53 [1572: Ch. 22]).

14. "Y antes que Inga Roca muriese, hizo amistades con Tocay Capac por medio de Mama Chicya, hija de Tocay Capac, que casó con Yaguar Guaca, y Inga Roca dió otra su hija, llamada Curi Occllo, por mujer á Tocay Capac" (Sarmiento de Gamboa 1906: 54 [1572: Ch. 22]).

15. This site is mentioned by Sarmiento de Gamboa (1906: 73 [1572: Ch. 35]). For a recent study of Huata, see Vera Robles (1998).

16. The site size is somewhat deceptive because the slopes of the mountain below the principal zones of buildings and domestic terraces are covered with small, irregular agricultural terraces that may have included some habitations.

17. "Y luego fue sobre los pueblos de Mohina y Pinagua, Casacancha y Rondocancha, cinco leguas pequeñas del Cuzco, que ya se habían puesto en libertad, aunque Yaguar Guaca los había destruido. Y los asoló y mató á los más de

los naturales y á sus cinches, que también en este tiempo se llamaban Muyna Pongo y Guaman Topa. Hízoseles esta guerra y crueldades, porque decían, que eran libres y no le habían de servir, ni ser sus vasallos" (Sarmiento de Gamboa 1906: 57–58 [1572: Ch. 25]).

18. Their name, however, lives on in a small village on the lower slopes of Pachatusan Mountain, above the ruins of Chokepukio.

19. "En tiempos pasados en el angostura del desaguadero de la laguna de Muyna estaua en el un lado, en unos edificios viejos, un pueblo que se decía Pinagua-Chuquimatero . . ." (Espinoza Soriano 1974: 205).

20. Our survey did find a much smaller site (Co. 129 [Pungurhuaylla]) with a wall built in a similar masonry style; however, the function of the wall is not known.

21. Some writers also report that the wife of Capac Yupanqui, Curi Hilpay, was from the Ayarmaca as well.

9. The Cuzco Valley during Imperial Inca Rule

1. *Saño* is Quechua for "clay."

2. Sample BM 930.

3. Sample ISGS 545.

4. 200 ± 80 BP, Sample ANU 5838.

5. Samples ANU 5839 and ANU 5840.

6. Samples AA 1530, AA 1407B, AA 2215, Ua 170, and Ua 1710.

7. Sample AA 34936.

8. There are also a number of descriptions of Inca ceramics found outside the Inca heartland, ranging from Ecuador to Argentina (for example, Jijón y Caamaño and Larrea M. 1918; Jijón y Caamaño 1934; Baca 1974, 1989; Meyers 1975; D'Altroy and Bishop 1990; Calderari 1991; Calderari and Williams 1991; D'Altroy 1992, 2001; Hayashida 1998, 1999; Costin 2001; Bray 2003).

9. Sample UCLA 1676G.

10. See Appendix: Samples SI 6987, SI 6988A, SI 6988B, and SI 6990.

11. Sample Ua 1709.

12. See Morris (1967, 1992), Earle et al. (1980), Earle and D'Altroy (1982), D'Altroy and Hastorf (1984), D'Altroy and Earle (1985), LeVine (1985, 1992), D'Altroy (1992).

13. "En este pueblo de Caxamarca fueron halladas ciertas casas llenas de ropa liada en fardos arrimados hasta los techos de las casas. Dicen que era depósito para bastecer el ejército. Los christianos tomaron la que quisieron, y todavía quedaron las casas tan llenas, que parecía no haber hecho falta la que fue tomada. La ropa es la mejor que en las Indias se ha visto; la mayor parte della es de lana muy delgada y prima, y otra de algodón de diversas colores y bien matizadas" (Xerez 1985: 116 [1534]).

14. "La ropa rica y escogida llevaban al Cuzco, y la demás

se ponía en los depósitos, y della se vestía la gente que andaba ocupada en los dichos servicios del inca . . ." (Santillán 1950: 68 [1564]).

15. "Hay casas donde se guardan las contribuciones que traen a los caciques sus tributarios. En alguna, se conservan más de cien mil pájaros resecados porque de sus plumas, de variadísimo colorido, se hacen vestimentas; y hay muchas casas destinadas a semejante almacenaje. Se guardan rodelas, adargas, planchas de cobre para revestir las paredes de las casas, cuchillos y otros utensilios, calzado, petos para soldados y todo ello en tal cantidad que no se concibe cómo se puede tributar en tal escala y con tanta variedad de cosas" (Sancho 1986: 137–138]).

16. "Contaré ahora de lo que en este Cuzco avía cuando en el entramos. Eran tantos los depósitos que avía de ropas muy delicadas y otras más bastas; depósitos de escaños; de comida; de coca; de plumas avía depósitos de una plumería tornasol que parecía oro muy fino; otras de tornasol verde dorado. Era la pluma muy menudita, de unos pajaritos poco mayores que cigarras, que por ser tan chiquitos los llaman pájaros tomines. Crían estos pajaritos solamente en el pecho esta pluma ya dicha, que será poco más que una uña donde la tienen. Avía tanto de ella enhilado en hilo de algodón, muy compuesto alrededor de unos corazones de maguey, hechos trozos de más de un palmo, metido en unas petacas. De esta pluma hacían vestidos que ponía espanto donde se podía auer tanta cantidad de este tornasol. Avía asimismo otras muchas plumas de diferentes colores para este efecto de hacer ropas que vestían los señores y señoras, y no otros, en los tiempos de sus fiestas. Avía también mantas hechas de chaquira de oro y de plata, que eran unas contecitas muy delicadas, que parecía cosa de espanto ver su hechura, porque estaba todo lleno de estas cuentas sin parecer hilo ninguno, a manera de ropa de red muy apretada. Asimismo para estas señoras eran estas ropas. Avía depósitos de zapatos hechos la suela de cabuya y lo de encima de el empeine del pié de lana muy fina de muchos colores, a manera de medios zapatones flamencos, sino que cubrían más el empeine del pie dos dedos bajo de la garganta. No podré decir los depósitos que vide de ropas de todos géneros que este reino hacían, que faltaría tiempo para vello y entendimiento para comprender tanta cosa. Muchos depósitos de barretas de cobre para las minas y de costales y sogas, de vasos de plata y platos. Decir de oro y plata que allí se halló era cosa de espanto . . ." (Pedro Pizarro 1986: 99–100 [1571]).

17. "Y assi el dicho Pachacuti Inca Yupanqui le haze la renunciaçión del reyno en su hijo Amaru Topa Inca, el qual jamas lo asepta, antes se aplica á las chacaras y á sus edeficios; y visto assi, el dicho Pachacuti Inca Yupanqui les dize al mayorazgo que si la quería que los dé el reyno á su ermano segundo Topa Inca Yupanqui . . .

Y en este tiempo començo aber gran hambre hasta siete años, sin que en esos siete años obiessen frutos de lo que sembraban. . . . En este tiempo, dizen que el dicho Amaru Topa Inca siempre en esos siete años de hambre los sacaba mucha comida de sus chácaras de Callachaca y Lucriocchullo; y más dicen, que de su chácaras jamas se apartaban nubes, llubiendoles siembre en anocheciendo, y assi dizen que no cayeyan yelos, milagro de nunca creer. . . . Este an hecho los *collcas* y troxes de las comidas, de mucho tiempo atrás . . ." (Santa Cruz Pachacuti Yamqui Salcamayhua 1950: 245–247 [ca. 1613]).

18. Niles (1984) provides a map of part of the site.

19. "Sobre el cerro, que de la parte de la ciudad es redondo y muy áspero, hay una fortaleza de tierra y de piedra muy hermosa; con sus ventanas grandes que miran á la ciudad y la hacen parecer más hermosa. Hay dentro de ella muchos aposentos y una torre principal en medio hecha á modo de cubo, con cuatro ó cinco cuerpos, uno encima de otro los aposentos y estancias de adentro son pequeños, y las piedras de que está hecha están muy bien labradas, y tan bien ajustadas unas con otras que no parece que tengan mezcla, y las piedras están tan lisas que parecen tablas acepilladas, con la trabazón en orden, al uso de España, una juntura en contra de otra. Tiene tantas estancias y torres que una persona no la podría ver toda en un día. Y muchos españoles que la han visto y han andado en Lombardía y en otros reinos extraños, dicen que no han visto otro edificio como esta fortaleza, ni castillo más fuerte. Podrían estar dentro cinco mil españoles; no se le puede dar batería, ni se puede minar, porque está colocada en una peña. De la parte de la ciudad que es un cerro muy áspero no hay más de una cerca: de la otra parte que es menos áspero hay tres, una más alta que otra, y la última de más adentro es la más alta de todas. La más linda cosa que puede verse de edificios en aquella tierra, son estas cercas, porque son de piedras tan grandes, que nadie que las vea, no dirá que hayan sido puestas allí por manos de hombres humanos, que son tan grandes como trozos de montañas y peñascos, que las hay de altura de treinta palmos, y otros tantos de largo, y otras de veinte y veinticinco, y otras de quince, pero no hay ninguna de ellas tan pequeña que la puedan llevar tres carretas; éstas no son piedras lisas, pero harto bien encajadas y trabadas unas con otras. Los españoles que las ven dicen, que ni el puente de Segovia, ni otro de los edificios que hicieron Hércules ni los Romanos, son cosa tan digna de verse como esto. La ciudad de Tarragona tiene algunas obras en sus murallas hechas por este estilo, pero no tan fuertes ni de piedras tan grandes; estas cercas van dando vuelta que si se les diera batería, no se les podría dar de frente sino al sesgo de las de afuera, estas cercas son de esta misma piedra, y entre muralla y muralla hay tierra y tanta que por encima pueden andar tres carretas juntas. Están hechas á modo de tres gradas, que la una comienza donde acaba la otra, y la

otra donde acaba la otra. Toda esta fortaleza era un depósito de armas, porras, lanzas, arcos, flechas, hachas, rodelas, jubones fuertes acoginados de algodón y otras armas de diversas maneras, y vestido para los soldados, recogidos aquí de todos los rumbos de la tierra sujeta á los señores del Cuzco. Tenían muchos colores, azules, amarillos y pardos y muchos otros para pintar; ropas, y mucho estaño y plomo, con otros metales, y mucha plata y algo de oro; muchas mantas y jubones acolchados para los hombres de guerra" (Sancho 1898: 409–411 [1534]).

20. "Pues volviendo al Cuzco, encima del, en un cerro tenían una fortaleza tan fuerte y tan cercada con piedras de cantería y con dos cubos muy altos. Avía piedras en esta cerca tan grandes y tan gruesas, que parecía cosa imposible ha bellas puesto manos, que avía algunas tan anchas como pequeños guadamecíes y de grosor de más de una braza tan juntas unas con otras y tan bien encajadas que una punta de un alfiler no se podía meter por las junturas. Era toda de terrados y açuteas. Avía tantos aposentos que cauían en ella mas de diez mil indios. Todos estos aposentos estaban ocupados y llenos de armas—lanzas, flechas, dardos macanas, rodelas, paueses que podrían ir cien indios de bajo de uno a manera de mantas, para tomar fuertes; muchos morriones que se ponían en las cabezas hechos de unas cañas muy tejidas y tan fuertes, que ninguna piedra ni golpe que en ellos les diese les podía hacer daño en las cabezas teniéndole puesto. Avía aquí en esta fortaleza muchas andas en que los señores andaban, como literas. Avía aquí muchos indios que guardaban estos depósitos, y para ver si en los ybiernos se llobían estos terrados y aposentos, para reparallos. Esta fortaleza era cosa impugnable y fuerte si tuviera agua, y de grandes laberintos y aposentos, que no se acauaran de ver ni de entender" (Pedro Pizarro 1986: 104–105 [1571]).

21. A very similar description is provided by Betanzos (1996: 69–70 [1557: Pt. 1, Ch. 16]) as well as by Sarmiento de Gamboa (1906: 101 [1572: Ch. 53]).

22. Mandóse que viniesen de las provincias que señalaron veinte mil hombres y que los pueblos les enviasen bastimiento necesario y si alguno adoleciese, entrando en su lugar otro, se volviese a su naturaleza, aunque estos indios no residían siempre en la obra sino tiempo limitado y viniendo otros salían ellos, por donde sentían poco el trabajo. Los cuatro mil de estos quebrantaban las pedrerías y sacaban las piedras, los seis mil las andaban trayendo con grandes maromas de cuero y de cabuya; los otros estaban abriendo la sanja y haciendo los cimientos, yendo algunos a cortar horcones y vigas para el enmaderamiento. Y para estar a su placer esta gente, hicieron su alojamiento cada parcialidad por sí, junto adonde se avía de hacer el edificio. Hoy día parecen las más de las paredes de las casas que tuvieron. Andaban veedores mirando cómo se hacían y maestros grandes y de mucho primor (Cieza de Leon 1996b: 147–148 [1554: Pt. 2, Bk. 51])

23. Verdaderamente es consideración ésta que con razón causa espanto y por donde se saca la multitud de gente que era menester para estas fábricas; porque vemos piedras de tan prodigiosa grandeza, que cien hombres no eran bastantes para labrar en un mes una sola; de donde se hace creíble lo que afirman ellos, y es que cuando se labraba la fortaleza del Cuzco, trabajaban en ella de ordinario treinta mil personas; y no es de maravillar, porque la falta de instrumentos, ingenios y maña forzosamente había de acrecentar el trabajo, y así lo hacían todo a fuerza de brazos.

Los instrumentos que tenían para cortar las piedras y labrarlas eran guijarros negros y duros de los ríos, con que labraban machacando más que cortando. Traíanlas, hasta donde era menester, arrastrando; y como carecían de grúas, ruedas e ingenios para subirlas, hacían un terrapleno escarpado arrimado a la obra, y por él rodando las subían; y cuanto iba ereciendo el edificio, tanto iban levantando el terrapleno; la cual traza vi usar en la catedral del Cuzco que se va edificando; porque como los peones que trabajan en la obra son indios, los dejan los maestros y arquitectos españoles que se acomoden a su uso, y ellos hacen para subir la piedra los dichos terraplenos, arrimando tierra a la pared hasta emparejar con lo alto della (Cobo 1964: 262 [1653: Bk. 14, Ch. 12]).

24. The original reads: "parecen las más de las paredes de las casas que tuvieron" (1996b: 148 [1554: Pt. 2, Ch. 51]).

25. Rowe (1944: 50) also documents this site.

26. The only other site in the Cuzco Valley to also contain large numbers of these three ceramic styles was Co. 21.

27. "La tardanza y pesadumbre con que los indios labraban las piedras para los edificios, derribaron todo lo que de cantería pulida estaba edificado dentro de las cercas, que no hay casa en la ciudad que no haya sido labrada con aquella piedra, a lo menos las que han labrado los españoles" (Garcilaso de la Vega 1960: 289 [1609: Pt. 1, Bk. 7, Ch. 29]).

28. See Dean (1998) for information concerning the demolition of Sacsayhuaman.

29. "Desde esta fortaleza se ven en torno de la ciudad muchas casas á un cuarto de legua y media legua, y una legua y en el valle que está en medio rodeado de cerros hay más de cinco mil casas, muchas de ellas son de placer y recreo de señores pasados y otras de los caciques de toda la tierra que residen de continuo en la ciudad. Las otras son casas ó almacenes llenos de mantas, lana, armas, metales y ropas, y de todas las cosas que se crían y fabrican en esta tierra" (Sancho 1998: 412 [1534]).

10. Inca Cuzco

1. Although the preservation of central Cuzco is now closely monitored, the exponential urban growth of Cuzco and its suburbs in the past twenty years has destroyed a

large number of important prehistoric sites that once surrounded the city.

2. Other researchers, most notably Harth-Terré (1962), Agurto Calvo (1980, 1987), Gasparini and Margolies (1980), Hyslop (1990), Rowe (1990), and Paredes García (1999), have also produced reconstructions of Inca Cuzco, but they differ in some details to the one presented here. Also see much earlier attempts to reconstruct Inca Cuzco, including those of Markham (1871), Squier (1877: opposite 429), and Uhle (Wurster 1999: 176–177). The fact that several alternative models of the former Inca capital can be derived from largely the same data sources is not surprising, given that our understanding of the Inca capital is fragmentary at best.

3. The earliest complete map of the city is an anonymous seventeenth-century plan held by the British Museum. The earliest partial map has been published by Rowe (1990). See Gutiérrez et al. (1981) for a discussion of other early Cuzco maps. Currently, the most accurate map of central Cuzco and its surviving Inca buildings is that produced by the National Institute of Culture of Cuzco (Plano Catastral de Registro Arqueológico y Monumental del Central Histórico del Cuzco 1979).

4. For more information on the nature of these shrines, their locations, and the social system through which they were maintained, see Bauer (1998).

5. The men left Cajamarca in mid-February and returned in mid-June.

6. Pedro Pizarro (1921: 207 [1571]) lists only two Spaniards (Martín Bueno and Pedro Martín de Moguer) and an unnamed Inca official. Cieza de León (1998: 224 [1554: Pt. 2, Ch. 5]) records the names of all three Spaniards (Martín Bueno, Pedro de Moguer, [Juan de] Zárate). Other writers, such as Zárate (1995 [1555]), who was then copied by Garcilaso de la Vega (1966: 287 [1609: Vol. 1, Bk. 5, Ch. 11]), incorrectly suggest that the expedition included Hernando de Soto and Pedro del Barco.

7. Xerez (1985: 72 [1534]) states that this official was a brother of Atahualpa.

8. Mena (1929: 36 [1534]).

9. "Dijo que la ciudad del Cuzco es tan grande como se ha dicho, y que está asentada en una ladera cerca del llano. Las calles muy bien concertadas y empedradas, y en ocho días que allí estuvieron no pudieron ver todo lo que allí había" (Xerez 1985: 149 [1534]).

10. Several so-called benches (or altars) were recovered during the early years of the conquest. See Pedro Pizarro (1921: 212 [1571]), Betanzos (1996: 11 [1557: Bk. 1, Ch. 2]), and Sarmiento de Gamboa (1906: 28 [1572: Ch. 7]).

11. "En otra casa muy grande hallaron muchos cántaros de barro cubiertos con hoja de oro: que pesaban mucho. No se los quisieron quebrar, por no enojar a los indios. En aquella casa estaban muchas mujeres: y estaban dos indios en manera de embalsamados: y junto con ellos estaba una mujer viva con una máscara de oro en la cara aventando con un aventador el polvo y las moscas: y ellos tenían en las manos un bastón muy rico de oro. La mujer no los consintió entrar dentro, sino se descalzasen: y descalzándose fueron a ver aquellos bultos secos: y les sacaron muchas piezas ricas: y no se las acabaron de sacar todas: porque el cacique Atabalipa les avía rogado que no se las sacasen diciendo que aquel era su padre el Cuzco: y por esto no osaron sacarle más" (Mena 1967: 93 [1534]).

12. "La ciudad del Cuzco por ser la principal de todas donde tenían su residencia los señores, es tan grande y tan hermosa que sería digna de verse aun en España, y toda llena de palacios de señores, porque en ella no vive gente pobre, y cada señor labra en ella su casa y asímismo todos los caciques, aunque . . . éstos no habitaban en ella continuo. La mayor parte de estas casas son de piedra y las otras tienen la mitad de la fachada de piedra; hay muchas casas de adobe, y están hechas con muy buen orden, hechas calles en forma de cruz, muy derechas, todas empedradas y por en medio de cada una va un caño de agua revestida de piedra. La falta que tienen es el ser angostas, porque de un lado del caño sólo pueden andar un hombre á caballo y otro del otro lado" (Sancho de la Hoz 1898: 407–408 [1534]).

13. "Verdaderamente era cosa digna de verse esta casa donde se fundía llena de tanto oro en planchas de ocho y diez libras cada una, y en vajilla; ollas y piezas de diversas figuras con que se servían aquellos señores, y entre otras cosas singulares eran muy de ver cuatro carneros de oro fino muy grandes, y diez ó doce figuras de mujer, del tamaño de las mujeres de aquella tierra, todas de oro fino, tan hermosas y bien hechas como si estuvieran vivas. Estas las tenían ellos en tanta veneración como si fueran señoras de todo el mundo, y vivas, y las vestían de ropas hermosas y finísimas, y las adoraban por Diosas, y les daban de comer y hablaban con ellas como si fueran mujeres de carne. . . . Todo este tesoro lo dividió y repartió el Gobernador entre los españoles que fueron al Cuzco y los que se quedaron en la ciudad de Xauxa, . . ." (Sancho de la Hoz 1898: 391–392 [1534]).

14. "En el mes de Marzo de 1534 ordenó el Gobernador que se reunieran en esta ciudad la mayor parte de los españoles que tenía consigo, é hizo un acta de fundación y formación del pueblo, diciendo que lo asentaba y fundaba en su mismo ser, y tomó posesión de él en medio de la plaza y en señal de fundar y comenzar á edificar el pueblo y colonia hizo ciertas ceremonias, según se contiene en el acta que se hizo, la que yo el escribano leí en voz alta á presencia de todos: y se puso el nombre á la ciudad 'la muy noble y gran ciudad del Cuzco,' y continuando la población dispuso la casa para la iglesia que había de hacerse en la dicha ciudad sus términos, límites y jurisdicción, y en seguida echó bando diciendo que podían venir á poblar aquí y serían recibidos por vecinos. . . ." (Sancho de la Hoz 1898: 392–393 [1534]).

15. Quechua: *cusi* = happy; *pata* = terrace.

16. Quechua: *haucay* = tranquil; *pata* = terrace.

17. The central plaza of Cuzco is not oriented along the cardinal directions. However, for the sake of conformity, I follow Garcilaso de la Vega's conventions in calling the northwest side of the plaza, the "north side"; the northeast side, "the east side"; the southeast side, "the south side"; and the southwest side, the "west side."

18. "Y así afirmaban que toda aquella plaza del Cuzco le sacaron la tierra propia y se llevó a otras partes por cosa de gran estima, y la hincharon de arena de la costa de la mar como hasta dos palmos y medio, en algunas partes más; sembraron por toda ella muchos vasos de oro y plata y ovejuelas y hombrecillos pequeños de lo mismo, lo cual se ha sacado en mucha cantidad, que todo lo hemos visto; de esta arena estaba toda la plaza cuando yo fui a gobernar aquella ciudad, y si fue verdad que aquella arena se trajo de ellos afirman y tienen puestos en sus registros, parecemé que será así que toda la tierra junta tuvo necesidad de entender en ello, porque la plaza es grande y no tiene número las cargas que en ella entraron, y la costa por lo más cerca está más de noventa leguas a lo que creo, y cierto yo me satisfice, porque todos dicen que aquel género de arena no le hay hasta la costa; que yo hice toda la información posible así entre indios como entre españoles, inquiriendo la razón de haberla traído, dicen haber sido por reverencia del Tiziviracocha, a quien ellos dirigen principalmente sus sacrificios . . . y es así que abriéndose los cimientos de la Iglesia Mayor del Cuzco, y siendo la arena que se hallaba ruin y lejos, dijeron los artífices que si no se tomaba la de la plaza, que sería mucha la costa, porque la que se hallaba era ruin y dificultosa de traer, y así yo la hice quitar toda, que fue grandísima cantidad, y la igualamos con otra tierra, lo cuál allá por sus opiniones sintieron los indios en extremo y no lo pagaron mal si lo pusiéramos en precio el dejar la plaza como se estaba, que después que lo entendí, la di de mejor voluntad a la iglesia y no hay duda si no que valió más de cuatro mil castellanos porque mucho más le costará traer y no de provecho, y con ella hice cuatro puentes de cantería en el mismo río de la ciudad, en que se ahorró mucho trabajo y costa porque fue muy gran cantidad, y otras obras que allí se hicieron de provecho, y lo principal fue quitarles la reverencia grande que se tenía a aquella plaza por esta razón" (Polo de Ondegardo 1990: 97–99 [1571]).

19. One of gold, one of silver, and one of spondylus shell.

20. For additional information on the Cuzco *ushnu*, see Zuidema (1980), Aveni (1981), and Hyslop (1990).

21. Cieza de León (1996b: 109 [1554: Pt. 2, Ch. 36]) describes the Cuzco *ushnu* as a cone-shaped stone covered with gold, an Anonymous Chronicler (1906: 158 [ca. 1570]) refers to it as a stone pillar, and Betanzos (1987: 52, 57 [1557:

Pt. 1, Ch. 11]) mentions a pointed rock covered with a strip of gold.

22. "Usno era un pilar de oro donde bevían al Sol en la plaça" (Albornoz 1984: 205 [ca. 1582]).

23. See Betanzos (1996: 190 [1557: Pt. 2, Ch. 1]), Sarmiento de Gamboa (1906: 104 [1572: Ch. 58]), Cabello de Valboa (1951: 361 [1586: Pt. 3, Ch. 21]), Cobo (1990: 58 [1653: Bk. 13, Ch. 13]), Murúa (1962: 77 [ca. 1615, Vol 1. Ch. 30]), and Pedro Pizarro (1921: 356 [1571]). Sarmiento de Gamboa (1906: 104 [1572: Ch. 58]) credits Huayna Capac's brother, Sinchi Roca, with building the Casana. This information is repeated by Cobo (1979: 153 [1653: Bk. 12, Ch. 16]).

24. "En muchas casas de las del Inca había galpones muy grandes de a doscientos pasos de largo y de cincuenta y sesenta de ancho, todo de una pieza que servían de plaza; en los cuales hacían sus fiestas y bailes, cuando el tiempo con aguas no les permitía estar en la plaza al descubierto. En la ciudad del Cuzco alcancé a ver cuatro galpones de éstos que aún estaban en pie en mi niñez. El uno estaba en Amarucancha, casas que fueron de Hernando Pizarro, donde hoy es el colegio de la santa Compañía de Jesús, y el otro estaba en Cassana, donde ahora son las tiendas de mi condiscípulo Juán de Cillorico, y el otro estaba en Collcampata, en las casas que fueron del Inca Paullu y de su hijo don Carlos, que también fué mi condiscípulo. Este galpón era el menor de todos cuatro, y el mayor era el de Cassana, que era capaz de tres mil personas: cosa increíble que hubiese madera que alcanzase a cubrir tan grandes piezas. El cuarto galpón es el que ahora sirve de iglesia catedral" (Garcilaso de la Vega 1960: 198 [1609: Pt. 1, Bk. 6, Ch. 4]).

25. The *Libro Primero del Cabildo . . .* (1965: 35 [1534]) confirms the fact that Juan de Pancorvo was assigned land in this area during the founding of Spanish Cuzco.

26. "La otra casa real, que estaba al poniente de Coracora, se llamaba Cassana, que quiere decir cosa para helar. Pusiéronle este nombre por admiración, dando a entender que tenía tan grandes y tan hermosos edificios, que habían de helar y pasmar al que los mirase con atención. . . . En mi tiempo abrieron los españoles una calle, que dividió las escuelas de las casas reales de la que llamaban Cassana; alcancé mucha parte de las paredes, que eran de cantería ricamente labrada, que mostraban haber sido aposentos reales y un hermosísimo galpón, que en tiempo de los Incas, en días lluviosos, servía de plaza para sus fiestas y bailes. Era tan grande, que muy holgadamente pudieran sesenta de a caballo jugar cañas dentro de él. Al convento de San Francisco vi en aquel galpón, que porque estaba lejos de lo poblado de los españoles se pasó a él desde el barrio Totocachi donde antes estaba. En el galpón tenían apartado para iglesia un gran pedazo capaz de mucha gente; luego

estaban las celdas, dormitorio y refitorio y las demás oficinas del convento; y si estuviese descubierto dentro pudieran hacer claustro. Dió el galpón y todo aquel sitio a los frailes Juan de Pancorvo, conquistador de los primeros, a quien cupo aquella casa real en el repartimiento que se hizo de las casas. Otros muchos españoles tuvieron parte en ellas; mas Juan de Pancorvo las compró todas a los principios cuando se daban de balde. . . . También vi derribar el galpón y hacer en el barrio Cassana las tiendas con sus portales como hoy están para morada de mercaderes y oficiales" (Garcilaso de la Vega 1960: 261 [1609: Pt. 1, Bk. 7, Ch. 10]).

27. *Galpón* is a West Indies term for a large building.

28. "Pues estando Hernando Pizarro en este galpón, en medio de las casas donde vivía, al ruido de la entrada que Almagro hizo en el Cuzco con su gente, Hernando Pizarro y los que con él estaban armados salieron y se pusieron a la puerta de este galpón. Pues llegado Almagro y su gente a querelle prender, estuvieron peleando un gran rato, que aunque los que estaban con Hernando Pizarro eran pocos, no les pudieron entrar. Tenía Hernando Pizarro consigo hasta veinte hombres, y Almagro *llevaba* más de trescientos, porque como he dicho, Hernando Pizarro no tenía más gente consigo a causa de las treguas que tenían puestas, y creyendo se guardarían. Hernán Ponce de León y [Gabriel de] Rroxas y otros malearon aquí a Hernando Pizarro y le faltaron, ellos y sus amigos, y por esta causa y por las treguas, entró Almagro tan a su *salvo,* que de otra manera hartas vidas costaran primero que entrara. Pues estando—como digo— peleando con Hernando Pizarro a la puerta de este galpón, y *hubiendo* Almagro herido algunos con saetas de los que Hernando Pizarro tenía consigo y visto que Hernando Pizarro no se quería rendir, Almagro mandó poner fuego a este galpón donde estaba Hernando Pizarro peleando, que era de paja, y hasta que ya el galpón empezaba a caerse abajo con el fuego, nunca Hernando Pizarro se quiso dar, . . ." (Pedro Pizarro 1986: 160–161 [1571]).

29. Other examples of such halls can be found in Huayna Capac's estate at Yucay (Niles 1999) and at the Inca site of Huaytara, and at Chinchero (Niles 1999).

30. Also see Esquivel y Navia (1980: 113 [1749]).

31. ". . . donde le tuvieron algunos días, hasta que aderezaron un cubo en Caxana, casas que eran del Marqués don Francisco Pizarro y adonde Hernando Pizarro estaba cuando le prendieron. Pues fortalecido este cubo, tapando ventanas y la puertas, dejando un postigo pequeño por donde cupiese un hombre, tapiado como digo este cubo, le metieron aquí. Estas casas tenían dos cubos, uno a un lado y otro a otro, quiero decir casi a las esquinas de esta cuadra. Estos cubos eran de cantería muy labrada, y muy fuertes; eran redondos, cubiertos de paja muy extrañamente puesta: salía el alar de la paja fuera de la pared una braza, que cuando llovía se favorecían los de a caballo que rondaban al amparo de este alar. Estas casas y aposentos eran de Guaina Capac. Quemaron estos cubos los indios de guerra cuando pusieron el cerco, con flechas y piedras ardiendo. Era tanta la paja que tenían, que tardaron en quemarse algunos días, digo antes que cayese la madera. Había hecho estos cubos terrados echándoles gruesos maderos arriba, y tierra encima, como *zuteas.* En uno de éstos tenían a Hernando Pizarro . . ." (Pedro Pizarro 1986: 161–162 [1571]).

32. See McElroy (1986) for additional information on these illustrations.

33. "La plaza de la ciudad era casi cuadrada, no grande ni pequeña. Aquella casa de Atabalica (*sic* Huayna Capac) que está en ella tenía dos torres de buen parecer, una portada rica chapada de pieza de plata y de otros metales . . ." (Estete 1924: 45 [1534]).

34. "La plaza es cuadrada y en su mayor parte llana, y empedrada de guijas: alrededor de ella hay cuatro casas de señores que son las principales de la ciudad, pintadas y labradas y de piedra, y la mejor de ellas es la casa de Guaynacaba, cacique viejo, y la puerta es de mármol blanco y encarnado y de otros colores, y tiene otros edificios de azoteas muy dignos de verse" (Sancho de la Hoz 1898: 408 [1534]).

35. [Ch-6:4] "La cuarta guaca tenía por nombre Guyana, y estaba en la puerta de Cajana: en ella se hacían sacrificios al viento para que no hiciese daño; y estaba hecho un hoyo en que se enterraban los sacrificios."

[Ch-6:5] "La quinta *guaca* era el palacio de Guaynacápac, llamado Cajana, dentro del cual había una laguna nombrada Ticcococha, que era adoratorio principal y adonde se hacían grandes sacrificios" (Cobo 1964: 172 [1653: Bk. 13, Ch. 13]).

36. Also see Esquivel y Navia 1980: 37 (1749).

37. [Ch-5:5] "La quinta *guaca* era un *buhío* llamado Coracora, en que dormía Inca Yupanqui, que es donde ahora están las casas de cabildo. Mandó el dicho Inca adorar aquel lugar y quemar en él ropas y carneros, y así se hacía" (Cobo 1964: 172 [1653: Bk. 13, Ch. 13]).

38. "Señaláronse a Gonzalo Piçarro dos solares en las casas donde agora avita con la delantera que tienen a la plaça por linderos el solar del Señor Gobernador y de la otra parte la fortaleza de Guaxacar" (*Libro Primero del Cabildo . . .* 1965: 33 [1534]).

39. "Yendo del barrio de las Escuelas al mediodía están dos barrios donde había dos casas reales que salían a la plaza principal. Tomaban todo el lienzo de la plaza; la una de ellas, que estaba al levante de la otra, se decía Coracora; quiere decir herbazales, porque aquel sitio era un gran herbazal, y la plaza que está delante era un tremedal o cenegal, y los Incas mandaron ponerla como está. Lo mismo dice Pedro de Cieza, capítulo XCII. En aquel herbazal fundó el rey Inca Roca su casa real por favorecer las escuelas, yendo muchas veces a ellas a oír los maestros. De la casa Coracora no alcancé nada, porque ya en mis tiempos estaba toda por el suelo; cupo en suerte,

cuando repartió la ciudad, a Gonzalo Pizarro, hermano del marqués don Francisco Pizarro, que fué uno de los que la ganaron. A este caballero conocí en el Cuzco después de la batalla de Huarina y antes de la de Sacsahuana; tratábame como a propio hijo; era yo de ocho a nueve años" (Garcilaso de la Vega 1960: 260 [1609, Pt. 1, Bk. 7, Ch. 10]).

40. "A Pizarro condenaron a cortar la cabeza por traidor y que le derribasen las casas que tenía en el Cuzco y sembrasen de sal y pusiesen un pilar de piedra con un letrero que dijese: 'Estas son las casas del traidor de Gonzalo Pizarro,' etc.

"Todo lo cual vi yo cumplido, y las casas eran las que le cupieron en el repartimiento que de aquella ciudad se hizo cuando la ganaron él y sus hermanos, y el sitio en lengua de indio se llamaba Coracora, que quiere decir herbazal" (Garcilaso de la Vega 1960: 391 [1609, Pt. 2, Bk. 5, Ch. 39]).

41. "Demás desto le mandaron confiscar sus bienes y derribarle y sembrarle de sal las casas que tenía en el Cuzco, poniendo en el solar un padrón con el mismo letrero, lo qual se executó aquel mismo día" (Zárate 1995: 374 [1555]).

42. This chapel was built to mark the miraculous triumph of the Spanish forces in Cuzco over the indigenous forces of Manco Inca.

43. "Señalose por casa del cabildo e fundicion el galpón grande questa en el anden encima la plaça" (*Libro Primero del Cabildo . . .* 1965: 33 [1534]).

44. See Cobo (1990: 57 [1653: Bk. 13, Ch. 13]), Albornoz (1984: 204 [ca. 1582]), and Molina (1989: 73 [ca. 1575]).

45. "Los indios mas valientes que venían escogidos para quemar la casa del Inca Viracocha, donde los españoles tenían su alojamiento, acudieron a ella con grándísimo ímpetu y le pegaron fuego desde lejos con flechas encendidas; quemáronla toda y no quedó cosa de ella. La sala grande que en ella había, que ahora es iglesia catedral, donde los cristianos tenían una capilla para oír misa, reservó Dios nuestro Señor del fuego . . ." (Garcilaso de la Vega 1960: 123 [1609: Pt. 2, Bk. 2, Ch. 24]).

46. Zuidema (1980) suggests that the largest hall was called Cuyusmanco. Niles (1999: 274–281), however, shows that the word *cuyusmanco* was the Quechua term for a specific type of large hall with a single large entrance on one end, and not the name of any particular building in Cuzco. Also see Murúa (1946 [1590]).

47. See Sarmiento de Gamboa (1906: 113 [1572: Ch. 63]), Cabello de Valboa (1951: 395 [1586: Ch. 24]), Murúa (1962: 123 [ca. 1615: Vol. 1, Ch. 43]), and Blas Valera (1950: 145 [ca. 1585]). In contrast, Garcilaso de la Vega (1966: 426–427, 701 [1609: Pt. 1, Bk. 7, Ch. 10; Pt. 2, Bk. 1, Ch. 32]) suggests that the Amarucancha belonged to Huayna Capac. This is unlikely, since it is well documented that Huayna Capac's palace was located in the Casana, on the other side of the plaza.

48. "Señalosele a Pedro de Ulloa el corral do esta la espalda (*sic palla*) del theniente Hernando de Soto, a las espaldas del solar de Lobillo" (*Libro Primero del Cabildo . . .* 1965: 35 [1534]).

49. Sarmiento de Gamboa (1906: 113 [1572: Ch. 63]) and Blas Valera (1950: 145 [ca. 1585]) also state that the Jesuits built their monastery on the Amarucancha.

50. From the description provided in the *Libro Primero del Cabildo . . .* (1965 [1534]), it does not appear that Mancio Sierra de Leguiçamo's original house lot was within the Amarucancha. Perhaps he, like Antonio Altamirano, owned more than one house in central Cuzco.

51. There may have been a number of small shrines within Amarucancha, as Cobo lists four shrines (Co. 1: 1, Co. 3: 1, Co. 3: 2, and Co 6: 1) in association with the house of Mancio Sierra de Leguiçamo (Bauer 1998).

52. Altamirano's other house was in the area of Pucamarca (Garcilaso de la Vega 1966: 424 [1609: Pt. 1, Bk. 7, Ch. 9]).

53. "Al cabo de la plaza, al mediodía de ella había otras dos casas reales; la que estaba cerca del arroyo, calle en medio, se llamaba Amarucancha, que es barrio de las culebras grandes, estaba de frente de Cassana. Fueron casas de Huayna Capac, ahora son de la santa Compañía de Jesús. Yo alcancé de ellas un galpón grande, aunque no tan grande como el de la Cassana. Alcancé también un hermosísimo cubo, redondo que estaba en la plaza delante de la casa. En otra parte diremos que aquel cubo, que por haber sido el primer aposento que los españoles tuvieron en aquella ciudad (además de su gran hermosura) fuera bien que lo sustentaran los ganadores de ella. No alcancé otra cosa que aquella casa real, toda la demás estaba por el suelo. En el primer repartimiento cupo lo principal de esta casa real, que era lo que salía a la plaza, a Hernando Pizarro, hermano del marqués don Francisco Pizarro, que también fue de los primeros ganadores de aquella ciudad. A este caballero vi en la corte de Madrid año de mil y quinientos y sesenta y dos. Otra parte cupo a Mancio Serra de Leguiçamo, de los primeros conquistadores. Otra parte a Antonio Altamirano, al cual conocí dos casas, debió de comprar la una de ellas. Otra parte se señaló para cárcel de españoles. Otra parte cupo a Alonso Mazuela, de los primeros conquistadores; después fue de Martín Dolmos. Otras partes cupieron a otros de los cuales no tengo memoria" (Garcilaso de la Vega 1960: 261–262 [1609: Pt. 1, Bk. 7, Ch. 10]).

54. According to the *Libro Primero del Cabildo . . .* (1965 [1534]), the following Spaniards were granted lots of land within Amarucancha in 1534: Hernando de Soto, Pedro de Ulloa, Juan Ruiz Lobillo, Gómez Mazuela, Antonio Altamirano, Diego del Castillo, (Bernaldino de) Valboa, and an unidentified individual named Astudillo.

55. "Todo lo cual vi yo en Cuzco, que en la casa real que

fué del Inca Huaynacapac en la parte que de ella cupo a Antonio Altamirano cuando repartieron aquella ciudad entre los conquistadores, en un cuarto de ella había caído un rayo en tiempo de Huaynacapac. Los indios le cerraron las puertas a piedra y lodo, tomáronlo por mal agüero para su rey; dijeron que se había de perder parte de su imperio, o acaecerle otra desgracia semejante; pues su padre el sol, señalaba su casa por lugar desdichado. Yo alcancé el cuarto cerrado, despúes lo reedificaron los españoles, y dentro en tres años cayó otro rayo y dió en el mismo cuarto, y lo quemó todo" (Garcilaso de la Vega 1960: 42 [1609: Pt. 1, Bk. 2, Ch. 1]).

56. "... hallaban tesoros dentro y fuera de aquella ciudad; que en una casa de las que en partición de ella dividieron los españoles, que era casa real, que llamaban Amarucancha, que fué de Antonio Altamirano, acaeció que trayendo un caballero en el patio unos galopes se le hundió al caballo un pie en un hoyo que antes de los golpes no lo había. Cuando fueron a ver de qué era el hoyo, si era alguna madre vieja que pasaba por la casa, hallaron que era la boca de un cántaro de oro de ocho o nueve arrobas, que los indios los hacen mayores y menores, en lugar de tinajas para cocer su brebaje, y con el cántaro hallaron muchas otras vasijas de oro y de plata que valieron mas de ochenta mil ducados" (Garcilaso de la Vega 1960: 90–91 [1609: Pt. 2, Bk. 2, Ch. 7]).

57. "Era un hermosísimo cubo redondo, que estaba de por sí antes de entrar en la casa. Yo le alcancé. Las paredes eran como de cuatro estados en alto, pero la techumbre tan alta, según la buena madera que en las casas reales gastaban, que estoy por decir, y no es encarecimiento, que igualaba en altura a cualquiera torre de las que en España he visto, sacada la de Sevilla. Estaba cubierto en redondo, como eran las paredes; encima de toda la techumbre, en lugar de mostrador del viento (porque los indios no miraban en vientos) tenía una pica muy alta y gruesa, que acrecentaba su altura y hermosura; tenía de hueco por derecho más de sesenta pies, llamaban la sunturhuasi, que es cosa o pieza aventajada. No había edificio alguno arrimado a él. En mis tiempos se derribó por desembarazar la plaza, como ahora está, porque entraba algo en ella, pero no pareciera mal la plaza con tal pieza a su lado, cuanto más que no le ocupaba nada. En este tiempo está en aquel sitio el colegio de la santa Compañía de Jesús como ya lo dijimos en otra parte" (Garcilaso de la Vega 1960: 60–61 [1609, Pt. 2, Bk. 1, Ch. 32]).

58. Guaman Poma de Ayala finished his *Primer nueva corónica* ... in 1615, when he was in his eighties. He would have been in his mid-twenties when Garcilaso de la Vega left Cuzco.

59. Also see Garcilaso de la Vega (1966: 799 [1609: Pt. 2, Bk. 2, Ch. 24]).

60. The *Libro Primero del Cabildo* ... (1965 [1534]) does not mention the Acllahuaci by name, but instead includes it within the area of the Hatuncancha. This is best illustrated in the description of Francisco Mejía's house lot. Mejía's holding is specifically recorded in the *Libro Primero del Cabildo* ... (1965: 34 [1534]) as within Hatuncancha, even though we know that he was awarded the portion of the Acllahuaci that bordered the plaza.

61. This street name is confirmed in the *Libro Primero del Cabildo* ... (1965 [1534]).

62. In the *Libro Primero del Cabildo* ... (1965: 34 [1534]) we read, "Señalóse a Francisco Mexía, regidor, un solar en Hatun Cancha que tiene por linderos puerta del dicho Hatun Cancha e de la otra parte la calle del Sol, e la plaça delantera que tiene hasta la callejuela de Apocamarca [*sic* Pucamarca] adelante e lo que faltare de traves que se le de largo."

63. "Al oriente de Amarucancha, la calle del Sol en medio, está el barrio llamado Acllahuasi, que es casa de escogidas, donde estaba el convento de las doncellas dedicadas al sol, de las cuales dimos larga cuenta en su lugar y de lo que yo alcancé de sus edificios resta decir que en el repartimiento cupo parte de aquella casa a Francisco Mejía, y fue lo que sale al lienzo de la plaza, que también se ha poblado de tiendas de mercaderes. Otra parte cupo a Pedro del Barco, y otra parte al licenciado de Gama, y otras a otros de que no me acuerdo" (Garcilaso de la Vega 1960: 262 [1609: Pt. 1, Bk. 7, Ch. 10]).

64. "Es así que un barrio de los de aquella ciudad se llamaba Acllahuasi, quiere decir, casa de escogidas; el barrio es el que está entre las dos calles que salen de la plaza mayor, y van al convento de Santo Domingo, que solía ser casa del sol. La una de las calles es la que sale del rincón de la plaza, a mano izquierda de la iglesia mayor, y va norte-sur. Cuando yo salí de aquella ciudad el año de mil y quinientos y sesenta, era esta calle la principal de los Mercaderes. La otra calle es la que sale del medio de la plaza donde dejé la cárcel, y va derecha al mismo convento dominico, también norte-sur. La frente de la casa salía a la plaza mayor, entre las dos calles dichas, y las espaldas de ella llegaban a la calle que las atraviesa de oriente a poniente; de manera que estaba hecha isla entre la plaza y las tres calles; quedaba entre ella y el templo del sol otra isla grandísima de casas, y una plaza grande que hay delante del templo" (Garcilaso de la Vega 1960: 121 [1609: Pt. 1, Bk. 4, Ch. 1]).

65. "Esta casa alcancé yo a ver yo entera de sus edificios, que sola ella y la del sol, que eran dos barrios, y otros cuatro galpones grandes que habían sido casas de los reyes Incas, respetaron los indios en su general levantamiento contra los españoles que no las quemaron, como quemaron todo lo demás de la ciudad, porque la una había sido casa del sol su dios, y la otra casa de sus mujeres, y las otras de sus reyes. Tenían entre otras grandezas de su edificio una calleja angosta, capaz de dos personas, la cual atravesaba toda la casa. Tenía la calleja muchos apartados a una mano y a otra, donde

había oficinas de la casa, donde trabajaban las mujeres de servicio. A cada puerta de aquéllas había porteras de mucho recaudo; en el último apartado al fin de la calleja estaban las mujeres del sol donde no entraba nadie. Tenía la casa su puerta principal como las que acá llaman puerta reglar; la cual no se abría sino para la reina y para recibir las que entraban para ser monjas. . . . En el repartimiento que los españoles hicieron para sus moradas de las casas reales de la ciudad del Cozco cuando la ganaron, cupo la mitad de este convento a Pedro del Barco, de quién adelante haremos mención, fue la parte de las oficinas, y la otra mitad cupo al Licenciado de la Gama, que yo alcancé en mis niñeces; y después fue de Diego Ortiz de Guzmán, caballero natural de Sevilla, que yo conocí y dejé vivo cuando vine a España" (Garcilaso de la Vega 1960: 122–123 [1609: Pt. 1, Bk. 4, Ch. 2]).

66. "Tiráronlas a todas las casas de la ciudad generalmente, sin respetar las casas reales; solamente reservaban la casa y templo del sol con todos los aposentos que tenía dentro. Y la casa de las vírgenes escogidas con las oficinas que habían de las cuatro calles adentro donde la casa estaba" (Garcilaso de la Vega 1960: 122 [1609: Pt. 2, Bk. 2, Ch. 24]).

67. "A los orones llaman pirua; son hechos de barro pisado con mucha paja. En tiempo de sus reyes los hacían con mucha curiosidad; eran largos más o menos conforme al altor de las paredes del aposento donde lo ponían; eran angostos y cuadrados y enterizos, que los debían de hacer con molde, y de diferentes tamaños. Hacíanlos por cuenta y medida unos mayores que otros, de a treinta hanegas, de a cincuenta y de a ciento, y de a doscientas más y menos como convenía hacerlos. Cada tamaño de orones estaba en su aposento de por sí, porque se habían hecho a medida de él; poníanlos arrimados a todas cuatro paredes y por medio del aposento; por sus hiladas dejaban calles entre unos y otros para henchirlos y vaciarlos a sus tiempos. No los mudaban de donde una vez los ponían. Para vaciar el orón hacían por la delantera de él unas ventanillas de una ochava en cuadro, abiertas por su cuenta y medida, para saber por ellas las hanegas que se habían sacado y las que quedaban, sin haberlas medido. De manera que por el tamaño de los orones sabía con mucha facilidad el maíz que en cada aposento y en cada depósito había; y por las ventanillas sabían lo que habían sacado y por lo que quedaba en cada orón; yo vi algunos de estos orones que quedaron del tiempo de los Incas, y eran de los más aventajados porque estaban en la casa de las vírgenes escogidas, mujeres del sol; y eran hechos para el servicio de aquellas mujeres. Cuando los vi era la casa de los hijos de Pedro del Barco, que fueron mis condiscípulos" (Garcilaso de la Vega 1960: 154 [1609: Pt. 1, Bk. 5, Ch. 5]).

68. This is the same Pedro del Barco that Zárate (1995

[1555]) and Garcilaso de la Vega (1966: 287 [1609: Pt. 1, Bk. 5, Ch. 11]) incorrectly include within the first Europeans to enter Cuzco.

69. The *Libro Primero del Cabildo . . .* (1965: 34 [1534]) indicates that Barco's house was tangent to Mejía's and the Street of the Sun. However, it is listed as being within Pucamarca.

70. Segovia is mentioned by Molina (1989: 59 [ca. 1575]) as having held a house lot in Pucamarca.

71. "Y en las casas de las vírgenes escogidas, en la parte que de ellas cupo a Pedro del Barco, que después la hubo un Hernando de Segovia, boticario que yo conocí, halló el Segovia acaso, sacando unos cimientos, un tesoro de setenta y dos mil ducados" (Garcilaso de la Vega 1960: 91 [1609: Pt. 2, Bk. 2, Ch. 7]).

72. Aerial photographs of the city (see Servicio Aerofotográfico Nacional: negative 8485-445 [1956]) suggest that the street now called Sta. Catalina Ancha could have once continued behind Sta. Catalina and the Jesuit church.

73. "[Un ejemplo] es un lienzo entero que permanece todavía en la ciudad del Cuzco, en el monasterio de Santa Catalina. Labraban estas paredes no derechas a plomo, sino tanto cuanto inclinadas para dentro. Las piedras son perfectamente cuadradas, pero de tal forma, que vienen a tener la misma hechura y labor que una piedra de anillo que los plateros llaman jaquelado, con dos órdenes de cantos y esquinas; de modo que entre dos piedras (destas ajustadas) queda formada una canal de los cantos menores y relevados de cada una. Y vese otro primor en esta obra, y es que no son iguales todas las piedras della, más que las de cada hilada entre sí, y como va subiendo la pared, van siendo menores, porque la segunda hilada consta de piedras más pequeñas que las de la primera, y las de la tercera son asimismo menores que las de la segunda; y por este orden van proporcionadamente disminuyéndose cuanto más sube la obra; y así, la pared sobredicha desta fábrica, que hasta hoy está en pie, teniendo los sillares de la primera hilada de un codo y más de diámetro, vienen a ser los postreros del tamaño de azulejos; y sube esta pared tres o cuatro estados en alto, la cual es la más artificiosa y de mayor primor de cuantas obras yo he visto de los Incas.

"Decimos que los indios no usaban de mezcla en estos edificios, sino que todos eran de piedra seca, . . . más no porque dejasen de estar por en medio unidas con alguna mezcla, que sí lo estaban, para henchir los huecos y afijar las piedras; y lo que echaban, era cierta greda colorada y muy pegajosa, que ellos llaman *llanca*, de que hay abundancia en la comarca del Cuzco; lo cual observé yo viendo derribar un pedazo de aquella pared del dicho monasterio de Santa Catalina, para edificar la iglesia que ahora tiene" (Cobo 1964: 261–262 [1653: Bk. 14, Ch. 12]).

74. ". . . la demás gente se aposentó en un galpón grande

que estaba junto a la plaza, y en Hatuncancha, que era un cercado grande que tenían que tenía sólo una entrada por la plaza: este cercado era de mamaconas, y auía en él muchos aposentos. En éstos que tengo dicho se aposentaron todos los españoles . . ." (Pedro Pizarro 1986: 88 [1571]).

75. "Hernando Pizarro y los capitanes se juntaban muchas veces a haber acuerdo sobre lo que harían, y unos decían que despoblásemos y saliésemos huyendo; otros, que nos metiésemos en Hatuncancha, que era un cercado muy grande donde todos pudiéramos estar, que (como tengo dicho) no tenía más de una puerta y cercado de cantería muy alta" (Pedro Pizarro 1986: 127 [1571]).

76. "En la plaza había una puerta donde había un monasterio que se llamaba Atuncancha, cercado todo de una muy hermosa cantería, dentro de la cual cerca había más de cien casas, donde residían los sacerdotes y ministros del templo y las mujeres que vivían castamente, a manera de religión, que llamaban por nombre mamaconas, las cuales eran en gran cantidad" (Estete 1924: 45 [ca. 1535]).

77. In the *Libro Primero del Cabildo . . .* (1965: 35 [1534]) we find, "Señalosele a Diego Maldonado donde esta un solar por lindero la calle de Candia y de Rocha."

78. "Al mediodía de la iglesia mayor, calle en medio, están las tiendas principales de los mercaderes mas caudalosos. . . . A las espaldas de las tiendas principales están las casas que fueron de Diego Maldonado, llamado el Rico, porque lo fue más que otro alguno de los del Perú; fue de los primeros conquistadores. En tiempo de los Incas se llamaba aquel sitio Hatuncancha; quiere decir barrio grande. Fueron casas de uno de los reyes llamado Inca Yupanqui" (Garcilaso de la Vega 1960: 260 [1609: Pt. 1, Bk. 7, Ch. 9]).

79. Wife of Topa Inca Yupanqui and mother of Huayna Capac.

80. [Ch-3:2] "La segunda *guaca* se decía Canchapacha: era una fuente que estaba en la calle de Diego Maldonado, a la cual hacían sacrificio por ciertas historias que los indios cuentan."

[Ch-3:3] "La tercera *guaca* era otra fuente llamada Ticicocha, que estaba dentro de la casa que fue del dicho Diego Maldonado. Fue esta fuente de la *Coya* o reina Mama Ocllo, en la cual se hacían muy grandes y ordinarios sacrificios, especialmente cuando querían pedir algo a la dicha Mama Ocllo, que fue la mujer más venerada que hubo entre estos indios" (Cobo 1964: 170 [1653: Bk. 13, Ch. 13]).

81. [Ch-4:2] "La segunda *guaca* se llamaba Púmui: estaba en un llano pequeño junto a la casa de Diego Maldonado. Fue adoratorio muy solemne, porque era tenido por causa del sueño; ofrecíanle todo género de sacrificios, y acudían a él por dos demandas: la una a rogar por los que no podían dormir, y la otra, que no muriesen durmiendo" (Cobo 1964: 171 [1653: Bk. 13, Ch. 13]).

82. "Lo mismo afirman que mandaba hacer el Inca cuando alguna mujer a quien él quería mucho fallecía en el Cuzco, que se traía tierra de su naturaleza para el sepulcro; también me satisface ser esto así porque declararon haber una sepultura en las casas del capitán Diego Maldonado labrada de cantería debajo de tierra, adonde se enterró una mujer del Inca natural de los yungas, la cuál hallamos bien honda y labrada desde tres estados de cantería muy prima y en cuadra como doce pies, y afirmaron ellos ser aquella arena de la costa de la mar, y sacada la arena, se halló solamente abajo un cuerpo en cierto hueco que en la sepultura había a un lado, que pareció probanza de lo que está dicho . . ." (Polo de Ondegardo 1990: 99 [1571]).

83. The *Libro Primero del Cabildo . . .* (1965: 34 [1534]) notes that Pedro del Barco was granted a house lot in Pucamarca. On the other hand, Garcilaso de la Vega states that Barco's land was within the Acllahuaci. This confusion may be the result of the fact that the *Libro Primero del Cabildo . . .* (1965: 34 [1534]) does not mention the Acllahuaci, but instead assigned the house lots within it to either Hatuncancha or Pucamarca.

84. Also see Van de Guchte (1990: 306–308), Hyslop (1990), and Bauer (1998: 138).

85. ". . . era una casa o templo diputado para los sacrificios del Pachayacháchic en el cual se sacrificaban niños y todo lo demás" (Cobo 1964: 172 [1653: Bk. 13, Ch. 13]).

86. Garcilaso de la Vega tells us that de la Gama owned part of the Acllahuaci and that his lot was later passed on to Diego Ortiz de Guzmán.

87. ". . . en las casas que fueron del licenciado de la Gama; en el cual estaba un ídolo del trueno, dicho Chucuylla" (Cobo 1964: 171–172 [1653: Bk. 13, Ch. 13]).

88. "Pucamarca quisuarcancha, que era la casa del hazedor y de los truenos" (Albornoz 1984: 204 [ca. 1582]).

89. This description of the Creator god is repeated in Cobo (1979: 135 [1654: Bk. 12, Ch. 12]).

90. Although Garcilaso de la Vega places the houses of Guzmán (Garcilaso de la Vega 1966: 197 [Pt. 1, Bk. 4, Ch. 2]) and Segovia (Garcilaso de la Vega 1966: 749 [Pt. 2, Bk. 2, Ch. 7]) in this same area of the city, he suggests that they were contained within the Acllahuaci.

91. Garcilaso de la Vega states that Hernando de Segovia bought the lot of Pedro del Barco.

92. ". . . mandó hacer las casas y templo de Quisuarcancha, que es por cima de las casas de Diego Hortiz de Guzmán, viniendo hacia la plaça del Cuzco, donde al presente vibe Hernán López de Segovia, donde puso el estatua del Hacedor de oro del tamaño de un muchacho de diez años; el qual hera figura de un hombre puesto en pie, el braço derecho alto con la mano casi cerrada y los dedos pulgares y seguros altos, como persona que estava mandando" (Molina 1989: 59 [ca. 1575]).

93. ". . . llevavan al Templo del Sol las figuras llamadas Chuquilla y Wiracocha que tenían su templo por sí en Pucamarca y Quisuarcancha, que son agora casas de doña Ysauel de Bobadilla . . ." (Molina 1989: 73 [ca. 1575]).

94. It is likely that Molina was present at the interviews conducted by Loarte.

95. Thunder had another temple in Totocachi.

96. A place labeled Cusicancha is also shown on Guaman Poma de Ayala's (1980: 303 [1615: 331 (332)]) map of Cuzco.

97. "Cusicancha pachamama, que era una casa donde nació Tupa Ynga Yupangui" (Albornoz 1984: 204 [ca. 1582]).

98. The *ayllu* (kin group) of Iñaca *panaca* were the descendants of Pachacuti Inca Yupanqui.

99. "Era el lugar donde nació Inca Yupanqui, frontero del templo de Coricancha, y por esta razón ofrecían allí los del ayllo Inacapanaca" (Cobo 1964: 171 [1653: Bk. 13, Ch. 13]).

100. Cobo (1990: 59 [1653: Bk. 13, Ch. 13]), Guaman Poma de Ayala (1980: 970 [1615: 1051 (1059)]), Loarte (1882: 234 [1572]), Betanzos (1987: 95 [1557: Pt. 1, Ch. 19]), Cabello de Valboa (1951: 353 [1586: Ch. 20]), and Albornoz (1984: 204 [ca. 1582]).

101. "Tenía también el trueno templo aparte en el barrio de Totocachi, en el cual estaba una estatua suya de oro en unas andas de lo mismo, que hizo el Inca Pachacútic en honor del trueno, y llamó Intiillapa; a la cual tomó por hermano, y mientras vivió la trajo consigo en la guerra. Fue tenido este ídolo en gran veneración y servido con grande majestad y aparato" (Cobo 1964: 160–161 [1653: Bk. 14, Ch. 7]).

11. The Coricancha

1. "El templo más rico, suntuoso y principal que había en este reino era el de la ciudad del Cuzco, el cual era tenido por cabeza y metrópoli de su falsa religión y por el santuario de más veneración que tenían estos indios, y como tal era frecuentado de todas las gentes del imperio de los Incas, que por devoción venían a él en romería. Llamábase *Coricancha,* que quiere decir 'casa de oro', por la incomparable riqueza de este metal, el que había enterrado por sus capillas y en las paredes, techo y altares. Era dedicado al sol, puesto caso que también estaban colocadas en él las estatuas del *Viracocha,* del trueno, de la luna y otros ídolos principales" (Cobo 1964: 168 [1653: Bk. 13, Ch. 12]).

2. Squier took two photographs of the Coricancha courtyard and combined them to make the etching shown in his book (McElroy 1986).

3. "Y luego los embio a unos bohios del sol en que ellos adoran. Estos bohios estavan de la parte que sale el sol chapados de oro de unas planchas grandes; y quanto mas les venia dando la sombra del sol tenian mas baxo oro en ellos. Los christianos fueron a los bohios: y sin ayuda ninguna

de indios (porque ellos no les querian ayudar porque era bohio del sol, diziendo que se moririan) los christianos determinaron con unas barretas de cobre de desguarnecer estos bohios: y assi los desguarnescieron según por su boca ellos lo dixeron" (Mena 1967: 93 [1534]).

4. Xerez also suggests that the roofs of these buildings were covered with gold, but this is not supported by other early accounts of the Coricancha.

5. "[Vieron] una casa del Cuzco tenía chapería de oro. Y que la casa es muy bien hecha y cuadrada y tiene de esquina a esquina trescientos y cincuenta pasos, y de las chapas de oro que esta casa tenía quitaron setecientas planchas, que una con otra tenían a quinientos pesos; y de otra casa quitaron los indios cantidad de doscientos mil pesos, y que por ser muy bajo no lo quisieron recibir, que tenía a siete o ocho quilates el peso; y que no vieron más casas chapadas de oro destas dos, porque los indios no les dejaron ver toda la ciudad. . . . Por manera que en todo el oro que traen vienen ciento y setenta y ocho cargas, y son las cargas de paligueres, que las traen cuatro indios, y que traen poca plata, y que el oro viene a los christianos poco a poco y detiniéndose, porque son menester muchos indios para ello, y los vienen recogiendo de pueblo en pueblo; y se cree que llegará a Caxamalca dentro de un mes. El oro que se ha dicho que venía del Cuzco entró en este pueblo de Caxamalca a trece días de junio del año sobredicho; y vinieron doscientas cargas de oro y veinte y cinco de plata; en el oro al parecer había más de ciento y treinta quintales; y después de haber venido esto, vinieron otras sesenta cargas de oro bajo; la mayor parte de todo esto eran planchas, a manera de tablas de cajas, de a tres y a cuatro palmos de largo. Esto quitaron de las paredes de los bohíos, y traían agujeros, que parece haber estado clavadas" (Xerez 1985: 149–150 [1534]).

6. Here Sancho could be referring to the palace of Huayna Capac, whom many of the earliest writers referred to as Cuzco. It seems, however, more likely that he was referring to the Coricancha.

7. "Llegaron los dos españoles que traían el oro del Cuzco y al punto se fundió una parte de él porque eran piezas pequeñas y muy finas, y montó á la suma de quinientas y tantas planchas de oro arrancadas de unas paredes de la casa del Cuzco, y las planchas más pequeñas pesaban cuatro ó cinco libras cada una y otras chapas de diez ó doce libras, con las cuales estaban cubiertas todas las paredes de aquel templo: trajeron también un asiento de oro muy fino, labrado en figura de escabel que pesó diez y ocho mil pesos. Trajeron asimismo una fuente toda de oro, muy sutilmente labrada que era muy de ver, así por el artificio de su trabajo como por la figura con que era hecha, y la de muchas otras piezas de vasos, ollas y platos que asimismo trajeron" (Sancho 1898: 310 [1534]).

8. "Pues recosido un golpe de oro de Quisquis juntó

haciendo quitar unas planchas de las casas del sol, que estaban encajadas en la pared en las piedras en toda la delantera de la casa" (Pedro Pizarro 1986: 59 [1571]).

9. Sancho estimates the slightly lower number of five hundred plates.

10. Xerez states that the seven hundred planks of fine gold weighted 500 pesos and that the total weight for the planks of lesser quality reached four times as such (i.e., 2,000 pesos).

11. Mena notes that after the arrival of the first installment of fine gold objects, another sixty loads of less fine gold entered Cajamarca, the greater part of which was in planks.

12. "Estas chapas o piezas de oro eran del tamaño y de la hechura de los espaldares de cuero que tienen las sillas de espaldas en que nos asentamos; de grueso tenía poco menos de un dedo, e yo vi de hartas" (Las Casas 1958: 193 [ca. 1550: Ch. 58]).

13. Betanzos (1996: 10–11, 277 [1557: Pt. 1, Ch. 2; Pt. 2, Ch. 277) and Sarmiento de Gamboa (1906: 28 [1572: Ch. 7]) incorrectly suggest that this bench came to Francisco Pizarro after the sacking of Cuzco.

14. "Delante del aposento donde dormía el sol tenían hecho un güerto pequeño, que sería como una era grande, donde sembraban a su tiempo maíz, regáuanlo a mano con agua que traían a cuestas para el sol, y al tiempo que celebraban sus fiestas, que era en el año tres veces—cuando sembraban las sementeras, y cuando las cosían, y cuando hacían orejones—henchían este güerto de cañas de maíz hechas de oro, con sus mazorcas y hojas al natural, como de maíz, todo de oro muy fino, las cuales tenían guardadas para poner en estos tiempos" (Pedro Pizarro 1986: 92 [1571]).

15. "Una caña de maíz de oro, de ley de catorce quilates, con tres hojas é dos mazorcas de oro, que pesó diez marcos é seis onzas cuatro ochavas" (Fernández de Alfaro 1904: 168 [1533]).

Xerez (1985: 152 [1534]) may also mention this maize stalk as it arrived in Cajamarca, writing, "Con el oro que aquí se trujo del Cuzco trujeron algunas pajas hechas de oro macizo con su espigueta hecha al cabo, propia como nasce en el campo" [With the gold that was brought here from Cuzco they brought some straws made of solid gold with finely made sikes, just like they grow in the fields].

16. "En las casas del Sol entramos y dijo Villaoma, que era a manera de sacerdote en su ley, 'como entráis aquí vosotros, que el que aquí ha de entrar ha de ayunar un año primero, y ha de entrar cargado con una cargo y descalzo'; y sin hacer caso de lo que dijo entramos dentro" (Trujillo 1948: 63–64 [1571]).

17. "Hallamos muchas ovejas de oro y mujeres y cántaros y jarros y otras piezas, muchas hallamos en todos los aposentos del monasterio al rededor del junto a las tejas

una plancha de oro tan ancha como un palmo. Esto lo tenían todos los aposentos del monasterio, . . ." (Ruiz de Arce 1933: 372 [ca. 1545]).

18. Garcilaso de la Vega suggests that there was a gold band surrounding the outside of the temple (1966: 181 [1609: Pt. 1, Bk. 3, Ch. 20]) as well as a second band in an interior courtyard (1966: 181 [1609: Pt. 1, Bk. 3, Ch. 21]). Like so much of Garcilaso de la Vega's account of the Temple of the Sun, this seems to be an exaggeration of what was really there.

19. "Tenían este sol en unas casas muy grandes, todas de cantería muy labradas . . . en la delantera della tenían una cinta de planchas de oro, de más de un palmo de anchor, encajadas en las piedras . . ." (Pedro Pizarro 1986: 91–92 [1571]).

20. "Y esto ansi hecho mandó Topa Yupangue que de aquel oro que ansi se había traído se hiciese una cinta ancha de dos palmos y medio y que fuese delgada y del gordor que es ahora un plato de estaño pequeño y esta cinta fuese tan larga cuanto era el redondo del aposento do el sol estaba y que ansi hecha la pusiesen en torno de aquel aposento del sol siendo puesta por la parte de afuera desde donde dice la paja de la cobertura hasta do la cantería es de la casa que sería lo que había de la paja a la cantería el anchor de aquella cinta de oro que ansi le mandaba poner" (Betanzos 1987: 136 [1557: Pt. 1, Ch. 28]).

21. See Ladrón de Guevara (1967) and Béjar Navarro (1990) for additional illustrations of these marks.

22. Garcilaso de la Vega suggests that there were four tabernacles, yet he only describes two in detail.

23. "Tenían sus molduras por las esquinas y por todo el hueco del tabernáculo. Y conforme a las molduras que en la piedra estaban hechas, así estaban forrados con tablones de oro, no sólo las paredes y lo alto mas también el suelo de los tabernáculos. . . .

"En dos tabernáculos de estos que estaban en un lienzo que miraba al oriente, me acuerdo que vi muchos agujeros en las molduras que estaban hechas en las piedras; las que estaban a las esquinas pasaban de un cabo a otro; las otras que estaban en el campo y espacio del tabernáculo no tenían más que estar señalados en la pared. A los indios y a los religiosos de la casa oí decir que en aquellos mismos lugares solían estar sobre el oro los engastes de las piedras finas en tiempo de aquella gentilidad" (Garcilaso de la Vega 1960: 115 [1609: Pt. 1, Bk. 3, Ch. 22]).

24. "Viniendo, pues, a la traza del templo, es de saber que el aposento del sol era lo que agora es la iglesia del divino Santo Domingo, que por no tener la precisa anchura y largura suya no la pongo aquí; la pieza, en cuanto su tamaño, vive hoy. Es labrada de cantería llana, muy prima y pulida.

"El altar mayor (digámoslo así para darnos a entender,

aunque aquellos indios no supieron hacer altar) estaba al oriente. La techumbre era de madera muy alta, porque tuviese mucha corriente; la cubija fué de paja, porque no alcanzaron a hacer teja" (Garcilaso de la Vega 1960: 112 [1609: Pt. 1. Bk. 3, Ch. 20]).

25. ". . . duraban en pie muchas paredes deste edificio; y en una esquina que estaba entera, se vía parte de una delgada lámina de plata en la juntura de dos piedras, la cual ví yo hartas veces" (Cobo 1964: 168 [1653: Bk. 13, Ch. 12]).

26. "Pasado el templo había un claustro de cuatro lienzos, el uno de ellos era el lienzo del templo. Por todo lo alto del claustro había una cenefa de un tablón de oro de más de una vara en ancho que servía de corona al claustro; en lugar de ella mandaron poner los españoles en memoria de la pasada otra cenefa blanca de yeso del anchor de la de oro, yo la dejé viva en las paredes que estaban en pie, y no se había derribado. Alderredor del claustro había cinco cuadras o aposentos grandes, cuadrados cada uno de por sí, no trabados con otros, cubiertos en forma de pirámide, de los cuales se hacían los otros tres lienzos del claustro" (Garcilaso de la Vega 1960: 113 [1609: Pt. 1, Bk. 3, Ch. 21]).

27. "De las cinco cuadras alcancé las tres que aún estaban en su antiguo ser de paredes y techumbre. Sólo les faltaban los tablones de oro y plata" (Garcilaso de la Vega 1960: 115 [1609: Pt. 1, Bk. 3, Ch. 22]).

28. See Gasparini and Margolies (1980) for a detailed discussion of the architectural changes that occurred at the site as a result of the reconstruction project. Additional information concerning the reconstruction can be found in Ladrón de Guevara (1967).

29. Also see Béjar Navarro (1990) for a reconstruction of the Coricancha.

30. "Hicieron en todo su reino estos Incas la misma división en que estaba repartida la ciudad del Cuzco, de *Hanan Cuzco* y *Hurin Cuzco;* dividiendo cada pueblo y cacicazgo en dos partes o bandos dichos *hanansaya* y *hurinsaya,* que suena el barrio alto y el barrio bajo, o la parte y bando superior y el bando inferior; y puesto caso que los nombres denotan desigualdad entre estos dos bandos, con todo eso, no la había más" (Cobo 1964: 112 [1653: Bk. 12, Ch. 24]).

31. "Del templo del sol salían, como de centro, ciertas líneas, que los indios llaman *Ceques;* y hacíanse cuatro partes conforme a los cuatro caminos reales que salían del Cuzco; y en cada uno de aquellos *ceques* estaban por su orden las *guacas* y adoratorios que había en el Cuzco y su comarca, como estaciones de lugares píos, cuya veneración era general a todas" (Cobo 1964: 169 [1653: Bk. 13, Ch. 13]).

32. Albornoz (1984: 205 [ca. 1582]) also includes this shrine in his list, but he provides a different description of it: "(#33) Guaracinci, una piedra labrada a la puerta del Sol" [Guaracinci, a worked stone in the door of the sun].

33. "La primera guaca se decía guaracince, la cual estaba en la plaza del templo del sol, llamada Chuquipampa (suena llano de oro); era un pedazuelo de llano que allí estaba, en el cual decían que se formaba el temblor de tierra. Hacían en ella sacrificios para que no temblase, y eran muy solemnes; porque, cuando temblaba la tierra, se mataban niños, y ordinariamente se quemaban carneros y ropa, y se enterraba oro y plata" (Cobo 1964: 170 [1653: Bk. 13, Ch. 13]).

34. Albornoz (1984: 204 [ca. 1582]) also describes this plaza but gives it a different name, writing: "(#2) Quillcai cancha, que era en la plaça ques agora de Santo Domingo" [Quillcai cancha, which was on the plaza which now is the plaza of Santo Domingo].

35. In the original: "plaza de sol" (Garcilaso de la Vega 1960: 260 [1609: Pt. 1, Bk. 7, Ch. 9]).

36. "A la primera nombraban Caritampucancha. Era una plazuela que está ahora dentro del convento de Santo Domingo, la cual tenían por opinión que era el primer lugar donde se asentó Manco Cápac en el sitio del Cuzco, cuando salió de Tampu. Ofrecíanse niños con todo lo demás" (Cobo 1964: 184 [1653: Bk. 13, Ch. 16]).

37. Albornoz (1984: 205 [ca. 1582]) also mentioned this brazier, writing, "(#32) Nina era un bezerro que siempre ardía" [Nina was a brazier that always burned].

38. "La primera se llamaba Nina, que era un brasero hecho de una piedra donde se encendía el fuego para los sacrificios, y no podían tomarlo de otra parte; estaba junto al templo del sol, y teníasele grande veneración y hacíansele sacrificios solemnes" (Cobo 1964: 170 [1653: Bk. 13, Ch. 13]).

39. "Las que residían en el templo del Cuzco tenían cuidado de encender y atizar el fuego que ardía en él para los sacrificios, el cual no se alimentaba con cualquiera leña, sino con una particular curiosamente labrada y pintada. Madrugaban todos los días a guisar de comer para el sol y sus ministros, y asomando por el horizonte y hiriendo con sus rayos en el Punchao, que era una figura del sol hecha de oro que estaba puesta enfrente del oriente, para que en saliendo el sol la bañase de su luz, le ofrecían la comida que le habían preparado, quemándola con cierta solemnidad y cantares" (Cobo 1964: 232–233 [1653: Bk. 13, Ch. 37]).

40. Also see Cobo (1990: 117 [1653: Bk. 13, Ch. 22]).

12. The Mummies of the Royal Inca

1. ". . . lo tenían de costumbre yrse a uisitar los muertos unos a otros, y hazían grandes bayles y borracheras. Algunas uezes yuan a casas de los uiuos, y los uiuos a las suyas" (Pedro Pizarro 1986: 52–53 [1571]). This statement was later copied by Cobo (1964 [1653]).

2. For other recent discussions of the Inca mummies, see Van de Guchte (1990), MacCormack (1991), Gose (1996), and Isbell (1997).

3. His first term lasted from 1558 until 1560; his second term ran from 1571 to 1572.

4. Another large-scale investigation occurred some thirteen years later, in 1572. This inquiry was led by Pedro Sarmiento de Gamboa, under orders from Viceroy Toledo, during Polo de Ondegardo's second term as corregidor of Cuzco.

5. "... que cuenta el licenciado Polo Ondegardo en su Relación, que por la averiguación que por orden suya hicieron los alcaldes indios en la ciudad del Cuzco, fueron traídos a su presencia de solos los moradores de aquella ciudad cuatrocientos y setenta y cinco hombres y mujeres que no tenían otro oficio, cada uno con los instrumentos que usaba" (Cobo 1964: 226 [1653: Bk. 13, Ch. 34]).

6. "Por lo cual, ha tenido siempre tanta autoridad la relación que por la averiguación de aquella junta hizo el sobredicho licenciado Polo, que en los concilios provinciales que se han celebrado en este reino, se abrazó cuanto ella contiene, así para la instrucción que se da a los curas de indios de sus ritos y supersticiones antiguas en orden a que se pongan toda diligencia y cuidado en extirparlas, como para resolver las dudas y dificultades que a cada paso se ofrecían a los principios sobre los matrimonios de los que se convertían a Nuestra Santa Fe; y esta relación tengo yo en mi poder, la misma que, firmada de su nombre, envió el licenciado Polo al arzobispo don Jerónimo Loaysa" (Cobo 1964: 59–60 [1653: Bk. 12, Ch. 2]).

7. "Pues en muchas partes, y creo que es en todas las que han podido, han sacado los cuerpos de sus difuntos de las iglesias y llevándolos al campo, a sus machays, que son las sepulturas de sus antepasados, y la causa que dan de sacallos de la iglesia, es como ellos dicen, Cuyaspa, por el amor que les tienen. En conclusión, para hacer concepto del miserable estado en que están y de la necesidad extrema que tienen de remedio y la facilidad y gusto con que le admiten, no es menester otro testimonio más que ver un día de las exhibiciones, que es cuando todos juntos traen todos los instrumentos de su idolatría. Parece un día de juicio; están repartidos en la plaza por ayllos y parcialidades; tienen consigo los cuerpos secos y enteros de sus antepasados, que en los llanos llaman Munaos y en la sierra Mallquis, y los cuerpos que han sacado de la iglesia, que parece que los vivos y los muertos vienen a juicio" (Arriaga 1999: 20–22 [1621: Ch. 1]).

8. "Visitó (Hernando de Avendaño) otros pueblos y descubrió en ellos muy grandes idolatrías y huacas, y entre ellos aquella tan famosa entre los indios y reverenciada de pueblos muy distantes, que era el cuerpo de un curaca antiquísimo llamado Liviacancharco, que se halló en un monte muy áspero, como una lengua del pueblo de San Cristóbal de Rapaz, en una cueva, debajo de un pabellón, con su huama o diadema de oro en la cabeza, vestido con siete camisetas muy finas de cumbi, que dicen los indios se las enviaron presentadas los reyes ingas antiguos. Este cuerpo como se halló y otro de un mayordomo suyo llamado Chuchu Michuy, que estaba en diferente lugar y era también muy reverenciado de los indios, se llevaron a Lima para que los viese el señor virrey y el señor arzobispo, y volviéndolos a los Andajes se hizo un solemne auto, convocando todos los pueblos de la provincia, y se quemaron estos cuerpos con otros muchas huacas y grande admiración y espanto de los indios" (Arriaga 1999: 18–19 [1621: Ch. 1]).

9. Acosta (1986 [1590]) paraphrases this description. Both of these accounts are most likely based on information provided by Polo de Ondegardo (1990 [1571]). For a similar, although independent, statement on the founding of the royal *panacas*, see Sancho (1917 [1534]).

10. "Otrosí, muerto el rey, no heredaba su casa y tesoro el príncipe, sino que se entregaba con el cuerpo del difunto al linaje que dejaba fundado, dedicándolo todo para el culto del dicho cuerpo y sustento de su familia; la cual, embalsamado el cuerpo del rey su padre, lo guardaba con toda su vajilla y alhajas, adorándolo por dios ellos y todos sus descendientes; de los cuales se iba entregando de mano en mano a los más principales, y éstos no se servían de la vajilla del rey muerto, sino cuando se hacía fiesta muy general del pueblo o lugar donde estaba depositado; y el sucesor en el reino ponía de nuevo casa, juntando para ella tesoro que dejar a los de su ayllu y linaje" (Cobo 1964: 66 [1653: Bk. 12, Ch. 4]).

11. In original: "tenían [los muertos] todo lo mejor de su reyno" (Pedro Pizarro 1986: 54 [1571]).

12. This statement was copied by Cobo (1990 [1653]). For a similar statement made by Huascar, see Betanzos (1996: 189 [1557])

13. Cobo (1990 [1653]) also presents this passage of Pedro Pizarro in his text.

14. "... los sacaban a la plaza sentándolos en ringle, cada uno según su antigüedad, y allí comían los criados y bebían y las criadas. Para los muertos hacíanles unas lumbres delante dellos de una leña que tenían labrada y cortada muy igual, y muy seca, y encendida ésta, quemaban aquí todo aquello que al muerto le habían puesto delante para que comiese de todo lo que ellos comían, que aquí en este fuego lo consumían. Tenían también delante de estos muertos unos canxilones grandes (que ellos llamaban birques) de oro, o de plata, o de barro, cada uno como quería, y aquí echaban la *chicha* que al muerto le daban, mostrándosela, convidando se unos muertos a otros, y los muertos a los vivos, y los vivos a los muertos. Pues llenos estos birques, los derramaban en una piedra redonda que tenían por ídolo, en mitad de la plaza y hecha alrededor una alberca pequeña donde se consumía por unos caños que ellos tenían hechos por debajo de tierra" (Pedro Pizarro 1986: 89–90 [1571]).

15. ". . . [Huayna Capac] mandó que ansi como fuese él entrando en las cosas destos señores que sus mamaconas y servicidores de tal señor cantasen su historia y hechos pasados y ansi como iba visitando los bultos y casas dellos como viese que le faltase alguna cosa íbasela dando y proveyendo y llegó a la de Ynga Yupangue y viendo el cantar de su historia los grandes hechos y ganados deste señor estúvose un mes haciendo grandes fiestas y sacrificios a este bulto de Ynga Yupangue su abuelo al cual bulto ofresció y dió grandes dones y dió mucha cantidad de mamaconas mujeres doncellas y ansi mismo muchos yanaconas y mandólos poblar en valles cercanos al Cuzco y que de allí trujesen el servicio de lo que ansi labrasen y criasen a la casa del Ynga Yupangue y ansi traían frutas y maíz nuevo y aves y ansi lo ponían delante del bulto de Ynga Yupangue como si vivo fuera con aquel acatamiento y reverencia que cuando era vivo le hacían y demás desto mandó que los soras y lucanas y changas de Andaguailas que fuesen deste bulto y a él sirviesen porque fueron las primeras provincias que este señor Ynga Yupangue en su vida conquistó y sujetó y esto hecho entró en la casa do estaba el bulto de su tío Yamque Yupangue y oída su historia en su canto y loa con mucho acatamiento le reverenció y le hizo sacrificios y proveyéndole y ofreciéndole grandes dones estuvo allí diez días y diole cierto repartimiento en Vilcas y de allí entró en casa de su padre que en historia y loa de su canto vio y supo sus hechos tan granados y de buen señor amigo de sujetar tierras y provincias" (Betanzos 1987: 182–183 [1557: Pt. 1, Ch. 41]).

16. "Guardaban estos cuerpos muertos los de la parentela, y teníanlos bien vestidos y aderezados, envueltos en gran cantidad de algodón, tapado el rostro, y no los mostraban sino por gran fiesta, ni los vían otros, de ordinario, más que aquellos a cuyo cargo estaba el aderezallos, guardallos y entender en su conservación; los cuales se sustentaban de la hacienda que para este efecto aplicaban los descendientes del difunto. Eran tenidos en gran veneración estos cuerpos embalsamados, y se les hacían sacrificios, a cada uno según su posibilidad; . . . cuidando dellos siempre los señores y cabezas de las parcialidades, y dedicándose toda la familia al culto de los suyos. Sacábanlos de allí muy acompañados a todas sus fiestas solemnes, y si no lo era tanto, sacaban en su lugar sus *guáuques*" (Cobo 1964: 163–164 [1653: Bk. 13, Ch.10]).

17. "Esto vine a entender yo cuando entramos la primera vez en el Cuzco, . . . pues a la partida un capitán de Mango Inca, que había de ir con él, vino a rogar al Marqués enviase a rogar a uno destos muertos que le diese por mujer una parienta suya, que estaba en su servicio. El Marqués me mandó a mí que fuese con don Martín, la lengua, a pedirle de su parte diese la india a este capitán. Pues creyendo yo que iba a hablar algún indio vivo, me llevaron a un bulto de estos muertos, donde estaba asentado dentro de unas andas,

que así los tenían; y el indio diputado que hablaba por él de un lado, y la india al otro, sentados cabe el muerto. Pues llegados que fuimos delante del muerto, la lengua le dijo el mensaje, y estando así un poco suspensos y callados, el indio miró a la india (entiendo yo que para saber su voluntad); pues después de haber estado así como digo, me respondieron ambos a dos diciendo que su señor el muerto decía que fuese así, que llevase la india el capitán ya dicho, pues lo quería el apo (que así llamaban al Marqués)" (Pedro Pizarro 1986: 53–54 [1571]).

18. ". . . que cada muerto de estos tenía señalado un indio principal y una india asimismo lo que este indio o india quería, decían ellos que era la voluntad de los muertos. Cuando tenía gana de comer o de beber, decían que los muertos querían lo mismo; si querían ir a holgarse a casa de otros muertos, decían lo mismo porque así lo tenían de costumbre irse a visitar los muertos unos a otros, y hacían grandes bailes y borracheras. Algunas veces iban a casas de los vivos, y los vivos a las suyas" (Pedro Pizarro 1986: 52–53 [1571]).

19. "Sacaban a la plaza para hacer esta fiesta todas las guacas ya dichas y los cuerpos de los incas señores y señoras difuntos, para beber con ellos, poniendo, los que avían sido señores de la parcialidad de Anan Cuzco en ella y a los de Hurin Cuzco en la suya, y así traían de comer y beber a los muertos como si estuvieran vivos diciendo: 'Cuando eras vivo solías comer y beber desto, reciba lo ahora tu anima y cómalo adoquiera que estuiere'" (Molina 1989: 111 [ca. 1575]).

20. "[P]ara lo cual se hacía un bulto de mantas con la figura que ellos ponerle querían, al cual llaman el nombre del rey ya muerto y salían estos bultos a ponerse en la plaza del Cuzco cuando se hacían sus fiestas y en rededor de cada bulto destos reyes estaban sus mujeres y criados y venían todos, aparejándole allí su comida y bebida, porque el demonio debía de hablar en aquellos bultos, pues que esto por ellos se usaba. Y cada bulto tenía sus truhanes o desidores que estaban con palabras alegres contentando al pueblo; y todo el tesoro cual señor tenía siendo vivo, se estaba en poder de sus criados y familiares y se sacaba a las fiestas semejantes con gran aparato; sin lo cual no dejaban de tener sus 'chacaras,' ques nombre de heredades, donde cojían sus maices y otros mantenimientos con que se sustentaban las mujeres con toda la demás familia destos señores que tenían bultos y memorias aunque ya eran muertos. Y cierto esta usanza fue harta parte para que en este reino oviese la suma tan grande de tesoros que se han visto por nuestros ojos; y a españoles conquistadores e oído que, cuando descubriendo las provincias del reino entraron en el Cuzco, había destos bultos, lo cual pareció ser verdad cuando dende a poco tiempo queriendo tomar la borla Mango Inca Yupangue, hijo de Guaynacapa, públicamente fueron sacados en la plaza del Cuzco a vista de todos los españoles e indios que en ella

en aquel tiempo estaban" (Cieza de León 1995: 29 [1554: Pt. 2, Ch. 11]).

21. "[S]eñaló y nombró [Pachacuti Inca Yupanqui] cierta cantidad de yanaconas y mamaconas y dioles tierras para en que sembrasen y cogiesen para el servicio destos bultos y ansi mismo señaló muchos ganados para los sacrificios que ansi se les habían de hacer y este servicio e tierras e ganado dió e repartió a cada bulto por sí e mandó que se tuviese gran cuidado el continuamente a la noche e a la mañana de dar de comer e beber a estos bultos y sacrificarlos para lo cual mandó e señaló que tuviesen cada uno de estos un mayordomo de los tales sirvientes que ansi le señaló que ansi mismo mandó a estos mayordomos e a cada uno por sí que luego hiciesen cantares los cuales cantasen estas mamaconas y yanaconas con los lores de los hechos de cada uno destos señores en sus días ansi hizo los cuales cantares ordinariamente todo tiempo que fiestas hubiese cantasen cada servicio de aquellos por su orden y concierto comenzando primero el tal cantar e historia e loa los de Mango Capac e que ansi fueron diciendo las tales mamaconas e servicio como los señores habían sucedido hasta allí y que aquella fuese la orden que se tuviese desde allí adelante para que de aquella manera hubiese memoria dellos e sus antigüedades . . . cuales bultos Ynga Yupangue mandó cuando ansi los mandó poner en los escaños que fuesen puestas en las cabezas unas diademas de plumas muy galanas de las cuales colgaban unas orejeras de oro y esto ansi puesto mandó que les pusiesen ansi mismo en las frentes a cada uno destos bultos unas patenas de oro e que siempre estuviesen estas mamaconas mujeres con unas plumas coloradas largas en las manos e atadas a unas varas con las cuales ojeasen las moscas que ansi en los bultos se asentasen el servicio de los cuales e que ansi se hiciese a estos bultos fuese muy limpio e que las mamaconas e yanaconas cada e cuando que delante de estos bultos paresciesen al servir o reverenciar otros cualesquiera que fuesen viniesen muy limpios e bien vestidos e con toda limpieza e reverencia e acatamiento estuviesen delante destos tales bultos y desta manera hizo este señor en esto dos cosas la una que hizo que sus pasados fuesen tenidos y acatados por dioses e que hubiese memoria dellos lo cual hizo porque entendía que lo mismo se haría del después de sus días" (Betanzos 1987: 86 [1557: Pt. 1, Ch. 17]).

22. In Quechua, the term *huauque* is used by a man to refer to his brother.

23. For the other Incas, Sarmiento de Gamboa simply writes that Polo de Ondegardo found the Inca's idol along with their mummy.

24. "[Sinchi Roca] dejó un ídolo de piedra, figura de pescado, llamado Guanachiri Amaru, que fue en su vida su ídolo guaoqui. El cual ídolo con el cuerpo de Cinchi Roca halló el licenciado Polo, siendo corregidor del Cuzco, en el pueblo de Bimbilla entre unas barretas de cobre, y el ídolo tenía su servicio de criados y tierras de sembrar" (Sarmiento de Gamboa 1906: 44 [1572: Ch. 15]).

25. "Halló el cuerpo deste inga el licenciado Polo en Totocachi, donde agora es la perroquia de señor Sant Blas de la ciudad del Cuzco, bien aderezado y guardado, y lo embió á Lima por mandado del marqués de Cañete virrey deste reino. El ídolo *guaoqui* deste inga se llamó *Indi illapa*; era de oro y muy grande, el cual en pedazos fué llevado á Caxamarca. Halló el dicho el licenciado Polo, casa, heredades, criados y mujeres deste ídolo *guaoqui*" (Sarmiento de Gamboa 1906: 94 [1572: Ch. 48]).

26. "Usaban en vida todos los reyes y señores de la casta de los Incas hacer cada uno su estatua que representase su misma persona, y con cierta solemnidad y ceremonias la tomaba por hermano, llamándola *guáuque*, que significa eso. Esta la hacían unos mayor, otros menor, y otros al propio de su tamaño y semejanza; unas eran labradas de oro, otras de plata, de palo, piedra o de otra materia. Los reyes ponían a sus *guáuques* casa y servicio, y aplicaban alguna hacienda para sustentación de los que los tenían a cargo; y mandaban al pueblo, y señaladamente a los de su linaje y parcialidad, que les hiciesen la misma reverencia, desde el día que los constituían, por hermanos suyos, que a sus propias personas. Eran estos ídolos tenidos en gran veneración mientras vivían los señores que representaban, y después de muertos se guardaban con sus cuerpos, y cuerpos e ídolos eran siempre igualmente respetados y servidos. Teniéndolos vestidos ricamente, y en las fiestas que, por no ser muy solemnes, no sacaban en público los cuerpos muertos de los señores, sacaban éstos sus *guáuques* o retratos. Era esta costumbre tan antigua, que si no fue entre ellos ficción, parece que venía desde que tienen memoria de sus cosas; y aunque comenzó por solo los reyes y grandes señores se fue con el tiempo extendiendo de manera, que cualquier hombre principal hacía estatua en vida o señalaba una piedra o ídolo, hecho de lo que le parecía, y lo tomaba por *guáuque*, y mandaba a los de su familia que lo tuviesen en su lugar mientras vivía, y después de muerto le hiciesen la misma veneración; con que vino a ser gran suma la destos ídolos en el Cuzco y su comarca; y fuera mucho mayor, sino que como se fue usando muy comúnmente de los más el ir dejando los menos principales, se fue perdiendo la memoria dellos con el tiempo. Mas los *guáuques* de los reyes Incas duraron hasta la venida de los españoles en la misma veneración que comenzaron, la cual era tan grande, que en todas sus necesidades se encomendaban a ellos las parcialidades que descendían de cuyos eran, y los llevaban en los ejércitos con toda la autoridad que podían, porque tenían creído que eran gran ayuda para sus victorias, y ponían gran espanto a los enemigos. A lo menos no hay duda sino que la gente de guerra iba muy confiada en su patrocinio, y

que hacía en ellas la imaginación gran operación, según los viejos afirman. A estas estatuas o *guáuques* hacían sacrificios muy notables y en mucha cantidad, y la opinión que dellas se tenía, era que en tanto durasen, tenían la misma fuerza que los cuerpos cuyos eran cuando estaban vivos. El tiempo que las tenían en la ciudad las ponían en compañía de los cuerpos, y adondequiera que las parcialidades y familias las llevaban, les hacían tanta honra como cuando vivía su original; y así les contribuían ofrendas para la gente que las tenía a cargo" (Cobo 1964: 162–163 [1653: Bk. 13, Ch. 9]).

27. After the conquest, Spaniards were keen to find lands dedicated to the Sun or other idols because these lands were reported to the local government as vacant and were often then reassigned as private Spanish holdings.

28. Still other accounts mention that gold statues were made in the likeness of the king. For example, Albornoz (1984: 205 [ca. 1582]) indicates that a golden statue of Topa Inca Yupanqui was kept in a building on the edge of the Plain of Anta (Bauer and Barrionuevo Orosco 1998).

29. "Hay otras imágenes hechas de yeso ó de barro las que solamente tienen los cabellos y uñas que se cortaba y los vestidos que se ponía, y son tan veneradas entre aquellas gentes como si fueran sus dioses" (Sancho 1898: 1419–1420 [1534: Ch. 19]).

30. ". . . teniendo esta nueva y se viese señor mandó luego hacer un bulto de sus mismas uñas y cabellos el cual imitaba a su persona y mandó que se llamase este bulto Ynga Guauquin que dice el hermano del Ynga y este bulto ansi hecho mandó que fuese puesto en unas andas y mandó a un criado suyo que se decia Chima que dando a este bulto que le sirviese y que tuviese cargo de guardarle y mirarle y dando a este bulto otros muchos mozos y servicio mandó que luego fuese tomado el bulto y llevado en sus andas por la posta a do sus capitanes estaban Chalcuchima y Quizquiz para que las provincias y gentes que sujetasen diesen obediencia a aquel bulto en lugar de su persona y ansi fue este bulto llevado y dado a los capitanes los cuales les recibieron y holgaron y muy mucho con él e hiciéronles muy muchos y muy grandes sacrificios y ansi servían y respetaban a este bulto como si fuera allí en persona el mesmo Atagualpa" (Betanzos 1987: 220 [1557: Pt. 2, Bk. 6]).

31. Angelina Yupanqui, born Cuxirimay Ocllo, was a wife of Atahualpa at the time of his death. She then became, for a short time, mistress to Francisco Pizarro. At the time when Betanzos was writing this passage, Angelina Yupanqui had become his own wife.

32. "[S]iendo ya muerto fue llevado a un pueblo que se llama Patallacta en el cual pueblo él había hecho edificar unas casas do su cuerpo fuese sepultado y sepultáronle metiendo su cuerpo debajo de tierra en una tinaja grande de barro nueva y él bien vestido y encima de su sepulcro mandó Ynga Yupangue que fuese puesto un bulto de oro hecho a su

semejanza y en su lugar a quien las gentes que allí fuesen adorasen en su nombre y luego fue puesto y de las uñas y cabellos que en su vida se cortaba mandó que fuese hecho un bulto el cual ansi fue hecho en aquel pueblo do el cuerpo estaba y de allí trujeron este bulto en unas andas a la ciudad del Cuzco muy suntuosamente a las fiestas de la ciudad el cual bulto pusieron en las casas de Topa Ynga Yupangue y cuando ansi fiestas había en la ciudad le sacaban a las tales fiestas con los demás bultos . . . y como el bulto fuese en la ciudad mandó Topa Ynga Yupangue que este bulto sacasen los de su mismo linaje a las fiestas que ansi hubiese en el Cuzco y que cuando ansi le sacasen le sacasen cantando las cosas que él hizo en su vida ansi en las guerras como en su ciudad y que ansi le sirviesen y reverenciasen y mudasen las ropas y vestidos como él los mudaba y era servido en su vida todo lo cual ansi fue hecho el cual bulto se llevó Mango Ynga de la ciudad del Cuzco cuando se alzó y el de oro que estaba encima de su sepultura por aviso que doña Angelina Yupangue dió del al marqués de don Francisco Pizarro le hubo el marqués con la demás riqueza que tenía" (Betanzos 1987: 149–150 [1557: Pt. 1, Ch. 32]).

33. "Ynga Yupangue mandó que tuviesen sus casas e pueblos y estancias en los valles e pueblos en torno de la ciudad del Cuzco e que estos y sus descendientes tuviesen siempre cuidado de servir a aquellos bultos a quien él los había dado y señalado todo lo cual fue ansi hecho desde entonces hasta el día de hoy que lo hacen oculta e secretamente e algunos públicos porque los españoles no entienden lo que es y estos tales bultos tienen metidos en orones que son topres en que acá se echan el maíz e la demás comida e otros en ollas y en tinajas grandes y en huecos de paredes y desta manera no los pueden topar" (Betanzos 1987: 86 [1557: Pt. 1, Ch. 17]).

34. The shrine of Huanacauri was believed to be one of Manco Capac brothers who had been converted to stone.

35. In original: "vestida y bien aderezada" (Cobo 1964: 67 [1653: Bk. 11, Ch. 4]).

36. Quechua: *inti* = sun.

37. Quechua: *acoy* = ill fortune; *wasi* = house.

38. Cobo (1979: 123 [1653: Bk. 12, Ch. 8]) indicates that the body and idol of Capac Yupanqui were found in a town near Cuzco.

39. Alternatively, it is possible that the idol and body of Mayta Capac were found in the village of Cayucache, located between Cuzco and Wimpillay, since Cobo (1979: 123 [1653: Bk. 12, Ch. 8]) indicates that most of his family lived there.

40. "Su cuerpo se halló bien aderezado y con mucha autoridad en un pueblezuelo de la comarca del Cuzco, llamado Rarapa, junto con un ídolo de piedra que lo representaba, del nombre de un ayllo Vica Quirao, y era muy honrado de los dicho ayllo y familia; la cual, allende

de la adoración y sacrificios ordinarios que le hacía, cuando había necesidad de agua para los sembrados, lo solía sacar en procesión vestido ricamente y cubierto el rostro, y llevarlo por los campos y punas; y tenían creído que era gran parte para que lloviera" (Cobo 1964: 73 [1653: Bk. 12, Ch. 9]).

41. "Estuvo depositado el cuerpo deste rey en Jaquijaguana, y teniendo noticias y rastro dél Gonzalo Pizarro, anduvo mucho tiempo buscándolo, por haber el gran tesoro que había fama estaba enterrado con él; y por descubrirle, quemó algunos indios, hombres y mujeres. Al cabo lo halló y gran suma de hacienda suya que le dieron los que lo guardaban. Hizo el dicho Pizarro quemar su cuerpo, mas los indios de su ayllo recogieron las cenizas, y con cierta confección las metieron en una tinajuela pequeña junto con el ídolo, que, como era de piedra, se lo dejaron los de Gonzalo Pizarro sin reparar de él. Después, al tiempo que el Licenciado Polo andaba descubriendo los cuerpos e ídolos de los Incas, en teniendo noticias de las cenizas e ídolo déste, lo mudaron los indios de donde antes estaba, escondiéndolo en muchas partes; porque, después que lo quemó Gonzalo Pizarro, le tuvieron en mayor veneración que antes. Ultimamente se puso tan buena diligencia, que fue hallado y sacado de poder de sus descendientes" (Cobo 1964: 77 [1653: Bk. 12, Ch. 11]).

42. The body of Pachacuti Inca Yupanqui was most likely stored in the site now called Kenko Grande (Bauer 1998: 50–51).

43. "[S]olo su cuerpo está el día de hoy en Patallacta el cual por sus miembros parece que era en su vida hombre de buen altor" (Betanzos 1987: 150 [1557: Pt. 1, Ch. 32]).

44. "Esta orden entendí yo cuando descubrí el cuerpo de Pachacutec Inca Yupanqui Inca, que fue uno de los que yo envié al Marqués a la ciudad de los Reyes, que estaba embalsamado y tan bien curado como todos vieron, que hallé con él el ídolo principal de la provincia de Andahuaylas, porque la conquistó éste y la metió debajo del dominio de los incas cuando venció a Valcuvilca el señor principal de ella, y le mató" (Polo de Ondegardo 1990: 86 [1571]).

45. "Fueron presos los señores y señoras del Cuzco que se hallaron ser amigos de Guascar, y también los ahorcaron en aquellos palos. Y luego fueron discurriendo por todas las casas de los ingas muertos pesquisando los que habían sido del bando de Guascar y enemigos de Atagualpa. Y hallaron, que la casa de Topa Inga Yupanqui había tenido con Guascar. Y Cuxi Yupanqui cometió el castigo desta casa á Chalco Chima y Quizquiz, los cuales prendieron luego al mayordomo de la casa y bulto de Topa Inga y á los de la casa, y ahorcólos á todos, y al cuerpo de Topa Inga hízolo quemar fuera del pueblo y á hacerle polvos. Y aun quemarle, mató muchas mamaconas y criados, que casi no dejó desta casa sino algunos, de quien no se hacía caso" (Sarmiento de Gamboa 1906: 122–123 [1572: Ch. 66]).

46. ". . . la fiesta acabada le hicieron al bulto de sus uñas y cabellos y fue desde allí adorado y tenido por señor al cual le hacían los sacrificios que ansi usaban hacer a los más señores muertos ya pasados y con aquella solemnidad y acatamiento que en si vivo [sic] fuera dándole a comer en sacrificio por sus horas y a beber según que comía y bebía cuando era vivo" (Betanzos 1987: 177 [1557: Pt. 1, Ch. 39]).

47. "A la muerte de Guayna Capac el cual como falleciese los señores que con él estaban le hicieron abrir y toda su carne sacar aderezándole porque no se dañase sin le quebrar hueso ninguno le aderezaron y curaron al sol y al aire y después de seco y curado vistiéronle de ropas preciadas y pusiéronle en unas andas ricas y bien aderezadas de pluma y oro y estando ya el cuerpo ansi enviáronle al Cuzco" (Betanzos 1987: 201 [1557: Pt. 1, Ch. 48]).

48. Elsewhere in his report, Xerez (1985: 85 [1534]) presents contradictory information, stating that the body of Huayna Capac was in a great hall in Cuzco.

49. Garcilaso de la Vega (1966: 578 [1609: Pt. 1, Bk. 9, Ch. 15]), who most likely garnered his information from Acosta, also states that Huayna Capac's heart was buried in Quito and that his embalmed body was returned to Cuzco. Cobo (1979 [1653]) repeats this claim in his chronicle.

50. "Su cuerpo se conserva en la ciudad del Cuzco ataviado con rica vestimenta; está muy bien conservado y sólo le falta la punta de la nariz. Hay allí también estatuas suyas hechas de estuco o yeso, con recortes de sus uñas y cabello y ataviadas con las ropas que usó en vida. Las gentes tienen a estas imágenes en tanta veneración como si fueran sus dioses. Sacan a menudo el cuerpo a la plaza acompañado de músicas y bailes y se están todo el día y la noche a su alrededor espantándole las moscas. Cuando alguno de los señores principales viene a ver al Cacique, va primero a rendir pleitesía a dichas estatuas y solo después al Cacique. Hacen con ellas tantas ceremonias que sería muy prolijo el escribirlas" (Sancho 1986: 142 [1534]).

51. "Entrados los españoles en esta tierra, hicieron grandes diligencias para descubrir un cuerpo, y aun no pocas violencias, por la fama de que tenía gran tesoro y que había de estar enterrado con su cuerpo o en los lugares que en vida más frecuentaba, porque ésta era costumbre antigua entre ellos. Al fin, por gran solicitud que se puso, y no con poco trabajo, fue hallado al tiempo que los cuerpos de los otros Incas. Hállose en el camino de la fortaleza, en una casa donde pareció haberle llevado la noche antes; que como los españoles iban ya por el rastro dándoles alcance, los indios que lo guardaban lo mudaron a muchas partes, y con traerlo con tanta priesa y sobresaltos de unos lugares a otros, siempre lo mudaban con cinco o seis ídolos en su compañía, a quienes hacían gran veneración, porque estaban persuadidos que entendían en la guarda del cuerpo del Inca" (Cobo 1964: 94 [1653: Bk. 12, Ch. 17]).

52. "Caminó el Inca con su ejército sin detenerse hasta Tumibamba; . . . mandó labrar un magnífico palacio para sí y templo para sus dioses, en el cual puso una estatua de su madre, toda de oro, gran cantidad de vajilla de plata y servicio de hombres y mujeres. Servían los Cañares de buena gana a la estatua de Mama Ocllo porque había parido en aquel lugar al rey Guayna Capac" (Cobo 1964: 90 [1653: Bk. 12, Ch. 16]).

53. "Entre otras cosas singulares eran de admirar cuatro grandes carneros de oro fino y diez o doce estatuas de mujeres, del tamaño que tienen las de esta tierra, todas realizadas en oro fino y tan bellas y bien hechas que parecían vivas. Tenían ellos a estas imágenes en tanta veneración como si estuviesen animadas y fueran señoras de todo el mundo; las vestían con bellos y finísimos trajes, las adoraban como a Diosas, les daban de comer y las hablaban cual si fuesen mujeres de carne y hueso" (Sancho 1986: 123–124 [1534]).

54. Garcilaso de la Vega's mother, Chimpu Ocllo, was a daughter of Huallpa Topa, who was a daughter of Huayna Capac.

55. ". . . habiendo de venirme a España, fui a la posada del licenciado Polo Ondegardo, natural de Salamanca, que era corregidor de aquella ciudad, a besarle las manos y despedirme de él para mi viaje. El cual, entre otros favores que me hizo, me dijo, 'Pues que vais a España, entrad en ese aposento; veréis algunos de los vuestros que he sacado a luz, para que llevéis que contar por allá.' En el aposento hallé cinco cuerpos de los reyes Incas: tres de varón y dos de mujer. El uno de ellos decían los indios que era este Inca Viracocha, mostraba bien su larga edad; tenía la cabeza blanca como la nieve. El segundo decían que era el gran Tupac Inca Yupanqui, que fue bisnieto de Viracocha Inca. El tercero era Huayna Capac, hijo de Tupac Inca Yupanqui y tataranieto del Inca Viracocha. Los dos últimos no mostraban haber vivido tanto; que aunque tenían canas, eran menos que las del Viracocha. La una de las mujeres era la reina Mama Runtu, mujer de este Inca Viracocha. La otra era la coya Mama Ocllo, madre de Huayna Capac, y es verisímile que los indios los tuviesen juntos después de muertos, marido y mujer, como vivieron en vida.

"Los cuerpos estaban tan enteros que no les faltaba cabello, ceja ni pestaña. Estaban con sus vestiduras como andaban en vida. Los *llautus* en las cabezas, sin más ornamento ni insignia de las reales. Estaban asentados, como suelen sentarse los indios y las indias; las manos tenían cruzadas sobre el pecho; la derecha sobre la izquierda, los ojos bajos, como que miraban al suelo. . . .

"Acuérdome que llegué a tocar un dedo de la mano de Huayna Capac; parecía que era de una estatua de palo, según estaba duro y fuerte. Los cuerpos pesaban tan poco, que cualquier indio los llevaba en brazos o en los hombros de casa en casa de los caballeros que los pedían para verlos.

Llevábanlos cubiertos con sábanas blancas; por las calles y plazas se arrodillaban los indios, haciéndoles reverencia con lágrimas y gemidos; y muchos españoles les quitaban la gorra, porque eran cuerpos de reyes, de lo cual quedaban los indios tan agradecidos, que no sabían cómo decirlo" (Garcilaso de la Vega 1960: 189–190 [1609: Pt. 1, Bk. 5, Ch. 29]).

56. See Sarmiento de Gamboa (1906: 59 [1572: Ch. 25]); Cobo (1979: 132 [1653: Bk. 12, Ch. 11]); Calancha (1981: 219 [1638: Bk. 1, Ch. 15]); Acosta (1986: 421, 429–430 [1590: Bk. 6, Ch. 20]).

57. See Sarmiento de Gamboa (1906: 102 [1572: Ch. 54]); Murúa (1962: 1: 62 [1611: Ch. 25]); Cobo (1979: 151 [1653: Bk. 12, Ch. 15]).

58. Alternatively, Rostworowski (1999: 33) suggests that there were some political advantages to be gained by Garcilaso de la Vega from stating that he saw these specific Incas in Cuzco. She concludes that Garcilaso de la Vega lied about his experience in the house of Polo de Ondegardo and substituted various names for those that were actually there.

59. This description of Pachacuti Inca Yupanqui is copied by Cobo (1979: 141 [1653: Bk. 12, Ch. 13]).

60. "Estaba el cuerpo [de Pachacuti Inca Yupanqui] tan entero y bien aderezado con cierto betún, que aparecía vivo. Los ojos tenía hechos de una telilla de oro, tan bien puestos, que no le hacían falta los naturales; y tenía en la cabeza una pedrada que le dieron en cierta guerra. Estaba cano y no le faltaba cabello, como si muriera aquel mismo día, habiendo más de sesenta u ochenta años que había muerto. Este cuerpo, con otros de Ingas, envió el dicho Polo a la ciudad de Lima, por mandado del Virrey Marqués de Cañete, que para desarraigar la idolatría del Cuzco, fue muy necesario; y en el hospital de San Andrés, han visto muchos españoles este cuerpo, con los demás, aunque ya están maltratados y gastados" (Acosta 1986: 423 [1590: Bk. 6, Ch. 21]).

61. Cobo (1979 [1653]) paraphrases this statement from Acosta.

62. "La madre de éste fue de gran estima; llamóse Mamaoclo. Los cuerpos de éste y del Guaynacapa, muy embalsamados y curados, envió a Lima, Polo . . ." (Acosta 1986: 424 [1590: Bk. 5, Ch. 22]).

63. ". . . y sacando el tesoro quemó el cuerpo, cuyas cenizas guardaron los Indios, y puestas en una tinajuela las adoravan. Estas cenizas y otros cuerpos enbió el Licenciado Polo a Lima en tiempo del primer Marqués de Canete, y están en un corral del Hospital de San Andrés" (Calancha 1981: 219 [1638: Bk. 1, Ch. 15]).

64. Polo de Ondegardo (1990: 86 [1571]) also uses this unusually long title (Pachacuti Inca Yupanqui Inca) for the ninth ruler.

65. The occurrence of copper bars with the mummy of Sinchi Roca is mentioned by Sarmiento de Gamboa (1906: 44 [1572: Ch. 15]).

66. "Doce ó trece años há, procuró [Polo de Ondegardo] con mucha diligencia y por diferentes medios descubrir los dichos cuerpos, para atajar el daño, y en efecto halló la mayor parte, así del ayllu de Hanan Cuzco como de Urin Cuzco, y algunos dellos embalsamados y tan frescos como cuando murieron; y cuatro del los, que fueron el de Guayna Capac y Amaru Topa Inga y Pachacuti Inga Yupanqui Inga, y á la madre de Guayna Capac, que se llamó Mama Ocllo, y los demás, halló enjaulados en unas jaulas de cobre, los cuales hizo enterrar secretamente; y con ellos descubrió las cenizas del cuerpo de Topa Inca Yupanqui, conservadas en una tinajuela envuelta en ropa rica y con sus insignias; porque este cuerpo había quemado Juan Pizarro . . . allende de hallar con los dichos cuerpos las guacas e ídolos principales de las provincias que cada uno habia conquistado, las cual eran asimismo notable estorbo de la conversión de estos naturales" (Ruiz de Navamuel 1882: 256–257 [1572]).

67. The body of Topa Inca Yupanqui was burned in 1533 by Atahualpa's forces when they captured Cuzco.

68. For information on Amaru Topa Inca, see Sarmiento de Gamboa (1906: 77, 84–86 [1572: Chs. 37, 42–43]), Santa Cruz Pachacuti Yamqui Salcamayhua (1950: 245–246 [ca. 1613]), Cabello de Valboa (1951: 334 [1586: Pt. 3, Ch. 18]), Murúa (1962: Vol. 1, p. 51 [1611: Bk. 1, Ch. 21]), and Cobo (1964: 83, 171, 173, 175 [1653: Bk. 12, Ch. 13; Bk. 13, Chs. 13–14]).

69. It is worth noting that even though Amaru Topa Inca played an important role in Inca history, Garcilaso de la Vega does not mention him. Perhaps Garcilaso de la Vega's lack of familiarity with Amaru Topa Inca played a role in his confusion between the mummies of Topa Inca Yupanqui and Amaru Topa Inca in the house of Polo de Ondegardo.

70. The street address is Jirón Huallaga No. 846, Distrito de El Cercado.

71. Other members of the research team included Antonio Coello Rodríguez, Patrick Ryan Williams, and Christopher Dayton.

13. Overview of the Inca Heartland

1. Ruiz de Arce (1933: 368 [ca. 1545]) also suggests that the city of Cuzco held about four thousand houses.

2. ". . . estaba este valle tan hermoso en edificios y población que en torno tenia, que era cosa de admirarse de ello, porque, aunque la ciudad en si no tenia mas de tres o cuatro mil casas, tenía en torno cuasi veinte mil. La fortaleza que estaba sobre la ciudad parecía desde a parte una gran fortaleza de las de España. Ahora la mayor parte de la ciudad está toda derribada y quemada. La fortaleza no tiene cuasi nada enhiesto." (Barrenechea 1959: 312–313 [1539])

BIBLIOGRAPHY

Abbott, Mark B., Mark W. Binford, Mark Brenner, and
    Kerry R. Kelts
1997   A 3500 ¹⁴C yr. high-resolution record of water-level
        changes in Lake Titicaca, Bolivia/Peru. *Quaternary
        Research* 47: 169–180.
Abbott, Mark B., Brent B. Wolfe, Ramon Aravena,
    Alexander P. Wolfe, and Geoffrey O. Seltzer
2000   Holocene hydrological reconstructions from stable
        isotopes and paleolimnology, Cordillera Real, Bo-
        livia. *Quaternary Science Reviews* 19: 1801–1820.
Acosta, José de
1954   De procurinda indorum salute o Predicación del
        evangelio en las Indias [1580]. In *Obras del P. José de
        Acosta de la Compañia de Jesús,* edited by P. Fran-
        cisco Mateos. Biblioteca de Autores Españoles
        (continuación), vol. 73, pp. 390–608. Madrid:
        Ediciones Atlas.
1986   *Historia natural y moral de las Indias* [1590]. Edited
        by José Alcina Franch. Madrid: Historia 16.
Agurto Calvo, Santiago
1980   *Cusco: Al traza urbana de la ciudad inca.* Cuzco:
        UNESCO, Instituto Nacional de Cultura del Perú.
1987   *Estudios acerca de la construcción, arquitectura y
        planeamiento incas.* Lima: Cámara Peruana de la
        Construcción.
Albarracín-Jordan, Juan, and James Edward Mathews
1990   *Asentimientos prehispánicos del Valle de Tiwanaku.*
        Vol. 1. La Paz, Bolivia: Producciones CIMA.
Albornoz, Cristóbal de
1967   Instrucción para descubrir todas las guacas del Pirú
        y sus camayos y haziendas [ca. 1582]. Edited by
        Pierre Duviols. *Journal de la Société des
        Américanistes* 56: 17–39.
1984   Instrucción para descubrir todas las guacas del Pirú
        y sus camayos y haziendas [ca. 1582]. In "Albornoz

y el espacio ritual andino prehispánico," edited by
        Pierre Duviols. *Revista Andina* 2 (1): 169–222.
Alcina Franch, José, M. Rivera, J. Galván, C. García
    Palacios, M. Guinea, B. Martínez-Caviro, L. J.
    Ramos, and T. Varela
1976   *Arqueología de Chinchero: Cerámica y otros
        materiales.* Memorias de la Misión Científica
        Española en Hispanoamérica, Vol. 3. Madrid:
        Ministerio de Asuntos Exteriores.
Aldenderfer, Mark
1989a   The Archaic Period in the south-central Andes.
        Journal of World Prehistory 3 (2): 117–158.
1989b   Archaic Period settlement patterns in the sierra of
        the Osmore basin. In *Ecology, settlement, and history
        in the Osmore drainage, Peru.* Edited by Don Rice,
        Charles Stanish, and Philip Scarr, pp. 129–166.
        BAR International Series 545 (I). Oxford: British
        Archaeological Reports.
1996   Reconocimiento arqueológico de la cuenca del Río
        Ilave. Report submitted to the Instituto Nacional
        de Cultura, Lima, Peru.
1997   Jiskairumoko: An early sedentary settlement in the
        southwestern Lake Titicaca basin. Paper presented
        at the 37th annual meeting of the Institute for
        Andean Studies, Berkeley, CA.
1998   *Montane foragers: Asana and the south-central Andean
        Archaic.* Iowa City: University of Iowa Press.
Aldenderfer, Mark S. (ed.)
n.d.   Quelcatani: *The prehistory of a pastoral lifeway on
        the high Puna.* Washington, D.C.: Smithsonian In-
        stitution Press.
Algaze, Guillermo
1992   *The Uruk world system: The dynamics of expansion of
        early Mesopotamian civilization.* Chicago: Univer-
        sity of Chicago Press.

Anderson, David G.
1994   *The Savannah River chiefdoms: Political change in the Late Prehistoric southeast.* Tuscaloosa: University of Alabama Press.

Angrand, Léonce
1972   *Imagen del Perú en el siglo XIX.* Lima: Editorial Carlos Milla Batres.

Anonymous Chronicler
1906   Discurso de la sucesión y gobierno de los yngas [ca. 1570]. In *Juicio de límites entre el Perú y Bolivia; prueba peruana presentada al gobierno de la República Argentina,* vol. 8, edited by Víctor M. Maúrtua, pp. 149–165. Madrid: Tipografía de los Hijos de M. G. Hernández.

Ansión, I.
1986   *El árbol y el bosque en la sociedad andina.* Lima: Instituto Nacional Forestal y Fauna–FAO.

Archivo Agrario: Miscelánea: Hacienda Larapa.
1596   Petición y petición aceptada de Catalina de Guevara Vda. de la Parroquia de San Sebastián. 1591–1596: f.348–349. Cuzco, Peru.

Arriaga, Pablo Joseph de
1968   *The extirpation of idolatry in Peru* [1621]. Translated and edited by L. Clark Keating. Lexington: University of Kentucky Press.

1999   *La extirpación de la idolatría del Pirú* [1621]. Cuzco, Peru: Centro de Estudios Regional Andinos.

Astete Victoria, Fernando
1983   Evidencias pre-cerámicas de Espinar. In *Arqueología Andina,* edited by Arminda M. Gibaja Oviedo, pp. 1–4. Cuzco: INC.

Avendaño, Fernando de
1904   Letter written in Lima (Los Reyes) on 3 April 1617. In *La imprenta en Lima (1584–1824),* vol. 1, edited by José Toribio Medina, pp. 380–383. Santiago de Chile: Impreso del autor.

Aveni, Anthony F.
1981   Horizon astronomy in Incaic Cuzco. In *Archaeoastronomy in the Americas,* edited by R. A. Williamson, pp. 305–318. Los Altos, Calif.: Ballena Press.

Baca C., Jenaro F.
1974   *Motivos de ornamentación de la cerámica inca Cusco.* Vol. 1. Camaná, Peru: Librería Studium S.A.

1989   *Motivos de ornamentación de la cerámica inca Cusco.* Vol. 2. Camaná, Peru: Librería Studium S.A.

Baker, Paul A., Geoffrey O. Seltzer, Sherilyn C. Fritz, Robert B. Dunbar, Matthew J. Grove, Pedro M. Tapia, Scott L. Cross, Harold D. Rowe, and James P. Broda
2001   The history of South American tropical precipitation for the past 25,000 years. *Science* 291: 640–643.

Barreda Murillo, Luis
1964   Primera excavación en Piquillacta. Tesis doctoral, Facultad de Historia, Universidad Nacional San Antonio Abad del Cuzco.

1973   *Las culturas inka y pre-inka de Cuzco.* Tesis, Facultad de Arqueología, Universidad Nacional San Antonio Abad del Cuzco.

1982   Asentamiento humano de los Qotakalli del Cuzco. In *Arqueología de Cuzco,* compiled by Italo Oberti Rodríguez, pp. 13–21. Cuzco: Instituto Nacional de Cultura.

1991   Historia y arqueología del Qosqo pre-inka. *Revista Municipal del Qosqo* 1 (2): 20–36.

Bauer, Brian S.
1987   Sistemas andinos de organización rural antes del establecimiento de reducciones: El ejemplo de Pacariqtambo (Perú). *Revista Andina* 9 (1): 197–210.

1989   Muyu Orqo y Ccoipa: Dos nuevos tipos de cerámica para la región del Cusco. *Revista Andina* 7 (2): 537–542.

1991   Pacariqtambo and the mythical origins of the Inca. *Latin American Antiquity* 2 (1): 7–26.

1992a   *The development of the Inca state.* Austin: University of Texas Press.

1992b   Investigaciones arqueológicas recientes en los asientos de Maukallaqta y Puma Orqo, departamento del Cusco, Perú. In *Avances en arqueología andina,* pp. 67–108. Cuzco: Centro de Estudios Regionales Andinos "Bartolomé de Las Casas."

1996   The legitimization of the Inca state in myth and ritual. *American Anthropologist* 98 (2): 327–337.

1998   *The sacred landscape of the Inca: The Cuzco ceque system.* Austin: University of Texas Press.

1999   *The early ceramics of the Inca heartland.* Fieldiana Anthropology, new series, no. 31. Chicago: Field Museum of Natural History.

2002   *Las antiguas tradiciones alfareras de la región del Cuzco.* Cuzco: Centro de Estudios Regionales Andinos "Bartolomé de Las Casas."

Bauer, Brian S., and Wilton Barrionuevo Orosco
1998   Reconstructing Andean shrine systems: A test case from the Anta region of Cuzco. *Andean Past* 5: 73–87. Edited by Monica Barnes, Daniel H. Sandweiss, and Brian S. Bauer. Ithaca, N.Y.: Cornell University Latin American Studies Program.

Bauer, Brian S., and R. Alan Covey
1999   The Cusco Valley Archaeological Survey Project. Presented at the 64th meeting of the Society for American Archaeology, Chicago (March 25–28).

2002   State development in the Inca heartland (Cuzco, Peru). *American Anthropologist* 10 (3): 846–864.

Bauer, Brian S., and David S. P. Dearborn
1995   *Astronomy and empire in the ancient Andes.* Austin: University of Texas Press.

Bauer, Brian S., and Bradford Jones
2003   *Early Intermediate and Middle Horizon ceramic styles of the Cuzco Valley.* Fieldiana Anthropology, new series, no. 34. Chicago: Field Museum of Natural History.

Bauer, Brian S., Bradford Jones, and Cindy Klink
n.d.   Excavations at Katapata. Unpublished research report.

Bauer, Brian S., and Charles Stanish
1990   *Killke and Killke-related pottery from Cuzco, Peru, in the Field Museum of Natural History.* Fieldiana Anthropology, new series, no. 15. Chicago: Field Museum of Natural History.
2001   *Ritual and pilgrimage in the ancient Andes: The Islands of the Sun and the Moon.* Austin: University of Texas Press.

Béjar Navarro, Raymundo
1990   *Arquitectura inka: El Templo del Sol o Corikanka.* Cuzco: Consejo Nacional de Ciencia y Tecnología.

Benavides Calle, Mario
1971   Análisis de la cerámica Huarpa. *Revista del Museo Nacional* (Lima) 37: 63–88.
1991   Cheqo Wasi, Huari. In *Huari administrative structure: Prehistoric monumental architecture and state government,* ed. William H. Isbell and Gordon F. McEwan, pp. 55–70. Washington, D.C.: Dumbarton Oaks Research Library and Collection.

Bengtsson, Lisbet
1998   *Prehistoric stonework in the Peruvian Andes: A case study at Ollantaytambo.* GOTARC series B, No. 10, Etnologiska studier 44. Göteborg: Etnografiska museet.

Betanzos, Juan de
1987   *Suma y narración de los incas* [1557]. Prólogo, transcripción y notas por María del Carmen Martín Rubio; estudios preliminares de Horacio Villanueva Urteaga, Demetrio Ramos y María del Carmen Martín Rubio. Madrid: Ediciones Atlas.
1996   *Narrative of the Incas* [1557]. Translated and edited by Roland Hamilton and Dana Buchanan from the Palma de Mallorca manuscript. Austin: University of Texas Press.

Billman, Brian
1996   The evolution of prehistoric political organization in the Moche Valley, Peru. Ph.D. dissertation, Department of Anthropology, University of California, Santa Barbara.

Binford, Michael, Mark Brenner, and Barbara Leyden
1996   Paleoecology and Tiwanaku ecosystems. In *Tiwanaku and its hinterland: Archaeology and paleo-* *ecology of an Andean civilization,* vol. 1, edited by Alan L. Kolata, pp. 89–108. Washington D.C.: Smithsonian Institution Press.

Binford, Michael, Alan L. Kolata, Mark Brenner, John W. Janusek, Matthew Seddon, Mark Abbott, and Jason Curtis
1997   Climate variation and the rise and fall of an Andean civilization. *Quaternary Research* 47: 235–248.

Bingham, Hiram
1915   Types of Machu Picchu pottery. *American Anthropologist* 17 (2): 257–271.
1922   *Inca land: Explorations in the highlands of Peru.* Cambridge, Mass.: Riverside Press.

Blanchard, Peter (ed.)
1991   *Markham in Peru: The travels of Clements R. Markham, 1852–1853.* Austin: University of Texas Press.

Blanton, Richard E., Gary M. Feinman, Stephen A. Kowalewski, and Linda M. Nicholas
1999   *Ancient Oaxaca.* Cambridge: Cambridge University Press.

Bray, Tamara L.
2003   Inka pottery as culinary equipment: Food, feasting, and gender in imperial state design. *Latin American Antiquity* 14 (1):3–28.

Browman, David
1970   Early Peruvian peasants: The culture history of a Central Highlands Valley. Ph.D. dissertation, Department of Anthropology, Harvard University.

Burger, Richard L.
1989   An overview of Peruvian archaeology (1976–1986). *Annual Review of Anthropology* 18: 37–69.

Burger, Richard L., and Frank Asaro
1979   Análisis de rasgos significativos en la obsidiana de los Andes Centrales. *Revista del Museo Nacional* (Lima) 43: 281–326.

Burger, Richard L., Frank Asaro, Paul Trawick, and Fred Stross
1998   The Alca obsidian source: The origins of raw material for Cuzco-type obsidian artifacts. *Andean Past* 5: 185–202. Edited by Monica Barnes, Daniel H. Sandweiss, and Brian S. Bauer. Ithaca, N.Y.: Cornell University Latin American Studies Program.

Burger, Richard L., Karen L. Chávez, and Sergio J. Chávez
2000   Through the glass darkly: Prehispanic obsidian procurement and exchange in Southern Peru and Northern Bolivia. *Journal of World Prehistory* 14 (3): 267–362.

Burleigh, Richard, Janet Ambers, and Keith Matthews
1983   British Museum natural radiocarbon measurements XVI. *Radiocarbon* 25 (1): 39–58.

Burns, Kathryn
1999   *Colonial habits: Convents and the spiritual economy of Cuzco, Peru.* Durham, N.C.: Duke University Press.

Cabello de Valboa, Miguel
1951   *Miscelánea antártica, una historia del Perú antiguo* [1586]. Edited by L. E. Valcárcel. Lima: Universidad Nacional Mayor de San Marcos, Instituto de Etnología.

Calancha, Antonio de la
1981   *Corónica moralizada del Orden de San Agustín en el Perú* [1638]. Edited by Ignacio Prado Pastor. Lima: Universidad Nacional Mayor de San Marcos, Editorial de la Universidad.

Calderari, Milena
1991   Estilos cerámicos incaicos de La Paya. In *Actas del XX Congreso Nacional de Arqueología Chilena,* vol. 2, pp. 151–164. Santiago de Chile: Museo Nacional de Historia Natural, Sociedad Chilena de Arqueología.

Calderari, Milena, and Verónica Williams
1991   Re-evaluación de los estilos cerámicos incaicos en el noroeste argentino. *Revista Comechingonia* 9: 73–95.

Candía Gómez, Alfredo
1992   Arquitectura de Qhataqasapatallaqta. Tesis presentado por Licenciado en arqueología, Universidad Nacional San Antonio Abad del Cuzco.

Casas, Bartolomé de Las
        See Las Casas, Bartolomé de

Chávez, Karen Lynne Mohr
1977   Marcavalle: The ceramics from an Early Horizon site in the Valley of Cusco, Peru, and implications for south highland socio-economic interaction. Ph.D. dissertation, Department of Anthropology, University of Pennsylvania.
1980   The archaeology of Marcavalle, an Early Horizon site in the Valley of Cuzco, Peru: Part I. *Baessler-Archiv,* neue Folge, 28 (2): 203–329.
1981a   The archaeology of Marcavalle, an Early Horizon site in the Valley of Cuzco, Peru: Part II. *Baessler-Archiv,* neue Folge, 29 (1): 107–205.
1981b   The archaeology of Marcavalle, an Early Horizon site in the Valley of Cuzco, Peru: Part III. *Baessler-Archiv,* neue Folge, 29 (1): 241–386.
1982   Resumen de los trabajos en Marcavalle. In *Arqueología de Cuzco,* compiled by I. Oberti R., pp. 1–8. Cuzco: Instituto Nacional de Cultura.
1985   Early Tiahuanaco-related ceremonial burners from Cuzco, Peru. *Diálogo Andino* (Arica, Chile: Departamento de Historia y Geografía, Universidad de Tarapacá) 4: 137–178.

Chávez, Sergio Jorge
1985   Ofrendas funerarias dentro de los límites meridionales del territorio Huari en el Departamento del Cuzco. *Diálogo Andino* (Arica, Chile: Departamento de Historia y Geografía, Universidad de Tarapacá) 4: 179–202.
1987   Funerary offerings from a Middle Horizon context in Pomacanchi, Cuzco. *Ñawpa Pacha* 22–23: 1–48.
1988   Archaeological reconnaissance in the Province of Chumbivilcas, south highlands of Peru. *Expedition* 30 (3): 27–38.

Chepstow-Lusty, Alex J., K. D. Bennett, J. Fjeldså, A. Kendall, W. Galiano, and A. Tupayachi Herrera
1997   When two worlds collide: Comparing human impact on fragile ecosystems before and after the Inca. *Tawantinsuyu* 3: 127–134.
1998   Tracing 4,000 years of environmental history in the Cuzco area, Peru, from the pollen record. *Mountain Research and Development* 18 (2): 159–172.

Chepstow-Lusty, Alex J., K. D. Bennett, V. R. Swisur, and A. Kendall
1996   4,000 years of human impact and vegetation change in the central Peruvian Andes—with events paralleling the Maya record? *Antiquity* 70: 824–833.

Chepstow-Lusty, Alex J., Michael R. Frogley, Brian S. Bauer, K. D. Bennett, M. B. Bush, T. A. Chutas, S. Goldsworthy, Alfredo Tupayachi Herrera, M. Leng, D.-D. Rousseau, K. Sabbe, G. Slean, and M. Sterken
2002   A tale of two lakes: Droughts, El Niños, and major cultural change during the last 5,000 years in the Cuzco region of Peru. In *Environmental catastrophes and recovery in the Holocene,* edited by S. Leroy and I. S. Stewart. Abstracts Volume, 28 August–2 September 2002. West London (UK): Brunel University.

Chepstow-Lusty, Alex J., Michael Frogley, Brian S. Bauer, and Alfredo Tupayachi Herrera
n.d.   A Late Holocene record of El Niño/arid events from the Cuzco region, Peru. Unpublished manuscript.

Chepstow-Lusty, Alex J., and Mark Winfield
2000   Agroforestry by the Inca: Lessons from the past. *Ambio* 29 (6): 322–328.

Chervin, M.
1902   Cranes, pointes de flèche en silex et instruments de pêche provenant de la baile d'Antofagasta: Momies des Hauts plateaux de la Bolivie. *Bulletins et mémoires de la Société d'Anthropologie de Paris* 5 (3): 700–704.
1908   Sur les photographies métriques du crane d'Atahualpa. *Anthropologie Bolivienne* 3: 108–109.

Cieza de León, Pedro de

1976   *The Incas of Pedro Cieza de León* [Part 1, 1553, and Part 2, 1554]. Translated by Harriet de Onís and edited by Victor W. von Hagen. Norman: University of Oklahoma Press.

1996a   *Crónica del Perú: Primera parte* [1553]. Introduction by Franklin Pease G. Y. and notes by Miguel Maticorena. Lima: Academia Nacional de la Historia and Pontificia Universidad Católica del Perú.

1996b   *Crónica del Perú: Segunda parte* [1554]. Introduction by Franklin Pease G. Y. and notes by Miguel Maticorena. Lima: Academia Nacional de la Historia and Pontificia Universidad Católica del Perú.

1998   *The discovery and conquest of Peru.* Edited and translated by Alexandra Parma Cook and Noble David Cook. Durham, N.C.: Duke University Press.

Clark, R.

1982   Point count estimate of charcoal in pollen preparations and thin sections of sediments. *Pollen and Spores* 24: 523–535.

Cobo, Bernabé

1964   *Historia del Nuevo Mundo* [1653]. In *Obras del P. Bernabé Cobo de la Compañía de Jesús,* edited by P. Francisco Mateos. Biblioteca de Autores Españoles (continuación), vols. 91 and 92. Madrid: Ediciones Atlas.

1979   *History of the Inca Empire: An account of the Indians' customs and their origin together with a treatise on Inca legends, history, and social institutions* [1653]. Translated and edited by Roland Hamilton. Austin: University of Texas Press.

1990   *Inca religion and customs* [1653]. Translated and edited by Roland Hamilton. Austin: University of Texas Press.

Comercio, El (Lima)

1952a   Hasta 5 kilos de oro ha dado el riachuelo de Huaroy-mayo que tiene intrigado al Cuzco. 6 August.

1952b   Motivo de investigación son los hallazgos de Batán-Orco. 8 August.

1952c   Huaqueros de Batán-Orco fueron puestos en libertad. 10 August.

1952d   No hay oro en Batán-Orco. Tumba pre-hispánica profanada contenía objetos valiosos. . . . Informe del visitador general de monumentos históricos. 19 August.

1952e   El Patronato arqueológico del Cuzco excavará en Batán-Orco. 21 August.

1952f   A pesar de todo, créese que Batán-Orco era un lavadero de oro. 26 August.

1952g   Tumba Tiahuanacu se halló en Batán-Orco. 16 September.

1952h   Informe de la Comisión del Patronato de Arqueología que investigó en Batán-Orco. 19 September.

1952i   Conchas marinas y turquesas hallaron en las últimas excavaciones de Batán-Orco. 21 September.

1952j   Láminas totémicas de oro se hallaron en Batán-Orco. 2 October.

1952k   El mamelón de Batán-Orco. 6 October.

Conrad, Geoffrey W.

1981   Cultural materialism, split inheritance, and the expansion of ancient Peruvian empires. *American Antiquity* 46 (1): 2–26.

Conrad, Geoffrey W., and Arthur A. Demarest

1984   *Religion and empire: The dynamics of Aztec and Inca expansionism.* Cambridge: Cambridge University Press.

Cook, Anita G.

1992   The stone ancestors: Idioms of imperial attire and rank among Huari figurines. *Latin American Antiquity* 3 (4): 341–364.

Cook, David Noble (ed.)

1975   *Tasa de la visita general de Francisco de Toledo.* Introduction by David Noble Cook. Lima: Universidad Nacional Mayor de San Marcos, Seminario de Historia Rural Andina.

Costin, Cathy Lynne

2001   Production and exchange of ceramics. In *Empire and Domestic Economy,* edited by Terence N. D'Altroy and Christine A. Hastorf, pp. 203–242. New York: Plenum.

Covey, R. Alan

2003   The Vilcanota Valley (Peru): Inka state formation and the evolution of imperial strategies. Ph.D. dissertation, University of Michigan, Department of Anthropology.

Cross, Scott L., Paul A. Baker, Geoffrey O. Seltzer, Sherilyn C. Fritz, and Robert B. Dunbar

2000   A new estimate of the Holocene lowstand level of Lake Titicaca, central Andes, and implications for tropical palaeohydrology. *Holocene* 10 (1): 21–32.

Cumpa Palacios, Claudio Víctor

1988   Prospección arqueológica en Qoripata. Tesis presentado por Bachiller en arqueología, Universidad Nacional San Antonio Abad del Cuzco.

D'Altroy, Terence N.

1992   *Provincial power in the Inka Empire.* Washington

D.C.: Smithsonian Institution Press.

2001 State goods in the domestic economy: The Inka ceramic assemblage. In *Empire and Domestic Economy*, edited by Terence N. D'Altroy and Christine A. Hastorf, pp. 243–264. New York: Plenum.

D'Altroy, Terence N., and Ronald A. Bishop

1990 The provincial organization of Inka ceramic production. *American Antiquity* 55: 120–138.

D'Altroy, Terence N., and Timothy K. Earle

1985 Staple finance, wealth finance, and storage in the Inka political economy (including comment and replay). *Current Anthropology* 25 (2): 187–206.

1992 Inka storage facilities in the Upper Mantaro Valley, Peru. In *Inka storage systems*, edited by Terry LeVine, pp. 176–205. Norman: University of Oklahoma Press.

D'Altroy, Terence N., and Christine A. Hastorf

1984 The distribution and contents of Inca state storehouses in the Xauxa region of Peru. *American Antiquity* 49 (2): 334–349.

1992 The architecture and the contents of Inka state storehouses in the Xauxa region of Peru. In *Inka storage systems*, edited by Terry LeVine, pp. 259–286. Norman: University of Oklahoma Press.

Davies, Nigel

1995 *The Incas*. Niwot: University Press of Colorado.

Dean, Carolyn S.

1998 Creating a ruin in Colonial Cusco: Sacsahuaman and what was made of it. *Andean Past* 5: 161–183. Edited by Monica Barnes, Daniel H. Sandweiss, and Brian S. Bauer. Ithaca, N.Y.: Cornell University Latin American Studies Program.

1999 *Inka bodies and the body of Christ: Corpus Christi in Colonial Cuzco, Peru*. Durham, N.C.: Duke University Press.

Dearborn, David S. P., Matthew T. Seddon, and Brian S. Bauer

1998 The Sanctuary of Titicaca: Where the Sun returns to Earth. *Latin American Antiquity* 9 (3): 240–258.

Demarest, Arthur A., and Geoffrey W. Conrad

1983 Ideological adaptation and the rise of the Aztec and Inca Empires. In *Civilization in the ancient Americas: Essays in honor of Gordon R. Willey*, edited by R. M. Leventhal and Alan L. Kolata, pp. 373–400. Albuquerque: University of New Mexico Press.

Dillehay, Tom

1984 A late Ice Age settlement in southern Chile. *Scientific American* 251 (4): 106–112, 117.

1989 *Monte Verde: A Late Pleistocene settlement in Chile*. Vol. 1, *Paleoenvironment and site context*. Washington, D.C.: Smithsonian Institution Press.

1997 *Monte Verde: A Late Pleistocene settlement in Chile*.

Vol. 2, *The archaeological context and interpretation*. Washington, D.C.: Smithsonian Institution Press.

Duviols, Pierre

1986 *Cultura andina y represión: Procesos y visitas de idolatrías y hechicerías Cajatambo, siglo XVII*. Archivos de Historia Andina Rural 5. Cuzco: Centro de Estudios Regionales Andinos "Bartolomé de Las Casas."

Dwyer, Edward Bridgeman

1971a The early Inca occupation of the Valley of Cuzco, Peru. Ph.D. dissertation, Department of Anthropology, University of California, Berkeley.

1971b A chanapata figure from Cuzco, Peru. *Ñawpa Pacha* (Berkeley) 9: 33–40.

Earle, Timothy K.

1997 *How chiefs come to power: The political economy in prehistory*. Stanford, Calif.: Stanford University Press.

Earle, Timothy K., and Terence N. D'Altroy

1982 Storage facilities and state finance in the Upper Mantaro Valley, Peru. In *Contexts for Prehistoric Exchange*, edited by J. E. Ericson and Timothy K. Earle, pp. 265–290. New York: Academic Press.

Earle, Timothy K., Terence N. D'Altroy, Christine A. Hastorf, Carterina Scott, Cathy L. Costin, Glenn S. Russell, and Elsie Sandefur

1988 *Investigations of Inka expansion and exchange*. Monograph 28. Institute of Archaeology, University of California, Los Angeles.

Earle, Timothy K., Terence N. D'Altroy, Catherine J. LeBlanc, Christine A. Hastorf, and Terry Y. LeVine

1980 Changing settlement patterns in the Upper Mantaro Valley, Peru. *Journal of New World Archaeology* 4: 1–49.

Early, Robert

1995 Excavation at Juchuy Aya Orqo, Marcacocha Basin, Patacancha Valley. Unpublished archaeological report. Witney, U.K.: The Cusichaca Trust.

Eaton, George F.

1916 The collection of osteological material from Machu Picchu. *Memoirs of the Connecticut Academy of Arts and Sciences* 5: 3–96.

Espinoza Martínez, Héctor

1983 Evidencia cultural del Horizonte Medio (Wari) Aqomoqo-Cuzco. In *Arqueología Andina*, edited by Arminda M. Gibaja Oviedo, pp. 16–22. Cuzco: Ediciones Instituto Nacional de Cultura.

Espinoza Soriano, Waldemar

1974 El hábitat de la etnia Pinagua, siglos XV y XVI. *Revista del Museo Nacional* (Lima) 40: 157–220.

1977 Los cuatro suyo del Cuzco, siglos XV y XVI. *Bulletin, Institut Français des Etudes Andines* 6: 3–4: 109–122.

Esquivel y Navia, Diego de

1980   *Noticias cronológicas de la gran ciudad del Cuzco* [1749]. Vols. 1 and 2. Edición, prólogo y notas de Félix Denegri Luna con la colaboración de Horacio Villanueva Urteaga y César Gutiérrez Muñoz. Lima: Fundación Augusto N. Wiese, Banco Wiese Ltdo.

Estete, Miguel de (attributed to)

1924   Noticia del Perú [ca. 1535]. In *Historia de los incas y conquista del Perú, vol. 8,* edited by Horacio H. Urteaga, pp. 3–56. Colección de Libros y Documentos Referentes a la Historia del Perú, 2d series. Lima: Imprenta y Librería Sanmartí.

1985   La relación del viaje que hizo el señor capitán Hernando Pizarro por mandado del señor Gobernador, su hermano, desde el pueblo de Caxamalca a Parcama y de allí a Jauja [1534]. Document contained within *Verdadera relación de la conquista del Perú,* by Francisco de Xerez, pp. 130–148. Madrid: Historia 16.

Fernández de Alfaro, Luis

1904   Relación del oro del Perú que recibimos de Hernando Pizarro que truxo en la nao que era maestre Pero Bernal, para Su Majestad, por el mes de Hebrero del año pasado de mil é quinientos é treinta é cuatro años, pesado por Hernand Alvarez, fiel de los pesos desta cibdad en la forma siquiente . . . [1534]. In *La imprenta en Lima (1584–1824),* vol. 1, edited by José Toribio Medina, pp. 163–172. Santiago de Chile: Impreso y grabado en casa del autor.

Flannery, Kent V.

1972   The cultural evolution of civilizations. *Annual Review of Ecology and Systematics* 3: 399–426.

Franco Inojosa, José María

1937   Informe sobre los restos arqueológicos de las cabeceras de Paucartambo. *Revista del Museo Nacional* (Lima) 6 (2): 255–277.

Gade, Daniel W.

1975   *Plants, man and the land in the Vilcanota Valley of Peru.* The Hague: Dr. W. Junk B. V.

Gade, Daniel W., and Mario Escobar Moscoso

1982   Village settlement and the colonial legacy in southern Peru. *Geographical Review* 72 (4): 430–449.

García, J. Uriel

1922   *Ciudad de los incas.* Cuzco: Estudios Arqueológicos.

Garcilaso de la Vega, Inca

1960   *Comentarios reales de los incas* [1609]. In *Obras completas del Inca Garcilaso de la Vega.* Biblioteca de Autores Españoles (continuación), vols. 132–135. Madrid: Ediciones Atlas.

1966   *Royal commentaries of the Incas and general history of Peru, parts 1 and 2* [1609]. Translated by Harold V. Livermore. Austin: University of Texas Press.

Gartner, William G.

1996   Book review of *The Tiwanaku: Portrait of an Andean Civilization,* by Alan L. Kolata. *Annals of the Association of American Geographers* 86: 153–156.

Gasparini, Graziano, and Luise Margolies

1980   *Inca architecture.* Translated by P. J. Lyon. Bloomington: Indiana University Press.

Gelles, Paul H.

1995   Equilibrium and extraction: Dual organization in the Andes. *American Ethnologist* 22 (4): 710–742.

Gibaja Oviedo, Arminda M.

1973   Arqueología de Choquepugio. Tesis, Facultad de Arqueología, Universidad Nacional San Antonio Abad del Cuzco.

1983   Arqueología de Choquepugio. In *Arqueología andina,* edited by Arminda M. Gibaja Oviedo, pp. 29–44. Cuzco: Ediciones Instituto Nacional de Cultura.

1984   Requencia cultural de Ollantaytambo. In *Current archaeological projects in the central Andes,* edited by A. Kendall, pp. 225–246. BAR International Series 210. Oxford: British Archaeological Reports.

Glowacki, Mary

1996   The Wari occupation of the Southern Highlands of Peru: A ceramic perspective from the site of Pikillacta. Ann Arbor: University Microfilms.

2002   The Huaro archaeological site complex: Rethinking the Huari occupation of Cuzco. In *Andean archaeology I: Variations of sociopolitical organization,* edited by William H. Isbell and Helaine Silverman, pp. 267–285. New York: Kkuwer Academic.

Glowacki, Mary, and Julinho Zapata

1998   The Wari occupation of Cuzco: Recent discoveries from the Huaro Valley. Paper presented at the 38th annual meeting of the Institute of Andean Studies, Berkeley, Calif.

González Corrales, José

1984   La arquitectura y cerámica killke del Cusco. In *Current archaeological projects in the central Andes,* edited by E. Ann Kendall, pp. 189–204. BAR International Series 210. Oxford: British Archaeological Reports.

Gose, Peter

1996   The past is a lower moiety: Diarchy, history, and divine kingship in the Inka Empire. *History and Anthropology* 9 (4): 383–414.

Gregory, Herbert E.

1916   A geologic reconnaissance of the Cuzco Valley. *American Journal of Science* 41 (241): 1–100.

Guaman Poma de Ayala, Felipe

1980   *El primer nueva corónica y buen gobierno* [1615]. Ed-

ited by John V. Murra and R. Adorno and translated by Jorge I. Urioste. 3 vols. Mexico City: Siglo
Veintiuno.

Gutiérrez, Ramón, Paulo de Azevedo, Graciela M.
Viñuelas, Esterzilda de Azevedo, and Rodolfo
Vallín

1981   *La casa cusqueña.* Resistencia, Argentina:
Departamento de Historia de la Arquitectura,
Universidad Nacional del Noreste.

Gutiérrez de Santa Clara, Pedro

1963   *Historia de las guerras civiles del Perú y de otros*
sucesos de las Indias (ca. 1600). Biblioteca de Autores
Españoles, vols. 165–167. Madrid: Ediciones Atlas.

Hampe Martínez, Teodoro

1982   Las momias de los incas en Lima. *Revista del Museo*
Nacional (Lima) 46: 405–418.

2000   Las momias de los inca en Lima: Estado de la
cuestión y perspectivas. Paper presented at the 50th
International Congress of Americanists, Warsaw,
Poland.

Hansen, Barbara C. S., Geoffrey O. Seltzer, and Herbert E.
Wright, Jr.

1994   Late Quaternary vegetational change in the central
Peruvian Andes. *Paleogeography, Paleoclimatology,*
Paleoecology 109: 263–285.

Haquehua Huaman, Wilbert, and Rubén Maqque Azorsa

1996   La cerámica de Cuave Moqo-Maras. Tesis de
Licenciatura, Facultad de Ciencias Sociales, Carrera
Profesional de Arqueología, Universidad Nacional
San Antonio Abad del Cuzco.

Harth-Terré, Emilio

1959   Pikillacta—Ciudad de pósitos y bastimentos del
imperio incaico. *Revista del Museo e Instituto*
Arqueológico 18: 3–19.

1962   Los últimos canteros incaicos. *Actas y trabajos del II*
Congreso Nacional de Historia del Perú. Vol. 2.
Lima: Centro de Estudios Histórico-Militares del
Perú.

Hastings, Charles M., and Michael E. Moseley

1975   The adobes of the Huaca del Sol and the Huaca de
la Luna. *American Antiquity* 40: 196–203.

Hayashida, Frances

1998   New insights into Inka pottery production. In
Andean ceramics: Technology, organization, and ap-
proaches, edited by Izumi Shimada, pp. 313–335.
MASCA Research Papers in Science and Archaeol-
ogy, Supplement to Vol. 15. Philadelphia: Museum
Applied Science Center for Archaeology, Museum
of Archaeology and Anthropology, University of
Pennsylvania.

1999   Style, technology, and state production: Inka pot-

tery manufacture in the Leche Valley, Peru. *Latin*
American Antiquity 10 (4): 337–352.

Heffernan, Kenneth

1989   Limatambo in late prehistory: Landscape archaeology and documentary images of Inca presence in
the periphery of Cuzco. Ph.D. dissertation, Department of Prehistory and Anthropology, Austra-
lian National University, Canberra.

Hemming, John

1970   *The conquest of the Incas.* New York: Harcourt
Brace Jovanovich.

Hemming, John, and Edward Ranney

1982   *Monuments of the Incas.* Boston: Little, Brown and
Co.

Hey, Gillian

1984   Early occupation on the Huillca Raccay promon-
tory site, Cusichaca: The archaeological evidence.
In *Current archaeological projects in the central*
Andes, edited by E. Ann Kendall, pp. 291–304.
BAR International Series 210. Oxford: British Ar-
chaeological Reports.

Hill, Samuel S.

1850   *Travels in Peru and Mexico.* London: Longman,
Green, Longman and Roberts.

Hollowell, J. Lee

1987   Precision cutting and fitting of stone in prehistoric
Andean walls. Unpublished Research Report
#2832-84, submitted to the National Geographic
Society, Washington, D.C.

Hunt, Patrick

1990   Inca volcanic stone provenance in the Cuzco province, Peru. *Institute of Archaeology Bulletin* 1: 24–36

Hutterer, Karl L., and William K. MacDonald

1982   *Houses built on scattered poles: Prehistory and ecology*
in Negros Oriental. Cebo City, Philippines: University of San Carlos.

Hyslop, John

1990   *Inka settlement planning.* Austin: University of
Texas Press.

Isbell, William H.

1977   *The rural foundation for urbanism: Economic and*
stylistic interaction between rural and urban commu-
nities in eighth-century Peru. Illinois Studies in Anthropology No. 10. Urbana: University of Illinois
Press.

1978   Environmental perturbations and the origin of the
Andean state. In *Social archaeology: Beyond subsis-*
tence and dating, edited by Charles Redman et al.,
pp. 303–314. New York: Academic Press.

1997   *Mummies and mortuary monuments.* Austin: University of Texas Press.

Isbell, William H., Christine Brewster-Wray, and Lynda Spickard

1991   Architecture and spatial organization in Huari. In *Huari administrative structure: Prehistoric monumental architecture and state government,* edited by William H. Isbell and Gordon F. McEwan, pp. 19–53. Washington, D.C.: Dumbarton Oaks Research Library and Collection.

Isbell, William H., and Gordon F. McEwan

1991   History of Huari studies and introduction of current interpretations. In *Huari administrative structure: Prehistoric monumental architecture and state government,* edited by William H. Isbell and Gordon F. McEwan, pp. 1–10. Washington, D.C.: Dumbarton Oaks Research Library and Collection.

Janusek, John Wayne

1994   State and local power in a prehispanic Andean polity: Changing patterns of urban residence in Tiwanaku and Lukurmata, Bolivia. Ph.D. dissertation, Department of Anthropology, University of Chicago.

Jijón y Caamaño, Jacinto

1934   *Los orígenes del Cuzco.* Quito: Imprenta de la Universidad Central.

Jijón y Caamaño, Jacinto, and Carlos Larrea M.

1918   Un cementerio incaico en Quito y notas acerca de los incas en el Ecuador. *Revista de la Sociedad Jurídico-Literaria* 20: 159–260.

Johannessen, Sissel, and Christine A. Hastorf

1990   A history of fuel management (A.D. 500 to the present) in the Mantaro Valley, Peru. *Journal of Ethnobiology* 10 (1): 61–90.

Jones, Bradford, Cindy Klink, and Brian S. Bauer

2001   The first inhabitants of the Cuzco Valley. Paper presented at the 66th annual meeting of the Society for American Archaeology, Denver, Colorado.

Julien, Catherine

1995   Documentación presentada por la ciudad del Cuzco sobre el terremoto de 1650. *Revista del Museo e Instituto de Arqueología* (Cuzco) 25: 293–373.

1999   History and art in translation: The *paños* and other objects collected by Francisco Toledo. *Colonial Latin American Review* 8 (1): 61–89.

2000   *Reading Inca history.* Iowa City: University of Iowa Press.

Kalafatovich, Carlos

1970   Geología del grupo arqueológico de la fortaleza de Saccsayhuaman y sus vecindades. *Revista Saqsaywaman* 1: 16–68.

Kaulicke, Peter (ed.)

1998   *Boletín de Arqueología PUCP Vol. 2: Perspectivas regionales del Período Formativo en el Perú.* Lima: Pontificia Universidad Católica del Perú.

Kendall, E. Ann

1974   Aspects of Inca architecture. Ph.D. dissertation, Institute of Archaeology, University of London.

1976   Preliminary report on ceramic data and the pre-Inca architectural remains of the (Lower) Urubamba Valley, Cuzco. *Baessler Archiv,* neue Folge, Band 24: 41–159.

1984   Archaeological investigations of Late Intermediate Period and Late Horizon Period at Cusichaca, Peru. In *Current archaeological projects in the central Andes,* edited by E. Ann Kendall, pp. 247–290. BAR International Series 210. Oxford: British Archaeological Reports.

1985   *Aspects of Inca architecture: Description, function, and chronology, parts 1 and 2.* BAR International Series 242. Oxford: British Archaeological Reports.

1996   An archaeological perspective for Late Intermediate Period Inca development in the Cuzco region. In *Structure, knowledge, and representation in the Andes,* edited by Gary Urton. *Journal of the Steward Anthropological Society* 24 (1–2): 121–156.

1997   *Proyecto Arqueológico Cusichaca, Cusco.* Lima: Gráfica Pacífico.

Kendall, E. Ann (ed.)

1992   *Arqueología y desarrollo rural: Infraestructura agrícola e hidráulica pre-hispánica presente y futuro.* Lima: The Cusichaca Trust, Asociación Gráfica Educativa.

Kidder, Alfred

1943   *Some early sites in the northern Lake Titicaca Basin.* Papers of the Peabody Museum of American Archaeology and Ethnology, vol. 27 (1). Cambridge, Mass.: Harvard University.

Klink, Cindy

1998   Proyecto Arcaico del Altiplano 1997: Prospección arqueológica en el valle del Río Huenque. Report submitted to the Instituto Nacional de Cultura, Lima.

1999   On the edge: Prehistoric trends on the Peruvian Altiplano rim. Paper presented at the 64th annual meeting of the Society for American Archaeology, Chicago.

n.d.   Archaic Period research in the Río Huenque valley, Peru. Manuscript.

Klink, Cindy. and Mark Aldenderfer

n.d.   A projectile point chronology for the south-central Andean highlands.

Klink, Cindy, Bradford Jones, and Brian S. Bauer

2001   The preceramic occupation of the Cuzco Valley. Paper presented at the 20th Northeast Andean Conference.

Knobloch, Patricia J.

1983   A study of the Andean Huari ceramics from the Early Intermediate Period to the Middle Horizon Epoch 1. Ph.D. dissertation, Department of Anthropology, State University of New York, Binghamton. Ann Arbor: University Microfilms.

1991   Stylistic date of ceramics from the Huari centers. In *Huari administrative structure: Prehistoric monumental architecture and state government,* edited by William H. Isbell and Gordon F. McEwan, pp. 247–258. Washington, D.C.: Dumbarton Oaks Research Library and Collection.

Kolata, Alan L.

1993   *The Tiwanaku: Portrait of an Andean civilization.* Oxford: Blackwell.

Kolata, Alan L. (ed.)

1996   *Tiwanaku and its hinterland: Archaeology and paleoecology of an Andean civilization.* Vol. 1, *Agroecology.* Washington, D.C.: Smithsonian Institution Press.

Kolata, Alan L., Michael W. Binford, Mark Brenner, John W. Janusek, and Charles Ortloff

2000   Environmental thresholds and the empirical reality of state collapse: A response to Erickson (1999). *Antiquity* 74: 424–426.

Kolata, Alan L., and Charles Ortloff

1996   Agroecological perspectives on the decline of the Tiwanaku State. In *Tiwanaku and its hinterland: Archaeology and paleoecology of an Andean civilization,* vol. 1, edited by Alan L. Kolata, pp. 181–201. Washington, D.C.: Smithsonian Institution Press.

Krueger, Howard W., and Francis C. Weeks

1966   Geochron Laboratories, Inc., radiocarbon measurements II. *Radiocarbon* 8: 142–160.

Kubler, George

1952   *Cuzco: Reconstrucción de la ciudad y restauración de sus monumentos.* Informe de la misión enviada por la UNESCO en 1951, Museos y Monumentos, III. Paris: UNESCO.

Ladrón de Guevara A., Oscar

1967   La restauración del Coricancha y Templo de Santo Domingo. *Revista del Museo e Instituto Arqueológico* 21: 29–95. Universidad Nacional San Antonio Abad del Cuzco.

La Lone, Mary

1985   Indian land tenure in southern Cuzco, Peru: From Inca to Colonial patterns. Ann Arbor: University Microfilms.

Lantarón Pfoccori, Lizandro F.

1988   Prospección arqueológica de la provincia de Chumbivilca. Tesis de Bachiller, Universidad Nacional San Antonio Abad del Cuzco.

Las Casas, Bartolomé de

1958   *Apologética historia* [ca. 1550]. In *Obras escogidas de Fray Bartolomé de Las Casas,* vol. 1, edited by Juan Pérez de Tudela Bueso. Biblioteca de Autores Españoles (continuación), vol. 106. Madrid: Ediciones Atlas.

Lawn, Barbara

1971   University of Pennsylvania radiocarbon dates XIV. *Radiocarbon* 13 (2): 363–377.

Lee, Vincent R.

1986   The building of Sacsayhuaman. *Ñawpa Pacha* 24: 49–60.

1998   Reconstructing the great hall at Inkallacta. *Andean Past* 5: 35–51. Edited by Monica Barnes, Daniel H. Sandweiss, and Brian S. Bauer. Ithaca, N.Y.: Cornell University Latin American Studies Program.

2000   *Forgotten Vilcabamba: Final stronghold of the Incas.* N.p.: Empire Publishing.

Lehmann-Nitsche, Robert

1928   Coricancha: El Templo del Sol en el Cuzco y las imágenes de su altar mayor. *Revista del Museo de La Plata* 31: 1–256.

LeVine, Terry Y.

1985   Inka administration in the Central Highlands: A comparative study. Ph.D. dissertation, Department of Anthropology, University of California, Los Angeles. Ann Arbor: University Microfilms.

1987   Inka labor service at the regional level: The functional reality. *Ethnohistory* 34 (1): 14–46.

LeVine, Terry Y. (ed.)

1992   *Inka storage systems.* Norman: University of Oklahoma Press.

Libro Primero del Cabildo de la Ciudad del Cuzco [1534]

1965   Edited by Raúl Rivera Serna. *Documenta* (Lima) 4: 441–480.

Liu, Chao Li, Kerry M. Riley, and Dennis D. Coleman

1986   Illinois State Geological Survey radiocarbon dates VIII. *Radiocarbon* 28 (1): 78–109.

Loarte, Gabriel de

1882   Información hecha en el Cuzco a 4 de enero de 1572. In *Informaciones acerca del señorío y gobierno de los incas hechas por mandado de Don Francisco de Toledo, Virrey del Perú, (1570–1572),* vol. 16, edited by Marcos Jiménez de la Espada, pp. 223–243. Colección de Libros Españoles Raros ó Curiosos. Madrid: Imprenta de Miguel Ginesta.

Lumbreras, Luis G.

1974a   *The peoples and cultures of ancient Peru.* Translated by Betty J. Meggers. Washington, D.C.: Smithsonian Institution Press.

1978   Acerca de la aparición del estado inka. In *El hombre y la cultura andina,* III Congreso Peruano, vol. 1, edited by Ramiro Matos M., pp. 101–109. Lima: Editora Lasontay.

Lunt, Sara W.

1984 An introduction to the pottery from the excavations at Cusichaca, Department of Cuzco, Peru. In *Current archaeological projects in the central Andes,* edited by E. Ann Kendall, pp. 307–322. BAR International Series 210. Oxford: British Archaeological Reports.

1987 Inca and pre-Inca pottery: Pottery from Cusichaca, Department of Cuzco, Peru. Ph.D. dissertation, Institute of Archaeology, University of London.

1988 The manufacture of the Inca aryballus. In *Recent studies in pre-Columbian archaeology,* edited by Nicholas J. Saunders and Olivier de Montmollin, pp. 489–511. BAR International Series 421 (ii). Oxford: British Archaeological Reports.

Lynch, Thomas F.

1980 *Guitarrero Cave: Early man in the Andes.* New York: Academic Press.

1999 The earliest South American lifeways. In *The Cambridge history of the native peoples of the Americas,* vol. 3, *South America, Part 1,* edited by Frank Salomon and Stuart B. Schwartz, pp. 188–263. Cambridge: Cambridge University Press.

MacCormack, Sabine

1991 *Religion in the Andes: Vision and imagination in early colonial Peru.* Princeton, N.J.: Princeton University Press.

MacNeish, Richard S., Robert K. Vierra, Antoinette Nelken-Terner, R. Lurine, and Angel García Cook

1980 *The prehistory of the Ayacucho basin, Peru.* Ann Arbor: University of Michigan Press.

Mannheim, Bruce

1991 *The language of the Inka since the European invasion.* Austin: University of Texas Press.

Marcoy, Paul

1875 *Travels in South America: From the Pacific Ocean to the Atlantic Ocean.* Vols. 1 and 2. New York: Scribner, Armstrong and Co.

Marcus, Joyce

1992 Dynamic cycles of Mesoamerican states: Political fluctuations in Mesoamerica. *National Geographic Research and Exploration* 8: 392–411.

1998 The peaks and valleys of ancient states: An extension of the dynamic model. In *Archaic states,* edited by Gary Feinman and Joyce Marcus, pp. 59–94. Santa Fe: School of American Research.

Marcus, Joyce, and Kent Flannery

1996 *Zapotec civilization: How urban society evolved in Mexico's Oaxaca Valley.* New York: Thames and Hudson.

Markham, Clements Robert

1856 *Cuzco: A journey to the ancient capital of Peru; with an account of the history, language, literature, and antiquities of the Incas. And Lima: A visit to the capital and provinces of modern Peru; with a sketch of the viceregal government, history of the republic, and a review of the literature and society of Peru.* London: Chapman and Hall.

1871 On the geographical position of the tribes which formed the Empire of the Incas. *Journal of the Royal Geographical Society* (London) 4: 281–338.

Matos M., Ramiro

1994 *Pumpu: Centro administrativo inka de la puna de Junín.* Lima: Editorial Horizonte.

McElroy, Keith

1986 Ephraim George Squier: Photography and the illustration of Peruvian antiquities. *History of Photography* 10 (2): 99–129.

McEwan, Gordon F.

1984 Investigaciones en la cuenca del Lucre, Cusco. *Gaceta Arqueológica Andina* 9: 12–15.

1987 *The Middle Horizon in the Valley of Cuzco, Peru: The impact of the Wari occupation of the Lucre Basin.* BAR International Series 372. Oxford: British Archaeological Reports.

1991 Investigations at the Pikillacta site: A provincial Huari center in the Valley of Cuzco. In *Huari administrative structure: Prehistoric monumental architecture and state government,* edited by William H. Isbell and Gordon F. McEwan, pp. 93–119. Washington, D.C.: Dumbarton Oaks Research Library and Collection.

1996 Archaeological investigations in Pikillacta, a Wari site in Peru. *Journal of Field Archaeology* 23: 169–186.

McEwan, Gordon F., Melissa Chatfield, and Arminda M. Gibaja Oviedo

2002 The archaeology of Inca origins: Excavations at Chokepukio, Cuzco, Peru. In *Andean archaeology I: Variations of sociopolitical organization,* edited by William H. Isbell and Helaine Silverman, pp. 287–301. New York: Kkuwer Academic.

McEwan, Gordon F., Arminda M. Gibaja Oviedo, and Melissa Chatfield

1995 Archaeology of the Chokepukio site: An investigation of the origin of the Inca civilization in the Valley of Cuzco, Peru. A report on the 1994 field season. *Tawantinsuyu* 1: 11–17.

Means, Philip A.

1931 *Ancient civilizations of the Andes.* New York: Charles Scribner's Sons.

Meddens, Frank M.

1989 Implications of camelid management and textile production for Huari. In *The nature of Wari: A reappraisal of the Middle Horizon Period in Peru,* edited by R. Michael Czwarno, Frank M. Meddens, and Alexandra Morgan, pp. 146–165. BAR International Series 525. Oxford: British Archaeological Reports.

Mena, Cristóbal de

1929 *The conquest of Peru, as recorded by a member of the Pizarro expedition* [1534]. Translated by Joseph H. Sinclair. New York: New York Public Library.

1967 La conquista del Perú [1534]. In *Las relaciones primitivas de la conquista del Perú,* edited by Raúl Porras Barrenechea, pp. 79–101. Lima: Instituto Raúl Porras Barrenechea, Universidad Nacional Mayor de San Marcos.

Menzel, Dorothy A.

1959 The Inca occupation of the south coast of Peru. *Southwestern Journal of Anthropology* 15 (2): 125–142.

Meyers, Albert

1975 Algunos problemas en la clasificación del estilo incaico. *Pumapunku* 8: 7–25.

Middendorf, Ernst F.

1895 *Peru: Beobachtungen und Studien über das Land und seine Bewohner.* Berlin: Gustav Schmidt.

1973 *Peru: Observaciones y estudios del país y sus habitantes durante una permanencia de veinticinco años* [1893]. Lima: Universidad Nacional Mayor de San Marcos.

Miller, George Robert

1979 An introduction to the ethnoarchaeology of the Andean camelids. Ph.D. dissertation, University of California, Berkeley. Ann Arbor: University Microfilms International.

Molina (el Cusqueño), Cristóbal de

1989 Relación de las fábulas i ritos de los Ingas . . . [ca. 1575]. In *Fábulas y mitos de los incas,* edited by Henrique Urbano and Pierre Duviols, pp. 47–134. Crónicas de América series. Madrid: Historia 16.

Montoya, Eduardo, Mary Glowacki, Julinho Zapata, and Pablo Mendoza

2000 A study in the production and distribution of Middle Horizon pottery of Cuzco, Peru. Final report for regional coordinated research program on nuclear analytical techniques in archaeological investigations. Washington, D.C.: International Atomic Energy Agency and Smithsonian Institution.

Morales, Ambrosio

1944 Documentos para la historia del Cuzco: Tumbas de los incas Sairi Tupac, D. Felipe Tupac Amaru, . . . y de la coya doña María Cusihuarcay. *Revista del Instituto Americano de Arte* (Cuzco) 3 (1): 13–21.

Morales Chocano, Daniel

1998 Importancia de las Salinas de San Blas durante el Período Formativo en la sierra central del Perú. In *Boletín de Arqueología PUCP: Perspectivas regionales del Período Formativo en el Perú* 2: 273–288.

Morris, Craig

1967 Storage in Tawantinsuyu. Ph.D. dissertation, Department of Anthropology, University of Chicago.

1992 The technology of highland Inka storage. In *Inka storage systems,* edited by Terry Y. LeVine, pp. 237–258. Norman: University of Oklahoma Press.

Morris, Craig, and Donald Thompson

1985 *Huánuco Pampa: An Inca city and its hinterland.* London: Thames and Hudson.

Moseley, Michael E.

2001 *The Incas and their ancestors: The archaeology of Peru.* London: Thames and Hudson.

Muelle, Jorge C.

1945 Pacarectambo: Apuntes de viaje. *Revista del Museo Nacional* (Lima) 14: 153–160.

Murra, John V.

1972 El "control vertical" de un máximo de pisos ecológicos en la economía de las sociedades andinas. In *Visita de la Provincia de León de Huánuco* (1562), edited by Iñigo Ortiz de Zúñiga, pp. 429–476. Huánuco: Universidad Hermilio Valdizán.

1984 Andean societies before 1532. In *The Cambridge history of Latin America,* vol. 1, pp. 59–90. Cambridge: Cambridge University Press.

1985 The limits and limitations of the "vertical archipelago" in the Andes. In *Andean ecology and civilization,* edited by Shozo Masuda, Izumi Shimada, and Craig Morris, pp. 15–20. Papers for the Wenner-Gren Foundation for Anthropological Research Symposium No. 91. Tokyo: University of Tokyo Press.

Murúa, Martín de

1946 *Historia del origen y genealogía real de los reyes incas del Perú* [1590]. Introduction and notes by Constantino Bayle. Biblioteca "Missionalia Hispánica," vol. 2. Madrid: Instituto Santo Toribio de Mogrovejo.

1962 *Historia general del Perú, origen y descendencia de los incas . . .* [ca. 1615]. 2 vols. Edited by M. Ballesteros-Garbrois. Biblioteca Americana Vetus. Madrid: Instituto Gonzalo Fernández de Oviedo.

Niles, Susan A.

1980a Civil and social engineers: Inca planning in the Cusco region. Ph.D. dissertation, Department of Anthropology, University of California, Berkeley. Ann Arbor: University Microfilms.

1980b   Pumamarca: A Late Intermediate Period site near Ollantaytambo. *Ñawpa Pacha* 18: 49–62.

1984   Architectural form and social function in Inca towns near Cuzco. In *Current archaeological projects in the central Andes: Some approaches and results,* edited by E. Ann Kendall, pp. 205–223. Oxford: BAR International Series 210.

1987   *Callachaca: Style and status in an Inca community.* Iowa City: University of Iowa Press.

1988   Looking for "lost" Inca palaces. *Expedition* 30 (3): 56–64.

1999   *The shape of Inca history: Narrative and architecture in an Andean empire.* Iowa City: University of Iowa Press.

Núñez, Lautaro, Martin Grosjean, and Isabel Cartajena

2002   Human occupations and climate change in the Puna de Atacama, Chile. *Science* 298: 821–824.

Núñez del Prado Béjar, Juan V.

1972   Dos nuevas estatuas de estilo Pucara halladas en Chumbivilcas, Perú. *Ñawpa Pacha* 9: 23–32.

Ocampo Conejeros, Baltasar

1907   *Account of the Province of Vilcapampa and a narrative of the execution of the Inca Tupac Amaru* [1610]. Translated by Clements Markham, vol. 22, pp. 203–247. London: Hakluyt Society.

Ortlieb, Luc, and José Macharé

1993   Former El Niño events: Records from western South America. *Global and Planetary Change* 7: 181–202.

Ortloff, Charles R., and Alan L. Kolata

1993   Climate and collapse: Agroecological perspectives on the decline of the Tiwanaku state. *Journal of Archaeological Science* 20: 195–221.

Oviedo, Gabriel de

1908   *Of what took place in the city of Cuzco . . .* [1573]. Translated by Clements Markham, vol. 23, pp. 401–409. London: Hakluyt Society.

Pachacuti Yamqui Salcamayhua, Juan de Santa Cruz
     See Santa Cruz Pachacuti Yamqui Salcamayhua, Juan de

Pardo, Luis A.

1938   Hacia una nueva clasificación de la cerámica cuzqueña del antiguo imperio de los incas, Perú. *Revista del Instituto Arqueológico del Cusco* 3 (4–5): 1–22.

1939   Arte peruano: Clasificación de la cerámica cuzqueña (época incaica). *Revista de la Sección Arqueológica de la Universidad Nacional del Cuzco* 4 (6–7): 3–27.

1941   Un hallazgo en la zona arqueológica del Ausangati (Cuzco). *Revista del Museo Nacional* (Lima) 10 (1): 110–112.

1946   La metrópoli de Paccarictambu: El adoratorio de Tamputtocco y el itinerario del camino seguido por los hermanos Ayar. *Revista del Instituto Arqueológico del Cusco* 2: 2–46.

1957   *Historia y arqueología del Cuzco.* 2 vols. Callao, Peru: Imprenta del Colegio Militar Leonico Pardo.

Paredes García, Mónica S.

1999   Registro informatizado de restos prehispánicos en el centro histórico de Cusco, diagnóstico e interpretación. Tesis, Facultad de Arqueología, Universidad Nacional San Antonio Abad del Cuzco.

Parsons, Jeffrey R., and Charles M. Hastings

1977   Prehispanic settlement patterns in the Upper Mantaro, Peru: A progress report for the 1976 field season. Unpublished report submitted to the Instituto Nacional de Cultura, Lima, and the National Science Foundation, Washington, D.C.

Parsons, Jeffrey R., Charles M. Hastings, and Ramiro Matos M.

2000a   *Prehispanic settlement patterns in the Upper Mantaro and Tarma Drainages, Junín, Peru.* Vol. 1, part 1, *The Tarama-Chinchaycocha region.* Ann Arbor: Museum of Anthropology, University of Michigan.

2000b   *Prehispanic settlement patterns in the Upper Mantaro and Tarma Drainages, Junín, Peru.* Vol. 1, part 2, *The Tarama-Chinchaycocha region.* Ann Arbor: Museum of Anthropology, University of Michigan.

Patterson, Thomas C.

1967   Current research, highland South America. *American Antiquity* 32 (1): 143–144.

1985   Exploitation and class formation in the Inca state. *Culture* 5 (1): 35–42.

Pauketat, Timothy

2000   The tragedy of the commoners. In *Agency in archaeology,* edited by M. A. Dobres and J. Robb, pp. 113–129. London: Routledge.

Paulson, Allison C.

1976   Environment and empire: Climate factors in prehistoric Andean culture change. *World Archaeology* 8 (2): 121–132.

Pearsall, D. M.

1980   Pachamachay ethnobotanical report: Plant utilization in a hunting base camp. In *Prehistoric hunters of the high Andes,* edited by John W. Rick, pp. 191–232. New York: Academic Press.

1983   Evaluating the stability of subsistence strategies by use of paleoethnobotanical data. *Journal of Ethnobiology* 3 (2): 121–137.

Pizarro, Pedro

1921   *Relation of the discovery and conquest of the kingdoms of Peru* [1571]. Translated and edited by Philip

Ainsworth Means. New York: The Cortés Society.

1986 *Relación del descubrimiento y conquista de los reinos del Perú* [1571]. Lima: Pontificia Universidad Católica del Perú.

Polo, José Toribio

1877 *Momias de los incas.* Documentos Literarios del Perú No. 10, pp. 371–378. Lima: Editorial Manuel de Orduizola.

Polo de Ondegardo, Juan

1916 *Instrucción contra las ceremonias y ritos que usan los indios conforme al tiempo de su infidelidad* [1567]. Edited by Horacio H. Urteaga. Colección de Libros y Documentos Referentes a la Historia del Perú, ser. 1, vol. 3 (Appendix A), pp. 189–204. Lima: Sanmartí.

1965 *On the errors and superstitions of the Indians, taken from the treatise and investigation done by Licentiate Polo* [1571]. Translated by A. Brunel, John V. Murra, and Sidney Muirden. New Haven, Conn.: Human Relations Area Files.

1990 Notables daños de no guardar a los indios sus fueros [1571]. In *El mundo de los incas,* edited by Laura González and Alicia Alonso, pp. 33–113. Madrid: Historia 16.

Poole, Deborah

1984 Ritual economic calendars in Paruro: The structure of representation in Andean ethnography. Ann Arbor: University Microfilms.

Porras Barrenechea, Raúl (ed.)

1959 *Cartas del Perú (1524–1543).* Lima: Sociedad de Bibliófilos Peruanos.

1967 *Las relaciones primitivas de la conquista del Perú.* Lima: Instituto Raúl Porras Barrenechea.

1992 *Antología del Cuzco.* Lima: Fundación M. J. Bustamante de la Fuente.

Pozzi-Escot B., Denise

1991 Conchapata: A community of potters. In *Huari administrative structure: Prehistoric monumental architecture and state government,* edited by William H. Isbell and Gordon F. McEwan, pp. 81–92. Washington, D.C.: Dumbarton Oaks Research Library and Collection.

Prescott, William

1847 *History of the conquest of Peru.* New York: Harper and Brothers.

Protzen, Jean-Pierre

1985 Inca quarrying and stonecutting. *JSAH* 44 (May): 161–182.

1986 Inca stonemasonry. *Scientific American* 254 (2): 94–105.

1991 *Inca architecture and construction at Ollantaytambo.* New York: Oxford University Press.

2000 Inca architecture. In *The Inca world: The development of pre-Columbian Peru, A.D. 1000–1534,* edited by Laura Minelli, pp. 193–217. Norman: University of Oklahoma Press.

Raimondi, Antonio

1874 *El Perú: Historia de la geografía del Perú.* Vol. 1. Lima: Imprenta del Estado.

Reichlen, Henry

1954 Découverte de tombes Tiahuanaco dans la région du Cuzco. *Journal de la Société des Américanistes* 47: 221–223.

Richardson, James B.

1994 *People of the Andes.* Washington, D.C.: Smithsonian Books.

Rick, John W.

1980 *Prehistoric hunters of the high Andes.* New York: Academic Press.

1988 The character and context of highland preceramic society. In *Peruvian prehistory,* edited by Richard W. Keatinge, pp. 3–40. Cambridge: Cambridge University Press.

Rivera Dorado, Miguel

1971a La cerámica Killke y la arqueología de Cuzco. *Revista Española de Antropología Americana* 6: 85–123.

1971b Diseños decorativos en la cerámica Killke. *Revista del Museo Nacional* (Lima) 37: 106–115.

1972 La cerámica de Cancha-Cancha, Cuzco, Perú. *Revista Dominicana de Arqueología y Antropología* 2 (2–3): 36–49.

1973 Aspectos tipológicos de la cerámica cuzqueña del Período Intermedio Tardío. In *Atti del 40 Congresso Internazionale degli Americanisti* 1: 353–362. Rome-Genoa: Tilgher.

Rivero y Ustáriz, Mariano Eduardo de, and Johann Jakob von Tschudi

1851 *Antigüedades peruanas.* Vienna, Austria: Imprenta Imperial de la Corte y del Estado.

1854 *Peruvian antiquities.* Translated by Francis L. Hawks. New York: Putnam and Co.

Rostworowski de Diez Canseco, María

1966 Las tierras reales y su mano de obra en el Tahuantinsuyu. XXXVI Congreso Internacional de Americanistas (Sevilla, 1964). *Actas y Memorias* (Sevilla) 2: 31–34.

1970 Los ayarmaca. *Revista del Museo Nacional* (Lima) 36: 58–101.

1978 Una hipótesis sobre el surtimiento del estado inca. In *Actas y trabajos del III congreso peruano "El hombre y la cultura andina,"* vol. 1, edited by Ramiro Matos M., pp. 89–100. Lima: Universidad Nacional Mayor de San Marcos.

1999   *History of the Inca realm.* Translated by Harry B. Iceland. Cambridge: Cambridge University Press.

Rowe, John H.

1943   Chanapata: La cultura pre-incaica del Cuzco. *Tupac Amaru* (Cuzco) 2 (2/3): 41–43.

1944   *An introduction to the archaeology of Cuzco.* Papers of the Peabody Museum of American Archaeology and Ethnology, vol. 27, no. 2. Cambridge, Mass.: Harvard University.

1946   Inca culture at the time of the Spanish Conquest. In *Handbook of South American Indians,* vol. 2, *The Andean civilizations,* edited by Julian Steward, pp. 183–330. Bureau of American Ethnology Bulletin, no. 143. Washington, D.C.: U.S. Government Printing Office.

1956   Archaeological explorations in southern Peru, 1954–1955. *American Antiquity* 22 (2): 135–150.

1962   Stages and periods in archaeological interpretation. *Southwestern Journal of Anthropology* 18 (1): 40–54.

1967   What kind of settlement was Inca Cuzco? *Ñawpa Pacha* 5: 59–75.

1976   El arte religioso del Cuzco en el Horizonte Temprano. *Ñawpa Pacha* 14: 1–20.

1990   El plano más antiguo del Cuzco. *Histórica* 14 (2): 367–377.

Rowe, John H., and Catherine T. Brandel

1971   Pucara-style pottery designs. *Ñawpa Pacha* 7–8: 1–16.

Rowe, John H., and Dorothy Menzel

1967   *Peruvian archaeology.* Palo Alto, Calif.: Peek Publications.

Ruiz de Arce, Juan

1933   Relación de servicios en Indias de don Juan Ruiz Arce, conquistador del Perú [ca. 1545]. *Boletín de la Real Academia de la Historia* (Madrid) 102: 327–384.

Ruiz de Navamuel, Alvaro

1882   La fe y testimonio que va puesta en los cuatro paños . . . [1572]. In *Informaciones acerca del señorío y gobierno de los incas hechas por mandado de Don Francisco de Toledo,* vol. 16, edited by Marcos Jiménez de la Espada, pp. 245–257. Colección de Libros Españoles Raros ó Curiosos. Madrid: Imprenta de Miguel Ginesta.

Rydén, Stig

1957   *Andean excavations I.* Publication No. 4. Stockholm: Ethnographical Museum of Sweden.

Salazar, Antonio

1867   Relación sobre el período de gobierno de los virreyes Don Francisco de Toledo y Don García Hurtado de Mendoza (1596). In *Colección de documentos inéditos relativos al descubrimiento, conquista y organización de las antiguas posesiones españolas de América y Oceanía,* vol. 8, pp. 212–421. Madrid: Imprenta de Frías y Compañía.

Sancho de la Hoz, Pedro

1898   *Relación de la conquista del Perú* [1534]. Vol. 8. Edited by Joaquín García Icazbalceta, pp. 309–423. Biblioteca de Autores Mexicanos. Mexico City: Imprenta de V. Agueros.

1917   *An account of the conquest of Peru* [1534]. Translated into English and annotated by Philip Ainsworth Means. New York: The Cortés Society.

1986   *La relación de Pedro Sancho.* Traducción, estudio preliminar y notas por Luis A. Arocena. Buenos Aires: Editorial Plus Ultra.

Sanders, William T.

1973   The significance of Pikillacta in Andean culture history. Occasional Papers in Anthropology 8: 380–428. University Park: Pennsylvania State University.

Sanders, William T., and Deborah L. Nichols

1988   Ecological theory and cultural evolution in the Valley of Oaxaca. *Current Anthropology* 29 (1): 33–80.

Sanders, William T., and Barbara J. Price

1968   *Mesoamerica: The evolution of a civilization.* New York: Random House.

Sandweiss, Daniel H., James B. Richardson, Elizabeth J. Reitz, Harold B. Rollins, and Kirk A. Maasch

1996   Geoarchaeological evidence from Peru for a 5000 years BP onset of El Niño. *Science* 273: 1531–1533.

San Román Luna, Wilbert

1979   Arqueología de Pomacanchi: Una introducción a su estudio. Tesis por Licenciado en Arqueología, Facultad de Ciencias Sociales, Universidad Nacional San Antonio Abad del Cuzco.

1983   Datos etnohistóricos de Pomacanchi. In *Arqueología andina,* edited by Arminda M. Gibaja Oviedo, pp. 66–75. Cuzco: Ediciones Instituto Nacional de Cultura.

2003   Análisis de la cerámica de Cusicancha, Cuzco. Paper presented at the Archaeology of Inca Cuzco Symposium (April 25–26), Peabody Museum, Yale University.

Santa Cruz Pachacuti Yamqui Salcamayhua, Juan de

1950   Relación de antigüedades deste Reyno del Perú [ca. 1613]. In *Tres relaciones de antigüedades peruanas,* edited by Marcos Jiménez de la Espada, pp. 207–281. Asunción, Paraguay: Editorial Guaranía.

1993   *Relación de antigüedades deste reyno del Pirú* [17th century]. Estudio etnohistórico y lingüístico de Pierre Duviols y César Itier. Cuzco: Centro de Estudios Regionales Andinos "Bartolomé de Las Casas."

Santillán, Hernando de

1950　Relación del origen, descendencia política y gobierno de los incas . . . [1564]. In *Tres relaciones de antigüedades peruanas,* edited by Marcos Jiménez de la Espada, pp. 33–131. Asunción, Paraguay: Editorial Guaranía.

Sarmiento de Gamboa, Pedro

1906　Segunda parte de la historia general llamada Indica . . . [1572]. In *Geschichte des Inkareiches von Pedro Sarmiento de Gamboa,* edited by Richard Pietschmann. Abhandlungen der Königlichen Gesellschaft der Wissenschaften zu Göttingen, Philologisch-Historische Klasse, neue Folge, vol. 6, no. 4. Berlin: Weidmannsche Buchhandlung.

Schaedel, Richard P.

1978　Early state of the Incas. In *The early state,* edited by Henri J. M. Claessen and Peter Skalnik, pp. 289–320. The Hague: Mouton.

Schreiber, Katharina J.

1987a　Conquest and consolidation: A comparison of the Wari and Inka occupation of a highland Peruvian valley. *American Antiquity* 52 (2): 266–284.

1987b　From state to empire: The expansion of Wari outside the Ayacucho Basin. In *The origins and development of the Andean state,* edited by J. Haas, S. Pozorski, and T. Pozorski, pp. 91–96. Cambridge: Cambridge University Press.

1991　Jincamocco: A Huari administrative center in the south central highlands of Peru. In *Huari administrative structure: Prehistoric monumental architecture and state government,* edited by William H. Isbell and Gordon F. McEwan, pp. 199–214. Washington, D.C.: Dumbarton Oaks Research Library and Collection.

1992　*Wari imperialism in Middle Horizon Peru.* Anthropological Papers No. 87. Ann Arbor: Museum of Anthropology, University of Michigan .

1999　Regional approaches to the study of prehistoric empires: Examples from Ayacucho and Nasca, Peru. In *Settlement pattern studies in the Americas,* edited by Brian Billman and Gary M. Feinman, pp. 160–171. Washington, D.C.: Smithsonian Institution Press.

Schwalb, Antje, Stephen J. Burns, and Kerry Kelts

1999　Holocene environments from stable isotope stratigraphy of ostracods and authigenic carbonate in Chilean Altiplano lakes. *Paleogeography, Paleoclimatology, Paleoecology* 148: 153–168.

Seler, Eduard

1893　*Peruanische Alterthümer, insbesondere altperuanische Gefass* . . . Berlin: E. Mertens.

Shimada, Izumi, Crystal Barker Schaaf, Lonnie G. Thompson, and Ellen Mosley-Thompson

1991　Cultural impacts of severe droughts in the prehistoric Andes: Applications of a 1,500-year ice core

precipitation record. *World Archaeology* 22 (3): 247–270.

Sidky, Homayun

1995　*Irrigation and state formation in Hunza: The anthropology of a hydraulic kingdom.* Lanham, Md.: University Press of America.

Silverman, Helaine

2002　*Ancient Nasca settlement and society.* Iowa City: University of Iowa Press.

Snead, James E.

1992　Imperial infrastructure and the Inka state storage system. In *Inka storage systems,* edited by Terry Y. LeVine, pp. 62–106. Norman: University of Oklahoma Press.

Spencer, Charles S., and Elsa M. Redmond

2001　Multilevel selection and political evolution in the Valley of Oaxaca, 500–100 B.C. *Journal of Anthropological Archaeology* 20 (2): 195–229.

Squier, E. George

1877　*Peru: Incidents of travel and exploration in the land of the Incas.* New York: Henry Holt.

Stanish, Charles

1998　Nonmarket imperialism in a prehispanic context: The Inca occupation of the Titicaca Basin. *Latin American Antiquity* 8 (3): 1–18.

2000　Negotiating rank in an imperial state: Lake Titicaca Basin elite under Inca and Spanish control. In *Hierarchies in action: Cui bono?* edited by Michael W. Diehl, pp. 317–339. Occasional Paper No. 27. Carbondale: Southern Illinois University Center for Archaeological Investigations.

2001　Regional research on the Inca. *Journal of Archaeological Research* 9 (3): 213–241.

2003　*Ancient Titicaca.* Los Angeles: University of California Press.

Stanish, Charles, Edmundo de la Vega M., Lee Steadman, Cecilia Chávez Justo, Kirk Lawrence Frye, Luperio Onofre Mamani, Matthew T. Seddon, and Percy Calisaya Chuquimia

1997　*Archaeological survey in the Juli-Desaguadero region of Lake Titicaca Basin, southern Peru.* Fieldiana Anthropology, new series, no. 29. Chicago: Field Museum of Natural History.

Stavig, Ward

1999　*The world of Túpac Amaru: Conflict, community, and identity in colonial Peru.* Lincoln: University of Nebraska Press.

Taca Chunga, Pedro

1990　Las cuevas y arte rupestre de Huayokhari en el valle Sagrado de los Inkas. *Saqsaywaman* (Cuzco: Instituto Departamental de Cultura) 1 (3): 21–38.

Thompson, Lonnie G., Mary E. Davis, Ellen Mosley-Thompson, and Kam-Biu Liu

1988   Pre-Incan agricultural activity recorded in dust layers in two tropical ice cores. *Nature* 336: 763–765.

Thompson, Lonnie G., and Ellen Mosley-Thompson

1987   Evidence of abrupt climatic change during the last 1,500 years recorded in ice cores from the tropical Quelccaya ice cap, Peru. In *Abrupt climatic change: Evidence and implications,* edited by Wolfgang H. Berger and Laurent D. Labeyrie, pp. 99–110. NATO ASI Series C, Vol. 216. Norwell, Mass.: D. Redel.

Thompson, Lonnie G., Ellen Mosley-Thompson, John F. Bolzan, and Bruce R. Koci

1985   A 1,500-year record of tropical precipitation in ice cores from the Quelccaya ice cap, Peru. *Science* 229: 971–973.

Thompson, Lonnie G., Ellen Mosley-Thompson, Willi Dansgaard, and Pieter Grootes

1986   The Little Ice Age as recorded in the stratigraphy of the tropical Quelccaya ice cap. *Science* 234: 361–364.

Thompson, Lonnie G., Ellen Mosley-Thompson, M. E. Davis, P.-N. Lin, Keith A. Henderson, Jihong Cole-Dai, John F. Bolzan, and Kam-Biu Liu

1995   Late glacial stage and Holocene tropical ice-core records from Huascaran, Peru. *Science* 269: 46–50.

Thompson, Lonnie G., Ellen Mosley-Thompson, and P. A. Thompson

1992   Reconstructing interannual climate variability from tropical and subtropical ice cores. In *El Niño: Historical and paleoclimatic aspects of the southern oscillation,* edited by Henry F. Díaz and Vera Markgraf. Cambridge: Cambridge University Press.

Toledo, Francisco de

1924   Carta de D. Francisco de Toledo, virrey del Perú, sobre la victoria obtenida en Vilcabamba . . . [1572]. In *Gobernantes del Perú: Cartas y papeles, siglo XVI, documentos del Archivo de Indias,* vol. 4, edited by D. Roberto Levillier, pp. 341–345. Colección de Publicaciones Históricas de la Biblioteca del Congreso Argentino. Madrid: Imprenta de Juan Pueyo.

1940   Informaciones que mandó levantar el Virrey Toledo sobre los incas . . . [1570–1572]. In *Don Francisco de Toledo, supremo organizador del Perú: Su vida, su obra (1515–1582),* vol. 2, edited by Roberto Levillier. Buenos Aires: Espasa-Calpe, S.A. See also Loarte, Gabriel de.

Topic, John R., and Theresa L. Topic

1985   El Horizonte Medio en Huamanchuco. *Revista del Museo Nacional* (Lima) 47: 13–52.

Torres Poblete, Nilo

1989   Sondeo arqueológico de Araway. Tesis por Licenciado en Arqueología, Facultad de Ciencias Sociales, Universidad Nacional San Antonio Abad del Cuzco.

Trujillo, Diego de

1948   *Relación del descubrimiento del reyno del Perú* [1571]. Edited by Raúl Porras Barrenechea. Seville: Imprenta de la Escuela de Estudios Hispano-Americanos.

Tschopik, Marion

1946   *Some notes on the archaeology of the Department of Puno.* Papers of the Peabody Museum of American Archaeology and Ethnology, vol. 27 (3). Cambridge: Harvard University.

Uhle, Friedrich Max

1912   Los orígenes de los incas. In *Actas del XVII Congreso Internacional de Americanistas,* pp. 302–352. Buenos Aires: Coni Hnos.

1930   El Templo del Sol de los incas en Cuzco [1905]. *Proceedings of the Twenty-third International Congress of Americanists,* pp. 291–295. New York: N.p.

Urton, Gary

1984   Chuta: El espacio de la práctica social en Pacariqtambo, Perú. *Revista Andina* 2 (1): 7–56.

1990   *The history of a myth: Pacariqtambo and the origin of the Inkas.* Austin: University of Texas Press.

Valcárcel, Luis E.

1934   Los trabajos arqueológicos en el Departamento del Cusco. Sajsawaman Redescubierto II. *Revista del Museo Nacional* (Lima) 3: 3–36, 211–233.

1935   Los trabajos arqueológicos en el Departamento del Cusco. Sajsawaman Redescubierto III–IV. *Revista del Museo Nacional* (Lima) 4: 1–24, 161–203.

1946   Cuzco archaeology. In *Handbook of South American Indians,* vol. 2, *The Andean civilizations,* edited by Julian Steward, pp. 177–182. Bulletin of the Bureau of American Ethnology, no. 143. Washington, D.C.: Smithsonian Institution Press.

Valencia Zegarra, Alfredo

1979   *Colección arqueológica Cusco de Max Uhle.* Cuzco: Centro de Investigación y Restauración de Bienes Monumentales, Instituto Nacional de Cultura-Cusco.

1984   Arqueología de Qolqampata. *Revista del Museo e Instituto de Arqueología* (Universidad Nacional San Antonio Abad del Cuzco) 23: 47–62.

Valencia Zegarra, Alfredo, and Arminda Gibaja Oviedo

1991   *Marcavalle: El rostro oculto del Cusco.* Cuzco: Instituto Regional de Cultura de la Región Inka.

1992   *Machu Picchu: La investigación y conservación del monumento arqueológico después de Hiram Bingham.* Cuzco: Municipalidad del Qosqo.

Valera, Blas
1950   De las costumbres antiguas de los naturales del Pirú [ca. 1585]. In *Tres relaciones de antigüedades peruanas,* edited by M. Jiménez de la Espada, pp. 135–203. Asunción, Paraguay: Editorial Guaranía.

Valverde, Vincente de
1959   Letter to the King of Spain dated 20 March 1539. In *Cartas del Peru (1524–1543),* edited by Raúl Porras Barrenechea, pp. 311–335. Lima: Sociedad de Bibliófilos Peruanos.

Van de Guchte, Maarten J.
1990   Carving the world: Inca monumental sculpture and landscape. Ann Arbor: University Microfilms.

Van Geel, Bas, J. Buurman, and H. T. Waterbolk.
1996   Archaeological and palaeoecological indications of an abrupt climate change in the Netherlands, and evidence of climatological teleconnections around 2650 B.P. *Journal of Quaternary Science* 11 (6): 451–460.

Vasco de Contreras y Valverde, Dean
1982   *Relación de la ciudad del Cusco* [1649]. Prologue and transcription by María del Carmen Martín Rubio. Cuzco: Imprenta Amauta.

Vázquez de Espinosa, Antonio
1948   *Compendio y descripción de las Indias Occidentales* [1629]. Transcribed from the original by Charles Upson Clark. Smithsonian Miscellaneous Collections, vol. 108. Washington, D.C.: Smithsonian Institution.

Vera Robles, Wilbert
1998   Wat'a (Anta): Una ocupación desde el Horizonte Temprano. Tesis presentado por Licenciado en arqueología, Universidad Nacional San Antonio Abad del Cuzco.

Villanueva Urteaga, Horacio
1971   Documentos sobre Yucay en el siglo XVI. *Revista del Archivo Histórico del Cuzco* 13: 1–148.

Wachtel, Nathan
1982   The *mitimas* of the Cochabamba Valley: The colonization policy of Huayna Capac. In *The Inca and Aztec states, 1400–1800: Anthropology and history,* edited by George A. Collier, Renato I. Rosaldo, and John D. Wirth, pp. 199–235. New York: Academic Press.

Wiener, Charles
1880   *Pérou et Bolivie: Récit de voyage suivi d'études archéologiques et ethnographiques et de notes sur l'écriture et les langues des populations indiennes.* Paris: Hachette et Cie.

Williams, Patrick Ryan
2002   Cerro Baúl: A Wari center on the Tiwanaku frontier. *Latin American Antiquity* 12 (1): 67–83.

Wilson, David J.
1988   *Prehispanic settlement patterns in the Lower Santa Valley, Peru.* Washington, D.C.: Smithsonian Institution Press.

Wing, Elizabeth S.
1978   Animal domestication in the Andes. *Advances in Andean Archaeology,* edited by David Browman, pp. 167–188. The Hague: Mouton.

Wurster, Wolfgang W.
1999   Technischer Plankatalog Beschreibung der einzelnen Blätter. In *Max Uhle (1856–1944) Pläne archäologischer Stätten im Andengebiet: Planos de sitios arqueológicos en el área andina,* edited by Wolfgang W. Wurster, pp. 121–191. Mainz am Rhein: Verlag Philipp von Zabern.

Xerez, Francisco de
1985   *Verdadera relación de la conquista del Perú* [1534]. Edited by Concepción Bravo. Madrid: Historia 16.

Yábar Moreno, Jorge
1959   La cultura pre-incaica de Chanapata. *Revista del Museo e Instituto de Arqueología* (Universidad Nacional San Antonio Abad del Cuzco) 18: 93–100.
1972   Época pre-inca de Chanapata. *Revista Saqsaywaman* 2: 211–233.
1982   Figurillas de la cultura pre-inka del Cuzco. In *Arqueología de Cuzco,* compiled by I. Oberti R., pp. 9–12. Cuzco: Instituto Nacional de Cultura.

Yamasaki, Fumio, Tatsuji Hamada, and Chikaako Fujiyama
1966   Riken natural radiocarbon measurements II. *Radiocarbon* 8: 324–339.

Zapata, Julinho
1997   Arquitectura y contextos funerarios Wari en Batan Urqu, Cusco. In *Boletín de Arqueología PUCP,* vol. 1, *La muerte en el antiguo Perú: Contextos y conceptos funerarios,* edited by Peter Kaulicke, pp. 165–206. Lima: Pontificia Universidad Católica del Perú.
1998   Los cerros sagrados: Panorama del Período Formativo en la cuenca del Vilcanota, Cuzco. In *Boletín de Arqueología PUCP,* vol. 2, *Perspectivas regionales del Período Formativo en el Perú,* pp. 307–336. Lima: Pontificia Universidad Católica del Perú.

Zárate, Agustín de
1995   *Historia del descubrimiento y conquista del Perú* [1555]. Edited by Franklin Pease y Teodoro Hampe Martínez. Pontificia Universidad Católica del Perú: Fondo Editorial.

Zárate, Rosario
1921   *El Cuzco y sus monumentos.* Lima: Sanmartí.

Zuidema, R. Tom
1964   *The ceque system of Cuzco: The social organization of the capital of the Inca.* Translated by Eva M.

Hooykaas. International Archives of Ethnography, supplement to vol. 50. Leiden: E. J. Brill.

1977   The Inca kinship system: A new theoretical view. In *Andean kinship and marriage,* edited by R. Bolton and E. Mayer, pp. 240–281. Washington, D.C.: American Anthropological Association, Special Publication No. 7.

1980   El Ushnu. *Revista de la Universidad Complutense, Madrid* 28 (117): 317–362.

1982   Catachillay: The role of the Pleiades and of the Southern Cross and δ and β Centauri in the calendar of the Incas. In *Ethnoastronomy and Archaeoastronomy in the American Tropics,* edited by Anthony F. Aveni and Gary Urton, pp. 203–229. New York: Annals of the New York Academy of Sciences, vol. 385.

1983   Hierarchy and space in Incaic social organization. *Ethnohistory* 30 (2): 49–75.

1986   Inka dynasty and irrigation: Another look at Andean concepts of history. In *Anthropological History of Andean Polities,* edited by John V. Murra, Nathan Wachtel, and Jacques Revel, pp. 177–200. Cambridge: Cambridge University Press.